Charles Thomas Marvin

The Region of the Eternal Fire

An Account of a Journey to the Petroleum Region of the Caspian in 1883

Charles Thomas Marvin

The Region of the Eternal Fire
An Account of a Journey to the Petroleum Region of the Caspian in 1883

ISBN/EAN: 9783744753593

Printed in Europe, USA, Canada, Australia, Japan

Cover: Foto ©Andreas Hilbeck / pixelio.de

More available books at **www.hansebooks.com**

THE REGION OF THE ETERNAL FIRE.

THE REGION

OF

THE ETERNAL FIRE

AN ACCOUNT OF

A JOURNEY TO THE PETROLEUM REGION OF THE CASPIAN IN 1883

BY

CHARLES MARVIN

AUTHOR OF

"THE RUSSIANS AT THE GATES OF HERAT," "RECONNOITRING CENTRAL ASIA" "ENGLAND AS A PETROLEUM POWER," "MERV, THE QUEEN OF THE WORLD," ETC.

NEW EDITION

Inscribed

TO

PROFESSOR A. H. KEANE,

AS A TOKEN OF APPRECIATION OF HIS EMINENT SERVICES TO SCIENCE,
AND THE GENEROUS, PATRIOTIC TONE
THAT HAS ALWAYS CHARACTERIZED HIS WRITINGS,
WHENEVER THEY HAVE TOUCHED UPON THAT GREAT EMPIRE,
WHOSE SECURITY IS NOW BEING MENACED
BY RUSSIA'S PROGRESS IN THE " REGION OF THE ETERNAL FIRE."

PREFACE TO THE POPULAR EDITION.

—o—

THE interest excited by the development of Russia's power in the Black Sea and Caspian, and the progress of the petroleum industry at Baku, has provoked a demand for a popular edition of the account of my travels published in 1884. So many have been the changes that have occurred since, that the task of revising the work has not been easy; and to meet the difficulty, so far as the petroleum section is concerned, an additional chapter has been appended, bringing the subject up to date.

GROSVENOR HOUSE, PLUMSTEAD COMMON, KENT,
    November, 1887.

PREFACE TO THE FIRST EDITION.

—o—

WHEN I proceeded to the Caucasus a few weeks after my return from attending the coronation of the Emperor Alexander III. at Moscow last year, I had no intention whatever of writing a book of travels. However, the interest which some letters about the Oil Fountains at Baku, appearing in the columns of the *Morning Post*, excited in various quarters, caused me to investigate more fully the Petroleum industry, and the result is now before the reader. If he be connected with the Petroleum trade, the data may be of value to him; if, on the other hand, he desires to know what Russia is doing in the Caspian, he may share with me the deep interest I feel in the Kerosine factor of the Central Asian problem.

The preparation of the work has involved an amount of labour I would not again readily undergo. A number of excellent publications have been issued in Russia on Baku, but there is not one giving in a clear condensed form the history of the Petroleum industry up to the present time; and it is during the last few years that the greatest changes have been made. Besides, therefore, extracting the pith of the literature dealing with the subject, I have been compelled to go through files of the

Baku and Tiflis newspapers since 1879, and "boil down" many hundred newspaper cuttings, reports, lectures, and official statistics that had accumulated on my hands in the interval; to say nothing of the contents of the notebook I took to Baku. Among the works I have consulted I would particularly call attention to those of Gospodin Gulishambaroff, undoubtedly the most prolific and impartial writer in Russia on the Petroleum industry. These comprise "The present condition of the Baku Petroleum Industry, with a plan of the Balakhani Plateau," "The present condition of the Baku refining industry, with a plan of the Black Town of Baku," both published in 1882; "The Bibliography of the Petroleum Industry," and "The heating of steamers and locomotives with Petroleum," published in 1883; besides a number of pamphlets: "Petroleum Fountains" (1879), "The Petroleum springs of Bradford" (1882), "The Oxokerit Industry in Galicia" (1882), and "The map of the Apsheron Peninsula," &c. Less valuable, because mainly of a polemical or theoretical character, are Sokolovsky's "Geological Investigation of Petroleum in the Caucasus" (1883), Markovnikoff and Ogloblin's "Researches into Caucasus Petroleum" (1883), Professor Mendelaieff's "Petroleum Industry in the North American State of Pennsylvania and the Caucasus" (1877), and Professor Letni's "Refining of Petroleum" (1875). The lectures of Ludwig Nobel, Gospodin Poletika, and Professor Lisenko, may be finally mentioned among those of the class which have yielded the richest amount of data.

In making these acknowledgments, I cannot refrain from appealing in turn to those who utilize this book for purposes of reference to condescend to mention the source. When I first took up the Central Asian Question, there was a complete dearth of data on the developing Caspian phase of it. The importance of that phase, further, was generally ignored. To render my opinions the more forcible, I weighted them heavily with original Russian facts. The result has been that since the fall of Geok Tepé and the annexation of Merv, many newspaper-writers and authors have displayed their considerate appreciation by appropriating both opinions and facts, without the slightest acknowledgment, and have passed them off as their own. Two flagrant instances, in particular, rankle in my memory. In September, 1883, the *Edinburgh Review* published an article on " Russian Railways in Asia," containing several pages of matter taken almost *en bloc* from my " Russians at Merv and Herat," without the slightest indication of the source ; and on the 25th January this year, a Mr. Robert Cust delivered a lecture at the " Royal United Service Institution " on the " Russians on the Caspian and Black Seas," embodying a large amount of information from the same source, as well as from my pamphlet " The Russian Railway to India," in which he left it to his audience to infer that the data about the railway had been collected by him during his journey to Baku, instead of from my writings. Mr. Cust arrived at Baku on a dark autumn night last year, and left early the next morning direct for Astrakhan. Such a flitting was hardly favourable to deep research, especially as he does not appear to have understood Russian.

To be plagiarized, I am told, is the fate of all authors who reach a certain eminence, and I suppose I ought to bear the infliction meekly. But my grievance is something more than a sentimental one. I am not a military officer or a government official, who may expect a reward for his exertions in the shape of a better appointment or a knighthood ; nor am I a party writer, receiving encouragement from any statesman. My works involve me in a pecuniary loss, and the only recompense I can hope for is a general reputation as a political writer. Consequently, when my books are pillaged of their contents I am not only robbed—let me hope heedlessly—of that reward, but further experience the discouragement of seeing public commendation bestowed in the wrong quarter. On this account, I cannot help registering a protest against the practice, and expressing a hope that if nameless writers resort to it, men of established reputation at least will avoid doing unto others what they themselves would be the first to cry out against, if done unto them.

CHARLES MARVIN.

GROSVENOR HOUSE, PLUMSTEAD COMMON, KENT
    June 10, 1884.

CONTENTS.

CHAPTER I.

FROM LONDON TO THE BLACK SEA.

PAGE

The old Worship of Fire at Baku; the new Diffusion of the Light throughout Europe and the East—The Way to Baku—Summer and Winter Routes—Equipment for the Journey—Pleasantest Time for Visiting the Caspian—Departure from London—The Flushing Route—The Westward Course of Cleanliness—Railway Arrangements in Germany—Berlin, Silesia, and Russian Poland—A Halt on the Austrian Frontier—Journey through Galicia—Crossing the Border into Russia—The Censor and Foreign Literature—The South Russian Railways—The Russian Poles—Jmerinka—A Sunday Morning's Ride Across the Russian Steppes—Arrival at Odessa 1

CHAPTER II.

ODESSA AND THE CORN TRADE.

A Change for the Better—A Sunday Morning in Odessa—The Town no longer an Ink-bottle in Winter and a Sand-box in Summer—Growth of Odessa—Its Position as the Capital of South Russia—The Export of Corn—Changes in the Trade—Competition of America and India—Dearness of Transport—The Elevator Question—Necessity for Organizing the Trade—Slow Growth of Railways in Russia—Outrun by India, Canada, and other Colonies—Trade between Odessa and the East—The Suez Canal—An Odessa Country House—Departure from Odessa for Batoum—Steamboat Arrangements—Daily Life on board a Black Sea Steamer—A German Preferable to a Russian as a Cabin Companion—Crossing over to the Crimea—Eupatoria 23

CHAPTER III.

THE RESTORATION OF SEVASTOPOL AND THE RUSSIAN FLEET.

PAGE

Sevastopol and its Harbour—The Progress of the Place—Its Rival Nicolaeff—Restoration of the Great Granite Docks—The Fortifications—The Dockyard of the Black Sea Steam Navigation Company—The Origin of the Company—Statistics respecting its Growth and Present Condition—New Ocean Liners for the Black Sea—The New Ironclads—Russian Cruisers—The Present Condition of the Russian Navy—Sir Edward Reed, the Naval Professor Holloway—Admiral Popoff his Patent Pill—The Fleet during the Russo-Turkish War—Fall of Popoff—The *Régime* of the Grand Duke Alexis—The Fleet of the Future—Sevastopol and the new Black Sea Fleet, and the Decadence of Turkey—Sevastopol as a Commercial Port—The new Route to Persia and Central Asia 41

CHAPTER IV.

GLIMPSES OF THE CRIMEA.

Departure from Sevastopol—Views of the Crimean Coast from on board the Steamer—The Crimean War—Ought we to be ashamed of it or not?—The Rivalry of England and Russia in the East—Real Importance of the Crimean War—Ought Russia to have Constantinople?—English Policy in Turkey—St. George's Monastery and Balaclava—Yalta as a Watering-place—The Grape-Cure—Life at Yalta—Visit to Theodosia—Kaffa in Olden Times—Wonderful Richness of the Crimea in the Middle Ages—What the Russians have done for Theodosia—The Beauty of the Black Sea—The Rat Fortress—The Defences of Kertch—Cannon Stolen and Sold from the Ramparts of the Fortress during the Turkish War 52

CHAPTER V.

A SECRET RUSSIAN MISSION TO CABUL.

Kertch and its Greek Antiquities—A Discovery made, not Classic, but Modern—The Jew who had been to Cabul—How he participated in Skobeleff's Campaign against Geok Tepé—Alikhanoff's Journey to Merv—Persons composing the Secret Russian Expedition to Cabul—Their Route through Central

PAGE

Asia—Samuel, the Interpreter, bound to Secrecy—What he saw at Cabul—English Soldiers with the Ameer's Troops—Loot from Geok Tepé—Caution displayed by Venkhovsky—Samuel's Description of Cabul—Afghan Opinion of the Russians—The Massacre after the Capture of Geok Tepé—Women Ravished—"It is better to be Silent in this World"—Description of a Secret Survey of Merv—The true Bearings of the Discovery of the Mission—Skobeleff's Memorandum on the Invasion of India—Russia now possesses a Survey of the direct Road from Herat to Cabul, which we know little or nothing about 64

CHAPTER VI.

CRUISING ALONG THE COAST OF THE CAUCASUS.

Departure from Kertch—The Romance of the Caucasus—Wanted, a Historian—The Conflict for the Possession of the Caucasus—Anapa—Its History—The Slave Trade, Old and New—Traffic in Young Girls—Novorossisk—The Colonization of the Stavropol Plains—Rapid Growth of Rostoff-on-the-Don—Future of Novorossisk—A Second Railway projected between the Caspian and Black Sea—Petroleum in the Taman Peninsula—The French Company at Novorossisk—Bartering Girls for Herrings—Journeying along the Coast—A happy, memorable Day—Soukhum Kalé—What the Turks did and did not do in 1877—Armed Mountaineers—Poti—Arrival at Batoum . . . 79

CHAPTER VII.

THE RUSSIANS AT BATOUM.

Batoum at Night—More Tame than Heroic—Difference between the Caucasus Army and the Army in India—Poti *versus* Batoum—Drawbacks of Poti—A Costly Mole—History and Future of the Port—Its Rival, Batoum—Extraordinary Development of the Place—The Turkish Defences—Secret Russian Armaments—New Batoum—Russian Improvements—The Bay of Batoum—New Harbour Works in Progress—Mr. Peacock, the British Consul—Benefit conferred on Russia by Europe in making Batoum a Free Port—The Contraband Trade at Batoum—The Caucasus Transit—How Smuggling is carried on—The Petroleum Export Trade at Batoum—Export of Oil in 1883—Future of Batoum 91

CHAPTER VIII.

BATOUM TO TIFLIS ACROSS THE LESSER CAUCASUS.

The Transcaucasian Railway and its Present and Prospective Ramifications—The old Trade Route from India to the Black Sea, *viâ* the Caspian and Lesser Caucasus revived by the Line—The future Rusian Railway to India—Luggage Troubles at Batoum—The Batoum Railway: Cost of Constructing it—Shower-Bath Railway Carriages—Lovely character of the Scenery—The Route must some day become popular with Tourists—Cheapness of Fruit along the Line—Tracking the Rion to its Source—Romantic Views—Crossing the Suram Pass—Heavy Gradients—A Two Thousand Feet Rise in Four Hours—The Projected Tunnel—Congestion of the Petroleum Traffic—Ludwig Nobel's Plan for Overcoming this—Remarkable Climatic Differences between the East and West Side of the Suram Pass—The Passengers on the Line to Tiflis 111

CHAPTER IX.

TIFLIS AS A POLITICAL AND MILITARY CENTRE.

Tiflis in the Autumn—Development of the City—One's Impressions of the Place depend upon whether one is proceeding East or West—The Administrative District of the Caucasus—What it Cost to Conquer it—Political and Strategical Position of Tiflis—Table of Annexations during the various Russian Sovereigns' Reigns—The Conquest of Central Asia—Tiflis compared with Indian Centres—The next War in the East—Value of Russian Assurances—The Approximation of Russia and India inevitable—Lesson Taught by the Annexation of Merv—The Principal Fact to be Remembered in regard to Tiflis—The Armenians: their Present and Future—Not so tame in Spirit as commonly imagined—Russian Interest in the Armenian Question—The Caucasus Deficit . . . 125

CHAPTER X.

FROM TIFLIS TO BAKU.

The New Railway from Tiflis to Baku—Strategical Results of the Construction—Departure from Tiflis—Transformation Scene the next Morning—Views of the Elisavetopol Steppes—The Caucasus Range—Mount Ararat—Refusal of the Armenians to believe that any Man has ever attained the Summit—Delights of a Morning Meal off a Water-Melon—The Melon as a Fruit—A free-and-easy Mode of Railway Travelling—Atrocious Pace on the Transcaucasian Railway—Deficit in working the Line—The Valley of the River Kura—The Transcaucasian Irrigation System—German Colonies in the Elisavetopol District—Adji Cabul, and the projected Russian Railway to Teheran—The Line described—The future Railways to the Persian Gulf and India—Alayat, the Second Terminus on the Caspian—A Night Ride along the Caspian Coast to the Apsheron Peninsula. . 138

CHAPTER XI.

BAKU AND ITS PETROLEUM SUPPLY, FROM THE EARLIEST TIMES.

Night and Morning Impressions of Baku—Hotels—The Shipping in the Bay—The Real Russian Base of Operations against India—Proposal for supplying the Town with Water from the Volga—Life at Baku—Stephen Gulishambaroff—The History of Baku—The Ancient Fire-Worshippers—Baku Petroleum during the Zoroastrian Period—Marco Polo and Baku Oil in the Middle Ages—Conquest of Baku by Peter the Great, and the Export of the Oil up the Volga—Jonas Hanway's Account of the Industry in the Time of George the Second—The Worship of the Everlasting Fires—Cooking Food and burning Lime with Hydro-Carbon Gas—Natural Kerosine—The Deposits on Holy Island and Tcheleken—Various English Travellers at Baku since the beginning of the present Century—Descriptions of the Place by Major Marsh, General Valentine Baker, Mr. Arthur Arnold, M.P., General Sir Frederic Goldsmid, Mr. O'Donovan, Mr. Gallenga, Professor A. H. Keane, and others —Reasons assigned for giving such Prominence to the Statements of so many English Authorities 154

CHAPTER XII.

THE PETROLEUM DISTRICTS OF RUSSIA.

Official Estimate of the Area of the Petroleum Region of Russia —Localities where the Oil Abounds—The Crimean Deposits— The Supply in the Taman Peninsula—Operations at Novorossisk, in the Ter and Tiflis Districts, and near Petrovsk—The Caspian Deposits—Setting the Sea on Fire—The Transcaspian

CONTENTS.

PAGE

Oil Fields—Enough to Supply the whole Russian Empire—A Modest Annexation—Description of the Baku Oil Region—The Surakhani and Balakhani Plateaux—Quantity of Petroleum Extracted up to now—Geological Characteristics of the Caspian Petroleum Region—Erroneous Deductions of Scientific Men—Ludwig Nobel's Theory of the Petroleum Deposits—Instances of Variations in the Supply of Oil from Contiguous Wells—The Vastness of the Baku Supply beyond the Reach of Controversy—Its Inexhaustibility—Relative Positions of the Baku and Pennsylvanian Supplies from Ports accessible to European Shipping 181

CHAPTER XIII.

A DRIVE TO THE OIL WELLS.

The Phaetons at Baku—Driving to Balakhani—The Salines of the Apsheron Peninsula—Passing the Black Town—The Gardens and Vineyards of the Peninsula—Aspect of the Great Droojba Fountain from Baku—The Pipe-lines—Too Clever by Half—Baku Oil Transport before the Pipe-line Period—Grandiose Schemes for Pipe-lines to Europe—The Projected Oleoduct to the Persian Gulf—Duty on Iron Pipes—Capacity of the Pipe-lines—Aspect of the Balakhani Oil Plateau—How America Gained Upon and Beat the Old Baku Oil Supply—Statistics of the Monopoly Period—Present Free Trade enjoyed by the Industry—The Excise Period—Recent Revolutions in the Trade—Stimulus given by the Swedish Engineers, Robert and Ludwig Nobel—Prices of Crude Petroleum for the last Twenty Years—Number of Drilled Wells—Effect of the Batoum Railway upon the Industry 194

CHAPTER XIV.

THE OIL FOUNTAINS OF BAKU.

Number of Wells in Baku and America compared—One Baku Well yielding more than all the American Wells put together—A Million's worth of Oil from a Single Well—Description of a Baku Petroleum Fountain—The Droojba Spouting Well—Mode of Boring for Oil—The Balakhani Drilled and Pumping Wells—Cost of Sinking a Well—Price of Land at the Oil Fields—The Kalpak, or Well-stopper—Storing the Oil—The

PAGE

History of the Oil Fountains during the last Ten Years— Subterranean Explosions—Six Hundred Gallons of Oil in Twenty-Four Hours—Enormous Waste of Petroleum—The Fire at Krasilnikoff's Wells—A Sand Volcano 400 Feet High— Account of the Droojba Fountain—A Liquid Grindstone— Gagging the Wells at Baku—Statistical Account of the Oil wasted by the Droojba Fountain—Science and the Oil Fountains at Baku—Their Effect on Commercial Men—Necessity of placing the Fountains under the Control of the State . 210

CHAPTER XV.

THE CASPIAN OIL REFINERIES.

The Black Town of Baku—The 200 Refineries of the Caspian— The Smokelessness of Petroleum Fuel depends upon the Apparatus and Care in Using it—A Lesson in Geography for English Statesmen—The Refinery of Nobel Brothers —Consumption of Kerosine in America—The Growth of the Trade—Qualities of the Various Kinds of Refined Petroleum Manufactured at Baku—Agitation for a Uniform Standard—Mode of Refining Petroleum—Table Showing the Productibility of 100 Gallons of Russian Crude Petroleum—The American and Baku Oil compared—Mr. Boverton Redwood's Analysis of Russian Kerosine—Condition of the Industry at Baku—The Fittings of a Refinery at Baku— Russian Lubricating Oil—Export of Kerosine to Europe— Future of the Lubricating Oil Trade—Medical Properties of Petroleum—Ozokerit Deposits East of the Caspian—Barbarous Waste of the Lighter Oils—Petroleum Dyes and Colours— Hydro-Carbon Gas at Surakhani—Natural Gas Stoves . . 234

CHAPTER XVI.

LIQUID FUEL.

Petroleum Furnaces no Novelty—Use of Oil Fuel in Ancient Times —Enormous Supply available at Baku—The Early Use of Hydro-Carbon Gas—Bricks of Oil—Invention of Oil-Burning Appliances in America—Aydon's Furnace—Shpakovsky's Discovery of the Value of Steam as a Pulverizer—Why Liquid Fuel has not been adopted in England and America—The Piracy of English Inventions by Russian Engineers in the Caspian Region—The First Liquid Fuel Steamer in the Caspian —Shpakovsky's Success—Improvements effected by Lenz the

CONTENTS.

PAGE

Inventor of the Apparatus now generally in Use on Board the Caspian Steamers—Flat-flame Pulverizers—Account of the Vessels using Lenz's Apparatus—The Oil-burning Locomotives on the Transcaucasian Railway—Brandt and Karapetoff's Pulverizers—The Rival Advantages of Oil and Coal—Experience in the Caspian—Crude Petroleum may be safely Used as well as Oil Refuse—Extension of the Use of Petroleum-burning Locomotives on Russian Railways—The Discovery of Oil in Beluchistan, and its Effect on the Russian Railway to India—Liquid Fuel in the Black Sea—Summary of its Merits—Prospects of Petroleum Fuel in the East—Satisfactory Results aready Achieved 251

CHAPTER XVII.

THE OIL KING OF BAKU.

The Most Important Factor of the Baku Oil Trade—"Beyond the Sea a Chicken may be Bought for a Farthing, but it Costs a Pound to Bring it Home"—Career of Ludwig Nobel—Origin of the Nobels—Invention of the Torpedo by Emmanuel Nobel, and of Dynamite by Alfred Nobel—How Ludwig Nobel acquired the Fortune with which he started Operations in Petroleum—Commencement of the Enterprise at Baku—Laying Down the First Pipe-line—Replacing Barrels with Cistern Steamers—Account of the Oil Fleet—The "Nine-Foot" Shallows of the Volga—Transporting the Oil from Baku to Tsaritzin—Inaugurating the Tank-Car System—Establishment of the Petroleum Network of Depôts throughout Russia—Mode of Distributing the Oil in the Provinces—Not a Drop Sold Except for Cash—Baku Kerosine in Germany—Prospects of the Trade Abroad—Statistical Description of the Present Position of Nobel Brothers' Petroleum Production Company—The World Does Not Know its Greatest Men—Russian Hatred of Foreigners—Character of Ludwig Nobel—His Remarkable Talents as an Engineer. 275

CHAPTER XVIII.

THE FUTURE OF THE CASPIAN PETROLEUM TRADE.

Repeated Crises of Late Years at Baku—Their Cause—Production of Russian Refined Petroleum by Nobel Brothers and other Firms—Russia beginning to Push the Petroleum Industry—New Combinations on the Volga—Statistics of the Import of

American Oil into Russia—The Russian Petroleum Trade and
the Markets of Germany and Austria—Prospects of Rivalry
with America—Projected Railways to Transport the Oil to
Europe—Petroleum Traffic on the Transcaucasian Railway in
1883—Export from Batoum and Poti—Progress of the Various
Branches of the Trade—New Markets in Southern Europe and
the East that may be expected to Fall to Russia once the
Batoum Route is Developed—The Cheaper the Oil the Larger
the Consumption—English Enterprise of the Past and the
Present—Whether we participate or not the Baku Petroleum
Region is sure to be Developed 299

CHAPTER XIX.

OLD PERSIA—NEW RUSSIA.

Sermons Preached by the Rocks at Baku—The Slovenly Persians of
To-day—Will the English some Day Become Pariahs in India?
—Russia Growing towards our Eastern Empire—We are Only
Sojourners in India, the Russians are Settlers in the Caspian
—The Material Growth of Russia More Fraught with Danger
to our Rule than her Military Operations in Central Asia—
Russia Becoming More Unassailable in Central Asia, while We
continue as Vulnerable as Ever in India—The Shortsightedness
of English Statesmen—The Caspian now a European Lake—
The Widening of the Boundaries of Europe—Its Significance—
The Waterway between London and Baku—The Population of
Baku ; Remarkable Growth—Tchernayeff's New Road to
Central Asia *viâ* the Mertvi Kultuk and Khiva—Discovery of
Petroleum along it—The Traffic on the Volga—Russia's Progress towards the Persian Gulf—Fate of Persia—The Baku
Road to India—Statistics of it—Disappearing Obstacles—The
Cossack Approach to India—Impossible to Prevent an Approximation of the Two Empires—The Duty of all Englishmen 312

CHAPTER XX.

1884-1887.

Rapid Development of Baku since 1883—Apathy of the British
Petroleum Trade—" The New Wonder of the World "—Fountains at Baku of Late Years—The 1,000-Ton Gusher—

	PAGE
Tagieff's Fountain—The Great Fountain of 1887—Production of Crude Oil—New Pipe-lines—Growth of Traffic on the Transcaucasian Railway—Trade at Batoum—The Conflict between the Crude Pipe-line and the Kerosine Pipe-line—The Pipe-line over the Suram Pass—Policy of the Russian Government—The Burmese Oil Fields—One Thousand Million Gallons of Lamp Oil manufactured every Year—The "Moloch of Paraffin"—Growth of Russian Power in the Caspian—The Afghan Boundary Settlement—"A Clerk in Epaulettes"—Russia and the Helmund	330

APPENDIX—

Skobeleff's Project for Invading India	349
Skobeleff on the Russian Position in Central Asia	362
The Russian Invasion of India in 1877 and 1884	367
Russia's Power of Seizing Herat	374
The Russian Annexation of Merv	388
What the Annexation of Merv means	401
The Caucasus View of the Invasion of India	403

LIST OF ILLUSTRATIONS.

—o—

1. Portrait of Author	*Frontispiece.*
2. The Petroleum Fields of Europe	*To face page* 1
3. Autograph of the Russian Interpreter to the Secret Cabul Mission	70
4. His Portrait	71
5. Batoum	*To face page* 90
6. The Batoum-Baku Railway Line	113
7. Section of the Poti-Tiflis Railway	119
8. The Transcaucasian Railway Station at Elisavetopol	*To face page* 141
9. The Future Russian Railway to Tcheran-Adji Cabul Station	*To face page* 149
10. The Transcaucasian Railway. View near Baku	,, ,, 154
11. Map of the Petroleum Region of the Caspian	,, ,, 181
12. Plan of the Pipe-lines at Baku	,, ,, 199
13. An Oil Fountain at Baku	,, ,, 210
14. Portrait of Ludwig Nobel	,, ,, 275
15. The Caspian Base of Operations against India—One of the Forty Oil Steamers	*To face page* 283
16. Map showing Nobel Brothers' network of Petroleum Depôts in Russia	*To face page* 288

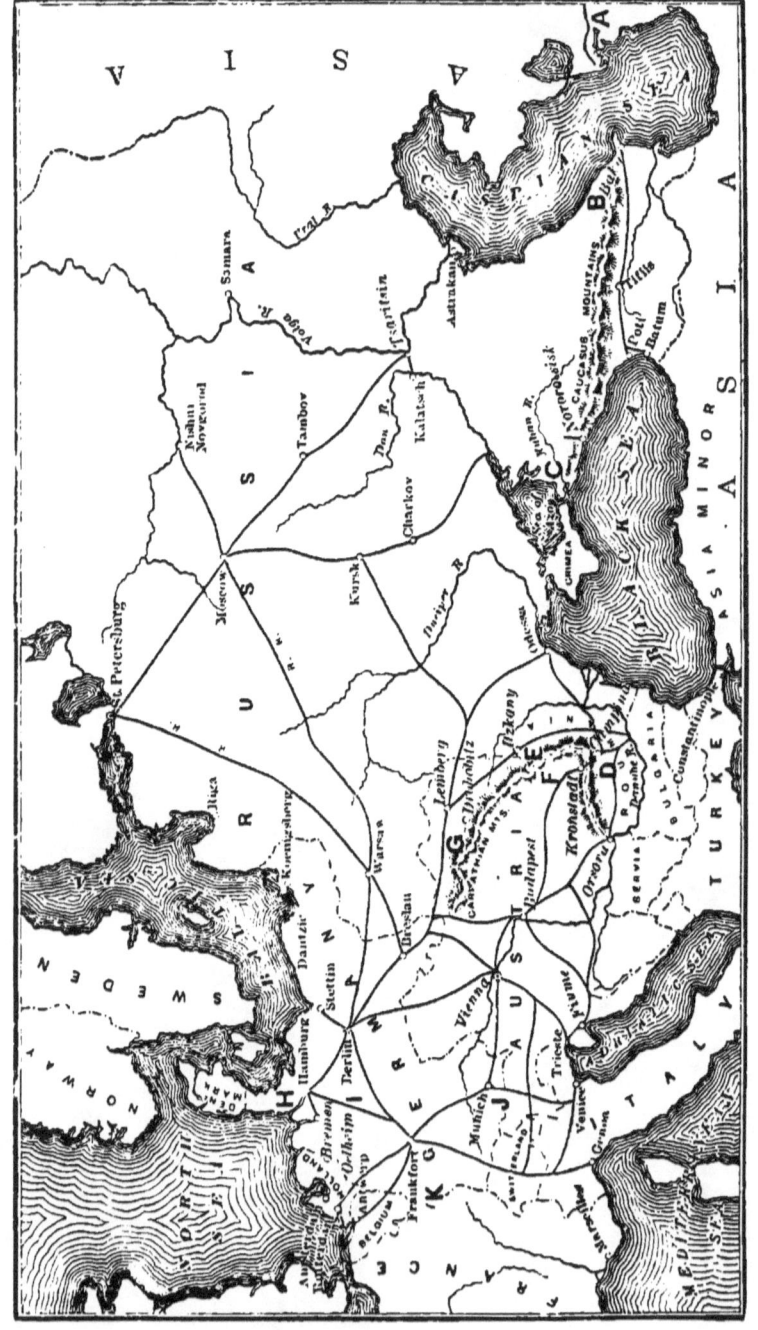

PLATE 2.—PETROLEUM FIELDS OF EUROPE.

A Transcaspian oil deposits. B Baku deposits. C Taman deposits. D Roumanian deposits. E and F Austro-Roumanian refineries.
G Galician deposits. H Hamburg refineries. I Refineries at Oelheim and Peino. J The Bavarian deposits. K Alsatian deposits.

THE
REGION OF THE ETERNAL FIRE.

CHAPTER I.

FROM LONDON TO THE BLACK SEA.

The old Worship of Fire at Baku; the new Diffusion of the Light throughout Europe and the East—The Way to Baku—Summer and Winter Routes—Equipment for the Journey—Pleasantest Time for Visiting the Caspian—Departure from London—The Flushing Route—The Westward Course of Cleanliness—Railway Arrangements in Germany—Berlin, Silesia, and Russian Poland—A Halt on the Austrian Frontier—Journey through Galicia—Crossing the Border into Russia—The Censor and Foreign Literature—The South Russian Railways—The Russian Poles—Jmerinka—A Sunday Morning's Ride Across the Russian Steppes—Arrival at Odessa.

A FEW years ago a solitary figure might have been daily seen on the shore of the Caspian Sea, worshipping a fire springing naturally from the petroleum gases in the ground. The devotee was a Parsee from India—the last of a series of priests who for more than 2,500 years had tended the sacred flame upon the spot. Round about his crumbling temple were rising greasy derricks and dingy kerosine distilleries—symbols of a fresh cult, the worship of mammon—but, absorbed in his devotions, the Parsee took no heed of the intruders. And so time passed on, and the last of the Fire-Worshippers died, and with him perished the flame that was older than history. And yet not so. The flickering light the Gueber priests had kept alive from the epoch of myths, had only quitted the ruined temple to reappear in a million brilliant jets throughout a region stretching for thousands of miles around Baku—in the cities of the icy north, in the teeming villages of middle Russia, here and there upon the southern steppes; lighting up the strongholds of the Caucasus, the caravanserais of Persia, the tents of Askabad and Merv; flaring in the furnaces of hundreds of steamers on the Caspian and Volga, and locomotives traversing the valleys of the Frosty Caucasus. The worship of the Eternal Fire in the Surakhani temple is dead; the Priest has left behind no followers; but the oil that dimly lit a shrine now illuminates an empire, and bids, ere long, to give light and heat to an entire hemisphere.

. . . .

From London to Baku is a distance of a little over 2,500 miles. The whole is traversed by steam. At present the journey occupies ten or eleven days, but this could be easily reduced by quickening the Russian communications. A twelvemonth ago, when the Russian Government sought to raise a loan in the European money markets, to cover the cost of constructing the Transcaucasian Railway, the late Mr. Edward Cazalet showed me a circular, ex-officially addressed to capitalists by the Minister of Finance, describing the completion of the railway as having brought Paris within six days' distance of Baku. This was anticipating history a bit, but there is very little doubt that before long it will be possible to do the journey from London to the Caspian in a week.

The direct route lies through Berlin, Odessa, Batoum, and Tiflis; but in the summer a very pleasant tour can be effected, with only a slightly increased expenditure of time, by proceeding by rail through Berlin, St. Petersburg, and Moscow to Nijni Novgorod, and then dropping down the Volga in a steamer to the Caspian; the return route being *viâ* Tiflis, Batoum, Odessa, and Vienna. This I should designate the best route of all. The Volga may also be struck at Tsaritzin by those who have less time to spare; or, one may journey by rail direct to Vladikavkaz, at the foot of the Caucasus, and thence post by road to Petrovsk on the Caspian, catching there the steamer to Baku, or, view the magnificent scenery of the Caucasus by proceeding through the Dariel Pass to Tiflis, whence the railway takes the traveller on to his destination. But these alternative routes to Baku, however attractive, are only summer ones. In winter-time the Volga is frozen to its mouth, the Caucasian passes are clogged with snow, and the traveller to Baku can hardly do better than take the direct route across the Black Sea. I myself travelled to Baku by this route, going and returning, but I had undertaken so many journeys through Russia previously, that there was little temptation to adopt a more circuitous road, even if circumstances had not been altogether hostile to any such notion.

As for equipment, so little is needed beyond the ordinary requirements of home travelling, that one might really start from Charing Cross with nothing except a spare suit of clothes and two or three changes of linen, and pick up at the well-stocked shops of Odessa, Batoum, or Baku whatever subsequently seemed necessary. In summer, a helmet should be taken, not omitting some pipeclay to clean it, as helmets rapidly soil, and Russians in the south are very particular about the spruceness of their head-gear. Or, better still, the traveller may leave behind the helmet and its inconvenient case, and purchase at Odessa one of those white caps which are universally worn by upper-class Russians and officers throughout South Russia, the Caucasus, and Central Asia. These have linen covers, which can be removed and washed, and besides looking always spruce, they are easily stowed away, are very comfortable, and provoke less notice than the helmet. A couple of white suits will be appreciated, and a light macintosh will be found useful at Batoum, where heavy rains are common all the year round. Any medicines the traveller may require may be easily obtained at the chemist shops in Russian towns, but as their drugs are sometimes dear and bad, it is as well to take a little quinine, some chlorodyne, and a few pills. But, providing he carefully avoids drinking water, the traveller may disregard any fears of ill-health during his journey. Batoum is the only place seriously affected with malaria, and his stay is not likely to be long there. Keating, of course, should not be forgotten by those who have sensitive skins; although this advice sounds like recommending the carrying of coal to Newcastle, since Transcaucasia is the district where the insect-killing Persian powder is produced. Small revolvers are invariably carried in the Caucasus.

The pleasantest time for visiting Baku is in the autumn, when the torrid heat of summer is over, and travelling is rendered enjoyable by the abundance of fruit in the Caucasus. Not many persons are likely to visit the region in winter; but all that is needed by those who do is a fur-lined coat, such as have been fashionable in London of late, a fur cap, and a pair of flannel-lined goloshes. As I have before stated, anything else the traveller fancies he wants he can readily obtain *en route*. He will naturally not omit to have his passport viséd by a Russian consul before leaving, or he will be stopped at the frontier. During his travels in Russia the passport must be handed over to the keeper of every hotel he stops at, to be registered by the local police, and before quitting the country he must obtain a notification (*sveedaitelstvo*) from the police that there is no crime against him, without which he will again render himself liable to be stopped at the border. This notification is usually obtained by the hotel-keeper of the last town the traveller stops at before leaving the country.

Travelling direct first-class, the journey from London to Baku costs about £35, including ordinary hotel and every other expense *en route*. The cost second-class is about £25, which includes first-class fare across the Black Sea, the second-class cabins being too unsatisfactory on the steamers. The Russian second-class carriages are not so good as those on the German lines, but persons travelling to the limits of Germany second-class can pay the excess fare and travel first on entering Russia. The money for the journey should be taken in English gold and notes, which may be readily changed at the principal Continental stations, or in the form of a letter of credit on a banking house at Odessa or Tiflis. In France 100 centimes make a franc, or 10d.; in Germany 100 pfennigs a mark, or 1s.; and in Russia 100 copecks (pronounced copeeks) a paper rouble, or 2s. The silver rouble is a myth; it disappeared from circulation years ago.

I have gone rather fully into these details, because there are a very large number of people interested in the petroleum trade anxious to avail themselves of the resources of Baku. If they will accept my word that it is as easy to go from London to the Caspian by the route I traversed as from London to Newcastle, they will perhaps be tempted to do what more than one Englishman has already done—go straight to Baku and make arrangements on the spot with the firms there for the opening up of business relations. A splendid market exists at Baku ready to be exploited, direct communication between it and England has just been established, and all that is needed is that English men of business should avail themselves of the new opening before Continental rivals appear upon the scene.

. . . . . .

I left London at half-past eight on Wednesday night, August 15, bound for Baku, *viâ* Berlin. On previous occasions I had made for the German capital by the Calais route, but this time I thought I would try the way by Flushing. It is an advantage of this route that if you are a good sailor, and the steamer is not crowded, you have an excellent night's rest, while, in addition, the travelling through Holland is superior to that on the wretched French railways. On the other hand, it is a serious disadvantage that when you reach Berlin you have only a quarter of an hour to change trains, purchase your ticket, and register your luggage; hence, besides standing a chance of losing your train, you have no time for either a wash and brush up or a supper.

The night was so boisterous that at the last moment I was inclined to change the route and proceed *viâ* Calais. However, never liking to alter my plans once they are formed, I kept to my original intention, and after an hour and a half's rapid spin found myself on the jetty at Queenboro', making for the steamer " Prince of Orange." The powerful vessels of the Zeeland Steamship Company are well adapted for service across the Channel on rough nights such as that on which I left England, and are certainly preferable to the older boats on the Calais route, on one of which I was last year ill from the time I left Dover until I reached Calais. On the same boat I should have probably been ill again, but in the case of the ,,Prince of Orange " I had a good supper while the luggage and mails were being hauled on board, and had already made myself snug and fallen into a heavy sleep before we were fairly in rough water. Shortly after midnight I was awakened by a deal of pitching and rolling, but with the exception of one particularly vicious jerk, which nearly deprived me at a stroke of what remained of my supper, I suffered no inconvenience, and slept again until the steward aroused me to say that we were close alongside Flushing.

Proceeding on deck, I found the vessel already made fast to the quay, and the passengers hurrying across it to the rambling station beyond. This is only of a temporary character, and doubtless will be made more convenient when the traffic settles down. The refreshment room is very inadequate for the requirements of the place, and when the steamer arrives crowded with passengers it must be almost impossible to get a comfortable meal. Even at the best of times, there is a scramble for the eggs and rolls and coffee.

Breakfast over, there was plenty of time to dawdle over one's toilet before the train drew into the station. Then the doors were opened, and the passengers made an unnecessary rush for the carriages, in which there was plenty of room for twice their number. A few minutes later all were comfortably seated, and instituting comparisons between the Dutch carriages and our own—not at all in favour of the latter—and then, shortly after seven, the train set off at a rattling speed in the direction of Berlin.

The morning was wet and cold, the landscape had a drenched look, as is the case half the year in Holland. But, in spite of this, it was impossible not to admire the beautiful trimness of the fields, the rows of stately trees lining the well-kept roads and canals, and the scrupulously clean and highly-painted cottages. The Dutch, I suppose, are the cleanest people in Europe. The further one travels east from Holland the dirtier the people become. The Germans are clean, but by no means so scrupulously clean as the Dutch. The people of East Germany are not so clean as those of West Germany.

As for the Russians, their dirt and squalor are proverbial. But even the Russians are as exemplary as the Dutch compared with the Armenians and Persians. The climax seems to be reached in Central Asia, where the nomads rarely wash themselves and their clothes, and a condition of person is attained which makes the reality a little different from the picture of handsome warriors and harem beauties drawn by the poets.

Chiefs of the Uzbek race
Waving their heron crests with martial grace,

sounds very pretty, but the traveller would do well to pack up some Keating when he puts his "Lalla Rookh" into the portmanteau.

The journey through Holland occupied us the whole morning, the German frontier being crossed shortly before mid-day. The landscape now lost its acute trimness, the canals disappeared, and fields of waving corn and orchards of ripening fruit succeeded the pasture-lands of Holland. Before long the smart military-looking German guard who had replaced the Dutch functionary at Goch appeared at the window, and handed in circulars printed in several languages, announcing that the passengers could either dine at Oberhausen during the half-hour's halt, or have the dinner handed into the carriage on trays to be eaten more comfortably during the journey. All the other passengers decided in favour of dining at the station, but I preferred the latter course, knowing from experience its advantages; and had the satisfaction of afterwards seeing the rest, who, owing to the train being behind time, had only twenty minutes at Oberhausen, gaze regretfully at the tranquil dinner I was enjoying in the carriage. To dine in the train in Germany is quite as cheap, and very much more convenient, than at the stations. Upon receiving your order, the guard affixes a label to the window, notifying the number of dinners required in the carriage, and when the train stops at the station, waiters dart forward with trays and deposit the corresponding number inside it. The tray is a bright, clean, electro-plated one, with a velvet covered rest to keep it steady on the knees, and contains in separate compartments some bouillon or soup, a veal cutlet, several slices of roast beef, two kinds of vegetables, some stewed fruit, and a half-pint bottle of white wine, accompanied by a new roll, a nice white napkin, and a couple of toothpicks. No one who has enjoyed such a dinner in Germany will begrudge the two and a half marks, or half-a-crown, which is exacted for it; and when he hands out the tray at the next large station, half an hour or three-quarters of an hour distant, he will be inclined to agree with me, as he leans back against the cushions to enjoy a cigar, that it would be cheaper even at double the price than a scrambling meal at a railway station.

At picturesque Minden, so full of historical associations, which we reached at about five o'clock, all the passengers got out except one, with whom I travelled the rest of the way to Berlin. When the distance is short, a carriageful of good-humoured, sociable passengers is very pleasant, but for a long journey one is enough for a sound conversation. In this instance my companion was a cultured German, the brother of a celebrated musician, settled in England, thanks to whose agreeable society the six hours' journey from Minden to Berlin was rapidly performed without any feeling of fatigue, and I was really sorry he could not accompany me further. There was one remark he made during the ride which made a great impression upon me. Discussing which was the greatest pleasure in life, he said, "I have tasted every possible enjoyment, for I had a gay youth and married late in life, but to my mind there is nothing that has ever occasioned me such an exquisite feeling as I experience when

I hear my little children running to the door to greet me on my arrival home." Poor fellow! he was proceeding to some German baths to undergo a tedious course of treatment for an internal disease, and from what he told me, I felt certain he would never see his children out of their infancy.

But even without his company the journey would have been pleasant enough, for, as I have before said in my works, Germany is the best country in Europe for railway travelling. The scenery is invariably charming, and this is particularly the case in passing through Hanover, and at the various stations there are plenty of waiters to hand round coffee, beer, wine, fruit, and other refreshments at the carriage door. I hope to be excused for dwelling rather strongly on the point of refreshments, but I mostly find that when people question me about undertaking a journey to Russia, their first inquiry is not about the scenery, but as to the character of the commissariat arrangements. After all, the best of scenery palls on an empty stomach. In Germany, one has good scenery and good living on the railway, and it is well to make the best of both, since in South Russia they are very indifferent.

Berlin reached, I alighted at the Schlessische Bahnhof, and seizing upon the sharpest looking of the blue-bloused porters, made him hurry my luggage below to the booking office. Here, while my portmanteau was being re-weighed, I secured a through ticket to Odessa; English gold, as usual in Germany, being taken as readily as the national currency, and then, hastening the registration of the luggage, darted back to the platform in time to catch the Breslau train. By tipping the guard I secured a carriage to myself, with a lavatory attached, and after ridding myself of the grime inseparable from prolonged railway travelling, made myself comfortable for the night.

When morning broke the train was already close to Breslau, and at six I was breakfasting at the rather comfortless station there. From Breslau to the frontier the railway traverses the Black Country of Germany, a region full of mines, ironworks, squalid towns and dirty villages. The rural scenery is flat and tame, and the ground carelessly cultivated. In Western Germany, round about Oberhausen and Dusseldorf, there is another Black Country; but the towns are clean there, the villages prosperous and picturesque, and the land well tilled. In the latter instance, however, the people are Teutons; in the former they are Slavs. The general features of Silesia are identical in appearance with those of the Polish provinces of Russia. If the region has a more prosperous look than the latter, the circumstance is due less to the Silesians themselves than to the constant efforts of Germany to ameliorate their lot.

Myslowitz, the frontier town, which we reached at midday, is as dull and as wretched a place as any in Silesia. There everybody alighted, and I was arranging to leave for Cracow by the one o'clock train, when I found that my luggage had been sent on by mistake to Oswiecim. The one o'clock train did not proceed to Cracow by this route, but by a shorter one, and although I might have had my luggage sent on to Cracow sealed up by telegraphing to Oswiecim, I thought it safer to go by the evening train. This involved spending at Myslowitz the five or six hours I had intended to pass in the pretty city of Cracow, but circumstances would not allow of my risking any delay over the luggage. I almost regretted my decision afterwards, when I began to explore the town. It is a strictly agricultural centre, of 2,000 inhabitants, with half-a-dozen indifferent shops in its ill-paved thoroughfares, and two or three inns. At the best of these latter I ordered dinner, and was surprised at the number of persons that dropped in to follow my example—some of them Germans and the others Poles—commercial travellers, traders, clerks, and so forth. They talked politics pretty freely, and their opinions were a fair sample of those prevailing in the town. Myslowitz is more disposed to see the rest of the Poles gathering under the German Eagle, than allying themselves with Panslavist Russia.

Years ago I had occasion to travel through and reside for a time in Russian Poland. The general features of provincial life in German and Russian Poland are the same; but I was particularly struck with one important difference, which will exercise a significant bearing on the future of the Poles. In Russian Poland, as elsewhere in Russia, education is at a very low ebb. Schools are rarely found in the villages, and only a minority of the children attend school in the towns. While I was eating my rumpsteak at Myslowitz—it was a very tender one, and deserves to be publicly mentioned—I saw crowds of little children running along the street merrily to school; not simply clean, tidy youngsters of the respectable classes, but also shorn-headed, barelegged, ragged little mortals of the London Arab description. Myslowitz is very much behind the rest of Germany in the race of civilization, but even there every child, however poor, has to go to school.

In German Poland the whole of the rising generation is being educated. To a great extent this is also the case, I believe, with the Poles in Galicia. In Russian Poland, on the other hand, the children are growing up as ignorant of the three R's as the majority of youngsters elsewhere in the Tsar's empire. Panslavism may be a very fine creed—for some of its advocates at Moscow, whom I personally know, I have a sincere esteem—but I cannot detect in it any attraction that should cause the educated Poles of Germany and Austria to throw in their lot with the ignorant and oppressed masses of Russia.

When I had finished dining at the inn at Myslowitz I went for a ramble in the country. As usual in Slavland, there was nothing in the landscape to invite a prolonged walk. Forest scenery one never tires of—had Myslowitz been one of the out-of-the-way stations of Northern Russia I should have quickly got rid of my six hours' *ennui* by exploring the woods, heedless of problematical wolves and inevitable mosquitos. But the surroundings of Myslowitz were similar to those that prevail throughout the whole of the southern parts of the great plain of Europe inhabited by the Slavs—oblong patches of vegetation stretching away over a flat expanse as far as the eye could see, with not a tree or a shrub to enliven the landscape. Even the most inveterate lover of country walks would rapidly tire of toiling along a dusty or muddy road, full of ruts, with nothing to see except everlasting patches of wheat, barley, oats, millet, and buckwheat. It is curious that the Teuton, wherever he goes, carries with him his love of trees and a bit of garden. The Slav, on the other hand, seems to prefer a desert. German colonies are scattered all over Russia, from the Baltic to the Caspian. If you are travelling through some of the southern districts intervening between those two seas, and are sick of traversing mile after mile of flat country, village after village of Slavs, without seeing a tree or a bush, you may rest assured if you hear that a German colony is near that you will find it buried in verdure.

Returning to the station, I made the rest of the time fly by writing until the train was ready to start. As usual in Germany, the railway officials were very obliging. One porter in particular—he who had caused my detention by sending on my luggage by the wrong train—attended me most assiduously, assisting me in arranging my writing materials on a table in the waiting-room, bringing me coffee, and continually dropping in to see how I was going on, until the first bell rang, when he carried me and my hand-luggage off to a *coupé* in the train he had secured for me. His unremitting exertions on my behalf even extended to licking for me the postage stamp he had obtained for the letter I had written—and taking it off afterwards, I imagine, for neither the letter nor the stamp ever reached its destination.

' From Myslowitz to the first station on the Austrian side of the frontier, Oswiecim, the journey occupies about an hour. I noticed that all the houses in the villages passed *en route*, in common with the whole of the buildings in Myslowitz, were loopholed. This may be said to be a regular feature of German frontier habitations, at any rate along the Austrian and Russian borders. Many of the loopholes bore obvious traces of having been hurriedly broken through the walls during former wars, but there must be some local regulation in force that keeps them open still, as they are all unclosed, and the whole of the new buildings that are constructed alongside the main roads or railways are furnished with musketry slits. Thanks to the prevalence of this system, the villages and towns in the German borderlands are capable of rapid defence against cavalry, and constitute a troublesome impediment to invaders.

Oswiecim is an important strategical point, for the Russian and German railway systems converge upon the point and join the Cracow-Vienna Railway. The station, however, is very insignificant; and more like a roadside refreshment-house than anything else, and the refreshments, like the officials, are very indifferent. I found my luggage waiting for me, and had it passed without any difficulty; then whiled away the hour we had to wait by drinking a tumbler of coffee with some Russians. When the train arrived I was particularly pleased with the handsome character of the Austrian carriages, and the urbanity of the guards. The carriages are on the American principle, and are fitted with every comfort, but have the defect of the gangway running through the centre of them instead of at one of the sides. By this means it is impossible to get a six-foot stretch at night. The best ordinary first-class carriages in Europe, in my opinion, are the new ones on the St. Petersburg-Moscow Railway. These are fitted with three rows of easy chairs, one along the centre of the carriage and the other two at the sides. By touching a bit of mechanism they let down and form a roomy six-foot bed with a pillow at the top. Eighteen or twenty persons can thus sleep in one carriage very comfortably.

Cracow was reached at ten o'clock, and sufficient time allowed for supper. Here the *coupé* I occupied lost its Russian occupants—a landowner's family from Kieff—and a countryman entered, Mr. Herbert Coxon, of the firm of James Coxon and Co., of Newcastle-on-Tyne. Mr. Coxon had conceived the idea of utilizing his holidays by taking a trip to Constantinople and the Caucasus, to see whether he could not arrange for a direct supply of Oriental carpets, now so fashionable in England. Had I not met him at Cracow he would have probably gone to Constantinople first, but he changed his plans on hearing I was bound for Baku, and shaped his course for the Caucasus. Thanks to this circumstance, I had as far as the Caspian a companion, whose never failing good humour, hearty manner, and huge capacity for enjoyment gave a zest to the journey and prevented it from becoming dull. On his return home Mr. Coxon published an interesting little work, recounting his experiences, entitled, "Oriental Carpets: how they are made and conveyed to Europe, with a narrative of a journey to the East in search of them." This deservedly proved a great success.

After an indifferent sleep, spoiled by the cramped position in which we were compelled to lie, we traversed the prosperous and picturesque city of Lemberg early in the morning, and about half-past ten o'clock reached Podvolotchisk, the frontier station. A brief halt, and then we crossed the Russian frontier and steamed slowly into Volotchisk, the first station on the Tsar's territory. This is not a very inviting place for one to make his first acquaintance with the Russian Empire. The station is small, with a wretched refreshment room to waste an hour in, no lavatory, and a very indifferent set of officials. Not that the latter bothered us much. They confiscated two or three copies of the *Newcastle Chronicle* and other English papers belonging to Mr. Coxon, but this was an exceptional instance of adherence to the regulations, as I have crossed the frontier several times with my portmanteau half full of books, pamphlets, and papers, and even in this instance, after the newspapers had been taken from Mr. Coxon's trunk, the same official turned to mine, adjoining it, and passed its literary contents without any question.

When I was proceeding last year to Moscow to visit the exhibition, I took with me half-a-dozen copies of my "Russian Advance towards India," which embodied the conversations with Russian statesmen I had contributed a few months earlier to the *Chronicle*. On the way to Berlin I travelled with an Englishman who had never been in Russia, and another who had been born and bred there, and was a merchant of quite thirty years' standing at St. Petersburg. The conversation turning upon the severity of the Censor, the latter said to the former, "They take everything from you at the frontier that is printed. I go to England every spring for my holidays, and when I return I deliver at the frontier all my books tied up together in brown paper, and afterwards apply for them at the Censor Office at St. Petersburg; otherwise, any attempt at concealment would lead to confiscation." I pooh-poohed such elaborate precautions, on the grounds that by delivering the books in a packet to the officials one compelled them to adhere to old regulations, which are rapidly dropping into abeyance, and are only enforced in exceptional instances. When I added that I had six copies alone of a political work on Russia, with passages referring to Prince Krapotkin, the merchant earnestly begged me to follow his example, and painted all manner of evil consequences that would ensue if I did not do so.

Arrived at the frontier, the case was put to the test. The six copies had been distributed throughout my luggage. Diving into one side of my portmanteau, the rummager produced one of the copies and handed it to the officer. I translated the title into Russ, and said it was simply a work on Central Asia. By this time the searcher had dipped again, and brought up a second copy to the surface. The officer examined its title and then handed them back to the man, who replaced them. Turning then to the other side of the portmanteau he brought up two more copies at a stroke. "This seems to be a favourite work of yours," observed the officer, with a certain amount of sarcasm. "Well, I suppose an author has an excuse for taking an interest in his own productions," I rejoined, pointing to the name at the foot of the title. "Oh, I see," replied the officer with a smile, and then turning to his subordinate said, "You need not search any more of this gentleman's luggage."

Had I followed the old merchant's advice I should have compelled the officer to keep to his instructions, whether he wished to or not; and besides bringing on myself the trouble of applying at the Censor Office for the books, would have probably failed to get them passed for several weeks, perhaps not until after my departure from Russia. How inconvenient this must have been will be seen from the following circumstance. A few days after my arrival Skobeleff died, and the *Novoe Vremya*, to which a copy had been sent, published a translation of all the matter in it referring to that general. This translation was copied into almost every other Russian newspaper. Subsequently it appeared in the pamphlet biographies that were sold by tens of thousands in the streets, and finally penetrated to every part of the empire, where there are Russian troops, in the little periodical "Reading for Soldiers," published under the auspices of the Government. Such publicity and the advantages it secured me would have been lost had the book been thrust into the Censor's hands. In general, it may be accepted as a rule that there is no regulation or law in Russia, however despotic, which may not be set aside with greater facility than the proverbial driving of a coach-and-four through an English Act of Parliament.

After our luggage was passed and our passports registered, we changed some gold into dirty but convenient Russian paper money at the official exchange office, and sat down to a little lunch before leaving. It is as well to make as good a meal as one can at Volotchisk, there being no buffet worthy of the name beyond until the train reaches Jmerinka, the junction for Kieff, at six in the evening. The intervening stations are as bad as any to be found in Russia. At Jmerinka, however, there is a very fine and remarkably cheap buffet, and plenty of time allowed for a good dinner. After arriving unwashed from Austria, the excellent lavatory, where a barber is kept, is a real luxury to the traveller.

Excluding Jmerinka, the Odessa-Volotchisk Railway has nothing to recommend it. It consists of a single line of metals laid on rotten sleepers, the rolling stock is dirty and uncomfortable, and the pace of the trains terribly slow. Easy-chair alarmists, who are fearful of Russia some day swooping down upon Austria, should take a trip along the Odessa Railway, after which they will return home convinced that it will be some time before Vienna needs a Magyar or Teutonic Sobieski to drive off the Cossack. A short time ago one of the leading German military papers instituted an elaborate statistical comparison of the Russian and German railway systems, the results of which were accurately worked out as follow. Russia suffers from the serious inconvenience that most of her frontier railways consist of only one line of metals, and that her stations are widely apart from one another, the minimum distance being twelve miles. In consequence of this she could only send to the frontier along each line twelve trains a day, while Germany could despatch sixteen. Russia has only seven lines extending to the frontier, Germany ten; Russia, therefore, could only send eighty-four trains per diem as compared with Germany's 160. In other words Germany could accumulate in five days nine army corps on the frontier, to confront which Russia could only concentrate four. This is the outcome of figures. But no one who has travelled on the Russian and German railways, and noticed the superiority of the Germans in working the traffic, will dispute for a moment that the comparison would, in reality, be very much more to the disadvantage of Russia. I have not by me the means for instituting exact comparisons between Austria and Russia, but I know that Austria is very much better able to invade her northern rival than for the latter to rush upon her. Russia is conscious that in a single-handed conflict she would get the worst of any encounter with the Germans, and she is not by any means sure, even in spite of the sympathy of the Slavs, that she would come gloriously out of a conflict with Austria. This consciousness is really the best guarantee for peace we have in Middle Europe at the present moment, for I suppose no one would seriously allege that Germany and Austria desire to meddle with Russia.

From the mid-day departure from Volotchisk until the evening arrival at Jmerinka, the train traverses an undulating country, which gradually becomes flatter and tamer the further one gets from the off-shoots of the Carpathians. The country is entirely devoted to the growing of corn and rearing of flocks and herds, but although identical in this respect with Galicia, the province of Podolia has none of the prosperous, progressive, and well-cultivated look of the former. The people are the same—save that the Podolians have a dash of Cossack and Tartar blood in them—their modes of living are almost identical; but the border line divides economical conditions enormously to the disadvantage of Russia's Slav subjects. The same is the case at every other point of the Russian frontier I have crossed in my time—prosperous well-built villages, well-cultivated fields, good roads, respectably-dressed intelligent peasants up to the very border of Germany and Austria; and then, directly afterwards, squalid villages, badly-tilled fields, wretched tracks, and dirty ignorant peasants on the Russian side. I do not say that the Poles in Germany and Austria do not suffer from many political and sentimental disadvantages, but there is certainly no material superiority in the neighbouring Russian provinces to cause them to ardently desire annexation to a Power, which still cherishes and exults over the evil deeds of the "butcher" Berg, and the "hangman" Mouravieff.

The afternoon ride from the frontier to Jmerinka was an extremely hot one, and we arrived at the station exhausted. The Volotchisk train went no further, and we had to wait more than an hour for the one running from Kieff to Odessa; allowing plenty of time for a good meal and a pleasant promenade on the platform afterwards, in the cool of the evening. I had hoped we should have had a good night's rest in the roomier

Kieff carriages, but when we left Jmerinka at seven o'clock there were so many passengers that there was no chance of getting a comfortable stretch. We were as uncomfortably packed for the night as in a crowded compartment on an English line.

From Jmerinka to Odessa, fifteen hours' journey, the railway traverses a real piece of steppe land—at places so flat that gazing from the window on either side of the carriage, it is often impossible to discern the slightest elevation or depression as far as the eye can reach. All around extends an interminable expanse of more or less cultivated land, unbroken by a single mound, landmark, tree, or shrub. Villages exist at intervals of many miles, but the stone or mud cabins have no gardens round them, no bushes, no trees. The whole country is a corn desert, terribly monotonous to look at in summer, and a fearful place for snowstorms in winter. I have traversed the steppes in almost every part of Russia, but those of Kherson are the flattest I have yet seen. For hours the next morning after quitting Austria we crawled through nothing but corn—here cut and standing in massive sheaves, there already carted away and the stubble ploughed up for the winter sowings, but mostly still untouched by the reaper. It is this region that absorbs the largest amount of the English agricultural machinery imported into Russia; for, in the southern-most steppes of Russia the population is scanty, labour relatively dear, and the harvest can only be won by the aid of machinery.

Being Sunday morning, there were very few peasants at work in the fields. As the train rattled slowly over the metals, we constantly passed parties of them in clumsy waggons, drawn by bullocks, going on visits to other villages or to some neighbouring market. For weeks there had been no rain in the district—the ground was cracked and parched, the ponds dried up, and in places the entire crop had been scorched off the ground. Huge dense clouds of black dust rose and enveloped the peasants as their waggons rumbled over the uneven roads, and even our train, jolting over the rotten sleepers, on which the metals were loosely pinned, provoked powdery emanations from the soil that filled the carriage with motes, and clogged the pores of our skin. Long before the hour that we should have sat down to breakfast in England, we were experiencing the exhausting effects of the heat, and longing for a bath to remove the coating of dust that had collected since our evening ablutions at Jmerinka. The railway carriage was provided with a lavatory, but it was so filthy that it was impossible to perform one's toilette in the place. I was sorry I had not brought with me a portable india-rubber basin and ewer, which could have been easily strapped with the rugs. There was plenty of water at the various stations, and abundance of time for lavatory operations either in the train, or, undisturbed by oscillations, during the numerous halts.

The nearer we got to Odessa the larger the stations became, and the greater the number of passengers. The latter consisted of peasants, mostly Cossack or Little Russian, with a considerable sprinkling of Jews. At one of the stations, where we had an eight o'clock tumbler of tea, the peasants had brought several waggon-loads of water melons to a spot near the platform, and did a brisk trade with the passengers by selling them at the rate of about a penny a-piece. Still crawling along at a miserable speed, the scenery never varying, we reached Odessa at last at ten in the morning, hungry, dirty, hot, and tired.

CHAPTER II.

ODESSA AND THE CORN TRADE.

A Change for the Better—A Sunday Morning in Odessa—The Town no longer an Ink-bottle in Winter and a Sand-box in Summer—Growth of Odessa—Its Position as the Capital of South Russia—The Export of Corn—Changes in the Trade—Competition of America and India—Dearness of Transport—The Elevator Question—Necessity for Organizing the Trade—Slow Growth of Railways in Russia—Outrun by India, Canada, and other Colonies—Trade between Odessa and the East—The Suez Canal—An Odessa Country House—Departure from Odessa for Batoum—Steamboat Arrangements—Daily Life on Board a Black Sea Steamer—A German Preferable to a Russian as a Cabin Companion—Crossing over to the Crimea—Eupatoria.

"COME, come, Mr. Marvin, if this is Russia, all I can say is, that it is a little bit more civilized than the Newcastle folk believe it to be," said C., an hour later, gazing with satisfaction at the breakfast table at the Hotel d'Europe. To this hotel we had driven direct from the station, and had enhanced the exhilaration produced by rattling along the leafy boulevards at a furious pace, breasting a glorious sea-breeze, by unlimited splashing and dabbling in cold water. Russians can wash themselves to their heart's content with a mere mugful of that liquid. Hence the quart-pot supply that stood in the bedrooms evidently represented what the Hotel d'Europe thought to be the extra allowance demanded by the more exacting nations of the West. However, this little defect was overcome by impressing all the servants we saw loitering about the spacious corridors, and ordering them to keep on bringing water in pans, pots, and ewers until further notice. By this means we accumulated in a few minutes a plentiful supply, and went at it as only Englishmen can who have experienced the craving for water that accompanies a long journey across a dusty and arid plain.

There are a number of good hotels at Odessa, but few equal the Hotel d'Europe for cleanliness, comfort, and luxury; while as regards site it is unsurpassable, situated as it is in front of a square on a height overlooking the harbour and sea, and catching the refreshing salt breeze blowing from the water. One could hardly be more comfortable in an English seaside hotel than at the Hotel d'Europe, and if the charges are higher than those of the other Odessa establishments, they do not exceed the general run of prices in England. The manager speaks English, and from the numerous English travellers calling there, knows our ways tolerably well. To any one arriving at Odessa from a journey to the East, it is an additional comfort to be able to get there the latest English newspapers.

Our breakfast was served up in a handsome spacious room, with a highly polished cool parquet floor, and windows and doorways decorated with palms and evergreens. Through the windows could be seen people passing to and fro in flat caps or helmets, and loose white summer clothing. The day was hot, and there was not a cloud in the intensely blue sky to intercept the heat of the southern sun; but as they passed the windows they evidently enjoyed as much as we did the cooling breeze from the sea. This, entering by doorway and window, ruffled pleasantly the cool clean white damask table-cloth, spread on a little table near a grove of evergreens, whereon were disposed delicious coffee and rolls, and a huge dish of ham and eggs, set off with handsome electro-plated ware and china, and a fresh uncut copy of the *Times* received by the last post from London. One might have searched a long while that pleasant Sunday morning to have found in any English town more agreeable arrangements for a breakfast, and, coming to it as we did, hungry from the Kherson plains, we thoroughly appreciated every feature of it.

Odessa has greatly improved since the primitive time of alternate mud and dust, which caused the poet Pushkin to compare it to an ink-bottle in winter and a sand-box in summer. Its broad quadrangular streets are well paved, and planted like boulevards with acacia; the lofty white houses, built of shell concrete obtained from neighbouring quarries, are enlivened by handsome shops. As a town it is better built and better paved than either St. Petersburg or Moscow, and in many other respects is more advanced than either of those capitals. When the poet Pushkin—the contemporary and admirer of Byron—dwelt in it, the city was still in its infancy, like Novorossisk, Poti, Batoum, and other points on the Caucasian coast to-day. There are yet persons living in South Russia who remember when Odessa had no existence, It is only ninety-five years ago since General de Ribas and the Russians stormed the insignificant fortress of Hadji Bey, and secured for the Empress Catherine the Great the port of Odessa, and it was not until several years after that assault that the conquerors began to develop the place. Once a start was made, however, the city grew amazingly; acquiring in its career Gallic characteristics, from the fact of its successive early governors, De Ribas, Richelieu, and Langeron, being Frenchmen. At the beginning of the present century its population was 2,000; it is now 190,000, and in point of size it ranks as fourth city in the Russian Empire, St. Petersburg coming first with 840,000 people, Moscow next with 625,000, Warsaw third with 340,000, and then

Odessa. If I add that it is distant 1,137 miles from St. Petersburg and 933 from Moscow, it will be seen that Odessa has very good reason to regard itself as the capital of South Russia.

Odessa has derived its rapid growth and prosperity largely from its export of corn. So long as the Turks held the whole of the coast of the Black Sea, agriculture in the provinces south of Moscow was cramped for want of an outlet. Directly Catherine the Great, however, secured the Black Sea littoral, the population began to spread over the southern plains, and their produce, added to that which filtered from the middle provinces down to the coast, gave plenty of lucrative trade to Odessa. Twenty years ago the total exports were valued at £4,000,000 sterling, of which the value of the grain was £3,000,000. In 1882, the grain export alone exceeded in value 100,000,000 roubles, or £10,000,000 sterling. This expansion in trade has been maintained in spite of the competition of Nicolaieff, Sevastopol, Rostoff, and other Azoff ports; to say nothing of the rivalry of America and India.

To deal satisfactorily with the Russian corn trade would require more space than I have at my disposal; yet the subject is an important one, for a corn crisis is more calculated to bring about a revolution in Russia than any sentimental desire for a constitution. Corn is still, as it has been for many generations, the staple product of the country. Until a few years ago Russia was really the granary of Europe. Forty per cent. of the corn consumed in England and on the Continent was supplied by Russia. Of this forty per cent., the larger proportion passed through the Black Sea ports. Those ports were closed during the Russo-Turkish war of 1877–78, and it was only with partial success that the export stream was diverted to the Baltic. The rise in the price of corn that ensued in consequence caused the United States, which for several years had been steadily gaining on Russia as a corn-exporting country, to redouble its efforts; the apparent certainty of a war between Russia and England exciting American enterprise to the utmost. In 1879 the United States not only overtook Russia, but shot ahead with 38,000,000 bushels to the good. The following year Russia's export of corn dropped at a lump from 180 million bushels to 104 millions, and although the next year she went ahead again with an export of 157 millions, the race was only maintained by accepting a ruinous price for the article.

That Russia will ever regain the monopoly she once enjoyed in the corn trade may be regarded as very improbable. Besides America, she has now another rival to deal with, equally powerful and still more dangerous. This is India. A decade ago India was thought very little of as a corn-exporting country. Even in 1879 General Annenkoff, in advocating the construction of a railway to India, so little foresaw the growth of the wheat trade there that one of his strongest arguments in favour of the line was the new market it would open up for Russian corn. As things now look, it is more probable that India will some day supply Russia with corn, rather than Russia India. In 1880 India exported 2,195,500 cwts. of wheat, in 1881 upwards of 7,444,449 cwts., while in 1882 the total reached 19,863,520 cwts. Formerly we traded most with Russia for wheat, but already in 1880 we purchased of her only to the extent of £1,568,261, as compared with £1,773,216 from India; while in 1881 the figures were as follow:—

WHEAT IMPORTED INTO ENGLAND.

	Cwts.	Value.
From India	7,308,842	£3,826,851
Russia	4,018,895	£2,171,372

Besides India, the dependencies of Australia and Canada are already the equals of Russia in exporting corn to England, and Egypt may be expected to become another, under English rule.

In this manner, the agricultural outlook of Russia cannot be regarded as a very satisfactory one. Good harvests are useless if no market can be found for the crops; and with corn, as with every other commodity, there is a point in its price below which it is not worth while to grow it. The Indian *ryot* can produce corn very much cheaper than the Russian *moujik*, and the English merchant can take it to market for him at half-a-dozen times less the cost than the Moscow *koopets*, or the Jewish intermediary at Odessa. A commission recently appointed to inquire into the export of Russian corn, found that it costs nine times as much to get a bushel of corn away from Odessa, reckoning all the charges from the field to the hold of the steamer, as it does a bushel of corn from the ordinary American outlets. For want of a proper system of transport it costs more to convey a sack of corn from the Odessa railway depôt to the steamer—a distance of a mile—than it does to convey a sack from Chicago to Liverpool. It is only by giving the Russian peasant the poorest price for his corn, that it can be sold low enough to cover the exorbitant transport charges, and compete with other grain in the markets of Europe.

This is a very serious matter, and in his budget report for the current year, the Minister of Finance, Professor Bungé, admitted the extremely unfavourable effects of English Colonial competition on Russian trade and Russian revenue. To improve matters he announced several fresh measures of a Protectionist character, but these were calculated to benefit the occasional manufacturer rather than the millions of peasants. Nothing in his report revealed that he had any consciousness of a great fact, that the only way to improve the position of the peasant and get him a better price for his corn is to diminish the transport charges.

For years there has been a talk of improving the railway system, but nothing has been done. When Professor Bungé held the chair of political economy at the Kieff University, he advocated the use of elevators, and in 1882, while discussing the subject of American competition with him, he told me he was then considering a scheme presented by the Duc de Morny for establishing elevators at Odessa and other South Russian ports. The project was drawn up in the name of the Duc and one other person, and the capital was fixed at the sum of $12\frac{1}{2}$ million of metallic roubles, or nearly £2,000,000 sterling. After some negotiation the scheme was withdrawn, and a fresh one substituted, in which the two French capitalists were reinforced by two Russians, Prince P. P. Demidoff, of San Donato, and Gospodin Duranoff, and two Americans, Messrs. Martin and Fisher. These six increased the capital to 25,000,000 roubles metallic, and added features to the project, to discuss which the Minister held a sort of congress of experts and delegates from various ports a few weeks ago. When the matter was put to the vote nearly all the members of the congress black-balled the notion of granting any foreign syndicate a monopoly, and in this condition things have remained up to now. In whatever form the elevator scheme be ultimately adopted, a considerable amount of time will be needed to get it into working order, and in the interval Russia will have lost still further her foothold in the European market, and India and our colonies will have proportionately gained upon her.

A deal of the corn exported from Odessa comes down the river Dniester in barges from the Kherson plain, but 52 per cent. is brought by the railroad. The fearful muddle the South Russian lines made of the transport of men and military material during the Russo-Turkish war is not yet forgotten—the same chaos prevails every year in transporting the corn to Odessa. Thousands and thousands of tons of corn rot every autumn at the railway stations, for want of shelter, while waiting to be conveyed to the coast. The slowness, inefficiency, and dearness of Russian railway transport compare most disadvantageously with that of America or India, although the transport service of India is susceptible of considerable improvement. This badness of railway transport tells as much on the price of corn as the relative insignificance of mileage in Russia. The United States possess over 100,000 miles of railway, while the Russian Empire, with twice the population, contains only 14,500 miles, or very little more than the States sometimes construct in a single year. India has a less mileage than Russia, about 10,500 miles being open for traffic; but, owing to better arrangements, the transport power of those 10,500 miles exceeds that of the 14,500 miles of Russia. In 1882 Russia only constructed 130 miles of railway; India built 373 miles.

In 1883 the deficits on the Russian railways, which the State had to make good, amounted to 13,500,000 roubles, or £1,350,000. This was the acknowledged loss, for no one in Russia or out of it regards the annual statement of the Russian Minister of Finance as being as worthy of confidence as a European budget. In India, on the other hand, to quote the financial statement of Mr. J. H. Cross in the House of Commons, August 22, 1883—in India, the railways were "the profitable branch of the productive works expenditure. In 1882 the receipts were £15,231,261, the expenses £7,580,549, and the net profits £7,650,712, or 5·37 per cent. on the total capital employed. In the matter of railway development India wants no help; she asks for nothing but permission to develop her own resources, and those who deny her that right incur a grave responsibility, which I have no wish to share."

From a financial point of view, Russia and India have had one drawback in common in the matter of railway construction; a large proportion of the lines have been built for strategical purposes. But Russia has had three other drawbacks, from which India has been exempt. All her railways have been badly constructed, all of them badly financed, and all of them badly worked. I know there are many defects in our Indian railways, but there is not one which is not tenfold worse in Russia. The result is, that while Russia is becoming every year saddled with a heavier deficit, India has already entered upon the stage when, to use the words of Mr. Cunningham,* railways must furnish her ere long with a "magnificent source of income." Every mile Russia builds adds to her indebtedness; every mile India builds improves her economical and financial condition. If Russia, by developing her armaments and extending her territory, is weakening our position in Asia, England, by constructing railways and growing corn in India, is weakening Russia's position in Europe. And this is a fact which the Secretary for Foreign Affairs should take cognizance of, as well as the Viceroy of India. A corn crisis may compel the Tsar to choose between a revolution at home and a conflict abroad. That conflict would naturally be waged with the country causing the crisis. Hence, a crisis in corn might lead to an expedition against India as well as a desire to possess Constantinople.

England is rapidly rendering the position of Russia intolerable. Both empires are progressing; but the progress of one is that of a lumbering stage-coach, and of the other that of a swift locomotive. The prosperity of Russia largely depends upon the export of certain products: corn, hides, tallow, wool, flax, hemp, and oil-seed. England, through India and her colonies, has become a formidable rival to Russia in every one of these articles.

* "British India and its Rulers," London, 1881, page 267.

There is nothing Russia produces which England is not producing more cheaply in some part of the world. Russia's exports, it is true, are still large; but the prices realized for the products are of such a low character that the economical condition of the Russian people is yearly becoming more serious. Not only is India building annually a greater mileage of railways than the whole Russian Empire, but Canada likewise constructs more, and also South Africa, Australia, and even New Zealand. Russia has no chance against these rivals, handicapped as she is with a costly and corrupt government, and an antiquated mode of agriculture, transport, and trade.

Against our colonies Russia entertains no animus. She believes they have no love for the mother country, and would hold aloof in the event of a conflict. As a rule, she ignores them in her tirades against England. But the case is different with India. She regards India, from one point of view, as the keystone of our commerce, and from another, as the vulnerable spot of our Empire. We are rich, not because we have certain characteristics that conduce to success, and hold with Free Trade, but because we remorselessly exploit India. Sever India from us, and our commerce would crumble to dust. There would then be an end to the Eastern Question and the paralyzing effect it exercises on Russian progress, and Russia would no longer have to contend with the rivalry of England in industry and commerce.

Such are some of the Russian considerations which, in my opinion, constitute a greater incentive on the part of our rival to upset our power in India, than either the love of military glory or any desire to possess our Asiatic empire. If Russia's views are illogical and erroneous, that does not detract in any way from their importance. Russia gazes across her plains towards India with her own eyes, not with ours, and if ever she attacks our power there it will be her own perceptions of the feasibility of the enterprise that will lure her on, and not the dogmatic assertions of English statesmen and generals respecting her rashness, stupidity, and impotence that will check her.

But, to get back to Odessa and its corn trade. Whatever may be the fluctuations in the export of grain, Odessa would appear to have a great future before it in connection with the new direct trade its merchants are opening up with the East. Formerly, before the Suez Canal was opened, much of the merchandise exported from Oriental countries to Russia was first conveyed to London or Hull, and thence transhipped to the Baltic. Most of the sea-borne tea reached Russia by this route. Now, however, goods from China and India are shipped direct to Odessa, to the injury of London trade, but to the benefit of the Russian consumer. Odessa, in short, is becoming a Russian Marseilles. The vessels of the Moscow Cruiser Committee have been largely instrumental in opening up this new trade, which is becoming more and more developed every year. Several powerful steamers have been built in England of late, over 300 feet long, for the new line the Black Sea Steam Navigation Company is establishing with the East. The result of this intercourse is, that Lascars are now seen at Odessa, and Russian seamen at Bombay.

The Russian Government takes great interest in these trade relations of Odessa with the East, and does its utmost to encourage them. Formerly, troops and exiles were sent to the Amoor region overland across Siberia, the journey taking sometimes a year and a half. Now they are all despatched to the Pacific by the steamers of the Moscow Cruiser Fleet and the Black Sea Navigation Company, and detachments of several hundred Russian troops pass through the Suez Canal at the time. This saves the troops and exiles many hardships, and gives Russian diplomatists grounds for blandly de-

D

claring that Russia possesses an important interest in the Suez Canal.

. . . . . .

After breakfast at the Hotel d'Europe, we went for a stroll along the Odessa boulevards. We had not gone far when we ran against Mr. Eles, an old friend of C.'s. Mr. Eles recently settled down in Odessa, and became a member of the well-known local shipping firm of Smeles, Eles, and Co. He had a charming *datcha* (country house), or *datch*, as English residents mostly call it, on the coast, a little way outside Odessa; and insisted on our spending the rest of the day with him. Not much pressing was needed to secure our acquiescence, for the best of Russian towns, and Odessa is one of the best, are more inviting outside than inside on a hot summer's day; and, besides, *datch* life possesses charms irresistible to those who have once tasted them. In Russia all of the urban population who can afford it migrate, bag and baggage, in the early spring to wooden "summer houses" in the forests or alongside the streams outside the towns, and do not return again until the autumn, when they coop themselves up inside three-brick walls, double windows, and treble doors for the winter. To dwell permanently in a *datch* the entire season is miserable, but an occasional visit is one of the pleasantest forms of "outing" that I know of. Mr. Eles's *datch* was a charming villa, perched on the edge of the cliffs, 150 feet high, overlooking the Black Sea. Behind were woods, gardens, and vineyards; in front of the broad balcony, with its magnificent umbrageous shelter of Virginia creepers, was an expanse of juniper bush, from which the cliffs fell away in broken terraces, covered with semi-tropical vegetation, to the very edge of the sea. An enjoyable swim preceded dinner, and afterwards we sat smoking on the balcony till nearly midnight—the moon shining brilliantly in the blue-black firmament, its rays impressing a gorgeous golden slant of light on the undulating surface of the sea; the surf breaking softly at the foot of the cliffs, the frogs piping with a muffled shrill noise in the distance, and the night birds uttering sharp cries occasionally as they darted about the garden.

The next morning we were up early, and after securing our berths on board the *Grand Duke Michael*, completed our preparations for our departure. At half-past two we drove down to the steamer with our luggage, and at three quitted the commodious harbour, leaving on the stone quay a motley assembly of passengers' friends, Cossack teamsters, drosky drivers, and fruit-sellers. In a few minutes we were passing through a score of English steamers lying idly in quarantine outside the artificial harbour, and then leaving in our rear Odessa—a handsome stately town seen from the water—were fairly out to sea.

As soon as the passengers were comfortably settled down, a loud ringing of the bell summoned them to dinner. The fares between the various Black Sea ports include meals for the first and second-class passengers. The deck passengers find for themselves, bringing on board their own huge loaves of black rye bread, and making heavy meals off them, with such additions as some slices of water melon or other fruit, and perhaps a bit of dried fish or stale meat, washed down with innumerable tumblers of tea, thinly brewed by means of hot water obtained from the steward. The newer steamers of the Black Sea Navigation Company contain regular accommodation below deck for the steerage passengers, but in the older vessels, like the *Grand Duke Michael*, they herd without any shelter, occupying two-thirds of the deck space. A more motley crew of Turks, Russians, Caucasians, Jews, and Greeks it would be difficult to find, or a more motley collection of baggage. So long as the weather is fine they do not experience much discomfort, being used to roughing it in the open air, but a heavy sea and drenching rain make things very miserable for these poor wretches.

The first-class fare from Odessa to Batoum is 39 roubles (£3 18s.); second-class, 30½ roubles (£3 1s.); and steerage, 13 roubles (£1 6s.). The first and second-class passengers receive the same food, and make use of the same deck, but the cabin and dining-saloon of the second-class passengers are less luxurious than those of the first, the company is more mixed, and, finally, the berths are situated in the fore part of the vessel amidst the evil-smelling steerage passengers. The fares may seem high for the journey, but I believe few who have travelled by the steamers of the company, and enjoyed the good living accorded them, have ever seriously regretted the cost on arrival at their destination.

As soon as the passengers are fairly awake in the morning, which with Russians is not much before eight or nine o'clock, tea and coffee, with bread and butter, and rusks, are served up in the saloon. At eleven o'clock the passengers meet for a light lunch, commencing, of course, with the inevitable *zakuska*, or dinette of the Russians—consisting of a glass of vodky, bitters, or absinthe, and a taste of raw herring, a sardine, a bit of cheese or sausage, two or three English pickles, some caviare on bread, dried salmon, and innumerable other little tit-bits calculated, according to Russian estimation, to give one an appetite. The *zakuska*, to my mind, is a grand institution, although it does not seem to flourish well out of Russia. During the Tsar's coronation some magnificent *zakuskas* were served up with the Imperial banquets and suppers, but my tenderest recollections are associated with one preceding a dinner given by the fifty special correspondents to their amiable Censor, Gospodin Vaganoff. A huge table literally groaned beneath the assortment of appetizers heaped upon it, and which could not have included less than a hundred different kinds of delicious tit-bits and forty or fifty stimulating drinks.

The *zakuska* disposed of, the clean and liveried stewards, whose unobtrusive attentiveness, by the way, impresses itself upon the traveller, hand round in succession sturgeon or some other kind of fish, cutlets or some made dish, cheese, confectionery, and grapes, melons, apples, nuts, and other fruit. Red and white wine of the Crimea, grown on the Company's own estates, and therefore real wine, free from adulteration, the passenger can drink as much as he likes; then, after a cup of coffee, he can go on deck and smoke, or play at chess in the cabin, with the calm self-satisfaction of a man who feels that he "has not done so bad for breakfast."

Dinner is served up at four in the afternoon. This consists of half a dozen excellent dishes, preceded by the *zakuska*, and accompanied by abundance of fruit and wine; and is equal to any *table d'hôte* dinner, in point of excellence and variety of cooking, obtainable at the Criterion or other leading restaurants in London. At eight or nine, tea and coffee, with rusks and rolls, are set forth again in the saloon, and when this is over, and the passenger retires to bed, he must be a very exacting mortal if he considers himself badly done by. Mr. Gallenga, the experienced special correspondent of the *Times*, has placed on record his conviction that nowhere in the world is such excellent "feeding" obtainable on board a steamer as on the vessels of the Black Sea Steam Navigation Company, and I can readily endorse his opinion. In no voyage round about the coast of England will a man find his inner and outer comfort better looked after, than has been the case for the last twenty years in the Black Sea.

The vessels of the Navigation Company maintain a perpetual service round the ports of the Black Sea, one running one way and one the other, and passing each other in their circular course near Batoum. Generally speaking, the steamers are crowded with passengers from Odessa as far as Kertch, but from the Sea of Azoff along the Caucasian coast, the most interesting part of the voyage, there are hardly any passengers at all, except steerage, and the traveller is thus able to enjoy the scenery without being incommoded by a crowd. The afternoon we left Odessa the saloon was full of people dining, but the fresh breeze we encountered when we got a little way out to sea soon thinned the tables, and hardly anybody at all turned up for the evening tea. Among the passengers was a Mr. Gibson, for many years in the employ of the Company, who was returning to Sevastopol, and he contributed to make the time pass rapidly away till he left us the next morning.

During the night the steamer caught it a little in running across the open sea to Cape Tarhankoutt, the first point attained of the Crimea, and the swell made nearly all the passengers sick, including a Russian who occupied part of my cabin. The voyage would have been pleasanter if Mr. C. and myself could have shared a cabin between us; but finding only single berths obtainable, we had been compelled to separate, which, as he did not speak Russian, was rather inconvenient for him. I tried hard to share a cabin with some German, on the principle that, whereas a German is only occasionally sick at sea, a Russian always is; but was unsuccessful. During the voyage it used to grieve me to see huge swaggering Russian officers come on board in full regimentals and decorations; I knew what their fate would be. But, as a rule, they took it quietly, retiring to their cabins as soon as they felt queer, and drawing a curtain over their undignified misery. Were England not an island, we should have innumerable Russian visitors, for we are heartily admired in Russia. But even the enthu-

siasm of Anglophiles cannot carry them across the
Channel. "Just fancy," said a well-known Russian
general to me once—"just fancy me, in full regimentals,
ignominiously leaning over the bulwark of a steamer and
vomiting. The bare recollection would prevent me ever
maintaining my composure before my troops again. No,
no, bridge over the Channel, or bore a hole under it, and
I will come and see you."

After daybreak we got well under cover of the coast
of the Crimea, and the rolling of the *Grand Duke Michael*
diminished. When the tea-bell rang at seven we were
already anchored in the roadstead of Eupatoria. The
town has a pretty appearance from the sea. The houses
are either built of a soft white stone, or of wood painted
white or yellow; the roofs are red or green, interspersed
with picturesque minarets. At the base are brown bare
hills, and towards Sevastopol stretch along the flat coast
fifty or sixty windmills clustered together, giving quite a
peculiar appearance to the place. Eupatoria possesses
deep historical interest to Englishmen, on account of
its being the first Russian point touched at and occupied by the Allies in the invasion of the Crimea. Concerning this occupation a funny incident is narrated by
Kinglake.

The English fleet arrived at Eupatoria on the 1st of
September, 1854, and the bright little town being defenceless, officers were sent to summon it. The governor was
an official personage in a high state of discipline. He
had before his eyes the armed navies of the Allies, with
the countless sails of their convoys; and to all that vast
armament he had nothing to oppose except the forms of
office. But to him the forms of office seemed all-sufficing,
and on them he still calmly relied; so, when the summons
was delivered, he insisted upon fumigating it, according
to the health regulations of the little port. When he
understood that the Western Powers intended to land,

he said that decidedly they might do so; but he explained that it would be necessary for them to land at the Lazaretto, and consider themselves in strict quarantine. The following day the place was occupied by a small body of English troops.

We only stopped long enough at Eupatoria to discharge a few barrels of merchandise into lighters, and take on board two or three passengers, and in less than an hour were off again. The comparative calmness of the sea had drawn on deck most of the passengers. These now promptly descended below again when the steamer stood out to sea, to strike straight across the bay to Sevastopol. Our course lay too far out, and the coast was too misty at the time, for us to distinctly discern where the Allies landed; but when we neared Sevastopol the steamer went close to the cliffs, and the brighter weather enabled us to follow the course of the troops from the Alma.

CHAPTER III.

THE RESTORATION OF SEVASTOPOL AND THE RUSSIAN FLEET.

Sevastopol and its Harbour—The Progress of the Place—Its Rival Nicolaeff—Restoration of the Great Granite Docks—The Fortifications—The Dockyard of the Black Sea Steam Navigation Company—The Origin of the Company—Statistics respecting its Growth and Present Condition—New Ocean Liners for the Black Sea—The new Ironclads—Russian Cruisers—The Present Condition of the Russian Navy—Sir Edward Reed, the Naval Professor Holloway—Admiral Popoff his Patent Pill—The Fleet during the Russo-Turkish War—Fall of Popoff—The *régime* of the Grand Duke Alexis—The Fleet of the Future—Sevastopol and the new Black Sea Fleet, and the Decadence of Turkey—Sevastopol as a Commercial Port—The new Route to Persia and Central Asia.

SEVASTOPOL has been so often described that I shall content myself with simply saying "ditto" to the many eminent authorities who, in language of more or less felicity, have declared it to be one of the most magnificent harbours in the world. Travellers often exaggerate what they see; but the chorus of encomium pronounced upon Sevastopol fails to create impressions which surpass the reality. I never imagined the harbour to be so splendid, the scenery so lovely. An impression prevails that the Allies knocked the place into ruins, and that little of its former glory remains; but it is impossible to enter the harbour, passing the huge granite forts on the left and the ugly earthworks on the right, without feeling surprised at there being so few perceivable traces of the great bombardment. Excluding the vast naked ruin of the naval barracks, which, being situated on a prominent cliff overlooking the harbour, arrests the attention the moment the batteries are passed, there is little to remind the traveller of the devastating effects of the siege.

As a matter of fact, Sevastopol has been looking up of late years, and before the close of the present decade will have recovered all its old prosperity and importance. The tearing up of the Treaty of Paris in 1871 was the first step towards the revival of Sevastopol; the completion, a few years later, of the Lozova-Sevastopol Railway, linking it with the Russian railway system, the second. In 1878 the earthworks that were erected at the mouth of the harbour, and the rows of torpedoes that blocked the channel, kept away the Turkish ironclad fleet from the place, as they would no doubt keep out an English fleet to-morrow. This defence—"successful defence," the Russians call it, although there was never any serious attack—gave Sevastopol the position again of a fortified harbour, and the security it accorded to Russian shipping during the war led the authorities to still further improve it. There was even a talk of dismantling Nicolaeff, and removing the dockyard there bodily back to Sevastopol, but more prudent counsellors suggested that it would be foolish to trust all the eggs in one basket again, and a decision was ultimately arrived at to retain Nicolaeff as it was, using it in the future as an auxiliary naval establishment.

During the last two years of Alexander II.'s reign the maladministration prevailing at the Russian Admiralty, by dissipating its pecuniary resources, checked the realization of the designs for re-establishing Sevastopol. The purer *régime* of the present High Admiral, however, has led to money being more freely forthcoming, and in excess of the heavy outlay on the four ironclads now in course of construction for the Black Sea fleet, a sum of a quarter of a million sterling has been expended in restoring the large stone docks that were once the glory of Sevastopol. When the Crimean War broke out it was estimated that £20,000,000 sterling had been spent upon the harbour works and the fleet, and £7,000,000 on the fortifications. The docks were the work of a British officer, Colonel Upton, who had employed 30,000 labourers to excavate them. Engineering and military science has advanced very much since those days, and, thanks to skilful appliances, a Russian engineer officer is now restoring with two or three thousand men what would have needed tens of thousands a generation ago. So also a few heavy guns suffice to do the work of the 1,200 guns the Russians were able to concentrate upon one spot when the Allied fleet appeared before Sevastopol in 1854. Throughout the whole of the town we saw men at work like ants raising fresh structures, removing ruins, laying out new streets, and making squares and gardens. A few years ago there were 70 per cent. of ruins to 30 per cent. of houses; to-day the figures are reversed, and there are only 30 per cent. of ruins left.

Our steamer stopped a couple of hours at Sevastopol, thus allowing us to have a ramble ashore and a sail across the harbour. Opposite the busy landing-place, with its stalls of cheap and luscious fruit, was the extensive yard belonging to the Black Sea Steam Navigation Company, where a deal of bustle was in progress, arising from the preparations for constructing the two new ironclads of the *Inflexible* type, *Tchesme* and *Sinope*, for the Black Sea fleet. Russia is well known as a country of contrarieties, but few things are more mysterious than that a company which cannot construct its own merchant steamers, should be deemed fit to entrust with the building of thick-ribbed ironclads.

The Black Sea Steam Navigation Company was established shortly after the Crimean War, with the object of evading the clause of the Treaty of Paris, limiting Russia's fleet to six steam vessels, of 800 tons maximum tonnage, by creating a flotilla of transports, capable of being turned into armed cruisers in time of war. The company receives a mileage subsidy, and up to the present time has drawn to the extent of nearly £3,000,000 sterling upon the Russian Treasury. A report that I have before me, published in 1881, states that its fleet then consisted of 76 steamers, of an aggregate of 78,162 tons, and 7,262 nominal horse-power. Of this fleet, costing 9,942,000 roubles, or a million sterling, not a single vessel had been constructed in Russia. The fleet burns 100,000 tons of coal a year, of which more than half is obtained from England, and the rest from the Donetz region, mostly from the company's own mines. The original 500 rouble shares of the company are now worth 750 roubles, and pay a dividend of 12 or 14 per cent. every year.

Before the Russo-Turkish War broke out in 1877, it was confidently anticipated that the company would render great assistance to the Government. In reality, it did very little at all. Several of its best steamers were purposely kept away from Russia when war became inevitable, and of the rest only two or three proved of any use as cruisers. This impotence caused great dissatisfaction in Russia, and the Press unanimously clamoured for a withdrawal of the subsidy; but the outcry neither affected the Government nor the company until the present Emperor ascended the throne. The new Ministers of the altered *régime* then took the matter up, and the result of the pressure they exercised was a decision on the part of the company to build a fresh fleet of steamers, of which nearly half a dozen have already been constructed on the Tyne. Of these some have been built by Messrs. Leslie, intended for the Batoum service, and others by Messrs. Mitchell, for the direct trade between Odessa and the East. A representative of the former is the *Pushkin*, 1,485 tons register, 265 feet long, 34 broad, and 24 deep, with engines of 300 nominal horse-power, or 1,616 indicated, steaming at fifteen knots, and having accommodation for 166 first and second-class passengers and 250 steerage. Her cost was £46,000. A typical vessel of the latter is the *Tsaritza*, which is 332 feet long, 37 feet broad, 27 feet deep, and cost £55,000. All the new vessels are most luxuriously fitted up, and whatever their future *rôle* in the next war may be, they will certainly in the interval conduce to the comfort of thousands of travellers in the Black Sea.

To repair its steamers, the company early after its formation spent £100,000 in constructing workshops on a site presented by the Government, and furnishing them with machinery from England. Up to last year another £100,000 had been expended in the same manner, and when it seemed likely that the company would secure the contract for the two new ironclads £40,000 more was allotted, making altogether nearly a quarter of a million expended on the dockyard. Some months ago the Russian Admiralty gave the company the order for the two new vessels, and the keel of the first has recently been laid in the presence of the Minister of Marine. The two vessels, for which the company will receive a payment of £643,500 sterling, are each 314 feet long, 69 feet broad, and 42 feet deep. Their plating will be 5 inches thick above water line, and 3 inches below; the turret having 14 inches of plating in front and 12 inches behind. The engines will be of 9,000 horse-power, and comprise 3 cylinders, 14 boilers, and 2 screws. Twelve heavy guns will be carried by the vessels—six 12-inch guns in three open casemates, and six 6-inch in closed casemates on the upper deck. The steel for the vessels is to be of Russian production, and the company has pledged itself to roll its own armour-plates. At present over 1,200 hands are employed at the company's establishment, and fresh men are being taken on every day. By 1885, the date fixed upon for the completion of the two ironclads, the Government should possess, through the instrumentality of the company, a quasi-State dockyard in fairly good working order. In excess, it is not improbable that it may build a dockyard of its own in the interval, for the use of the men-of-war wintering at Sevastopol.

So much for the Black Sea Steam Navigation Company, whose headquarters may be regarded as temporarily fixed at Sevastopol, although most of its trade is done at Odessa. Sevastopol also serves as the headquarters of the Moscow Cruiser Fleet, consisting of half a dozen powerful steamers purchased during the war scare of 1878, or since then, and which have performed a useful service in showing the Navigation Company how to open up the direct trade between Russia and the East. Towards the cruiser movement Russia subscribed half a million sterling in 1878-79. The vessels this money enabled the promoters to secure were first used as transports, and then as merchantmen, the armaments being placed in store at Sevastopol while the vessels were engaged in commerce. In course of time, as might have been expected, the committee grew tired of its duties and neglected them, and the managers of the undertaking were beginning to run into debt, when, a few months ago, the Government stepped in and annexed the concern to the Black Sea Fleet; thereby adding materially to a branch in which it was deficient. The steamers are now used as troopships between South Russia and the Caucasus, and South Russia and the Pacific. One of them recently conveyed 3,800 time-expired troops from Batoum to Sevastopol.

It is impossible to quit the subject of the naval progress of Sevastopol without saying a few words about the Black Sea Fleet. The public have not yet forgotten the wolf-cry Sir Edward Reed raised in 1872, and again in 1875, respecting the frigate *Peter the |Great* and the circular ironclads or *popoffkas*. For years Sir Edward Reed posed as a naval Professor 'Holloway; Admiral Popoff was his patent pill. By jumbling up matters which were correct with matters which were wholly imaginary—to put the advertising in no stronger light —Sir Edward Reed conferred naval prestige on Russia which that country did not deserve, and which disappeared in smoke the moment the imaginary armaments of the northern Power were summoned to confront a real enemy.

I have no space to deal with all the causes that led to this impotence, so humiliating to Russia, so contrary to the traditions of a fleet which Englishmen had helped to establish, and with whose triumphs so many English names are associated. If Sir Edward Reed's gross laudation of the fleet had been advantageous to Russian diplomacy during the period preceding the war, its collapse directly afterwards gave a blow to its prestige from which it has not yet recovered. The very praises heaped so unstintedly upon the fleet helped to deepen the disgrace attending its failure. Russians could not bear to hear the names of Popoff and Reed mentioned, for they were conscious that but for the support given by the English constructor to his Russian *confrère*, the latter would have never gained such an ascendency at the Admiralty, and acquired power to dissipate the naval funds over unspeakably foolish hobbies. Had Sir Edward Reed shown himself at Cronstadt in 1877 he would have been grossly insulted, perhaps lynched. As far as the Press dared, it unsparingly assailed the Popoff *régime*, and exposed the gross maladministration which, in effect, was more to blame for Russia's impotence than climatic drawbacks, and the absence of cheap iron, cheap coal, and skilled labour. But, in spite of the protests of the *Golos* and other papers, things went on from bad to worse, and the fleet had become a by-word in Russia for disorganization and disorder when Alexander II. suddenly died, and a sweeping change took place in all the departments of State. The brothers of the old Tsar retired from office; the brothers of the new one took their place. Vladimir succeeded Nicholas in the control of the army; Constantine gave up to Alexis the charge of the fleet.

The change was gladly welcomed in Russia, and the public expectation of improvement was speedily justified by events. The Russian Admiralty was exposed to a thorough reorganization. Admiral Popoff was first to go. So great was the confusion found to be, that considerable time was needed to put things to rights, without attempting to develop the fleet. As Minister of Marine, the Grand Duke Alexis chose Admiral Shestakoff, who had been commander of the *Svetlana*, the frigate which had taken him to America ten years earlier, when the old Emperor wished to break off a secret marriage he had contracted with the niece of the Minister of Finance, Baron Reutern. More recently, Shestakoff had acted as naval attaché in Southern Europe, and before taking office had made a tour of inspection of the great dockyards of the West, including those of this country. Directly afterwards, Admiral Pestchuroff, another energetic officer, was sent to the Black Sea to supersede Admiral Arkas, a man who had let things drift, and had covered himself with ridicule during the Turkish war by continually issuing magniloquent despatches on dry land, signed " Arkas, Commander-in-Chief of all the Russian ports and squadrons in the Black Sea "—a title hardly suited to times when no squadron existed, and no port was free from the Turkish blockade.

Having at length restored a little order in the navy, the Grand Duke Alexis began to think of creating a new Russian fleet. Two armoured frigate cruisers were commenced on the Neva, of which one, the *Vladimir Monomarchus*, is already in commission, and the second, the *Dmitri Donskoi*, soon will be; and then the order was given for four ironclads for the Black Sea Fleet—two, as stated, to be built at Sevastopol, and two at Nicolaeff. Orders were also given for half a dozen sea-going torpedo boats to firms abroad.

To sum up, the position in the Black Sea is this: that Russia will possess in two or three years' time a full-grown town at Sevastopol, with a subsidized dockyard capable of turning out ironclads, and probably a State dockyard as well; together with the old large granite docks restored, and an iron floating dock capable of sustaining the largest ship of war. By the beginning of 1886 she will have afloat at Sevastopol a squadron of four ironclads, incomparably stronger than the vessels of the Ottoman fleet, and collectively able, with the projected six new gunboats and twelve sea-going torpedo boats, to prevent any Turkish squadron entering the Black Sea. For cruiser or transport purposes she will have at least twelve ocean-liners, comprising the steamers already constructed or projected of the Navigation Company and the vessels of the Moscow Fleet. What aims Russia may have in view in developing her Black Sea Fleet need not be discussed. Suffice it to call attention to the fact that Turkish naval supremacy in the Black Sea, which contributed so materially to prolong the last struggle, is rapidly dying away, and that ere long the power will pass completely to Russia, who, with her masked stronghold at Batoum, her railway to Kars—also to be finished in a few years' time—and her dominant position in the Balkans, may be expected to adopt a very much more arrogant attitude in regard to Turkish affairs than she is content to do to-day.

But whatever may be the power and the prestige of armaments, I have always considered that Turkey has to dread more the material rather than the naval and military progress of Russia. Sevastopol, in excess of recovering its position as a dockyard, is becoming a great commercial outlet. This is the case also with Nicolaeff, where trade has developed with such remarkable strides of late years that the place could forego the support of the navy. In 1880 the exports from Sevastopol were valued at 5,943,022 roubles; the chief article being corn. Last year the total was 9,888,706 roubles. At present the shipping arrangements are very bad, but improvements are impending, and these may be expected to be accelerated by the growth of the new line of communication which is rendering Sevastopol the Brindisi of Russia.

A glance at the map will show that Sevastopol is the nearest Russian port for Batoum, and many Russians already prefer taking their departure from it instead of from Odessa, which latter involves twenty hours' additional sea journey. A few months ago an express service was started between Moscow and Sevastopol, the distance, 945 miles, being done in forty-seven hours. More recently, the enterprising and unsubsidized Greek firm of Rodokanaki conceived the idea of running steamers direct between Sevastopol and Batoum, instead of taking passengers round to Kertch and coasting slowly down to that port, as is at present the practice with the Navigation Company. Three steamers have been ordered in England for this service, and when they are placed on the line nearly all the passenger traffic between Russia and Transcaucasia, Central Asia, and Persia, may be expected to pass through Sevastopol.

Thus Sevastopol has a great future before it, and will

doubtless restore itself without needing any particular coddling on the part of the Government. Like Odessa, Nicolaeff, Rostoff-on-the-Don, Taganrog, and half a dozen other places on the Black Sea littoral, Sevastopol is being pushed into prominence by the expansion of the population and the trade at its rear. If, as many believe, and myself among them, Russia is yielding to the Teuton in Poland and along the Baltic, she is making up for it by bulging out in the direction of the Black Sea and Caucasus. Therein lies the real danger to Constantinople.

CHAPTER IV.

GLIMPSES OF THE CRIMEA.

Departure from Sevastopol—Views of the Crimean Coast from on board the Steamer—The Crimean War. Ought we to be ashamed of it or not ?—The Rivalry of England and Russia in the East—Real Importance of the Crimean War—Ought Russia to have Constantinople ?—English Policy in Turkey—St. George's Monastery and Balaclava—Yalta as a Watering-Place—The Grape-Cure—Life at Yalta—Visit to Theodosia—Kaffa in Olden Times—Wonderful Richness of the Crimea in the Middle Ages—What the Russians have done for Theodosia—The Beauty of the Black Sea—The Rat Fortress—The Defences of Kertch—Cannon Stolen and Sold from the Ramparts of the Fortress during the Turkish War.

WE left Sevastopol at two o'clock in the afternoon, a military band, bound for Kertch, playing a warlike tune, and, with the numerous boats passing across the bay from the north side, filled with white-coated soldiers with their bayonets fixed, bringing back our memories to the period of the siege. As we steamed out of the harbour, and worked our way round the coast in the direction of Balaclava, catching numerous glimpses as we did so of the trench-traversed heights where the English and the French fought out their great struggle with the Russians, the heroic associations of the place summoned all on deck, and more than one grey-headed survivor of the conflict pointed out to eager crowds the sites of the most cherished events of the beleaguerment. That there were Englishmen on board made no difference to the narrators. Ignorant of their presence, or perhaps ignoring it, they and their hearers discussed the operations of the siege with that tolerance which is so characteristic of Russians. They were beaten, they said, because the Allies had the superiority in the long run of skill, money, and military resources ; but, after all, the tenacity with which they held Sevastopol was something to be proud of.

It has become the fashion to depreciate the Crimean war, and to speak of it as something for Englishmen to be ashamed of.* I do not share that feeling. Regarded as a whole, an Englishman certainly cannot but view with vexation the blundering of the chiefs, the cruel muddle and stupid mismanagement that cost us so many lives, and the unpatriotic jealousies which led to Kars being abandoned, in spite of its heroic defence, to Russia. That our soldiers fought with invincible bravery is very inadequate consolation, for the world knew well enough before what tough assailants we are, and there is no need for us to embark in campaigns such as the Crimean war simply to advertise our courage. From this point of view, treating the matter in a military sense, Englishmen cannot regard the Crimean war with unqualified satisfaction. But this is not the ground on which

---

* The Duke of Argyll denounced this canting spirit in a most creditable manner in his speech on the Russian annexation of Merv, March 10, 1884 :—" I have the honour, and a great honour I deem it, of being one of the very few survivors of the Cabinet which fought the Crimean war. Unlike many other members of the Liberal party, who are never tired of denouncing that war as either a great folly or a great crime, I have never been ashamed of the part which the English Government took on that occasion. We did not fight for the resurrection of Turkey. I, for one, never would. We fought for the great principle that, whatever the fate of Turkey might be, it was not to rest in the hands of Russia, but was a question to be decided by Europe, not by Russia, not by secret treaties and conventions giving her the power to do what she pleases when she pleases. That was the principle for which we fought, and it is the principle which I, for one, should be ready to fight for again."

the war is being attacked nowadays. It is asserted that the war was a stupid, senseless war, because politically nothing of permanent value was gained by it. It would have been better, in short, to have left the Turks to their fate, instead of involving ourselves in a struggle which, after all, has failed to save the Ottoman Empire from the danger of extinction.

This is an opinion which I do not think any one can hold who has really at heart the interests of our Empire, and is acquainted with the features of its progress during the last thirty years. To be plain, the English and the Russians have been rivals in Asia for more than half a century, and leaving undiscussed the causes of the rivalry, we have to face the fact that however much our statesmen may aim at peace at any price, and at being left alone, the competition will become more acute every year. The mere expansion of the two Empires, apart from schemes of conquest, real or imaginary, on the part of Russia, is bringing the two Asiatic frontiers together; and I do not believe that a junction can be effected without leading to serious dangers, which we ought to prudently guard against by making our position as strong as possible. Thanks to the check the Crimean war undoubtedly inflicted on Russia, the English have had breathing time to consolidate their position in the East, and the longer Russia is kept from acquiring the whole of the Black Sea and Constantinople, the better prepared we shall be to confront her in any conflict which may arise in the future out of the rival interests of the two peoples. But for the Crimean war we should have been seriously handicapped in establishing our power in the East, and we have therefore to thank those statesmen who gave the check to Russia for that start in the race for empire, which is rendering the English the strongest people in the world. In his recent work on Egypt, Mr. Mackenzie Wallace urged that we should permanently occupy Egypt, and, as a sop to Russia, resign to her Constantinople. I do not approve of this. By all means render Egypt by degrees another India, but let us keep Russia out of Constantinople as long as we can. If the concession of Constantinople to Russia would put an end to the rivalry of the two peoples, and afford a guarantee of permanent friendship, I would let Russia occupy the city at once. No one desires more than I do that England and Russia should be friends. But the gift of Constantinople to Russia would no more put an end to the rivalry of the two peoples in Asia—in China, in Central Asia, in Persia, and Asia Minor—than the presentation of Madagascar to France would suspend Anglo-Gallic rivalry on the Congo or in Tonquin. Hence, however much we may secretly nourish the conviction that Constantinople will ultimately fall to Russia, we should strive to keep it out of her hands as long as we can.

About a couple of hours' steaming brought us abreast of St. George's Monastery and Balaclava; but by this time the passengers had exhausted their interest in the siege, and were busy down below dining. The saloon was crowded with passengers, all the tables being occupied, for Sevastopol is the nearest railway terminus to Yalta, the fashionable and flourishing watering-place of South Russia. After dinner all hurried on deck, to escape the intense heat and view the Crimean scenery, the best of which is seen from Balaclava to Theodosia. The huge solid blocks of mountain rising sheer out of the sea to the height of three or four thousand feet, afford continually scenes of a stupendous and picturesque character, and render the evening's journey along this part of the Black Sea full of interest. Unfortunately for the Russians, when we reached Cape Aia, and left the shelter of the mountains for less protected water, the intense heat was suddenly dispersed by a fierce blast, which made the steamer lively, and sent most of the passengers in a melancholy mood to their bunks, there to remain until at nine o'clock the steward conveyed to them the cheering intelligence that the vessel had arrived at Yalta, and that tea was on the table.

By this time it was already pitch dark, and there being no jetty at Yalta we did not go ashore. On my return home the steamer reached Yalta early in the morning, and stopped long enough for me to have a look at a seaside resort, which has been well described by Mr. Gallenga as "one of the most beautiful watering-places in the world." It is a place of singular beauty, reminding one of Oban, but beating it out and out. When the late Emperor died, the palace he had built at Livadia, three versts from Yalta, was closed, and many believed that the prosperity of the place was at an end. But the reverse has proved to be the case. Yalta is becoming yearly a more and more favourite Russian seaside resort, and acquiring attractions which in time will doubtless provoke a rush of visitors from Europe. The two new monster hotels—Edinburgh and Russia—on the seashore, and the numerous villas on the hills at the rear, testify, without any reference to statistics, to the growing prosperity of Yalta. Were the railway system extended from Sevastopol to Yalta, and the Russians spared the fears of a few hours' sea trip, the number of visitors would immensely increase, for the air has the curative powers of that of Switzerland, the scenery is enchanting —particularly to the dwellers of the flat and frozen plains of Russia, and innumerable miracles are said to have been wrought by the "grape cure," for which the Crimea is famous.

All day long, at home in lodgings, in the streets, in the shops, in the baths, on the quay, and in the public gardens, people may be seen eating grapes. The ground is everywhere littered with grape-skins. By eating very little else than grapes and bread, and leading an outdoor life, invalids are able to get rid of many ailments, and return home full of gratitude to Yalta. Of all cures, the grape cure is certainly the pleasantest, especially when carried out amid such charming surroundings as those of the Crimea. The grapes are extremely large, and there are many varieties of them, of which the dearest does not cost more than twopence a pound. Scoffers affirm that it is the moderate living, the outdoor life, and the absence of worry and responsibility, that effect the cure rather than the grapes; but, without arguing this point, it is certain that the system benefits by the infusion of grape juice into it. There is but one defect to it; the acid in the fruit is apt to tell on the teeth after a person has been eating grapes for a few weeks, but the evil is not discovered until the patient has gone away from Yalta recovered in health, and when it is found out the true cause of the mischief is rarely guessed by the sufferer.

Nearly all the Russian Grand Dukes possess villas along the coast, stretching away from here in the direction of Sevastopol, and most of the nobility also. All of them are charmingly situated, and often surrounded by beautiful gardens; and these being open to the public when their owners are away, there are plenty of drives to amuse the visitor. For those fond of climbing there is good amusement in scaling the cliffs towering in the background above Yalta, and shooting may be had in the vicinity. To a certain degree, Englishmen must make their own pleasures in places like Yalta, because the Continental notion of recreation differs widely from our own. After a drive or two to Alupka or Alushta, and a trip to Livadia, the Russian is satisfied with what he has seen of the exterior of Yalta, and settles down for the rest of his stay to a daily lounge on the quay in the morning, a nap between lunch and dinner at the hotel, and a promenade in the public gardens until midnight. Occasionally during the season Yalta is visited by a dramatic troupe, and the circus, with Jewish performers, is a permanent feature of the place; in excess of which, there are weekly concerts and frequent balls. For those who have time to spare, and are tired of Nice and Mentone, a trip to Yalta, achievable in five days, should be an agreeable outing. Ignorance of Russian is no bar to the journey, as French and German are generally understood at Yalta, and there are plenty of good-natured, hospitable Russians, with more time on their hands than they know what to do with, who are only too ready to assist a stranger. In spite of the political quarrelling between the two countries, English people are the most popular foreigners in Russia, and the nationality of an Englishman is a passport to good treatment wherever he travels in that country. It is only in Central Asia that his presence is objected to, and there are not many who want to take a holiday trip as far as that. If such halt at Yalta they are not likely to wish to go beyond.

We turned in before the steamer left Yalta, and were awakened shortly after midnight by the violent rolling of the vessel, the banging of loose water-cans and handbags about the cabin, and the groans of the unlucky passengers. The steamer was in the midst of a storm, and, as usual, every Russian was deadly sick. Commiseration for them kept me awake some time, but at length I fell asleep, and when I aroused myself again it was eight o'clock, and the vessel was in calm, deep water, alongside the Theodosia jetty. It is a feature of Black Sea travelling that the misery of being afloat in stormy weather is mitigated by the frequent runs into port, and the shelter accorded by the mountains. Under the most unfavourable circumstances, the nervous passenger may count on the certainty of securing a tolerable number of comfortable meals in the course of a journey round the sea.

Theodosia is famous for two things : its ancient ruins, and the gallery of modern pictures of the painter Aivasovsky, who possesses a charming villa on a prominent point overlooking the bay. Russians always rush to see the pictures, and the passengers on board the *Grand Duke Michael* were no exception to the rule. But it occurred to me that while I might some day see the pictures in London (Aivasovsky often displays them on the Continent), I might never hope to have Theodosia brought to my door; so I spent the few hours going and returning in exploring the ruins of the place. Not that I love ruins *as* ruins, for I prefer new things to old, but for the sake of forming an estimate of the political future of Theodosia.

It is easy to see, even before landing, that Theodosia must have once been a remarkable city. From the bay, with its anchorage of eight to ten fathoms of water, there is a grand view of tier upon tier of stone houses, with bits of garden wall constantly cropping up in their midst; and, stretching far away, higher and higher upon the heights to the rear, may be readily detected ruins of villages, mounds of rubbish, and tumuli raised by the ancient Greeks. Broken, dirty, dusty, ruined as Theodosia now is, there was a time when it was called the Granary of Greece, and shipped, according to classic tradition, 3,000,000 bushels of corn in one year. Considering the size of vessels in those days, an immense amount of shipping must have been employed upon the task, even if we regard the figure as exaggerated, and reduce it. During the second, or Genoese epoch of its career, Theodosia, or Kaffa, as it was called, flourished to such a degree that when the Turks took it in 1475, after two centuries of Italian prosperity, they dubbed it "Yarin Stanbol," or "Half Stamboul," because its size gave it a right to rank next to Constantinople. When Chardin visited the place two centuries ago, there were more than 4,000 houses and 80,000 people in Theodosia, and 400 ships in the bay. A century later the Russians took it, and every stupidity and crime bad government can be guilty of was experienced by Theodosia under their rule. All the grand public buildings were pulled down, the magnificent mosques destroyed, the beautiful Genoese walls torn to pieces, and the inhabitants ill-treated till they forsook the place, carrying its trade away with them. Over and over again during the twenty-five hundred years that have elapsed since the Milesians colonized the site, Theodosia has been bombarded from sea and besieged by land, but no enemies, Greeks, Genoese, Venetians, Turks, or Tartars, ever desecrated it so wantonly and ruthlessly as the Russians did after they placed it under their administration, even if we include the unnecessary and heartless banging Hobart Pasha gave it in 1878. The arch-vandal Kasnatchaeff, from whose unscrupulous hand nothing was saved, not only destroyed the beauty of the town, but turned the environs into a desert by cutting down all the woods, the orchards, and the gardens. Gazing from the sea at the bare and bleak mountain side, it is difficult to realize that the country once bore the fruitful aspect of Devon and Kent.

The Russians of to-day have done little to repair the ravages wrought by their fathers, however much they may deplore and disown their vandalism. Theodosia is commonly spoken of as a "fashionable watering-place," but it possesses nothing to deserve such a designation. Ill-paved, inundated with dust, with one drowsy public garden, a wretched hotel or two, a filthy strand along the waterside, and water full of rank sea-weed and sewage, it offers no inducement to tempt Russians, who are good judges of luxury, from resorting to Nice, Mentone, Eastbourne, and Ostend. The only Russians who really visit it are people who cannot afford to go farther in search of a watering-place, or like a couple on board, deceived by a fictitious reputation and "taken in." Perhaps, in the distant future, Theodosia may become a clean and thriving little port; but there is at present no speedy likelihood of its attaining afresh the wonderful pitch of prosperity and power it enjoyed under the Greeks and Genoese.

After a couple of hours' stay the steamer quitted Theodosia in the direction of Kertch. The view of Theodosia as one crosses Kaffa Bay is very fine. Besides the panorama of the port, there are to the right and left magnificent configurations of the Crimean mountains, which dwell on one's memory many a day. I do not know what impressions the scenery had on the Russians, but knowing the North well, I could not help asking myself—How can men be content to dwell on the sullen and marshy shores of the Baltic when they have such a splendid sea in the South? To have asked the question of the passengers, however, would have been cruel, for the "splendid sea," directly we got away from the shelter of the mountains, began to tumble the steamer about, and before long the bunks were full, and nobody was left to enjoy the lunch but the English passengers on board. In the afternoon the wind almost blew a gale, and the deck passengers had a miserable time of it. After passing Cape Tash Kyryk the cliffs diminished in height, and became grey and sullen, like those of Dorset. The only striking bit of scenery the whole afternoon was the curious Ship Rocks, lofty sharp masses of rock starting out of the water a couple of miles from land, and appearing in the distance exactly like a ship in full sail. The Tartars call them the Sytchan Kalch, or Rat Fortress. When we got well into the Straits of Yenckale the sea grew calmer, and the passengers began to troop on deck, to find dinner over and cleared away, and the steamer abreast of the fortress of Petropavlovsky.

This fortress was erected after the Crimean War by General Todleben, on the site of the batteries silenced and captured by the Allies, when they invaded Kertch in 1855 with 15,000 troops. It has been described as a combination of masked batteries and covered ways extending over two miles, the casemates being masked by massive earthworks supported in their rear with buttresses of masonry. At the foot of the cape are a number of embrasure batteries, at present mounting 150 guns; and at the top is the citadel, Fort Todleben, whence the fire is directed by means of telegraphic communication, the entire view to seaward being comprehended in a camera. In the opinion of Commander Buchan Telfer, R.N., "fortifications one-fifth of the size of Petropavlovsky, and a few torpedoes, would have sufficed to defend the entrance, half a mile in width, between the Touzla bank and the works. When it is considered that this fortress might be invested by an enemy without a mighty effort, and the supply of water at the rear cut off, it is difficult to conceive the object with which these enormous defences have been erected, defences necessitating in time of war a garrison of many thousand men. A second Sevastopol has been raised, without the advantages of a good port."

During the Turkish War the defences of Kertch were left untouched by Hobart Pasha, who evidently thought them too strong for his ironclads, and the only event of the campaign was a court-martial on a number of officers of the garrison, caught removing some of the guns and ammunition from the batteries, and selling them to a professional receiver of stolen goods at Kertch. The inquiry into this little peccadillo extended over a long period; but revelations being threatened compromising the higher authorities of the place, it was suddenly suspended, and the delinquents let off, except, of course, the small fry: the watchmen, carters, and so forth, who were promptly deported to Siberia. "Just like Russia!"

exclaims the reader. But such abuses of justice are not peculiar to Russia alone. The rich and the powerful of all countries are privileged thieves. In every land the petty pilferer, whose chief incentive to crime is his poverty, is heavily and wrathfully punished, while the nobleman who steals common-land, the official who receives bribes or appropriates public funds, and the capitalist who thrives on bubble companies, are invariably allowed to enjoy their plunder.

Two miles beyond the fortified cape lies Kertch. On our way we passed thirty steamers, mostly English, idling in quarantine.

CHAPTER V.

A SECRET RUSSIAN MISSION TO CABUL.

Kertch and its Greek Antiquities—A Discovery made, not Classic, but Modern—The Jew who had been to Cabul—How he participated in Skobeleff's Campaign against Geok Tepé—Alikhanoff's Journey to Merv—Persons composing the Secret Russian Expedition to Cabul—Their Route through Central Asia—Samuel, the Interpreter, bound to Secrecy—What he saw at Cabul—English Soldiers with the Ameer's Troops—Loot from Geok Tepé—Caution displayed by Venkhovsky—Samuel's Description of Cabul—Afghan Opinion of the Russians—The Massacre after the Capture of Geok Tepé—Women Ravished—"It is better to be Silent in this World"—Description of a Secret Survey of Merv—The true Bearings of the Discovery of the Mission—Skobeleff's Memorandum on the Invasion of India—Russia now possesses a Survey of the direct Road from Herat to Cabul, which we know little or nothing about.

NOBODY goes to Kertch without writing about its Greek antiquities, or carrying away some of them with him. A pleasant little place, it contains enough Greek remains in the vicinity to satisfy the most inveterate archæologist. By mounting to the top of the limestone slope on which the town is built, a fine view is obtained of a range of hills running away inland seven or eight miles, studded with tumuli. Every bit of elevated ground for miles and miles round Kertch possesses these excrescences, and as a large proportion have been excavated at some time or other, they remind one of the barnacle growth on oysters. The panorama of the bay is grand, and it is flattering to the Englishman's pride that most of the year round nearly all the large shipping in it should fly the Union Jack; to the Greek or Italian, however, the spectacle must be full of melancholy. There was a time when all the shipping was Greek. There was another epoch when most of it hailed from Genoa. Now the English flag prevails, although the Russians have held the place a century. In course of time, when the coal of the Donetz valley and the iron beds of Kherson are more developed, the Russians may build their own iron ships, and themselves carry their wares to foreign markets. For the moment, the foreign transport trade of the Don and the Azoff is chiefly in English hands.

Kertch has never forgotten that it was once the capital of the Kingdom of the Bosphorus. In its traditions it is far more Greek than Russian. Everybody has something to say about King Mithridates, whose "arm-chair" is one of the most prominent features of the locality; and near which antiquities are constantly being brought to light. Few places have yielded more Greek treasures, or a richer and finer assortment than Kertch. They, however, are not to be seen there, but at St. Petersburg, where they constitute one of the sights of the imperial Hermitage. The small museum at the town itself is only a sort of temporary depository—the antiquities exhumed being kept in it until the accumulation reaches a certain point, when the treasures are carefully overhauled and the pick of them sent to the Russian capital. Many people make a livelihood by digging for antiquities, which are still plentiful, in spite of successive rulers, Khazars and Tartars, Genoese and Turks, and finally Russians, having pillaged the tumuli for centuries.

It was seven in the evening when the *Grand Duke Michael* was made fast to the jetty at Kertch, and as the steamer did not leave for the coast of the Caucasus until midnight, those passengers who were bound for Batoum were able to pass a pleasant evening ashore. It was too dark to visit the Greek ruins outside the town, or to hope of seeing much even of Kertch itself; but anything was better than being cooped up on board the steamer, and, at the worst, we thought a few antiquities might be picked up at the shops to take back to England. The sequel proved that Kertch contained other things of importance besides musty Greek relics, and that at this out-of-the-way corner of the Black Sea, of all places in the world, I was fated to make a discovery throwing a vivid light upon Russia's secret relations with Cabul. The party comprised myself, Mr. Coxon, and another Englishman on board, Mr. Cail. Making our way to the market, we loaded ourselves with grapes, here obtainable for a penny a pound, and then, by chance, roamed into a broad thoroughfare, which proved to be the Woronzoff Street (*Vorontsovskaya Oolitza*), the principal street in the town. Having walked a short distance along this, on the right-hand side, we noticed two or three antiquities exposed in a small shop, belonging to a working jeweller. Entering the place, we examined them, but found them both indifferent and dear; upon which the man said that if we cared to accompany him he would take us to a German's, where we should find plenty of cheaper specimens. The German's shop was situated in the same street, on the opposite side of the way, and proved to be a large hardware establishment, with an assortment of antiquities in one corner—vases, bottles, images, coins, &c., obtained from the tumuli outside Kertch. The proprietor spoke a little English.

We made a selection, and, while bargaining, our guide inquired where we were bound to by the steamer, and on my telling him that my ultimate destination might possibly be Krasnovodsk or Kizil Arvat, said that he knew both places well, and, in fact, the greater part of Central Asia, having travelled to Askabad and Merv, Herat and Cabul, and other places. I pricked up my ears at this. When had he been to Cabul? Last year, was his answer; he had been interpreter to a Russian mission to the Ameer Abdurrahman Khan. This was the first I had heard of any Russian expedition to Afghanistan in 1882. Nothing was known about it in England. It was clear that if this man was telling the truth, there was some basis for the reports that had been continually coming from Afghanistan respecting the presence of secret Russian agents at Herat and Cabul.

Leaving Mr. Cail, who spoke German, to settle the bargain with the German shopkeeper, I commenced to closely interrogate the man. As we pursued an eager interrogation I do not know who seemed more astonished —myself, that this working jeweller at Kertch should have turned out to be a secret Russian agent recently returned from Cabul, or himself, that a person who had never been beyond the Caspian should know so much about what the Russians had been doing there for the last five years. Probably, for months past he had come in contact with no one who cared a rap what he had seen and done in Central Asia, and now that he had met with some one who knew all about Skobeleff's siege at Geok Tepé, in which he had participated, and who could fight over again the conflict with him, he was delighted at his experience being appreciated, and was only too ready to talk of old times. In the course of a few moments the following particulars transpired.

During Skobeleff's expedition against the Turcomans, 1880-81, he accompanied the army to Geok Tepé as a sutler. He was perfectly familiar with the incidents of the siege, and described all the leading events and the principal actors in them with a minuteness that could have only resulted from personal participation in the campaign. The day after the storm of Geok Tepé he assisted in the pillage of the Tekké fortress, and secured a large number of valuable carpets, which, however, were taken from him by the military authorities. After the pacification of the country he resided at Askabad until the early part of 1882, and the probability of this was borne out by his account of Lessar's surveys and Alikhanoff's journey to Merv in disguise. He told me many things about Alikhanoff, which I knew to be correct; that he had once been a major, but had been reduced to the ranks for fighting a duel; that the Merv Tekkés had been so hostile to his caravan that the Russians had abandoned their goods at Merv in a panic; that his companions had been Lieutenant Sokoloff and the trader Gospodin Kosikh, together with other details that could have only been obtained at Askabad, and which he recounted without the slightest prompting or pressing.

On the 27th of January (Russian style), 1882, he set out from Askabad for Cabul. The party consisted of three persons, all disguised—Captain Venkhovsky, of the Engineers, who had been attached to General Glonkhovsky's survey of the old bed of the Amu Daria (Oxus), and spoke Turki and Pushtoo (he had once before visited Afghanistan); Prince Khilkoff, manager of the Transcaspian Railway; and finally himself, Samuel, a Jew. Venkhovsky was the envoy; he, Samuel, acted as interpreter, and was disguised as a travelling watchmaker and jeweller. Leaving Askabad, they proceeded to Merv, where they stopped fourteen days. Then they went to Khiva, afterwards to Bokhara, and then back over the Oxus and the mountains to Herat, which was reached in March. From Herat they proceeded direct to Cabul, where they stayed eight days in May. Returning by the same way, they reached Herat again June 10 (o.s.), and spent there also eight days.

Questioned as to what he did at Cabul, he said he could not tell me; as, on his return to Askabad, he had been compelled to sign a paper that he would never divulge what he had interpreted during his travels. Finding my interrogations on this point made him suspicious, I said I quite understood how he was placed, and changed the conversation to Turcoman carpets, of which he said he had some specimens from Merv and Geok Tepé. After a time I resumed the talk about his travels, and got him to write in Russ in my pocket-book the name of the envoy, Venkhovsky, that there might be no doubt about it. The second Russian's name he had forgotten, but he bore the title of prince.

After he had thought for a few seconds, I asked if it was Eristoff, the name of an enterprising Transcaspian petroleum pioneer.

"No," replied Samuel, "it was not he. Eristoff was a Georgian. The person I mean was a Russian prince, who spoke many languages, including English."

"Was it Khilkoff?"

"That's the name," replied the Jew, "Prince Khilkoff. Travelling about so much makes one forget and mix up names. Khilkoff was controller of the Transcaspian Railway. He was once in America, and worked as a locomotive driver. He is now in Bulgaria, Minister of Railways. He promised me a situation if he got the appointment, but he has forgotten me, I suppose."

These personal details of Khilkoff were perfectly accurate. To them he added others which need not be repeated here. Nearly the whole of the conversation was carried on in Russ; but he repeatedly dropped into German, and this induced me to ask Mr. Cail, who spoke that language, to also question him on the subject. To him he readily repeated much that he had related to me. He said he spoke most of the Central Asian dialects, and also French and German, but no English. Altogether he had spent four years in the Transcaspian region. While with the Russian expedition in Afghanistan he received 100 roubles a month. His name, at my request, he wrote in my pocket-book. First he wrote "Samuel" in French characters, and then began "watchmaker" in German—"Uhr . . ."—but I checked him, and told him to write it in Russian. Thereupon he wrote "Samoilo. Watchmaker. Vorontsovsky Street. Own House. Kertch."

[facsimile of handwritten note in Russian:]

Самойло Часовой Мастеръ. въ Керчи на Воронцовской Улицѣ. Въ собственномъ Домѣ.

The above is a *fac-simile* of what he wrote in my pocket-book.

On my expressing a desire to see a photograph of himself in the costume he wore at Cabul, and also some Turcoman carpets, he said that if we would proceed to his shop, and wait while he closed it for the night, he would go home and bring them to us in a public garden near. We accordingly repaired to his shop, where Messrs. Coxon and Cail bought some Persian krans mounted as studs, and I obtained a coin picked up in Geok Tepé. When he had packed up the few articles of jewellery displayed in the window to take home, we proceeded to a garden near the Fruit Market. He excused himself that he could not take us to his house, on the score that his wife and children were probably asleep. In a quarter of an hour's time he joined us again with another Jew. He had a tolerably good specimen of a small Merv carpet, for which he asked 15 roubles, and another from Geok Tepé, for which he wanted six. He showed us two photographs—one of himself in the costume he wore at Khiva (Turcoman dress), and the other showing the dress he wore at Cabul. The latter, he said, was taken at Askabad, and had printed on the back in Russ—"M. M. Sarkisiantz. In Akhal-Tekké." It was

a vignette, of which the above is a reproduction, and represented him wearing a tall, white, conical, sheep skin cap of the Turcoman pattern, and a striped Bokharan *Khalat*.

I asked him to give me the photograph, but he refused. It was the only copy he had got. The negative was at Askabad, and I could easily get a duplicate there. If I failed he would give it me on my return—a promise he kept on my paying him a visit on my way home. In case I went to Krasnovodsk and Kizil Arvat he gave me the names of two persons who would lodge me there—Gospodin Cohen, at the former place, and Biliani at the latter.

By this time it was already late, and we had to make our way back to the steamer. Both while walking to the garden, and during our stay in it, Mr. Cail closely questioned the man on all essential points in German, Samuel giving ready replies to the questions, and accompanying them with details that rendered it impossible to doubt that he had visited the places mentioned by him. The only portion of his story that was at all difficult to understand, was a statement that he had seen a number of English soldiers at Cabul, saying with Oriental looseness first that there were a hundred there, then fifty or so. He did not know whether they spoke Pushtoo or not. The guard of six men placed over the party during its stay at Cabul contained two of these English soldiers. He did not speak to them at all, and as his impression of their nationality apparently arose from their appearance and dress, they may have been the regular troops of the Ameer's army, in uniforms cut after the European fashion, such as several times misled our own troops during the Afghan war by their similarity to our own. He persisted in calling them English soldiers—they were not Indian troops, he was certain, and I was sorry afterwards I had not had time to interrogate him more fully on this point. He mentioned having in 1882 seen at Askabad an Englishman, who spoke Russian fluently. This was probably Mr. Condie Stephen, of the British Legation at Teheran, who was sent that year to report upon the condition of the Perso-Turcoman frontier. While at Cabul he said that the Russians had to be very careful in what they said and did, and from motives of prudence, to avoid arousing the proverbial suspiciousness of the Afghans, did not ask too many questions, or confer privately with one another before them.

The whole story was so very curious that, in order to set at rest any doubts that might be raised as to the authenticity of my account of it, I drew up a statement the next morning, embodying the above, which Messrs. Coxon and Cail signed. Fortunately, Mr. Gardiner, the British Vice-Consul at Poti, joined the vessel at Kertch, and they were able to discuss and attest its accuracy in his presence. Subsequently the statement was read over to Mr. D. R. Peacock, the British Consul at Batoum, who has an extensive knowledge of politics in the Caucasus. He said it was impossible to seriously doubt the general truthfulness of the man's story. From motives of prudence I did not send home by post the statement to be published, but kept it in my pocket-book, to add to it if circumstances should lead to my calling at Kertch and seeing the man on my return journey. On Thursday, September 15th, I found myself at sunrise again at Kertch, and the steamer *Tsarevna* not leaving before half-past ten, I passed the early hours in exploring the ruins of Kertch, and at eight o'clock made my way to the shop of the Jew. Mr. Coxon, who happened to be again travelling by the steamer, accompanied me.

I found the watchmaker already at work in his shop. After a few minutes' conversation at the door, he invited us to go to his house, a small stone building with a large yard attached, situate about five minutes' walk from the Woronzoff Street. It was poorly furnished. His wife was out shopping, but returned after a while.

I began questioning him further about his travels in Central Asia, in the course of which he produced a number of articles he had brought from that region— several carpets, some pierced with bullets and bought with other loot from the soldiers at Geok Tepé; the ornamented travelling sack, of carpet material, which contained his food and was strapped behind him when he rode to Merv; a couple of belts he bought at Khiva, the robe (very dirty and worn) he was disguised in during the Cabul journey, and various other things. While he was showing these I interrogated him closely about the English soldiers he said he had seen at Cabul, but could not disabuse him of the belief that they were Englishmen. He told me he had not come in actual contact with them. He had only seen them at a distance. He had not even spoken with the two attached to the Afghan guard placed over the Russian expedition, having been cautioned by Venkhovsky to avoid asking questions. The Russians had hardly spoken to the Afghan guard at all, they were so apprehensive of exciting their hostility. The alleged English soldiers could be readily distinguished from the Afghan troops, both by their dress and physiognomy. They wore high boots and blue tunics. It was an Afghan who told him they were English soldiers. They seemed to be on the best terms with the Afghans. He saw them walking and talking together like "chums." The Afghans treated them as brothers, not as foreigners.

The Russian expedition went by the direct road from Herat to Cabul, traversing mountains. They rode on horses. During the journey Prince Khilkoff kept a diary; he had two large books, in which he made notes. He was continually making them while on the road, writing down every feature of it. On the arrival of the mission at Cabul the Ameer was particularly friendly. Venkhovsky and Khilkoff dined twice with him. On the occasion of the first interview Venkhovsky gave the Ameer a packet—he, Samuel, could not tell me the contents of the despatches, nor did I press him. He said he had no idea of the nature of the communications. Letters were continually passing between the Ameer and Venkhovsky during the stay of the expedition at

Cabul, and when it left the latter took away another packet with him.

The Ameer he described as a fine, stout man, reminding him in burliness of Bismarck. He treated the Russians with every possible respect, and wanted them to go to Candahar, but, owing to tribal disturbances along the road, Venkhovsky thought it wiser to defer the visit. The principal negotiations between the Ameer and the Russian mission were carried on by a Khivan Usbeg at the Ameer's court. He had forgotten his name; he spoke Russian a little, and was very fond of women. Samuel described Cabul as a charming city. If he had not had a wife he would have settled down there as a watchmaker. He would go there again to-morrow if anybody wanted him. There was plenty of fruit at Cabul, and he had never visited a place where such splendid kishliks [or kabobs, small bits of meat roasted on skewers] were to be had. The Afghans cook them at Cabul "in the English fashion, with plenty of blood in the meat." He saw the places outside Cabul "where the Afghans repeatedly defeated General Roberts," and the crosses above our soldiers' graves. The Afghans have a high opinion of the Russians, and are inclined to be very friendly with them. He would undertake to travel in any part of Afghanistan.

When we returned to the steamer he accompanied us, carrying a Turcoman carpet Mr. Coxon had purchased of him. He said it was one of the spoils of Geok Tepé. He described the siege of the fortress as a dreadful affair; the Tekkés fought with such determination that the Russians several times thought they would have to retreat. When the fortress was captured, and the Turcomans streamed out across the plain, the carnage was fearful. One thousand Russians cut down 8,000 Turcomans—men, women, and children— in a few hours. The whole country was covered with corpses; "the morning after the battle they lay in rows like freshly mown hay, as they had been swept down by the mitrailleurs and artillery. He himself saw babies bayonetted or slashed to pieces. Many women were ravished before being killed." On my mentioning that Skobeleff had solemnly assured me none had been ravished, he replied energetically, " Lots were. They were ravished by the soldiers before my eyes. He may not have known it. I could tell you many horrible things that took place, but (tapping his lips significantly with his forefinger) it is better to be silent in this world. The plunder from Geok Tepé was immense. The troops were allowed to get drunk, plunder, and kill for three days after the assault."

I mentioned that Mr. Cail had carried away the impression from the last interview that he, Samuel, had served as interpreter to Skobeleff during the siege. He denied this. He had been a sutler, pure and simple. He had, however, acted as interpreter to Prince Khilkoff after the war. On my asking if he had no other name besides Samuel, he replied that his family name was Gourovitch, but that he was commonly known as Samuel at Kertch. He wrote his name in my pocket-book. I should add that I made no secret of my personality. What he told me was given openly, not in confidence. As he disclosed to me nothing respecting what he was bound to keep secret, I can do him no harm in giving his statements in full. On the steamer I showed him some of the illustrations appearing in my last work, "The Russians at Merv and Herat." The picture of the "Northern Gate of Merv" (page 194) delighted him.

"How many times have I gone up and down that road," he said. "We used to go about the fortress, scanning it, disguised as Tekkés. Do you know that inside the fortress, behind the wall, there are forty

English cannon?" I replied that they were not English, but Persian ones, thirty-two in number, captured from the army of Sultan Murad Mirza in 1861. "Then if they are not English, they are of English manufacture," rejoined Samuel.

The third bell now ringing, to warn the public that the steamer was about to start, he bade me goodbye, and went ashore.

. . . . .

I have no wish to give undue prominence to Venkhovsky's secret mission to Cabul, but I cannot dismiss the subject without a few remarks. When the discovery was made at Kertch, rumours were reaching India from Cabul that Russian agents had repeatedly visited Afghanistan since our treaty of peace with the Ameer, and that a secret representative was still there. Samuel's story proved for the first time without doubt that there had been at least one secret mission to Cabul since 1881, and thereby gave an air of probability to the statement that others had been there also. This was something.

But the true bearings of Venkhovsky's mission can only be understood by a reference to the condition of political affairs at the time it reached Cabul. Europe, in the early part of 1882, was in a state of agitation. The rising in Herzegovina had found England's sympathy to rest with Austria, and General Skobeleff, chagrined at Mr. Gladstone's falling off, had used ominous language at the famous Geok Tepé banquet with reference to Vienna and India. Already, even then, the Egyptian Question was exciting rival ambitions among the European Powers, and Russia had taken up a diplomatic attitude decidedly hostile to this country. If Venkhovsky's mission had a political aim, the time was certainly well chosen for preparing the ground in Central Asia for operations against India, in the event of a necessity arising to coerce England in Europe.

But whether the expedition had a political purport or not, it was certainly attended with geographical results of the highest importance. There is, I believe, no published march-route existing of the direct road between Herat and Cabul. The road has never yet been traversed by an English explorer, and we know so little about it that Colonel Malleson, in his admirable "Herat," goes back to 1506 for a description of the highway! In 1875 General Sir Charles MacGregor made preparations for effecting the survey, but was foolishly hindered from doing so by the over-scrupulous and timid officials at Simla at the very moment he was setting out from Meshed. Thus we have no survey of a road which has been carefully investigated and mapped by a couple of clever Russian officers, in a country which we were assured when Candahar was evacuated would remain wholly under our influence. So little is this the case that Russia can send officers riding hither and thither throughout Afghanistan and maintain agents at Cabul, while we, who are paying the Ameer £120,000 a year and giving him armaments to fit out a fresh army, are forbidden to send not only any agent to his capital, but even solitary English officers or merchants across the frontier. Such a policy is, on the face of it, a foolish one. An independent Afghanistan is an idle dream. The Gladstone Government are simply pandering to the treachery of a prince who has given no real evidence whatever that he is loyally disposed towards England, or that he would be her ally in the event of complications with Russia.

CHAPTER VI.

CRUISING ALONG THE COAST OF THE CAUCASUS.

Departure from Kertch—The Romance of the Caucasus—Wanted, a Historian—The Conflict for the Possession of the Caucasus—Anapa—Its History—The Slave Trade, Old and New—Traffic in Young Girls—Novorossisk—The Colonization of the Stavropol Plains—Rapid Growth of Rostoff-on-the-Don—Future of Novorossisk—A Second Railway projected between the Caspian and Black Sea—Petroleum in the Taman Peninsula—The French Company at Novorossisk—Bartering Girls for Herrings—Journeying along the Coast—A happy, memorable Day—Soukhum Kalé—What the Turks did and did not do in 1877—Armed Mountaineers—Poti—Arrival at Batoum.

WE left Kertch at midnight, the moon shining brightly upon the angry waters of the bay, and a wild wind blowing. Several times during the night I was awakened by the tossing of the vessel, but when a sudden cessation of motion finally aroused me at daybreak, and I looked out of the porthole, I found the weather calm and bright again, and the *Grand Duke Michael* anchored in the beautiful bay of Anapa.

From this point really commences the modern, exciting, romantic part of the Caucasian coast. The Taman Peninsula, and, as a matter of fact, the whole of the region on both sides of the Straits of Yenekale, are full of classical associations. A whole volume might be written upon the rise and fall of the Greek colonies, which at one period rendered the entrance to the Sea of Azoff busier and more flourishing than any part of the Russian littoral at the present day. For those who hate classical history, and prefer that of the Middle Ages, the same region is full of mute memorials of the wonderful trade centres established by the Genoese. But, once we get away from the lower ground round about the Straits, and reach the mountains of the Caucasus, practically commencing at Anapa, the interest henceforth is neither classical nor Genoese, but arises from the modern fearful struggle which the chivalry of the Caucasus waged against desperate odds until the other day. The story of that struggle has yet to be written by some sympathetic historian. A finer subject an earnest and ambitious writer could hardly desire. For a period of two centuries there is not a decade without its campaign, and at times there are a dozen in as many years. Pitched battles and sieges occur by hundreds; of skirmishes, reconnaissances, raids, and ambushes there are thousands. Generation after generation of yellow-haired Russians swarm to the Caucasus and pierce its defiles by land, or invade the coast and attack its flanks from the Caspian and the Black Sea, and one after the other the Persian, the Turk, and the Caucasian go down before them; the latter the toughest resister of the three, and maintaining for a solid century such a defence as we can find no parallel for in ancient or modern history. Considering the marvellous character of that racial conflict, it is remarkable that neither in English nor in Russian is there any work extant describing from beginning to end the conquest of the Caucasus. Abundance of materials lie scattered through European works of travel; and as for Russia, it would take years to go through the records, the narratives, and the fragmentary histories in the Library of the General Staff and other great collections of books. Yes, the materials are numerous and accessible enough, but neither in Russia nor out of it does there seem to be any man anxious to gain a reputation for himself by evolving a history out of them.

Every inch of the Caucasus is full of memories of war and romance. Anapa, which lay so quiet before us that calm August morning, looking like a little vignette composed of a few new staring-white Russian buildings, a lot of dingy native houses, a church or two, a ruined earthwork with roads and paths running remorselessly over it, and wearing away its outlines, a long stretch of flat coast towards Kertch, and perpendicular hills 200 feet high in the background towards the Caucasus, has been the centre of many a stirring scene. Founded exactly a century ago by the Turks, it has been attacked five times, besieged thrice, and completely ravaged and destroyed four times. Two of its sieges any seaport might be proud of. The first was of six weeks' duration, in 1791, when General Goudavitch took the place by assault, to be himself directly afterwards driven out by the Turks and the mountaineers; and the second lasted three months, the town in 1828 defying the combined sea and land forces of General Prince Menshikoff, and the Scotchman, Admiral Creig. Since then Anapa has remained a Russian possession, its evacuation for strategical reasons during the Crimean war being only of a temporary character. As a fortified post it is no longer of any importance. The Circassians were long ago exterminated at the rear, and their places have not yet been taken by fresh settlers from Russia. Its trade amounts to a quarter of a million sterling a year, and is not likely to increase very much, owing to the unsheltered character of the port and its bad anchorage. For those who do not care for war and commerce, Anapa may perhaps excite interest as the port whence in the good old Turkish times hundreds of lovely girls used to be shipped to the harems of Constantinople.

The good old Turkish times are gone, yet slavery still flourishes in the Black Sea. Swift sailing vessels no longer scud across its dark waters to the Bosphorus with captive Circassian maids on board, but the trade in female flesh is still carried on between the Russian ports and Constantinople by means of the steamers of the Black Sea Navigation Company. The slave dealers are Jews; the victims attractive Russian girls, inveigled to Turkey under the pretence of obtaining situations there, or some other pretext. Hundreds of girls thus lose their virtue and freedom every year. At Constantinople there are schools where Russian girls purchased or kidnapped from their parents in childhood are regularly reared, and ultimately sold into Turkish harems. In justice to the Russian authorities, it is but right to say that every effort has been made of late to put down the trade, and more than one slave dealer has been sent to Siberia; but the traffic in young girls is an evil which is not readily crushed, and if it flourishes at intervals in London, in the midst of our morality, the reader can imagine the difficulties impeding its suppression in the Euxine.

We did not stop long at Anapa, and were away again by seven o'clock, steaming along the beautiful coast, and enjoying the magnificent mountain scenery, which from this point does not cease all the way to Batoum. Thirty miles south-east of Anapa we passed Soudjuk Kalé, or Dry Sausage Fort, at the entrance to Novorossisk Bay, once a powerful Turkish stronghold, but now a crumbling ruin. Eight thousand out of fifteen thousand Russians perished in 1836 in trying to establish their hold upon the place, and the survivors experienced fearful sufferings from floods, famine, and the attacks of the Circassians in their retreat to Anapa. Novorossisk Bay is one of the finest in the Black Sea. It is between eight and nine miles in circumference, possessing great depth of water and excellent anchorage, and is completely land-locked, except to the south-east. There it might be easily rendered secure by a mole, and being protected on the land-side from violent winds by the mountains around it, the bay would then become a magnificent outport for the produce of Cis-Caucasia.

About seventeen or eighteen years ago, with some such aim in view, the Russians abandoned Soudjuk Kalé, and started a settlement further back in the bay, to which they gave the name of Novorossisk—New Russia. It is this that now gives the designation to the bay. But beyond shifting the seat of administration from one spot to another the Russians have done little to render the place worthy of its magniloquent title. Novorossisk is neither new nor Russian. It consists of simply a few hundred miserable stone houses, and two or three good ones, scattered over a large area of ground, with a miserable sleepy bazaar in the centre. The streets, although carefully designed, have never been paved; the grand stone quay of the future still exists on paper. In the meanwhile, goods are loaded or discharged by lighter, although the expenditure of a few thousand roubles would give the place the convenience of a pier. It is a question whether, for commercial purposes, Novorossisk is not worse than the Soudjuk Kalé it supplanted.

But, none the less, Novorossisk really is a place of the future. The population of Russia is swelling out towards the Caucasus. The steppes of Stavropol are losing their pastoral character and becoming agricultural. The Cossack element is being engulfed by the swarms of peasants from Penza, Riazan, and Koursk. Those steppes have a larger area than the whole of England. Their fertility is proverbial. Already the new-comers have demonstrated the natural fitness of the region for the cultivation of corn. During the last five years the products of the Kouban have increased 50 per cent., and the settlers can now export 400,000 tons of grain. Of the 500,000 tons of bread-stuffs conveyed by the railway to Rostoff-on-the-Don in 1882 for shipment abroad, 300,000 tons were despatched from the upper part of the line, in the *rayon* of the Kavkazskoi station, whence it is projected to run a line to Novorossisk.

At present nearly all the Stavropol corn and wool runs the wrong way to the sea. The Rostoff-Vladikavkaz Railway, passing through the heart of the country, draws the traffic in a north-westerly direction to the mouth of the Don. Forty years ago Rostoff was a wooden village, with a couple of stone houses for the headman and the priest. It has now a fixed population of 70,000 people, which during the navigation season is extended to more than double that number, and it transacts a trade of quite seven millions sterling a year. Its prosperity is largely due to the produce it sucks and exports from the Cis-Caucasian region. But Rostoff is a very inconvenient outport. It is situated twenty miles from the mouth of the shallowest river in Europe, and has to ship all its stuff in lighters; and further, it is enclosed by ice quite four months out of the twelve. Did the Stavropol produce, instead of flowing towards the Don, make direct for the Black Sea at Novorossisk, it would not have half so far to go by rail, its outport would be a day nearer Europe, and not only would no lighters be needed, but the navigation would be open the whole year round. From the mouth of the Don to Novorossisk the coast of the Cis-Caucasian region is not indented by a single good harbour; but Novorossisk makes up for this by offering to commerce a bay capacious enough for the largest possible traffic. The two factors needed to render Novorossisk a second Odessa are a railway into the interior, and the quays and piers essential to every port.

The Russian Government is perfectly well aware of the wants of Novorossisk, and has already taken the initial steps for dealing with them. A railway, standing almost first on the list of those to be next constructed, will run from Novorossisk to some station about midway between

Rostoff and Vladikavkaz. This will be 172½ miles long, and will cost, with £150,000 for improving the port, £1,400,000 sterling, and require a couple of years to construct. From Vesler, a station near Vladikavkaz, another line is projected to the Caspian port of Petrovsk, 163 miles long, costing £1,600,000. This would establish direct communication between the Caspian and the Black Sea, north of the Caucasus, parallel with that already existing between Baku and Batoum, to the south of it. If, as already projected, the Petrovsk line were pushed on to Baku, another excellent outlet would be afforded by Novorossisk for Caspian petroleum. Last autumn official surveys were made for this line, and when subsequently the Minister of Railways, General Possiet, visited Novorossisk, he promised the inhabitants the first section of the network should be taken in hand as soon as possible. When his promise is carried into effect, Novorossisk will rapidly take a prominent place among the ports of the world.*

The Stavropol plains produce wool and corn; the coast jutting towards the west, and forming one of the jaws of the Sea of Azoff, is rich in petroleum oil. The naphtha springs of the Taman Peninsula were known to the world so long ago as in the time of the ancient Greeks. In modern times they have been visited by many eminent scientific men, and their copiousness is beyond question. The exact area over which the springs extend has not yet been accurately defined; but, generally speaking, the entire Taman Peninsula may be accepted as an oil-bearing region, and has only remained undeveloped because of the crushing effects of the abundant supply at Baku. A

* The railway is now finished, and the commercial port, which is to cost £380,000, is well in hand. Tapping as it does the petroleum region of Cis-Caucasia, a great future may be predicted for the place. A new town is rapidly growing, and military importance has been given to Novorossisk by the location there of a battalion of troops. There is also a talk of making it a naval station.

few years ago a French company was formed to develop the deposits sixty miles inland of Novorossisk. The management was confided to an American, who had previously created some talk by a scheme for pumping petroleum through a pipe from the Caspian to the Black Sea. At his instigation, a pipe, sixty miles long, was laid down between the wells inland of Novorossisk and a refinery on Novorossisk Bay. Last year there was a quarrel between himself and the directors, and he left the concern, which does not seem to have been a very successful undertaking. While I was on shore exploring Novorossisk, a carriage full of Frenchmen drove into the place from the refinery, and had much to say about the capabilities of the Taman petroleum supply. But, while sharing the belief that the deposits there are as large as those of America, I cannot see that they have any chance for the moment against those of Baku; at least, not until the inland railway is constructed, and obviates such costly items of expenditure as laying down sixty miles of piping. An American petroleum engineer, whom I met in the Caucasus, and who is thoroughly acquainted with Pennsylvania, the Taman Peninsula, and Baku, assured me that nothing existing in the world can approach the Baku supply in copiousness and ease of extraction. He had no interest at all in Baku, and his opinion was quite impartial.*

After a couple of hours at Novorossisk the steamer continued its voyage. Twenty miles from Novorossisk we passed Ghelendjik, which is considered the snuggest and safest harbour on the coast of the Caucasus. Then came Pshad and Tuapse, ports where in former times the Genoese traders used to exchange dried-fish, wine, and

* In 1886 the quantity of crude oil produced in the Kuban region was a little over 4,250,000 gallons, of which 4,000,000 were raised in the Ilsky district. A considerable proportion was shipped to Marseilles.

salt for girls for the harems of Turkey and Egypt. It seems cruel that beauty should have been sold for a tub of salt or a barrel of herrings, but in principle the transaction was no worse than the occasional transfer of girls nowadays by virtuous and Christian mothers to the possessors of greasy bank-books and tarnished coronets. We did not stop at any of these ports, but steamed steadily along the coast, about a mile from it, the whole of the afternoon and evening.

I think this was the most enjoyable part of the journey. The sea was without a ripple or a wave—it was like a placid mountain lake. The ample awning effectually protected us from the blazing sun, shining from a firmament of blue, in which there was not the vestige of a cloud. To share the spacious accommodation of the vessel there were not more than half a dozen persons, forming among themselves a pleasant little yachting party. All day long the scenery never ceased to be magnificent—stupendous cliffs rising sheer out of the water into tree-clad, cloud-capped cones, stretching far away out of sight in the background, and here and there lovely little dells and valleys inviting the navigator to go ashore. Not a sign of culture visible anywhere except at tiny ports—nothing but virgin forests and trackless mountains; both enjoyed without the slightest discomfort, and with luxurious meals at intervals, such as probably no millionaire cruising in his own yacht in the Mediterranean would have been able to surpass. I would sooner live that day over again than attend half a dozen Imperial coronations.

We stopped at two or three places during the night, and after breakfast the next morning halted at Monastyr, or Monastery, where, in excess of the edifice giving the port its name, were several white buildings peeping out from the dense forests covering the whole of the country. Here a score or more pilgrims, men and women, went ashore to do penance and pray, and make their way back, perhaps, by the return steamer. It was like a scene from the Middle Ages, to see the lay brothers rowing the pilgrims, with their wallets and their staves, across the placid bay towards the monastery, at the entrance of which were monks and devotees waiting to receive them.

In an hour's time we reached Soukhum Kalé, a place which in English hands would have long ago recovered some of that importance it possessed in Pliny's time, when to the " opulent city of Dioscurias resorted people speaking seventy different languages." Soukhum was fearfully pulled about during the last war. The Turks landed several thousand men at the port, which General Kratchenkoff abandoned without firing a shot; and might have exercised a powerful effect on the fate of the struggle in Armenia if they had pushed a little inland, especially as the Russians were retreating at the moment from Kars, and the Daghestan tribes were rising against them. But the Turks contented themselves with doing less than they had even done during the Crimean war, when they had also landed a similar fruitless expedition at Soukhum Kalé, and remained quiescent until the struggle was over. As in 1856, so in 1878, the Turks in evacuating Soukhum Kalé left nothing but dirt, disease, and ruin behind them. Fearing the vengeance of the Russians, nearly all the natives fled with them, and the country round about the port became depopulated. Recently some of the houses have been rebuilt, but every street is disfigured with ruins. The bones of hundreds of cattle mark the site where the Abkazians slaughtered their herds to prevent them falling alive into the hands of the Russians. The fever and the stench which these carcases produced still lurk in the air, and check the return of many of the inhabitants to the place. The garrison is kept under canvas on a mountain to the rear. In process of time the town may be expected to recover itself and thrive, but much will depend upon the fulfilment of a long projected scheme for connecting Soukhum with the Poti-Tiflis Railway, and the colonization of the adjacent region. The line is designed to run from Soukhum to the Novosenaki station of the Poti-Tiflis Railway. It would be 114 versts, or about 80 miles long, and would enable travellers journeying from Europe to Tiflis to save nearly half a day by landing there instead of going on to Batoum. Soukhum Kalé is situated on a very fine bay, which engineering science properly applied—not misdirected, as in the case of Poti—could easily render a safe and commodious port. In his "Summer Tour in Russia," Mr. Gallenga speaks most erroneously of there being "no" good ports between Kertch and Trebizond, but with a few improvements Soukhum Kalé could be made, if not as good as Novorossisk, at least sufficiently convenient for all the trade that might be expected to pass through it. Pending the construction of the railway, the Russians are fronting the place with a fine stone quay.

We took aboard a good many deck passengers at Soukhum—Georgians, Mingrelians, Imeretians, and other Caucasian natives, all in their national dress, and armed to the teeth. Watching these mountaineers affords constant amusement to the traveller. Their warlike dress and demeanour, and the assortment of weapons every one of them with any pretensions to breeding carries about with him, remind the traveller very forcibly on his arrival at Soukhum or Poti from Odessa that he has left the land where Keating's insect powder is the only defensive weapon needed, and that he would do well to look out his revolver. It is curious that the Russians, who act invariably in a very systematic manner in crushing the hostile spirit of the people they conquer, should have never sought to disarm the inhabitants of the Caucasus.

Many of the tribes dwelling between Soukhum and Batoum have revolted times out of number, and even now secretly perpetrate acts of brigandage on the high road; but no attempt is made to take their weapons from them, and they go about Soukhum and Batoum armed to the teeth with Berdan, revolver and silver-hilted dagger, securing respect from unarmed Russians and terrifying timid European tourists. But if their aspect is warlike, they are a very different class of people from the Afghans or Kurds. Provided he treats them well, and forbears from travelling past their villages at the dead of night, the tourist can rely upon "doing" the Caucasus in almost perfect safety. As a rule, their weapons are mainly kept for show or hunting purposes, and if he is a keen sportsman the traveller will be well treated and assisted wherever he goes.

Leaving Soukhum Kalé at eleven o'clock, we coasted pleasantly alongside the mountains—separated from the sea by a swampy beach—all day, and at six in the evening passed Poti, of which from the water little is seen beyond a house or two projecting above a forest marsh. On board the *Grand Duke Michael* were many passengers bound for Poti, but instead of landing them there, the vessel carried them on to Batoum, where they had to wait until the following day and return by a smaller steamer. This roundabout way of doing business has been going on for years, without the Black Sea Steam Navigation Company adopting the simple expedient of having a tug to meet the steamer outside Poti to take off the passengers and mails, or the Russian Government compelling it to respond to the clamour of the public to be treated with greater regard for its convenience. Three hours later we arrived at Batoum.

PLATE 5.—BATOUM.

CHAPTER VII.

THE RUSSIANS AT BATOUM.

Batoum at Night—More Tame than Heroic—Difference between the Caucasus Army and the Army in India—Poti *versus* Batoum—Drawbacks of Poti—A Costly Mole—History and Future of the Port—Its Rival, Batoum—Extraordinary Development of the Place—The Turkish Defences—Secret Russian Armaments—New Batoum—Russian Improvements—The Bay of Batoum—New Harbour Works in Progress—Mr. Peacock, the British Consul—Benefit conferred on Russia by Europe in making Batoum a Free Port—The Contraband Trade at Batoum—The Caucasus Transit—How Smuggling is Carried on—The Petroleum Export Trade at Batoum—Export of Oil in 1883—Future of Batoum.

It was about nine o'clock at night (Aug. 24) when the *Grand Duke Michael* entered Batoum harbour, and took up a station alongside the wooden jetty. Up to that moment we had had excellent weather, but the rain now fell in torrents. "At Batoum," said a resident to us, putting on his macintosh, "it always rains, just as at Baku rain never falls at all." This was a somewhat exaggerated way of putting the case, but, generally speaking, for the greater part of the year, wet weather prevails in the Batoum corner of the Black Sea, while extreme dryness is the characteristic of the Caspian at Baku. The backbone of the Lesser Caucasus, running south-west of the Great Caucasus range, divides the Transcaucasian region into two wholly different climates —as widely diverse in their characteristics as Devonshire and Sahara. Batoum catches the rain from the heavily-laden clouds from the Black Sea striking against the mountains at its rear, while Baku lies entirely open to the desiccating effects of the heat radiating from the sands of Central Asia.

The captain wanted us to stop on board the vessel all night; but we had been cooped up from Monday till Friday, and were only too glad to get ashore. Selecting some of the bare-legged, ragged, Turkish-looking *mushirs*, or porters, crowding the head of the pier, we made them shoulder our luggage, and filed off in the direction of the *Hôtel de France*, situated about three minutes' walk from the landing-stage. In any other country the train for Tiflis and the interior of the Caucasus would have been arranged to leave immediately after the arrival of the steamer, but in Russia time is a commodity of no value. Hence the steamer arrives at Batoum at nine at night, and the train leaves at eight or nine the next morning. On this account, passengers are compelled to pass a night at Batoum, and this circumstance has given rise to two hotels, the *Hôtel de France* and the *Hôtel d'Europe*. The former is the larger establishment, and is located in an extensive and commodious building close to the station. The rooms are well furnished; the charges are high, but not exorbitant; and a decent dinner can be had any time up to midnight. The chief drawback is a want of civility, arising probably from the fact that the majority of travellers only pass a night there, and never repeat their visit. In course of time the break at Batoum will no doubt be done away with, and the journey to Baku will then be shortened by half a day.

From what we had heard, we considered ourselves in jeopardy from attack on our persons and property the moment we got ashore. Revolvers were disposed in our pockets ready for action, and with a stout oak cudgel apiece we mounted guard over the *mushirs*, keeping one eye on them, that they did not bolt into the darkness with our effects, and the other on the black expanse around us, in case ferocious footpads should suddenly start up and bar the way. These exaggerated precautions, we afterwards found, were altogether unnecessary. Batoum is as tame as any ordinary foreign port, and the traveller who lands there is safer with the *mushirs* than the foreigner usually is who confides himself to the tender mercies of wherrymen and waterside porters on the river Thames. Outside Batoum, in the savage and inaccessible mountains, robbers exist and frequently attack the sportsman or the traveller on the post-road; but, although street robberies and burglaries are not unknown at Batoum, the place is probably quite as safe to live in as any port on the Continent.

Arrived at the hotel, we secured our rooms, gave up our passports to be registered, and adjourned for supper to the dining saloon, where we found about a score of officers and officials assembled and boisterously enjoying themselves. Only a battalion or so of troops is maintained inside the free port of Batoum; the rest of the garrison is established in force outside, where it guards the arsenal of eighteen and twenty-five ton guns and other weapons lying ready to be despatched into the place the moment Russia declares war next time against Turkey, or tears up the Berlin Treaty. Close to the pier are corrugated iron barracks for several thousand troops. These were almost entirely unoccupied while I was there, but late in the autumn they are crowded with recruits arriving at Batoum from Russia to join the army of the Caucasus, and in winter by time-expired soldiers on their way home. The army of the Caucasus is very different in one important essential from our own in India—excluding the irregular cavalry, the whole of the troops are Russians. The Caucasus contains no Sepoys. On the other hand, while we in

India do our utmost to prevent the Indian gentry entering the army, or if they do, place a limit to their promotion, the Russians throw every inducement in the way of the gentry of the Caucasus to encourage them to accept military employment. The result of our system is, to provoke a deal of discontent among Indian gentlemen anxious to follow the only career which seems to them fit for persons of their standing, while the result of the Russian plan is, to interest the nobles of the Caucasus in the maintenance of Russian rule. The fact of thousands of recruits and time-expired soldiers passing through Batoum every year, exercises an important effect upon the business of the place.

The next morning was nice and bright, and we spent a pleasant day exploring Batoum. I was astonished at the remarkable activity everywhere apparent. Houses and shops were being built by hundreds, and there was every evidence that in a few years nothing will be left of the old Turkish town ceded in 1878. Before another decade is past, Batoum will have become a great commercial outport, and the Sevastopol of the Southern Euxine.

For more than a year a discussion has raged in the Russian press as to the merits and prospects of the rival ports of Poti and Batoum, both of which are connected by railway with Tiflis and the Caspian. In England we should leave the two ports to fight out their own futures; but in Russia the State always exercises large control over the development of new centres of commerce, and as much therefore depends upon the support of the Government as excellence of site. At the present moment Batoum is the favourite port, and Poti can only hope to retain its position in the event of the new outlet proving too small for the requirements of trade.

Poti has gained an evil reputation from two causes—the prevalence of malaria, and the costliness of its mole.

These drawbacks have rendered it malodorous both to the Russian public, which can never refer to the place without expressions of disgust, and to the Russian Government, from whose treasury 9,000,000 roubles have passed to improve the port without the port being proportionately any the better for the outlay. There was a time when Poti was very differently thought of. Great expectations were entertained of its becoming the Odessa of the Caucasian side of the Euxine. After the Crimean war the favour which the Government had shown to Soukhum Kalé was withdrawn, and every effort was made to develop Poti. In 1863 a scheme was taken in hand for running out a mole to the sea, in such a manner as to afford accommodation and safety to a large number of steamers in bad weather. The river Rion, on which Poti is situated, has too little water on the 8-ft. bar at its mouth to allow of the entrance of vessels of large capacity, and when the weather is at all windy outside no communication can be maintained between the shore and the shipping in the roadstead. It was to overcome this serious defect that the mole was planned, and if nothing has come of the project, the Russian Government cannot be accused of not having spent enough money over it.

More than twenty years have elapsed since the first stone of the mole was laid with pomp by the engineers at Poti, and the work is still as far off completion as ever. In the interval, the undertaking has been carried on by a whole series of engineers and contractors, all of whom have retired after a few years with fortunes, leaving the mole to be continued by needy successors. As originally designed, the harbour works were to have cost only about £200,000, but nearly a million sterling has vanished and Poti has nothing to show for it. It is said that the original plan was radically wrong, and that the Government has never had the moral courage to revoke or revise it; but the more likely supposition is, that the authorities mainly concerned have never bothered themselves about the defects of the undertaking, but have contented themselves with enriching themselves out of it. How many times confident expectations have been announced of the work coming to an end in a couple of years, it would be difficult to say. The only thing that is certain is, that the grants have always come to an end long before the expiration of the period over which the expenditure of them was fixed to spread. When the Poti-Tiflis Railway was completed at the close of the Khivan war, extra energy was infused into the undertaking, but nothing came of it; and after the spurt was over the works languished until the Turkish conflict, since when they have been suspended altogether. Originally the mole was to have been 6ft. above high water mark, and to have been constructed of blocks of stone weighing not less than three tons. After a while the height was raised to 16ft., and the size of the blocks of stone to thirty tons. Not long ago a storm occurred, during which twenty of these 30-ton blocks were carried away by the sea, together with a couple of massive cranes, weighing 100 tons apiece. To render the mole of any use it would have to be carried out fifty yards from its present halting point, or else a costly breakwater constructed. While the Government is making up its mind what to do, the plant of the harbour construction works is rotting or being swallowed up by the sea, and the foundering of a steamer and a number of coasting craft the other day proved that what there is of the mole is useless for the protection of shipping. The local opinion is, that now that Batoum has been connected by railway with Tiflis, Poti will be allowed to go to ruin.

Already, owing to the revocation of free transit across the Caucasus, the place wears a languishing aspect.

Very little business is being done, and many merchants are leaving the port for good. The stoppage of the free transit of European goods to the East, a measure sanctioned by the Tsar during the Coronation, against the recommendations of his leading Ministers, and intended as a solace and gift to the merchants of Moscow, then complaining of bad trade, has certainly failed to produce the effect it was intended; the despatch of Russian goods on a large scale, in place of the prohibited European ones, to Persia and Central Asia has not yet commenced, while the traffic receipts of the Transcaucasian Railway Company have fallen seriously. The people of Poti are very angry at the concession made to the merchants of Moscow, and no wonder, since, besides losing their transit business, they can get nothing for their houses and land, and find themselves in many instances absolutely ruined.

Poti has never been a favourite place with travellers, who have always hurried from it by the first train or post-cart. A guide book says that it is very dangerous to pass even one night in Poti, owing to its malaria, at which extreme criticism the inhabitants are very indignant, affirming that even if fever is prevalent at Poti, it is a better fever to catch than the fever at Soukhum Kalé or Batoum, because the victim recovers from it sooner. Situated on marshy ground at a river mouth, and surrounded by impenetrable forests, its only two advantages over Batoum are that it has plenty of flat ground round about to allow of expansion, and is twenty-four and a half miles nearer Tiflis and Baku. These, in my opinion, are sufficient to prevent the pessimist views about the place being ever entirely realized. Batoum is not a large port; it cannot be increased in size beyond a certain point; and the inconvenience that will then arise will drive trade back again to Poti. The fact of the Black Sea Navigation Company having recently applied for harbour lands at Poti, after transferring its operations entirely to Batoum, is an indication of a reaction which may assume encouraging dimensions at no distant date. Poti may not become a second Odessa, but it will never descend to the decayed condition of an Anapa and Soudjuk Kalé.

As regards Batoum, so rapid has been its transformation under Russian rule, and so quickly are changes succeeding one another now, that any traveller who visited the place anterior to the war of 1877–78 would probably fail to recognize it. A railway has been cut right through the town to a capacious pier stretching some distance out to sea. Streets are being laid out, and when I was there were being excavated for laying on water. New houses are rising everywhere like mushrooms. Scores of shops, well fronted and filled with the wares of the West, are crushing out of existence the miserable little booths common to Batoum in its Turkish days. Everywhere builders are at work. There must have been at least 200 houses and shops in course of erection last autumn, and the building is being carried out on a regular plan, the hovels of the Armenian inhabitants being remorselessly cut down to allow of the formation of wide rectangular streets, and no mercy being shown to mosques or any structure that bars the way. Where the Turkish outposts were placed by Dervish Pasha in 1877 a surburban station occupies the ground. A busy kerosine canning factory has sprung up alongside the Turkish redoubts. On the hills country residences are being erected. Along the shore, on the Anatolian side, is a regular suburb, almost as big as old Batoum, consisting of corrugated iron barracks for troops, and scores of two-storey stone residences for the military and administrative staff. In a few years' time nothing will be left of the Batoum of the Turks, and Russia will possess on the south-east coast of the Black Sea a well-built, well-drained, and well-lit town, ranking next to Odessa as a commercial port in time of peace and next to Sevastopol as a naval station in time of war. The commerce of the place is growing with gigantic strides, largely due to its privileges as a free port. As regards purposes of war, the defences of the Turks—defences which Russia herself could never overcome—are still unrazed, large bodies of troops are assembled on the spot, and if the Treaty of Berlin has been fulfilled to the letter by mounting no Russian cannon on the Ottoman fortifications, it has been broken in the spirit by collecting them in an arsenal outside the boundary of the free port, whence in a few hours they could be dragged to the defences and placed in position.

Respecting the fortifications an anecdote is current at Batoum, which well illustrates how the Government is acting in the matter. The principal Turkish position, the casemated redoubt immediately controlling the harbour and alongside which the pier runs out to sea, some time ago began to show signs of decay; thereupon tenders were invited to repair the place. One of the local contractors, a Russian, sent in an estimate headed "Repairs to fortifications." In a day or two he was summoned to the Military Control office, and was there informed that such a heading would never do. "There are no fortifications in Batoum," said the general, "they are forbidden by the Treaty of Berlin. Adopt as a heading, therefore, and use throughout the words—'Garrison barrack repairs.'"

Formerly Batoum consisted of 800 or 900 shops and houses, and about the only two-storey one was that of the Russian Vice-Consul. There must now be quite a couple of hundred two-storey buildings, besides several three-storey structures used as hotels and Government offices. In Turkish days, the ground either belonged to Allah or the Sultan. When Dervish Pasha evacuated the place, he and his officials reaped a neat little sum by selling the land at any price to anybody who cared to make the investment. Even after they were gone, money was made by the Turkish officials at Trebizond by selling titles, dated back, to Armenian speculators. At present, owing to the demand, land can hardly be bought at any reasonable price, while builders exact exorbitant sums for erecting anything upon it. Besides the impulse given to building by the trade produced by the *porto franco*, there is another reason which acts as a stimulus. New Batoum is being built on a regular plan, and as the streets develop themselves the authorities take possession of the land between the new houses to form the highway. If there is nothing on the land, the proprietors get nothing for it. The slightest habitation, however, gives a right to compensation, and to secure this, structures are being run up everywhere, the officials apparently controlling their growth only where they happen to be of brick or stone. It is said that the officials are not above setting fire to the native quarters now and again, so as to get rid of the structures and secure the land for nothing. How far this is true I had no means of ascertaining, and do not repeat the statement as correct, but it is certain that improvements are being carried out with an amount of despotic energy which fanatic improvers of London would envy. Every obstruction goes down before the will of the Governor and his officials, and if redress from grievances cannot be secured from them, there is nothing to be done by the sufferers but submit. No appeal can be made beyond.

Batoum undoubtedly possesses a splendid port—the drawback is that there is not much of it. Respecting the question of size, there was a deal of wrangling in 1878, when the Earl of Beaconsfield had to find an excuse for relinquishing it to Russia, and when, to speak a little plainer than is customary in these kid-glove days of ours, there was a considerable amount of hard swearing on both sides over the matter. To the traveller fresh from the magnificent bays of Sevastopol and Novorossisk, the first thought that strikes him as he mounts one of the hills and surveys the place is—What a small port is Batoum! The promontory forming the bay is really altogether insignificant, and the present harbour looks as though a score of vessels would fill it. But although small naturally, Batoum is capable of being considerably extended, and, as a matter of fact, the Minister of Marine and the Minister of Ways of Communication, who visited the place at the end of 1883, have sanctioned a scheme for enlarging the port, at a cost of half a million sterling. The promontory is to be continued further out to sea, and on the opposite side of the bay a long mole is to be established, which will very considerably enlarge the area of the harbour. When these works are finished Batoum will answer the present requirements of trade, and become an excellent outlet for the petroleum of Baku. According to some persons the trade will eventually be too much for the size of the port, which is obviously incapable of extension beyond a certain point. But, in that case, Poti can be called in as an auxiliary, and afterwards the neglected port of Soukhum Kalé, giving the Transcaucasian trade route three outlets in the Euxine.

Like Poti, Batoum suffers a little from fever, but the evil will probably disappear in a year or two with the draining of the marshes outside the town. In 1881 the Russian Government assigned £7,500 for this purpose, and sent to supervise the works General Jilinsky, who had rendered himself famous by draining the Pinsk marshes. The trenches and canals in connection with the undertaking were being cut while I was there, and when finished Batoum will be a tolerably healthy place to live in. Thanks to its being a free port, foreign produce and manufactured goods can be purchased in abundance cheaper than at Odessa, and a man can really make himself very comfortable in the place. If, as is anticipated, the transport of petroleum from Batoum to the European market be effected by English oil-carrying steamers, an English colony will spring up in the town. Already there are several Englishmen on the spot; among them Mr. Peacock, the vice-consul, whose consular report on Baku petroleum won him so much reputation two years ago. Mr. Peacock is a very intelligent and active man of thirty-six, a first-rate Russian scholar, having been educated in Russia, and is, I believe, married to a Russian wife. While very appreciative of Russia, he is extremely zealous on behalf of the interests of his own country, and in this manner maintains a universal popularity at Batoum without detriment to his duties as consul. The great difficulty English statesmen usually have to contend with is, to secure impartial representatives abroad. English ambassadors and consuls either write up or write down the country they live in. Their despatches and reports have nearly always to be taken *cum grano salis*. It seems to be quite natural for Englishmen to take sides. An objective survey is beyond the power of most of them. Mr. Peacock is free from this common defect, and is making a special study of the Caucasus, which should render him of extreme value to the Foreign Office when the Armenian Question crops up in an active form. Not that the Foreign Office may be expected to utilize his services in that case. In all probability, when he becomes ripe for any important post in Russia, where his Russian knowledge would be of use, he will be packed off to Pekin or Pernambuco. Mr. Peacock had just come back from Kars, and was strongly impressed with the necessity for constructing the Euphrates Valley railway before Russia acquires an overshadowing influence in Turkish Armenia. If any one could capitalize all the money and time that have been wasted over that project during a miserable controversy extending over the last twenty years, he would need no guarantee from the Government. He would possess enough funds to carry out the scheme alone.

The rapid development of Batoum has proceeded from two causes—its privileges as a free port, and the remarkable progress of the petroleum industry at Baku. When the Treaty of Berlin was signed, its framers probably thought that the formation of Batoum into a free port would impede Russian growth in this part of Transcaucasia. Quite the contrary has been the case. If Batoum had been given to Russia without any restrictions, it would certainly have been made a strong naval port, but it would almost as equally assuredly have failed to become a great mercantile centre. Batoum protects Poti, but Poti does not protect Batoum. Had Russia acquired Batoum unreservedly she would have made commerce remain at Poti, and used Batoum exclusively as a naval station. The harbour would have been left as it is—small, although powerfully defended; and the town that would have grown around it would have consisted almost exclusively of the residences of officials. No commercial resources could have grown up. Surrounded by natural disadvantages, Poti would have embarrassed and checked trade as it has always done, and Batoum would have exercised influence simply through the prestige of its military and naval strength. But, by forcing Batoum to be a free port, Europe has laid the foundations of a great commercial emporium, which will soon have trading ramifications all over Anatolia, and exercise influence which Poti could never have hoped to enjoy, and which even a fortified Batoum would have failed to secure. Generally speaking, the commercial growth of a vigorous European community is more fatal to the security of its Asiatic neighbours than the maintenance of armies and fleets. From Batoum to the Bosphorus the Turkish coast is so unprotected that, provided she had a stronger fleet than the Ottomans, Russia could do pretty well what she liked along it. Such a fleet she will have in two years' time. By the end of that period also she will possess at Batoum most of the resources of a great naval station, together with a flourishing town, with magazines and shipping to enhance its strength. Had Batoum been given freely to Russia she would have had in 1886 only a well-fortified harbour to renew her historical struggle with Turkey. As it is, she will have a fortified harbour —the forts are all there, and the guns and munitions of war are gathered just outside the boundary of the port, ready to be brought in at a minute's notice—plus a town full of traders' stores, bristling with factories, and well provided with shipping. Russians are very sore at the *porto franco* imposed upon Batoum, and universally condemn it; but it seems to me that Europe has conferred thereby upon Russia a benefit which will some day produce significant military results.

When the Russians took over Batoum the population was very small and very poor, and nearly the whole of the inhabitants of the interior, as is well known, migrated to Turkey. As only a few colonists have arrived to replace the latter, and no manufactories except a kerosine-canning works have yet been established, it would appear difficult at first sight to explain the remarkable trade that has sprung up in a few short years. Huge shops are rising like mushrooms; their fronts are crammed with goods from Europe. The population of the place is small; the garrison is poor; yet every street resounds with the hum of business. When you land from the Odessa steamer, you are not allowed to return to the vessel without your effects being rigorously examined. When you walk through the town to the boundary of the free port, you cannot pass beyond without a second investigation taking place. Theoretically, therefore, all that comes into Batoum of a dutiable character—and what is not dutiable in Russia?—should be consumed at Batoum, or, nearly all of it, for there is, after all, a trifling per centage of goods which passes regularly through the Custom House. That trifling per centage, however, cannot in any way explain the amazing development of the place. The explanation must be found elsewhere. It will be discovered, perhaps, in a few figures.

The year before last 10,000 tons of fruit, fresh and dried, were imported to Batoum from Turkey. Of this amount 35 tons were transhipped to Russia, and paid the regular duty. During the year Batoum sent to Russian ports, as Russian-raised duty-free produce, 25,000 tons of fruit. Now, it is clear a town of a few thousand inhabitants could not consume 9,965 tons of fruit in a year, or raise—for the orchards and gardens are few—25,000 tons. It is tolerably certain, therefore, that the 25,000 tons sent to Russia included more of the 10,000 tons of Turkish fruit than the 35 tons duly registered, and that there were other shipments from abroad that passed through Batoum to Russia without paying a fraction of duty. The official value—a low one—of the 25,000 tons of fruit that Batoum reshipped to Russia was £72,598, and if nearly the whole of this was in reality contraband the loss in duty alone was £10,000. What was the case with fruit was the case also with a large number of other articles. If official returns of the imports and exports represented a real state of things, the inhabitants of Batoum would eat more, drink more, smoke more, wear out more clothes, purchase richer garments, and manufacture more goods than the inhabitants of any city in the world. Yet, whatever may be the story told by figures, facts go dead the other way. The Batoumtsi are wretched eaters—it is difficult to get a good square meal in the place; they are rarely seen drunk; their garments are common or shabby; and so far from producing anything, their whole time seems to be spent in unpacking and packing bales and boxes. If you stop long at Batoum you see the contents of the innumerable shops constantly being replenished, and in the warehouses all manner of goods entering in one kind of package and disappearing in another. Yet the houses at Batoum are meagrely furnished, the owners seem to purchase little, and it is certain that the goods that are sold and disappear are not purchased by them, or secretly stored up in their cellars or lofts. Last year Batoum sent to Odessa 125,000 roubles' worth of certain fabrics as foreign goods, paying duty upon them, and 725,000 roubles' worth of the same fabrics, as being of Batoum manufacture, paying no duty. Yet there is no manufactory in the place, except for making cans for kerosine. In one word, Batoum is a contraband centre, and fortunes are being made by taking advantage of its privileges as a free port to introduce without paying duty all manner of European wares into Russia.

This explains the bazaar-like character of Batoum, and the extraordinary expansion of its trade. In excess of its contraband intercourse with Russia, it carries on a lucrative smuggling trade in a smaller way with the Caucasus, which has recently received a great impetus by the suppression of the free transit of goods to Persia formerly enjoyed by Europe. Up to the present summer foreign goods could be landed and sealed at Poti, and conveyed thence across the Caucasus to Tiflis for Tabreez, or Baku for Astrabad, without paying duty to Russia. Envying the trade Europe carried on by this means with the East, Russia resolved to seize it for herself by suppressing the transit, and compelling Western wares to take the long and roundabout caravan route *viâ* Trebizond. One of her reasons for doing this was the alleged prevalence of an extensive system of smuggling, in connection with the transit across the Caucasus. Last summer the free transit was finally abolished, and the main result of this would appear to be, that all the old smuggling has been transferred to Batoum. The *modus operandi* of the wholesale smuggling is kept a secret, but that of the retail is obvious enough. Every night large numbers of Armenian and other merchants arrive by the Tiflis and Baku train, with very little baggage. Every morning the train leaves for Tiflis and Baku, swarming with Armenian and other merchants, who require a host of native porters to convey their luggage to the station. For quite an hour before the train leaves, the station is crammed with merchants and their *mushirs*, all groaning beneath the weight of bales and packs. In advance of mounting the platform all luggage has to be examined by Custom House officials, and this is done amidst a scene of confusion and din impossible to describe. The curious part of the affair is, that all the packs opened reveal nothing but dirty clothes when the officials poke their hands into them, and that the revenue benefits little or nothing by the investigation. Yet, if the packs were properly rummaged, it would no doubt be found that they consisted largely of manufactured goods wrapped in a few old garments, and that much of the confusion and din is a farce arranged between the officials and the contrabandists to make appear that the examination is a genuine one. Thanks to this system of smuggling, pedlars recruit their packs with the greatest ease, and whole consignments of goods make their way to Tiflis. Things are so cheap at Batoum compared with Tiflis, that a man who wants a new outfit can pay his expenses there and back and leave a margin of profit besides by taking a trip to the free port to get them.*

It may be said that smuggling is a precarious thing for a town to thrive upon, and that if a purer atmosphere were introduced, Batoum would at once be subjected to depression and decay. Odessa was once a free port, but it had at the back of it an immense area of corn land, which extended its prosperity after its contraband trade was extinguished by the abrogation of the *porto-franco* privileges. At the rear of Batoum is nothing but uninhabited hills, which cannot be readily colonized by the peasants of Russia, accustomed to a different climate. Malaria has already killed off or driven away many settlers who arrived after its first occupation, and, at present at least, the Government has no intention of rendering the country inland fit for European life by sanitary improvements. But there is one thing that Batoum possesses which seems likely not only to enhance its present trade, but also to sustain it if smuggling ever falls off. That thing is the best harbour on the Black Sea coast for the exportation of Caspian oil, and a railway already conveying to it consignments of petroleum from Baku. The petroleum export trade was in an embryotic condition when I was at Batoum, and it has hardly yet assumed definite form. Still, although the railway from Baku to Batoum was not opened until May, and the oil traffic did not commence for some time after, 8,301,289 gallons of Baku petroleum products were shipped from Batoum in 1883. The total number of vessels clearing Batoum in January 1884 was 140.

* A few weeks ago, a correspondent of the *Moscow Gazette* at Tiflis described the visit of a pedlar to his house, with packs full of contraband goods from Batoum. The authorities subsequently made a raid upon the bazaar, and brought to light many thousand roubles' worth of smuggled goods, including hundreds of Persian carpets secretly introduced from Tabreez without paying the heavy duty.

The export trade showed an increase last year upon 1882 of £250,000 to foreign countries, and £135,000 to Russian ports. The increase was largely due to the export of oil, which found its way from Batoum to almost every part of Europe, and laid the foundations of what must some day become an enormous trade.

At present there is only one packing establishment at Batoum. The kerosine brought in tank-cars from Baku is there barrelled or canned, and shipped to the Continent and the East. Nobel Brothers and other large firms, however, have bought sites for factories, and in a few years' time there will be a score or more in active existence. If the trade makes anything like the progress it has achieved in the Caspian and on the Volga, we may expect to see Batoum a great, prosperous, populous port in less than a decade, and fleets of cistern oil steamers conveying Baku petroleum from its harbour to every part of the West and the East.

. . . .

Since this was written Batoum has ceased to be a free port, Russia having in July 1886 repudiated the 59th Article of the Treaty of Berlin. While sharing the indignation which this breach of international engagements provoked among English statesmen of all parties, I did not hesitate to point out (*Contemporary Review*, August 1886), that the free port had proved to be a serious impediment to the petroleum trade, as well as a contraband centre, and that Russia in consequence was justified in her desire to see the obnoxious 59th Article cancelled. The change has inflicted no harm on British commerce, while, on the other hand, the removal of the cordon has allowed the port to expand freely, to the satisfaction of Russia. Numerous canning factories have sprung into existence, many storage reservoirs for oil and piers have been erected, and Batoum has become the principal petroleum port of Europe. The exports from

Batoum to foreign countries in 1885 comprised 24,000,000 gallons of refined petroleum, 330,000 gallons of lubricating oil, and 532,000 gallons of astatki, or about 25,000,000 gallons altogether. In 1886 this total was doubled.

More than a dozen tank steamers now run regularly between Batoum and the ports of Europe, and the petroleum export trade of the port, only in its infancy when I was there in 1883, is now firmly established. In the meanwhile Russia's naval power has developed, and the desire to make use of Batoum as a dockyard for the fleet has led to fears that ere long the Government may summarily divert the commerce of the Transcaucasian railway to Poti, and employ Batoum solely for naval purposes. It is a well-known fact that the Tiflis authorities have repeatedly recommended this course. However, before this is done, another Tiflis wish may be realized and the Russian flag be planted at Trebizond, where a dockyard could be formed without interfering with commerce in the least, and, in that case, Batoum could be left exclusively to petroleum.

CHAPTER VIII.

BATOUM TO TIFLIS ACROSS THE LESSER CAUCASUS.

The Transcaucasian Railway and its Present and Prospective Ramifications—The old Trade Route from India to the Black Sea, viâ the Caspian and Lesser Caucasus revived by the Line—The future Russian Railway to India—Luggage Troubles at Batoum—The Batoum Railway; Cost of constructing it—Shower-bath Railway Carriages—Lovely Character of the Scenery—The Route must some day become popular with Tourists--Cheapness of Fruit along the Line—Tracking the Rion to its Source—Romantic Views—Crossing the Suram Pass—Heavy Gradients—A Two Thousand Feet Rise in Four Hours—The Projected Tunnel—Congestion of the Petroleum Traffic—Ludwig Nobel's Plan for Overcoming this—Remarkable Climatic Differences between the East and West Side of the Suram Pass—The Passengers on the Line to Tiflis.

THE Transcaucasian Railway, connecting Batoum on the Black Sea with Baku on the Caspian, is 561½ miles long. Poti, which was originally intended to be the Black Sea terminus, is 24½ miles nearer the Caspian than Batoum. The section from Poti to Tiflis, 196 miles, which owes its construction entirely to English enterprise, capital, and skill, was commenced in 1871, and opened for traffic a few years afterwards. The section from Tiflis to Baku, 341 miles, was taken in hand soon after the conclusion of the Russo-Turkish war in 1878, and completed a few months ago. The branch line joining Batoum to the railway at Samtredi, 65⅓ miles distant, was also finished at the same time. The railway possesses only one other offshoot, running a short distance to Kutais, whence it is now being pushed on 25 miles further, to the coal fields of Tkvibooli.* A project, already sanctioned by the Government, is expected to be shortly carried out for making a branch from Tiflis to Kars, a distance of 200 miles, at a cost of £3,050,000 sterling. Another scheme is also being pushed for running a line from Adji-Cabul station, near Baku, to Resht, in Persia; thence to be extended to Teheran. This would complete steam communication between London and the capital of the Shahs.

Starting from the Black Sea, the Transcaucasian Railway winds its way up the sinuous valley of the river Rion until it reaches its source in the ridge of the Lesser Caucasus, whence, after traversing the latter at a height of 3,200 feet above the level of the ocean, it descends along the valley of the river Kura to the Caspian Sea. It thus pursues the old trade route by which, according to Pliny, the wares of the East used to find their way to Europe. Immediately opposite Baku, on the other side of the Caspian, commences the Transcaspian Railroad, running 144 miles to Kizil Arvat. From here to Sibi, the first railway station on the Indian frontier, is a distance of 1,122 miles.† It is in this direction that the shortest and quickest railway to India will some day be constructed. The old trade route mentioned by Pliny ran from India to Cabul, then over the Hindoo Koosh to the Oxus near Balkh, whence the wares floated down the river towards the Caspian, and made their way by the Kura and Rion to a point where Poti now stands. But this route was taken to ensure the use of a waterway running with occasional breaks from Balkh to the Black Sea. Owing to geological changes, there is now no waterway whatever between the Oxus region and the Caspian,

* This is now opened for traffic.
† The completion of the Russian line to Merv, and the Indian line to Pishin, reduces the distance now to about 700 miles.

nor is there any need to construct one solely to reopen the old trade route, since the line selected by Annenkoff for his railway to India traverses low hills, steppes, and easy valleys, instead of the frightful passes, 15,000 feet high, separating Cabul from the Oxus. The extension of

THE BATOUM-BAKU RAILWAY LINE.

the railway system to India promises a great future for the Batoum-Baku line, even apart from the trade it will attract from Persia and Asia Minor. It is this circumstance that renders the petroleum supply of the Caspian of such vital importance to Russia. Baku will be able to furnish for ages oil fuel for the locomotives running on the Transcaucasian line and its extensions, while the vast deposits east of Krasnovodsk will render a similar service to the Transcaspian Railway, penetrating to Turkmenia, Afghanistan, and India.

Probably no railway in Europe offers such climatic contrasts in its course as that between Batoum and Baku. You begin the journey in Devonshire, you end it in Sahara. The scenery for most of the way is magnificent, and if it grows tamer towards the end, the characteristics of the desert sweeping round to the Apsheron Peninsula are so utterly different from anything to be seen elsewhere in Europe, that they cannot fail to deeply interest the traveller.

We left Batoum on Sunday, August 26th, and experienced a disagreeable amount of bother at the railway station. This is a small temporary wooden structure, close to the pier and the hotel, and possesses no accommodation whatever for the rigorous examination of passenger luggage insisted on by the Custom House authorities. Batoum being a free port, all dutiable goods are liable to be taxed on quitting it for the Caucasus; the examination takes place in Batoum itself before the train starts, and when the new station is built will probably be conducted in as orderly a fashion as elsewhere in Russia. At present the hustling to which the traveller is subjected in leaving Batoum by train or steamer, is sufficient to overcome the calmest temper. Much trouble will be avoided by the traveller if he restricts himself to a little hand luggage, and allows his portmanteau to be sealed and kept in the Custom House while he remains at Batoum. This will protect him also if he lands at a second Russian port after leaving Batoum. Where he fails to adopt this course, a few fifteen copeck pieces judiciously placed at the corners of his portmanteau, within easy reach of the rummager's fingers when that functionary dives down for dutiable goods, will save him a deal of trouble, and perhaps expense, should he happen to have any Persian embroideries with him.

Delivered from the confusion of the Customs' inspection, we took our seats in the train, which consisted of about eight or ten carriages on the American principle, and at eight o'clock bade adieu to Batoum. The morning was very wet, and the rain fell in torrents. The mountains at the rear of Batoum were buried in huge lowering masses of black clouds. Our course lay along the marshes for a few miles, and then leaving behind the Tzikiuzeri lines, six miles from Batoum, where Dervish Pasha held his ground so successfully during the last war, we began pushing our way through the spurs of the mountains frowning over the sea-shore. The scenery at this part is very fine. The mountain sides are covered with rhododendrons, laurels, hazels, and ferns, growing in a rich loose soil, and sustained by an atmosphere which for the greater part of the year is hot and moist, like that of a greenhouse. For nearly an hour the locomotive runs alongside the bay, over a road, at every step mounting higher, formed by alternate scarp and tunnel. This section was the most difficult to construct, and occasioned the loss of hundreds of lives from fever and scurvy. Out of six months there were only fifty days that the men could work, owing to the incessant rains. Even now the road is far from satisfactory, the scarping being so badly formed in places that storms frequently wash it away. Considering that the line was chiefly constructed as a military one, it is an obvious defect that it should be exposed for so many miles to bombardment from the enemy's shipping, or to destruction by any enterprising landing party. A line further inland, however, could not have been constructed without an immense outlay on tunnels and steep gradients, to say nothing of a delay of years in connecting Batoum with the Poti-Tiflis Railway. As it was, the $65\frac{1}{2}$ miles of line from Batoum to the junction at Samtredi cost 6,531,864 roubles, or £653,186 sterling, being at the rate of about £10,000 a mile. The line consists of only a single row of metals, the stations are of a very ordinary character and wide apart, and the rolling-stock is altogether insignificant.

The higher we mounted the heavier became the rain, which beat so fiercely against the windows, and streamed down the panes with such copiousness, that we could not see any of the scenery on the sea-side. Before long it forced its way through the roof in half a dozen places, and kept us well employed in dodging the cascades. The carriages leaked like sieves. The first and second-class carriages were particularly bad in this respect, the composite one I was in being so porous that only one seat was dry in it, and the rain poured through the roof in places in a regular stream. Had the passengers been civilized enough to possess umbrellas, the curious spectacle would no doubt have been witnessed of their sitting in the carriage with their umbrellas up. Outwardly, the carriages were well enough built—for the convenience of their arrangements, and their numerous little comforts, they would have gained a prize in any English exhibition of rolling-stock; but there was not a door that would shut without terrific banging; not a window that would move up and down without a groan or a curse; not a ventilator that would open if shut, or would shut if open; and, in short, there was not a movable fitting that was not warped or otherwise out of gear. The cause of this extraordinary condition of things I soon discovered after a little inquiry. From Poti and Batoum to Tiflis the line runs through a region in which, as far as the Suram Pass, where the Lesser Caucasus is traversed, the climate is always more or less moist and wet. It is rare that the rolling-stock runs through the country without getting a wetting. On the other hand, from Tiflis to Baku the region grows drier the further east one advances, until in approaching the Caspian the line traverses a desert where rain scarcely ever falls, where the heat is sometimes terrific, and where the dryness of the air is such that timber shrivels, and cracks, and warps under its influence. One day soddened with rain, another day passing through the temperature of an oven, it would be difficult for even the best built rolling-stock to remain unaffected. As for that of the Trans-caucasian Railway, which was built at Riga, it is simply going to rack and ruin as fast as it can, and nothing is being done by the company to arrest its decay, or in any way to improve matters.

But for the drawback of having to dodge the rivulets from the roof, and attend to the erratic movements of doors and windows, all of which would not keep closed on the windy side, and would not remain open on the other, we should have enjoyed undisturbed the magnificent scenery passed on our way from Batoum to the Poti line at Samtredi, and thence in the journey up the Rion Valley and the ascent to the Suram Pass. For splendid sea views, for ever-varying magnificent forest and mountain scenery, and for the interest imparted to the landscape by the constant presence of Mingrelian, Imeretian, and other mountaineers, all more or less picturesquely habited and armed, this railway journey is the most striking and most beautiful in Europe, and must sooner or later become a favourite one with English tourists. Now that the Baku line is open, a summer tour of a month's duration *viâ* the Dutch flats, the romantic Rhine, the primitive Carpathians, and the unique Russian steppes to Odessa, occupying four days; the Crimea and Caucasian coasts to Batoum, and across Transcaucasia to Baku, taking a week; thence up the Caspian and Volga to Nijni Novgorod, and by railway home *viâ* Moscow, St. Petersburg, and Warsaw, using up the rest of the time, has become such a simple performance that it is bound in time to become a popular tour. I have said already that the mere coasting alone round the lovely scenery of the Crimea and Caucasia is worth the fatigue of the railway journey to Odessa; the same might with equal truth be said of the trip from Batoum to Tiflis. The stations are good; plenty of time is allowed at the excellent buffets to enjoy good living on the way; the pace is slow enough for the traveller to appreciate the beauty of the scenery; and he not only has plenty of time at the constant stoppages to stretch his limbs at the stations, but can purchase at most of them freshly-picked fruit at fabulously cheap rates—a huge water melon for a penny, a rope of grapes, consisting of bunches strung on ropes like onions and weighing two or three pounds, for five farthings, a handful of peaches for a halfpenny, and a pocketful of delicious filberts for a farthing. At nearly every station there is a regular bazaar, where not only fruit can be bought, but poultry, game, and other provisions. In connection with this very peculiar feature of the Batoum-Tiflis Railway, it is noteworthy that alongside and round about stations which, when originally built, contained no habitation near them, rows of shops have sprung up, attaining the proportions in one or two instances of large bazaars. In this manner the stations are becoming encompassed by markets, and facilities are afforded for trade *en route* to be witnessed nowhere else in Russia. Between Batoum and Tiflis the train is so crowded, and there is such a large traffic on both sides of the Suram Pass, that the Company ought to run several through trains a day instead of simply one every twenty-four hours. Under English or American railway administration the Transcaucasian region would develop rapidly, but what growth there is seems to be rather in spite of it. After a couple of hours' travelling we cleared the confines of Gouria, and at eleven o'clock reached the junction station of Samtredi, where we had twenty minutes for lunch, and picked up the passengers from Poti. Here we came in contact with the more settled part of the Transcaucasian Railway. Hitherto we had passed newly annexed mountains and forests, with merely a bare little station here and there, and occasionally a tiny village. Passengers were neither picked up nor put down. Henceforth to Tiflis, however, there was plenty of bustle, and new-comers experienced a difficulty in getting a seat.

Two stations beyond Samtredi is Rion, whence a branch line takes the traveller in seventeen minutes to Kutais, the capital of Imeritia. From here to the top of Suram Pass, five hours' journey,

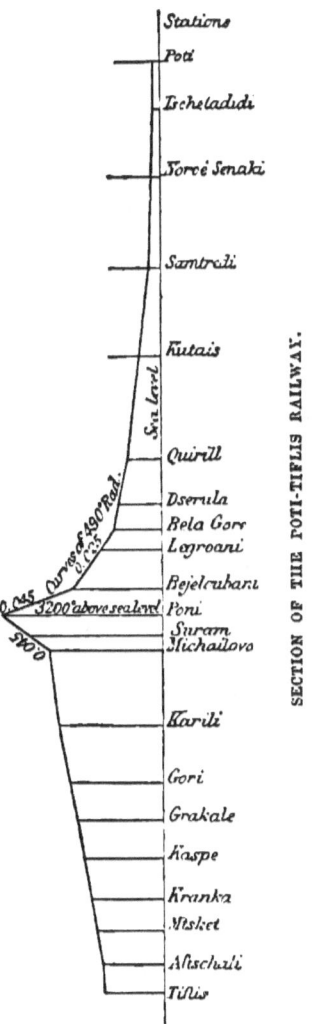

the scenery never ceases to excite interest. The railway runs along the river Rion, tracking it to its very source, three thousand feet above the level of the sea. For the most part the railway keeps to the right-hand side of the river, and the fine old military macadamized road to the left: cloud-topped mountains tower above both. Villages perched upon precipices, or down on the river bank, are constantly passed; the military road is enlivened by groups of horsemen in the warlike Mingrelian costume; now and again a caravan of camels is seen, and at every strategical bend are the ruins of some old fort or castle, the stones of which, if they could speak, would tell many a story of romance, war, and chivalry. For magnificent and romantic scenery, this part of the journey will compare with the Rhine from Coblentz to Cologne; in my opinion, it beats it. The presence of handsome armed horsemen, like the knights of old, imparts to the journey up the Rion an interest which is altogether lacking in the case of the Rhine.

As the train approaches the Suram the inclines become very steep. The topmost station is Poni, 3,200 feet above the level of the sea. In climbing up this point and descending from it, the gradients for more than eight miles are one foot in 22¼. During the four hours' journey from Quirill, on the Rion side, to Michaelova on that of the Kura, the train rises a height of 2,000 feet.* Three engines, one a 60-ton Fairlie, are employed to haul the train up to the top of the pass and ease it down the other side. The operation is naturally slow, but the magnificence of the scenery repays the traveller for the delay.

---

* The line starts from Batoum and Poti at 18 feet above the sea-level. From Poti for 40 miles the railway traverses a swamp, after which the line rises with gradients from 1 in 125 to 1 in 70, with curves of from 200 feet to 250 feet. Beyond this the gradients are 1 in 45 and 1 in 40, and finally the profile changes to 1 in 22¼, landing at the Poni station, at the top of the Suram Pass, 3,200 feet above the sea-level. After leaving Poni the line goes down a few miles at 1 in 22¼, after which the grades grow slighter. Beyond Gori, to Tiflis, they are comparatively easy, and thenceforth the line is virtually level to the Caspian.

Commercially, the traversing of the pass by such steep gradients is a mistake, however grand the railway may be from an engineering point of view. Only a few trucks or carriages can be taken over the pass at a time, and the line being a single one, this will inevitably lead to a congestion of the traffic the moment the petroleum trade assumes large proportions. It is but right to say that the English engineers who constructed the line urged a tunnel instead of a crossing, and the Tiflis authorities long ago regretted that they did not listen to their advice. The forty miles of gradients involve a special extra outlay of £55,000 yearly, or nearly £1,400 a mile to keep it in order. As this sum would be more than sufficient to pay 5 per cent. guaranteed interest on the £1,000,000 needed to construct a tunnel, there is very little doubt that before long the latter will be excavated. Of course, this would be a work of years, which is a serious matter for the petroleum trade, but, in the meanwhile, Mr. Ludwig Nobel suggested that the congestion in the oil traffic should be relieved by running a pipe-line over the pass. The trains from Baku would deposit the oil in reservoirs on the east side of the Lesser Caucasus, whence it would be pumped to the top of the pass. From here its own gravity would carry it down to the bottom, and a considerable distance beyond, and it could then be carried on again in oil-trucks to its destination. The idea is excellent, and it has this great advantage, that it would form a section of the pipe-line that will some day run from Baku to Batoum.*

Poni station was reached at half-past six. I do not know any place that would give a person a better idea of

---

* The tunnel is now being bored, and the new loop line avoiding the pass will be finished in two years' time. The Russian Government has also sanctioned the laying down of a kerosine pipe-line over the Suram Pass. This will be nearly 40 miles long, and will greatly relieve the traffic.

a watershed, or impress upon him more clearly the difference in climate and scenery produced by a range of mountains. Up to the top of the pass, on the Rion side, he has forests, bushes, grass, and creepers growing with the utmost luxuriance under the influence of the humid climate of the Black Sea littoral. From the station at Poni, he has before him, in the direction of Tiflis, a grand panorama of mountain tops—forming, as it were, a plain of cones—all more or less bare and bleak in appearance. The cold here is very sensible; we should have enjoyed our greatcoats. Directly the descent commences, and the new valley, that of the Kura, begins to broaden out, there is a perceptible decrease in the luxuriance of vegetation; and although the vale of Georgia, as far as Tiflis, is considered equal to any part of Italy in fertility of soil and softness of climate, this change continues to deepen until even at Tiflis vegetation is only maintained by means of artificial irrigation. The rainfall on the Tiflis side of the Suram Pass is three times less than on the Poti side.

Half an hour's ride from Poni brought us to the extensive camp at Suram, where many thousand troops are maintained in the fresh and invigorating climate of the highlands. Russia maintains the principal part of the army of the Caucasus in and about Tiflis, and the valley stretching up to the Suram. Food is everywhere abundant and cheap there, and by keeping the men well in hand in a central spot she can throw them forward to Kars, or right and left respectively to the Black Sea and the Caspian. At the station next to Suram, Michaelova, the train stopped long enough for the passengers to partake of dinner at the excellent buffet, and then there were no more prolonged halts till we got to Tiflis. It was quite dark when we left Michaelova, and if we had not returned the same way we should have missed the beautiful scenery extending between it and the Georgian capital. Vineyards and maize fields, villages and ruined castles, mark the entire course. At all the stations grapes can be had for two or three farthings a pound, and a capful of pears or peaches for a penny or twopence. In the Caucasus there are nearly 300,000 acres devoted to the culture of the vine, and the quantity of wine produced every year does not fall far short of 35,000,000 gallons. Of this more than a third is grown in the Rion region. The wine is pronounced by experts to be of excellent quality, although it is not manufactured with sufficient skill to enable it to keep long. Throughout the Caucasus it is transported in skins, and is sold at the innumerable wine-shops from sixpence a bottle upwards. Although fond of wine, I must admit I rapidly grew tired of it, and while at Baku preferred the Russo-Bavarian light beer, brought from Astrakhan and Kazan. In all parts of Russia the wines of the Crimea and the Caucasus can be bought very cheap, and are invariably unadulterated. The Russians, as a rule, despise them, although recent investigations have revealed that much of the French and German wine sold throughout the country at a heavy price is nothing more than the native article, adulterated and labelled with foreign brands.

Our train became very crowded as we approached Tiflis, and we had plenty of opportunities of studying the varieties of natives with whom we came in contact. If dress and demeanour afford any criterion of the civilization of a country, Georgia is ahead of any other part of Russia; on no other line in the Empire will the traveller find so many respectable and intelligent people in the second and third-class carriages as during the journey from Poti to Tiflis. The men of the Caucasus are proverbially handsome. Some of them I saw were superbly beautiful. I am sorry I cannot say as much of the women. I did not see a pretty face the whole time I was in the Caucasus. As for the women in Georgia, they seem to have been grossly overrated; their round flat caps and Roman noses had the aggravating effect on me that Dickens ascribes to Pip in " Great Expectations."

We had left in the morning Batoum deluged with rain; we arrived at Tiflis just before midnight, and found the place parched with heat and overwhelmed with dust. The phaeton that conveyed us and our luggage to the London Hotel (Gostinnitza London) stirred up dense clouds as it rattled over the ill-paved streets. Like all Russian stations, that of Tiflis is situated right outside the town, and we had a couple of miles to drive before we reached our destination, and made ourselves comfortable for the night.

CHAPTER IX.

TIFLIS AS A POLITICAL AND MILITARY CENTRE.

Tiflis in the Autumn—Development of the City—One's Impressions of the Place depend upon whether one is proceeding East or West—The Administrative District of the Caucasus—What it Cost to Conquer it—Political and Strategical Position of Tiflis—Table of Annexations during the various Russian Sovereigns' Reigns—The Conquest of Central Asia—Tiflis compared with Indian Centres—The next War in the East—Value of Russian Assurances—The Approximation of Russia and India inevitable—Lesson taught by the Annexation of Merv—The Principal Fact to be Remembered gard to Tiflis—The Armenians: their Present and Future—Not so tame in Spirit as commonly imagined—Russian Interest in the Armenian Question—The Caucasus Deficit.

As nobody goes to the Caucasus without paying a visit to Tiflis, that city has been so often and so well described that there is no need of my devoting much attention to it. Situated 1,350 feet above the level of the sea, and exposed to the dry winds from the east, it is naturally inclined to aridity; a defect which has been increased by denuding all the mountains round about of trees. The morning after our arrival the wind tore with such force down the valley, and carried with it such clouds of grit, that we were cruelly reminded of a dusty March wind at home. Hot and dry in summer, Tiflis, however, is a delightful place in winter, and its mild and bracing atmosphere then is calculated to have an invigorating effect on the officials charged with the government of the Caucasus.

We found plenty of progress observable. The builder is busy in every part of the city, and not only are old houses being replaced by new ones, forming handsome thoroughfares, but suburbs are being developed on a very extensive scale. Situated on an unnavigable mountain torrent, which cuts too deeply into the rock to allow of the water being any ornament to the city, Tiflis straggles over a considerable space of ground, and is never at any point very far away from the country. All around it the mountain sides are bare and brown; nothing grows on them but a little camel thorn and here and there a juniper bush. Even in the town itself cultivation is only maintained by an elaborate system of artificial irrigation; not a tree or a shrub can be kept alive in the arid soil of the place without being daily attended to with the watering-can or water-cart. Thanks to this, Tiflis has a somewhat desolate look, which would be appalling but for the boulevards of stately poplars and the green gardens in the German quarter. The care which these Teuton settlers display in keeping fresh the verdant aspect of their colony contrasts remarkably with the apathy of the Russians, who do little or nothing to extend cultivation in the Georgian capital. Except where the Germans abound, the city is dry and dusty, and a most undesirable place of residence in the summer months. During this period hot arid winds often blow across the hill-sides upon Tiflis with a desiccating force, which I can only compare to a concentrated easterly wind. These produce an unceasing longing for drink and a cooling bath—the latter a luxury almost unattainable, owing to the Kura river being little more than an open sewer. When there is no wind at all the atmosphere is cool and agreeable. Happening to point out to a Russian officer the generally arid aspect of Tiflis, he said that one's impression of the Georgian capital depends largely on the direction from which the traveller arrives. Coming from the Black Sea coast, where constant rains drench the Anatolian and Caucasian ranges, and encourage the growth of magnificent forests and rank vegetation of a semi-tropical character, Tiflis strikes the traveller as having a scorched and withered aspect. But if he arrives from the south or the east, from Erivan or Baku, where the country is almost entirely devoid of verdure, and nothing grows without irrigation except the camel thorn, the impression is altogether different. So far from seeing no vegetation, his eye seeks out and is refreshed by the trees and shrubs scattered here and there—the German colony seems to him quite a little paradise. This will account for most travellers arriving at Tiflis from the Caspian or Persia describing the place as "enchanting." Those who touch it in journeying the other way, from west to east, mostly, so far as my memory goes, either discover no attractions in Tiflis, or else ignore them.

The administrative district of the Caucasus consists of the region north and south of the Caucasus range, from nearly the mouth of the Don to Batoum, and from the mouth of the Kuma to the Persian border, and possesses an area (186,000 square miles) half as large again as the British Isles. This is exclusive of the territory newly annexed beyond the Caspian, the boundaries of which on the Khivan and Turcoman side are not exactly determined, but which comprise, if we add Mangishlak and other districts governed from Tiflis, an area of about the same dimensions. Thus the Governor-General at Tiflis rules an area larger than Germany and the British Isles put together, with England a second time thrown in; and a population, inclusive of the Turcomans, of $6\frac{1}{4}$ millions, or not quite twice the population of London. To conquer this area took Russia more than 150 years; it cost her from beginning to end the lives of more troops than we spent in acquiring the whole of our Empire;

and to maintain order she keeps within its boundaries to-day a force considerably larger than the English army in India, involving, with other expenses, an annual deficit of not less than a million sterling.

Several circumstances contribute to render Tiflis the proper capital of this appanage of the Russian Crown. It has the largest population by a long way of any of the towns lying south of Rostoff, at the mouth of the Don, and Astrakhan, at the mouth of the Volga. If we leave out Bagdad, which lies too far south to be included in these comparisons, it is larger, in point of inhabitants, than any town in Asiatic Turkey; Erzeroum, the only extensive place lying between it and Constantinople, having less than half the population. Added to this, it occupies a good central position, politically and commercially, being situated at the cross road of the trade flowing from the Caspian to the Black Sea, east and west, and from Asia to Europe in a northerly direction *viâ* the sole split in the Caucasus ridge from sea to sea— the Dariel Pass. It was this strategical quality that so greatly facilitated the conquest of the country, once Russia had occupied Tiflis. In 1800 she took possession of the town "in the interests of humanity and order." Once settled in Georgia she pushed out down the valley of the Kura to the Caspian, and conquered all she now holds from Persia. Afterwards she turned her arms the other way, down the valley of the Rion to the Black Sea, and annexed all her present dominions there from Turkey. Transcaucasia conquered from sea to sea, she set to work at the rear to subjugate the Caucasus itself—a tough bit of business, seeing that from the Black Sea to the Caspian the mountains were 700 miles long by 100 broad, and covering an area nearly half as large again as England. For thirty years a quarter of a million troops were employed on this undertaking, and in the end Russia only attained her aim by annihilating or expelling the population. The struggle came to a close in 1862, and, excluding the column the Caucasus sent to co-operate in the Khivan expedition eleven years later, the army enjoyed a rest until the war of 1877. This war increased the area of the Caucasian territory by the addition of Kars and Batoum, and then came the three years' conflict in Turkmenia, resulting in the annexation of Askabad and the opening up to the Tiflis officials of a grand vista of political influence in Central Asia.*

While Russia had been conquering the Caucasus, she had also been engaged further east, on the confines of her Orenberg base, in conflicts with the Kirghiz and other steppe tribes. Directly the Caucasian struggle ended, fighting in earnest commenced in Central Asia, and continued with but very few breaks almost up to the Turkish war. The result of that conflict was the formation of the province of Turkestan, a province which attracted an extraordinary amount of attention in Eng-

* The following table shows the relative annexations in the Caucasus made by various Russian sovereigns:—

Sovereign.	Date.	Territory Annexed.	Area in sq. versts.
Elizabeth	1748	Osetin Country	1,900
Catherine II.	1783	Kuban	58,700
Paul	1801	Georgia	44,600
Alexander I.	1803	Mingrelia	9,500
	1804	Imeretia	14,200
	1810	Gouria	1,900
	1813	Ganjin, Karabah, Baku, Derbent, &c., by Gulistan Treaty	66,800
	1817–23	Tchetchni and Kabarda	16,200
Nicholas	1828	Erivan Nakhitchevan, &c., by Treaty of Turkmantchi	23,300
	1829	Poti, and other Turkish territory, by Treaty of Adrianople	4,900
		Later annexations	55,100
Alexander II.	1857–59	Daghestan	9,400
	1859–64	Tcherkess Country	13,600
	1878	Batoum and Kars	23,000

land in the course of its development, overshadowing completely the Caucasus; but which, since the conquest of Geok Tepé in 1881, has fallen out of the race and provoked but little interest. The Transcaspian region, which stretches up to the confines of Khiva and Afghanistan, is administered from Tiflis, not from Tashkent. It is from this base that any future movements will be made in the direction of India. Turkestan and Tashkent may be treated with a certain amount of indifference for the moment, but we are bound to keep a watch upon the Caucasus and Tiflis, because the officials there control Russia's relations with Afghanistan, Persia, and Asiatic Turkey, and their forces may some day be set in motion against Herat, Teheran, or Constantinople.

Tiflis is thus a place of the future. It will figure largely whenever the Central Asian or Eastern Questions crop up afresh in an active form. The Caucasus cannot stand comparison in population with India, but it holds its own against the neighbouring states. Tiflis has 105,000 inhabitants: we have twenty towns with a larger population in India. After Tiflis comes Yekaterinodar, with 32,500 people. Including these two, the Caucasus possesses only twenty-one towns of more than 10,000 inhabitants. We have 1,360 such towns in India. But while the Caucasus, the possible base of future operations against India, is so insignificant in point of people and developed resources compared with the English dependency, it compares favourably with Persia, Afghanistan, and Asiatic Turkey. The Governor-General rules more people than either the Shah or the Ameer, and nearly as many as the Sultan does in his Asiatic dominions. These three States are bitter enemies to one another, and would never combine. The Caucasus is thus qualified to crush each of them in succession.

But it is a mistake to regard the Caucasus as figuring

single-handed in the next conflict in the East. From what I have said of the growth of Russia's fleet at Sevastopol, we may expect to see, in the course of a few years, the Tsar powerful enough to keep the Turks from quitting the Bosphorus. In that case, all the ports and garrisons of South Russia, and the new fleet of transports growing up in the Black Sea, could co-operate in any movement upon Asiatic Turkey or Roumelia for the seizure of Constantinople. When we get to the Caspian I trust to be able to clearly demonstrate that, thanks to the development of the railway and steamer service in that region, Russia will be able herself to render powerful assistance to the Caucasus in any operations either against Persia, or, through Afghanistan, against India. I do not wish it to be supposed that I accuse Russia of nourishing at the present moment aggressive designs against our supremacy in the East. Throughout the whole of my journey in the Caucasus I was everywhere assured, and assured by all classes, that Russia had no wish to invade India. The same was repeated to me over and over again by the most eminent Russians of the day I came in contact with at the Tsar's coronation. I should be sorry to cast any doubt upon the genuine character of these assurances. But the policy of great States is determined, not by the good wishes or the good intentions of individuals, but by the exigencies of national growth, the aspirations of races, and the idiosyncracies of statesmen. When a nominal settlement of the Central Asian Question was arrived at in 1881, by Russia annexing Askabad and fixing the Persian boundary on one side of the region, and by England withdrawing from Candahar on the other, we were told there was to be no more meddling with the intervening country by either Power, and that both England and Russia were to do their best to avoid any departure from the new arrangement. What has been the actual result?

Russia has observed the compact by suddenly seizing Merv; Russian travellers and secret agents have penetrated to Herat and Cabul; and reconnoitring columns have been pushed out close to Sarakhs. England, on her part, has given a subsidy of £120,000 a year to the Ameer to bring him under her influence; she has strengthened her outposts beyond Quetta, which place further she has annexed, and she has established a protectorate over Beluchistan. When such a pacific Emperor as the present Tsar is believed to be does these things, and such a violent defender of Masterly Inactivity as Mr. Gladstone follows suit, the question naturally arises whether it is possible to prevent by earthly means the apparently inevitable gravitation of the frontiers of the English and Russian Empires towards each other in Central Asia? All that is left for poor mortals to do, who have no influence on the issue of the game, is to hope that the junction may be effected by peaceful means, and that good may come to both countries from the contact of the Sepoy and Cossack.*

* The sudden annexation of Merv demonstrated pretty clearly the value of good wishes and assurances, and the English public is not disposed to give heed to them any more. During my interviews with Russian statesmen and generals in 1882, nearly all of them ridiculed the notion of an early annexation of Merv. The crowning triumph of Geok Tepé had rendered the Merv Tekkés sufficiently well behaved for Russian purposes. Yet, without any actual provocation, for the Merv Tekkés were becoming a tranquil tribe, the Tsar suddenly sent a military force to within striking distance of Merv, and, by the sudden apparition of this force, at a moment when the Merv Tekkés believed peace to be prevailing, and were unprepared for war, coerced them into submission. To talk of "voluntary submission" under such circumstances is to utter a deliberate untruth. Merv was carried by a *coup de main.* How little even Russians themselves anticipated such a bold stroke on the part of their Government, was illustrated by a letter I received from a Russian author at Tiflis the day before the annexation, in which, after informing me he had read my "Russians at Merv and Herat," he proceeded to point out the groundlessness of my charges of aggression—"Russia," he said, "had no desire

I hope I shall be excused for dwelling upon the political aspect of Tiflis. The city has been excellently described archæologically by Commander Buchan Telfer in his "Crimea and Transcaucasia;" General Valentine Baker, Major Marsh, Mr. Mounsey, and many others have recorded their *impressions de voyage;* and both Mr. O'Donovan and Mr. Gallenga have given clever word pictures of the place in their books. But the political features of Tiflis have been, without exception, wholly ignored since Tashkent came into prominence, and much blundering has arisen in the management of our relations with the East from English statesmen mixing up Turkmenia with Turkestan, and treating it as an appanage of the latter, instead of belonging to the Caucasus. If I have made it clear that Tiflis is the capital not only of the Caucasus, but of the Caspian also, and the region beyond the Caspian stretching to Khiva and Merv, I shall be successful, perhaps, in persuading politicians to leave off concerning themselves too much about Tashkent and Samarcand, and focus their whole attention upon Tiflis, Krasnovodsk, Askabad, Sarakhs, and Herat —the real highway of Russian operations against India.

But if the future of the Central Asian Question is largely in the keeping of Tiflis, the fate of the Armenian people is still more so. Before the commencement of the present century, Tiflis was the capital of the kingdom of Georgia. Politically it has since been the capital of the Russian appanage of the Caucasus. Racially, however, it is really the capital of the Armenian people, and in the future it will play an important part in connection with this aspect. Of the 105,000 inhabitants of Tiflis, the Georgians number 23,000, the Russians 30,000, and the Armenians 37,000. The

whatever to meddle with Merv, or to advance a step further towards India." Events the next morning proved pretty conclusively to the contrary.

latter have the commerce of the place in their hands; they control five-sevenths of the votes in the municipal council; and through their representatives in the army and administration they exercise a powerful and increasing influence over the administration of the Caucasus. There are also several thousand German settlers at Tiflis.

The latter are descendants of a number of Wurtembergers who migrated to Russia to escape religious oppression, and founded what is now the finest and the most flourishing quarter of Tiflis. They still speak their own language, wear their own Teuton dress, and display the same hostility towards Russians generally which is a common feature of German colonists in the Tsar's dominions. Equally difficult to assimilate or absorb is the Persian element, occupying the lower and dirtier part of Tiflis, constituting in point of crowdedness and squalor as great a contrast to the German quarter as St. Giles to Belgravia. The Armenians are quite different from the Germans and Persians. They readily adopt Russian ways and Russian dress. With few exceptions they speak Russian as readily as their mother tongue, and many of them have even discarded the latter for the guttural language of their conquerors. So far as I can gather, this conformation of the Armenian race to the Russian is in the main entirely spontaneous. As a matter of fact, the Armenians are a race without a nationality and without a head. Unlike the Persians, they have no Shah to look towards to encourage them to resist assimilation, and they have not that keen love of the Fatherland which keeps the Germans in Russia from denationalizing themselves. Too weak to form a State of their own, even if they had any political tendency that way, which they have not, their only course is to throw in their lot with that of Russia. Some writers have described them as the Jews of the Caucasus, owing to their love of trade, and an alleged dislike for warlike pursuits. But the comparison is not a good one. In the first place, the Armenians, generally speaking, possess a fine physique, which the Jews rarely have, above all in Russia; and this cannot but secure them respect from the Russians. In the second place, the Armenian is far from being as mild as the Hebrew, and is apt to return an insult with a telling backhander. That writers are wrong who speak of the Armenians as an oppressed trading class, unfit for independence because unable, owing to lack of spirit, to assert it, is proved with tolerable conclusiveness by the number of excellent Armenian Generals military operations have produced in the Caucasus. General Lazareff, who stormed Kars, General Tergoukasoff, who so ably led the Erivan column, and General Loris Melikoff, who, after successfully controlling the Russian operations, was summoned to rule Russia itself, were all three of them Armenians. The best officers, and the best officials Russia possesses in the Caucasus are of Armenian birth. The commerce of the region is almost entirely in Armenian hands. So rapidly is the Armenian element in Tiflis gaining upon the others that ere long Tiflis will fairly merit the title of being the capital of the Armenian race.

Such being the case, it is easy for the reader to understand the interest which Tiflis takes in the progress of events in the Armenian provinces of Turkey. The most oppressed and pacific people in Asiatic Turkey are the 760,000 Armenian subjects of the Sultan. The atrocious treatment which they have experienced since 1878 at the hands of the Turks, is too sorrowful and sickening a subject for me to dilate upon here. They exercise no power; their development is checked; and the hatred they entertain towards the Turks renders them a source of weakness to the country. In Russia and the Caucasus there are 850,000 Armenians, who are treated as equals of the Russians, enjoy every privilege the latter possess, and can rise to any post in the State, as witness the autocratic powers conferred on Loris Melikoff in 1880. Tiflis is the centre of their commercial and literary activity; the Presses there are continually turning out translations of the masterpieces of European literature; and they maintain four monthly reviews—the *Ararat, Nordz, Aikikan,* and *Ashkar,* and four newspapers, the *Mshak, Megoo, Psak,* and *Gortz.* The latter possess correspondents throughout Asiatic Turkey, and serve as a mouthpiece for their grievances. It is quite natural, therefore, that Tiflis should manifest a deep interest in what goes on in our Asia Minor Protectorate. To Tiflis, Erzeroum is a sort of second Bulgaria, which the next conflict should place in her keeping. The Armenians there watch events at Erzeroum as keenly as the Russians used to regard them in the Balkan provinces. Every Turkish outrage is exaggerated, and made a peg for agitation by the Armenian Press, and it is affirmed that the Russian higher authorities are not altogether innocent of stimulating the feeling against Turkey. As for the local officials, a fresh crusade would be exceedingly popular.

The Caucasus is a grand military base for Russia. From it radiate roads to the most important objective points in the East. No barrier now exists to a direct march from Tiflis and Kars upon Constantinople. By taking a direction a little more to the south, a Caucasian army can cut the trade routes of Asia Minor and occupy the Euphrates valley, through which England will some day require to make a railway to India. A third highway takes an invading force to Teheran to stamp out the Persian monarchy, and push down to the Persian Gulf. By proceeding due east, across the Caspian, two parallel roads are open to a Caucasian advance upon Herat, either *viâ* Astrabad and Meshed, or Krasnovodsk, Askabad and Sarakhs; and the reader does not need to be reminded where an army would ultimately get to, if it marched beyond Herat.

The Caucasus base, garrisoned by 150,000 troops in time of peace and 350,000 in time of war, is not maintained without a heavy drain on the Russian Exchequer. The deficit, as I have said, is never less than a million a year. But this large figure could be easily reduced to a considerable extent by carrying out the long promised administrative reforms. Besides having to support a huge army, the Caucasus is required to maintain a swarm of heavily paid functionaries, several times in excess of its wants, and notorious even in Russia for possessing the worst traits of an ill-regulated bureaucracy. The Orenburg base was "revised" in 1880, and after a host of incapable and corrupt officials had been pensioned or punished, the staff was cut down, and the annual deficit extinguished. Last year Turkestan underwent a similar purging, and although in this case the deficit was not altogether removed, still it was very much lessened, and the administrative service rendered of greater utility to the natives. The turn of the Caucasus will come next. One of these days a Senator will go forth from St. Petersburg armed with full powers, and those officials who have been lazy and corrupt will shake in their shoes and have a very bad time of it,

CHAPTER X.

FROM TIFLIS TO BAKU.

The New Railway from Tiflis to Baku—Strategical Results of the
Construction—Departure from Tiflis—Transformation Scene the
next Morning—Views of the Elisavetopol Steppes—The Caucasus
Range—Mount Ararat—Refusal of the Armenians to believe that
any Man has ever attained the Summit—Delights of a Morning
Meal off a Water-melon—The Melon as a Fruit—A free-and-easy
mode of Railway Travelling—Atrocious Pace on the Transcaucasian
Railway—Deficit in working the Line—The Valley of the River
Kura—The Transcaucasian Irrigation System—German Colonies
in the Elisavetopol District—Adji Cabul, and the projected
Russian Railway to Teheran—The Line described—The future
Railways to the Persian Gulf and India—Alayat, the Second Terminus on the Caspian—A Night Ride along the Caspian Coast to
the Apsheron Peninsula.

WHEN the war of 1877-78 broke out between Russia and
Turkey, it took the former Power nearly a month to
move troops from the Caspian littoral to Tiflis. A few
months later, when the tribes in Daghestan rose against
the Russians and menaced the security of the region
about Petrovsk, it occupied a relieving force three weeks
to get from Tiflis to the Caspian, even with extraordinary
efforts on the part of the commanding general. A few
months ago the new railway to Baku was opened for
traffic, and all this hard travelling was at once reduced
to a matter of twenty-two hours. In this manner, the
journey from one sea to the other, across Transcaucasia,
which a decade ago occupied, travelling express, nearly
a fortnight, has been reduced to thirty-six hours, and

might, if the present slow service were accelerated, be shortened to within the limits of a day. In the interval Turkey has done nothing to improve her communications between her capital and Armenia. Russia, therefore, has increased her power in Transcaucasia to an extent that must tell with crushing effect on the issue of the next campaign. This circumstance alone would almost justify the deficit incurred by constructing the railway from Batoum to Baku. But the new railway has done something more than merely enable Russia to throw her military resources with equal facility towards the Caspian or Black Sea, and ahead into Armenia—it has laid open to Europe the immense petroleum supply of Baku, and secured Russia the market of the world for it. It was a misfortune for me, perhaps, that I saw the Baku railway rather early in its career. It had only been opened a month or two, and while the old Persian goods' traffic had been suddenly snatched from it by the suppression of the European transit trade across the Caucasus, the arrangements for the despatch of petroleum had not been sufficiently matured to allow of the deficiency being made good. Hence we travelled the 341 miles from Tiflis to Baku with only a score of passengers, and met only a similar return consignment and a couple of oil trains the whole of the way—traffic insufficient to pay the expenses of the odd forty-one miles, let alone the remaining three hundred.*

* In four years the traffic has increased so rapidly, and to such a volume that the railway is quite unable to cope with it. Irrespective of the petroleum traffic, goods now pour along the line from Turkestan and Persia, while the products of the Caucasus are largely exported to Europe. The export of corn to Europe last year blocked the line for weeks and attained a total of nearly 200,000 tons, and of manganese ore over 60,000 tons were shipped from Poti. The traffic in 1883 amounted to about 280,000 tons; in 1884 it had grown to 400,000 tons; in 1885 to nearly 600,000 tons, and in 1886 to more than 900,000 tons; about two-thirds of the latter consisting of petro-

The train from Batoum arrives at Tiflis at 10.25 at night and leaves at 11.11. The greater part of the passengers quit it there, and the few that go further on alight for the most part at the town of Elisavetopol. We had no difficulty, therefore, in securing excellent seats and making ourselves comfortable for the night. The carriages on the line have an ingenious arrangement for sleeping, which might be easily copied in our English carriages. The cushioned back lifts up like the leaf of a table, and enables a person to lie down full length above the ordinary seat. These we found such excellent couches that we passed Elisavetopol at half-past six the next morning fast asleep, and did not wake until we were approaching the Adjinaoor steppe, a couple of hours later on.

Quite a transformation scene greeted us when we put our heads out of the window. We were traversing a country which bore no resemblance to anything we had previously passed through since our departure from London. Around us was a sort of plain of fuller's earth—so dry was the loam that it seemed as though one might dig for yards without coming upon a vestige of moisture. Dotting it here and there were small straggling oases of trees, enclosing a thatched village, and connected one with the other by a low ridge running across the plain, marking the course of an irrigation canal. Now and again we passed one of these canals, the turbid waters of which were sluggishly moving at the bottom of a deep and arid cutting. Occasionally flocks and herds could be seen browsing on the scanty grass close to the oases, the shepherds protected from the

leum products. In 1883 the traffic receipts reached 3,458,000 roubles; in 1886 the sum exceeded 8,500,000 roubles. When the Transcaspian railway is finished to Samarcand, the Transcaucasian line will be the regular highway between Central Asia and Europe. Already Penjdeh fleeces are sent viâ Baku and Batoum to Marseilles.

The Transcaucasian Railway.—Station at Elisavetpol.

fierce rays of the sun by a thatch over a dwarf conning post constructed on the trunk of a tree. The plain itself bore no vegetation, except a little camel thorn, on which alongside a track camels from a halted caravan could be seen at times feeding. Once or twice we passed horsemen riding across the country—fierce and swarthy men, with Eastern khalats, or robes like dressing-gowns and a huge black sheepskin buzbee. Most of them carried a rifle, and all of them a dagger, for the lower valley of the Kura is still notorious for its brigandage, owing to its proximity to the unsettled Kurdish border of Persia. Such was the aspect of the plain which stretched away on both sides of the railway to a mountain ridge; one of them—the Caucasus—running in an even course parallel with the line, and the other, flanking the Persian side, more broken and intermittent. The Caucasus had a very different appearance from what it had borne before. It was brown, bare, and treeless; the cones were no longer green, but seemed to reflect the sun with a silvery lustre. A person inexperienced in mountains would have calculated the distance of the ridge from the railway at ten or fifteen miles. In reality, it was between sixty and seventy. One of the cones we had just passed was the Kamatzna Dagh, 11,445 feet high, and in front was the Bazar Douz, rearing its head above the level of ocean 14,722 feet.

Mount Ararat, which lies a few days south of Tiflis, is only a little more than two thousand feet higher than this. Travelling in our carriage was a young Armenian engineer, who was reading a recently published Armenian book upon Mount Ararat. The cause of its issue had been the publication of a work at St. Petersburg by a Russian professor, describing his partial ascent of the mountain. The Armenian book, written by one of the Armenian monks on the spot, denied the truthfulness of the professor's statements, and asserted that no one had ever placed his foot on the summit. This, by the way, the Armenians have repeatedly asserted since Parrot first effected the ascent in 1829. Since then Aftronomoff, Behrens, Abich, Seymour, Tchodsko, Khanyloff, Stuart, C. C. Tucker, and Bryce have either stood on the actual summit, or at a height within a few feet of it. Still, prejudice is hard to kill, and the Armenians having made up their minds that the mountain has never been ascended since the time of Noah, and that its summit will never be attained by mortal man to the end of time, are ready to argue the matter against all comers in the face of the clearest evidence to the contrary.

The Armenian was a very intelligent fellow. He was being trained at Moscow by the Government as a railway engineer, and was gaining experience during the vacation by travelling with a free pass over the Caucasian railroads. Some day, when these railroads push their way into Persia, Afghanistan, and Turkey, the Government will possess in the person of this Armenian and others of the same nationality, skilled engineers capable of making all the arrangements with the natives of the districts through which the lines will pass.

Had we been up early we should have been able to have breakfasted at Elisavetopol Station, where the train stops for twenty minutes, at an excellent buffet. As it was, we were only able to get a glass of tea and a stale roll at one of the small stations. This, however, was better than nothing, considering the sultriness of the morning; and when we followed it at the next station with a capital wash and brush up in the solitary waiting-room, and then in the roomy carriage attacked with our pen-knives a huge water-melon, weighing eight or ten pounds, and bought for a penny, I was quite ready to admit the force of C.'s remark—could luxurious travelling be carried to further lengths in the East?

Throughout the Kura Valley I do not know any fruit

that surpasses the water-melon. Grapes which can be bought for almost nothing with their delicate bloom on in the humid valley of the Rion, too often reach the traveller in the dusty valley of the Kura gritty and fly-blown. It is unpleasant also to eat grapes after they have been packed in dirty baskets and handled by dirty Asiatics. But the dust and the fly cannot get at the water-melon; its tough skin is proof against bruises and dirt, and it retains its freshness long after the pear and the apricot have become stale and rotten. Gently removing the top, we helped ourselves to thick horizontal slices, and I think the friends of C. and myself would have been amused if they had seen us afterwards, sleeves turned up, holding the slices with both hands out of the window and taking huge bites at the pulp, while the juice descended in showers on the dusty earth below. When we had eaten of it till we could eat no more, we replaced the top and stowed the melon away in a cool corner of the carriage, whither we resorted whenever we felt thirsty—it being impossible closer to Baku to get water-melons at the stations. At Baku itself they are again abundant, being brought by barge-loads from the Volga. Throughout the whole of South Russia water-melons are wonderfully abundant. Generally speaking, they may be bought for 1d. or 2d. apiece, although they cost 6d. to 1s. 6d. at Moscow and St. Petersburg, and I have often seen half-a-crown demanded at Covent Garden. In some parts of South Russia, as, for instance, in the province of Tamboff, where I lived six months among the peasants some years ago, the water-melon is used as an alternative crop—wheat being sown the first year, millet or buckwheat the next, and water melons or cucumbers the third. In the Caucasus they are commonly grown amidst the maize. The people of South Russia practically live on bread and melons during the summer, and this is the case all the way to Merv. At the close of the season they are salted in tubs for winter eating. The water-melon is essentially a fruit for a hot climate. On a hot day it is simply delicious. But it never seems to me palatable in cold, dull weather, even in Asia, and I always avoid it in England, where it is not only out of place in our chilly climate, but never possesses the juiciness and flavour of the water-melon of the East. As a rule, the hotter the climate the better the water-melon. It attains its largest size, I believe, at Merv, the Turcomans having been accustomed for generations to grow it on manure heaps. To those who have never seen the water-melon in perfection, the sweet melon of the English hothouse can convey no idea of the fruit; the two are as widely dissimilar as the pear and the grape. The sweet melon is only occasionally grown in Russia and the Caucasus, and is eaten as a luxury, not as a quencher of thirst and article of diet, like the water-melon.

The free-and-easy mode of travelling on the Baku Railway was very pleasant. There were not more than a score of passengers in the entire train, and one could walk from one end to the other through the almost deserted carriages and enjoy every variety of seat, window, and travelling companion. The abundance of unoccupied seats about me made me feel as though I were journeying in an empty church. At the stations we took up no passengers, and set none down. Half a dozen officials were usually on the platform to meet us, and when the train stopped half a dozen alighted from it—supervisors inspecting the different branches of railway organization. These chatted and gossiped for five minutes and then they got into the train, which went on slowly again. The regular passengers for the most part slept; they only concerned themselves about the station when a buffet was there. All the stations, as also the watch-houses along the line, are beautifully built of fine grey marble. Most of the former have commodious waiting-rooms, fitted with lavatories and mirrors, luxuries of which the trains themselves on this line are deficient.

The pace we went at was atrociously slow. Including stoppages, the average rate from Tiflis to Baku was little more than fifteen miles an hour. It has not been improved since, and there is no prospect at present of any alteration for the better. The Transcaucasian Railway is notoriously ill-managed. The greater portion of its shares are held by a group of Russian bankers, who content themselves with the Government guarantee and care very little for the efficiency of the line. The 341 miles from Tiflis to Baku cost 34,000,000 roubles (£3,400,000), or about £10,000 a mile, including £1,005,447 spent on rolling-stock and metals, ordered by the Government of various Russian firms. The rolling-stock on the line was altogether insignificant in September; but arrangements are now being made to extend it. But the extension will be less in the shape of passenger trains than cars for conveying petroleum. For some time to come the passenger service will remain as it is. The Transcaucasian Railway, with its ramifications, has an extent of about 640 miles. Over this in September last it only carried 68,653 passengers; the united fares of which were under £9,500. The total receipts of goods and passenger traffic were £32,612, or on an average £1,087 a day. This is a mere trifle for a line costing altogether £7,000,000 sterling to construct, and which will need two or three millions more to render it thoroughly efficient.

The Kura valley, down which we travelled, occupies what was once a fiord or inlet of the Caspian. Ages ago the southern part of the Caucasian isthmus, now forming the Russian province of Transcaucasia, probably consisted of little more than a narrow ridge of mountains, with the

L

Caspian running close in towards it on the one side and the Black Sea on the other. Two things are tolerably clear in connection with this opinion. Pliny's account of the trade that used to pass across the ridge from the Caspian to the Black Sea indicates that there were great water facilities on both sides of it, while modern observation has shown that the rivers occupying the two inlets—the Rion and the Kura—are yearly becoming more and more clogged in their course, and thrusting out their deltas further into the Black Sea and Caspian. In ancient times the Rion was navigable for 100 miles: at present it has barely two feet at low water, and during the flood season can only be ascended by small craft for thirty miles. The delta of the Kura encroached fifty square miles on the Caspian during the period from 1830 to 1860.

As far as Tiflis, the Kura is little more than a rapid mountain stream, with a rocky bed formed in a very deep cutting. Afterwards it rapidly increases in size, and from 450 miles from its mouth is navigable for vessels drawing four feet of water. Viewed from the railway, the lower valley of the Kura has a desiccated appearance, the arid loamy plain possessing vegetation only alongside the river or the canals running out from it. The discharge of the Kura, with the Aras, is 25,000 cubic feet per second in summer. If this were distributed over the Mogan and Karabagh steppes, 5,000,000 acres of rich soil would be rendered fit for cultivation.

In ancient times the valley was intersected by a whole series of irrigation canals, one of which was nearly 100 miles long. The invasion of Djengis Khan, and the subsequent raids of the mountaineers, laid the whole of them in ruins. More recently, the wholesale destruction of forests has led to a further desiccation of the country. The environs of Tiflis, formerly woody, have now the aspect of a desert. A recent Russian report cited nearly

100 settlements in Transcaucasia which had been abandoned, owing to the failure of the water supply in their respective districts. One of these settlements, now a waste, contained formerly 2,000 inhabitants. The serious character of the evil has frequently engaged the attention of the Government during the last twenty years. In 1860 the Governor-General of the Caucasus, Prince Bariatinsky, availed himself of the services of two English engineers, Messrs. Bell and Gabbe, who spent six years in surveying the valleys of the Kura and Aras, and drew up an exhaustive report on the irrigation of the country, which still excites the admiration of the Russian engineering profession. Messrs. Bell and Gabbe (the latter is now dead) divided the scheme into three sections, and provided for the gradual irrigation of about $5\frac{1}{2}$ millions of acres by means of 3,000 miles of irrigation canals; but nothing has been done to carry their project into effect. Climatically, the Kura valley is altogether Persian in its characteristics. Rain rarely falls, drought prevails for months together, and vegetation is only maintained by ceaseless activity in keeping in proper order a vast system of irrigation. In the valley where there is water there is life; willows and pollards grow along the watercourses, poplars and plane-trees give shade on their banks, and inside the area, enclosed by the outer main irrigation canal, a ramification of channels carries existence to maize fields, orchards, and vineyards. The soil is everywhere of a splendid quality—the arid plain is just as rich as the greenest spot in the oases; but without water nothing can grow except the camel-thorn. If the mountain streams supplying the irrigation canal system of the Kura valley were dammed up, and their water diverted for a week or two, the whole country would become as dreary a waste as the Kara Kum in Central Asia. On the other hand, if the Government would repeat on a larger scale what has already been

done in the Elisavetopol section of it, the valley could support many millions.

The whole surface of the province of Elisavetopol is dotted with tree-rimmed oases; hidden away in the foliage and vegetation of which are the wood and mud dwellings of the natives. The herds and flocks of each settlement graze on the plain outside. Where so much water is needed to preserve alive the vegetation, and the supply is so limited, constant quarrels may be expected between villages situated on the same main irrigation canal. If the higher villages take too much water the lower ones have to go short, and in the same manner if, of the quantity drawn off from the canal for the village supply, one family takes more than it ought, other families have to suffer. Hence conflicts are of constant occurrence in Elisavetopol, and the Cossack gendarmes controlling the agricultural districts have ever to be on the alert. Yet there is conclusive evidence that with a little better supervision on the part of the authorities, these quarrels might not only be prevented, but also such a supply given to the country as would put an end to all competition. Scattered about Elisavetopol are a number of German colonies. In these colonies quarrels for water are unknown, and they never experience drought. This is ascribed to the excellence of their water arrangements, and the care they take to maintain an independent supply of their own for the summer by establishing reservoirs to catch the winter rains. A little while ago an irrigation commission was sent from Russia to report upon the water supply of the whole country between Tiflis and the Caspian Sea. In its report the members declared that with a more scientific system of rain-storing and irrigation, the cultivable area of Elisavetopol might be easily trebled, and this without resorting to the expensive underground canals or *karezes*, at present largely employed to preserve the water from

PLATE 9.—FUTURE RUSSIAN RAILWAY TO TEHERAN. ABDI-CABUL STATION.

the prevailing desiccating winds from the Caspian. Some day their recommendation will, no doubt, be carried into effect.

Although the hot season was virtually at a close, we found the weather extremely warm towards the middle of the day. On the platform the heat of the sun was almost unendurable. At half-past three we arrived at Adji-Cabul, where the train stopped twenty minutes for the passengers to dine. The station is a particularly fine one, and the platform is well shaded by a handsome roof running from one end to the other. The buffet, however, is very indifferent, the food being cooked in a coarse and greasy manner, and the cook using his dirty fingers, instead of a fork, in serving out the cutlets. This, and the swarm of flies, took away the little appetite the heat had left me.

Adji-Cabul lies close to the junction of the Aras with the Kura. Formerly the two rivers entered the Caspian by separate mouths, but in comparatively modern times they coalesced, and every year push their outlet further into the Caspian, forming loamy plains like the Mogan steppe. Adji-Cabul is a place with a future, although to-day it consists only of a station and barracks for the employés, and a track or two, disappearing across the plain in the direction of distant villages. From here, at some future period, will run the railway to Teheran. The establishment of direct railway communication between the English and Persian capitals may seem at first sight a long way off, but in reality it is more within measurable distance than many people imagine, as a few facts will show.

From Adji-Cabul to Resht the distance is about 350 miles, the country the whole way being very rich and fertile, and in the first section, through the Mogan steppe, petroleum running all over the ground, and having the reputation of being as plentiful as at Baku. The engineering works would not be of a very serious character, on account of the line following the coast. From Resht to Teheran, 200 miles, a French company has a concession for running a line, and a short time ago was reported to be making preparations for carrying out the scheme. In the event of its falling through, the Russians would be willing to construct the section.

In this manner, by constructing a line 550 miles long, at a cost of between three and four millions, Teheran would be joined by railway with Tiflis and Batoum, and steam communication would be established between the capital of the Shahs and the civilized world. From London to Teheran the journey would occupy eleven days, which might be reduced to nine if the Russian service were accelerated. Apart from the Persian traffic the line would attract to the Transcaucasian Railway, the Russians are sanguine that a very large trade would be done in exporting Baku oil to Persia. The line would be cheaply worked, one of the heaviest items in railway expenditure, fuel, being obtainable for next to nothing at Baku, and lubricating oil, another expensive item, being abundant also at a nominal price.

Of course, there would still remain the break between the Transcaucasian-Teheran Railway and the Russian and European network. Two schemes exist to join them together. One would extend the Vladikavkaz line direct to Tiflis, and the other turn off east to the Caspian at Petrovsk, and then proceed along the coast to Baku. The first would be the shortest, but the passage of the Caucasus range is attended with enormous engineering difficulties. The 111 miles needed to connect the two points would cost £4,250,000 sterling, or nearly £40,000 a mile, and would involve the construction of a series of tunnels, of which one, $8\frac{1}{2}$ miles long, would be the work of years. In its present mood the Russian Government is decidedly averse to the undertaking. On the other hand, only last autumn the whole country from Vladikavkaz to Baku was surveyed for the alternative route, which although three or four times longer, would not cost so much, and besides opening up a rich and fertile country, fit for Russian colonization, instead of mountain peaks, would afford a fresh outlet for Baku petroleum, the unlimited conveyance of which to Batoum, as already stated, is impeded by the difficult Suram Pass. When General Possiet, the Minister of Railways, was at Baku last November, he intimated to a deputation of petroleum firms that the Vladikavkaz-Petrovsk line would be one of the first to be taken in hand, so impressed was he with its importance. The line would be constructed by the Rostoff-Vladikavkaz railway company, and would thus in no way draw upon the energies of the Transcaucasian company, and prevent its attention being directed towards Resht and Teheran.

Without being unduly sanguine, we may regard a Russian railway to Teheran as a certainty in the course of a few years. This will bring North Persia completely under Russian influence, and no doubt give Russian trade a preponderance in that region. Further extensions are not sufficiently near consummation to be scanned at length. They would be two — from Teheran to the Persian Gulf, and from Teheran to Herat and India. Respecting the former, *via* Ispahan and Shiraz to Bushire, 714 miles long, which would create a new road from Europe to India, my impression is strong that it would be some time before Russia would push such an enterprise, because it would open up Persia to English influence and trade from the Persian Gulf. The second, from Teheran to Meshed (550 miles), and thence to Herat (230 miles), or, in all, 780 miles, would be equally discountenanced by Russia; since it would pass through Persian territory and solidify Persian rule, while being 257 miles longer than the link necessary to join the

Transcaspian Railway at Kizil Arvat with Herat *viâ* Sarakhs. Until the Russian Transcaspian Railway is completed to Herat and India, Russia may therefore be expected to give no support to the extension of the Persian railway system beyond Teheran.

Whatever may be the development of the railway network in the Caucasus region, one fact stands out sky-high above cloudy controversy—that is, that the Baku petroleum region occupies a grand position for supplying the lines with fuel and light and lubricating oil, to say nothing of trade with the towns and villages of Persia. Adji-Cabul acts as the station for Shemakha, a town which ruled the Baku region until destroyed by an earthquake. From there to Baku, a distance of seventy-two miles, petroleum exists nearly the whole of the way.

After leaving Adji-Cabul, the country loses almost all traces of settlement, and we traversed a barren expanse for an hour. We then reached the shore of the Caspian at Alayat. This' is another place of the future. The railway touches the Caspian there before sweeping round to Baku, fifty miles distant; the intention being to establish a port on the site of Alayat Bay. The Transcaucasian Railway will then have two outlets in the Caspian Sea—Baku and Alayat, corresponding with the two in the Black Sea, Poti and Batoum. There is a certain amount of activity observable at Alayat, owing to the operations of a French company engaged in boring for oil. In excess, 400 plots of petroleum ground have found purchasers in the locality. There is a small buffet at the station, where an excellent tea may be made. Afterwards there are no refreshments until the train reaches Baku.

From Alayat to Baku, three hours' journey, the country is a sheer desert. The ground consists of a little sand or loam, thinly spread over the rock, and produces only the prickly camel-thorn. The mountains running towards the Apsheron peninsula bear every evidence of volcanic origin. At one place there is a very remarkable monument of an earthquake, the plain having opened at one period and thrown up thousands of blocks of stone, closing afterwards and leaving a structure like the breakwater at Suez, lying along the flat plain with an extinct mud volcano at each extremity. Numerous salt lakes are passed—the salt glistening in the parched depressions like snow. Here and there are black blotches, marking the site of a petroleum spring. In constructing this section many navvies perished from the excessive heat and dryness; just as many perished at the other extremity of the line near Batoum from the opposite cause. Often for six months together not a drop of rain moistens the parched rocks of Baku.

After the intense heat of the day, it was pleasant to gaze at the waves breaking on the Caspian shore, and sniff the fresh breeze blowing from the sea. Not a ship or boat, or any evidence of human activity, could be detected on the sea; the only sign of life was a few waterfowl flying along the shingle. The stations we stopped at now were as desolate as their surroundings. I don't think we took up a passenger the whole fifty miles. After a while it grew dark, and we began to see in the distance the lights of Balakhani. The ozone from the sea gave place to the smell of naphtha; the plashing of the waves was succeeded by the shrill piping of myriads of crickets; and above us we saw for the first time the magnificent Oriental array of stars, affording such a lovely canopy at nights to Eastern deserts—not simply shining overhead as at home, but reaching almost down to the ground on every side, and possessing a brilliancy never seen in England. While we were still engaged admiring them the train began to slacken speed, and a few minutes after eight we slowly crawled into Baku.

CHAPTER XI.

BAKU AND ITS PETROLEUM SUPPLY, FROM THE EARLIEST TIMES.

Night and Morning Impressions of Baku—Hotels—The Shipping in the Bay—The Real Russian Base of Operations against India—Proposal for supplying the Town with Water from the Volga—Life at Baku—Stephen Gulishambaroff—The History of Baku—The Ancient Fire-Worshippers—Baku Petroleum during the Zoroastrian Period—Marco Polo and Baku Oil in the Middle Ages—Conquest of Baku by Peter the Great, and the Export of the Oil up the Volga—Jonas Hanway's Account of the Industry in the Time of George the Second—The Worship of the Everlasting Fires—Cooking Food and burning Lime with Hydro-Carbon Gas—Natural Kerosine—The Deposits on Holy Island and Tcheleken—Various English Travellers at Baku since the beginning of the Present Century—Descriptions of the Place by Major Marsh, General Valentine Baker, Mr. Arthur Arnold, M.P., General Sir Frederic Goldsmid, Mr. O'Donovan, Mr. Gallenga, Professor A. H. Keane, and others—Reason assigned for giving such Prominence to the Statements of so many English Authorities.

MY first acquaintance with Baku was not of a very encouraging character. The train dropped us at a wretched little shanty station in the midst of a wilderness, and, confiding ourselves with great misgivings to a Tartar phaeton-driver, we were bumped for a couple of miles over a perfect curiosity in the way of bad roads, the surface consisting of alternate sand and rock, full of fearful ruts and undulating like a sea. When at length we reached the town, the driver took us through gloomy streets of low, forbidding houses, and landed us at an hotel, the

PLATE 10.—TRANSCAUCASIAN RAILWAY: VIEW NEAR BAKU.

London, of which perhaps the least said the better, since it proved to be a villanous *café chantant*, and as dirty a *gostinnitza* as it has been my fortune, or misfortune, to put up at in the course of my many travels in Russia. But, in justice to Baku, I must say that we saw it under very disadvantageous circumstances. An Italian, arriving in London in a dense November fog, and putting up for the night in Wapping, would not send off by the next post a very flattering or very accurate account of the metropolis. As regards Baku, a railway terminus is now completed close to the town, which, for beauty of design and excellence of accommodation, is one of the finest in Russia. From the station to the best part of Baku a regular stone-paved road is being constructed, and if the traveller remembers to ask for the Hôtel d'Europe (Yevropaisky Gostinnitza), or the Hôtel Dominique (Gostinnitza Dominik), he will find at either very decent accommodation. Of course, Baku being so far east and its civilization so new, he cannot expect to be as well lodged as he would in London; but at either of the two hotels I mention, and particularly as regards the former, he will find spacious and tolerably comfortable rooms, and a *cuisine* which might be worse and is gradually becoming better. That we should have gone to such a den as the London at all, was due to an ill-natured passenger who travelled with us from Tiflis, and who, I think, must have maliciously misled us.

But the next morning, when we got about a bit, we found Baku to be a very different place, not only from our bad impression of the night before, but from the good impressions previously prevailing.

Baku, indeed, fairly amazed me. The numerous reports that had appeared in the Russian Press of late years, describing and extolling its progress, had prepared me for a spectacle of rapid development, but I must confess that I had no idea Baku was such a large place. To most English people, the Caspian is a sort of Dead Sea. They think there is little or no activity there. They forget that it is the natural outlet of the stream of life, of commerce, and of progress flowing down the Volga—the main artery of the Russian Empire. To such people a glimpse of Baku would be what Dick Swiveller would term a "regular stunner." What was ten years ago a sleepy Persian town is to-day a thriving city. There is more building activity visible at Baku than in any other place in the Russian Empire. It possesses more shipping of its own than Odessa or Cronstadt, and it has commenced the construction of a fine stone quay, of which about a mile is open for traffic, which beats the quay of the Neva at St. Petersburg, and is no unworthy rival of the Thames Embankment. Already the principal town and port of the Caspian, Baku in a few years' time will be the leading commercial centre of the Caucasus, and a dangerous competitor of Tiflis. How significant a bearing its development has on the future of the Central Asian Question may be seen by a glance at the map. Krasnovodsk is often spoken of as the base of the new Transcaspian movement towards India, and being a small place that movement is decried. But this is a misconception arising from putting the base on the wrong side of the sea. Baku is the base of the new movement, not Krasnovodsk. It is from Baku that troops are sent, supplies despatched, and munitions of war furnished for the garrisons in Akhal and Merv. Krasnovodsk is only a point *en route*. Baku people refer to it as merely "across the water," a trifling run of sixteen hours by steamer; isolated and distant a few years ago, but now "as close as in the palm of your hand;" having a telegraph cable to join it to Baku, a Government ferry service, and a railway beyond to carry on troops to within a short distance of the outposts of Central Asia.

Baku is situated on a magnificent bay, in the shape of

a crescent, seven miles across from point to point, and about fifteen in circumference. Across the mouth of the bay, well out to sea, is disposed an island, much in the same fashion as the Plymouth breakwater, thoroughly protecting it from adverse winds, and enabling it to give secure anchorage to thousands of vessels. I was astonished at the amount of shipping lying in the bay. Several hundred vessels were riding at anchor, and a large number of big steamers, many 200 feet long, were taking in oil or other cargoes at the twenty-five long piers which stretch out into various parts of the bay. Starting from the extremity of the Black Town, where the petroleum is refined, one can walk a good eight miles along the strand or quay, with shipping always on one side and buildings on the other; and everywhere there is just as much activity as on the strand of the Volga at Nijni during the busy period of the Great Fair. From one end of the town to the other, we saw the character of Baku being transformed. Everywhere old houses were being pulled down and new ones being built; streets were being laid out in regular lines, and paved with stone or asphalte; the wretched booths of the Persians were being replaced by spacious Russian shops; and the great old Persian fortress was being exhumed from the mass of surrounding buildings, and laid bare to the gaze of the world. Much of this improvement had been in progress before the Batoum railway was opened, but the movement has been accelerated since, and in two or three years, Baku will be a new city, with most of the comforts and luxuries of civilization, including even tramways, for the construction of which a syndicate is now being formed in Russia. As the place develops, its disadvantages—the heat, dust, absence of good water, rainlessness and the want of vegetation—will be largely mitigated. In regard to the water, for instance, Ludwig Nobel has offered that, for a moderate sum, his oil steamers shall bring back fresh water from the Volga, which, on arrival, could be pumped into a reservoir, purified, and distributed throughout the town. The adoption of such an arrangement would provide Baku with an abundant water-supply, and not only enable the inhabitants to use it freely in their homes, but permit of the irrigation of gardens on an extensive scale.

At Baku one can make himself tolerably comfortable during a short stay, and obtain anything in the shops he may have forgotten in starting on his journey. Amusements there are none, beyond spending the evening over cards or billiards in the select town clubs—to which admission is readily obtained—located near the Governor's house. The bay is full of fish, and there are plenty of craft to sail in. Moored off the new quay are the Caspian Baths, an excellent roomy structure, where for a few pence one can bathe under the most favourable circumstances, or make it a base for a pleasant swim in the bay. The water in the Caspian is clear and salty, and for the greater part of the year maintains just the temperature that suits most people's taste. There are only two drawbacks—the bay is so full of fish that one never loses the impression that he is in an aquarium; and when the wind lies in a particular direction, it blows inland the oil spouting up to the surface outside, causing a black scum to gather on the top of the water and prevent bathing for a day or two. The Governor's house is situated on the quay, and his Excellency is always ready to receive any day travellers visiting Baku. Such visits should be made in the morning, and it is better that the caller should wear a dress-coat—Russian officials in the Caucasus being more particular on this point than those at St. Petersburg or Moscow. Close to the Hôtel d'Europe is the Baku branch of the Imperial Russian Technical Society, where maps of the petroleum region and all the books published dealing with it may be seen, and the stranger placed in communication with the principal experts in Baku. Equally close is the office of Nobel Brothers, the creators of the prosperity of modern Baku, the manager of whose concern, Mr. Gustav Törnudd, will not only afford the traveller every assistance in viewing the huge establishment under his control, but will impart to him clearer and more impartial information respecting the local petroleum industry than any other manager in the place. Mr. Törnudd was once at Penn's engineering works, and speaks English fluently. The leading authority on Baku petroleum, Gospodin Stephen Gulishambaroff, is at present residing at Tiflis. There is probably no writer living who has a wider knowledge of the petroleum industry of the world than he has. A few Americans may have a better acquaintance with their own special industry, but none of them know anything about Baku. Gulishambaroff, on his part, has not only investigated the American oil region on behalf of the Russian Government, but has visited the petroleum districts of Galicia, &c., as well, besides having compiled a bibliography of the works in various languages dealing with petroleum, which is a masterpiece of its kind.

The cause of the progress and prosperity of Baku is oil—petroleum or rock oil, than which there is not a more copious or older known supply in the world. In England we are accustomed to regard the petroleum trade as a new branch of the world's commerce; yet for 2,500 years Baku has been famous for its marvellous springs of petroleum, and we have historical evidence that for nearly 1,000 years its oil resources have been drawn upon for the benefit of surrounding nations. It is noteworthy that at every epoch its petroleum supply has been spoken of as enormous and inexhaustible, and that there has never occurred in the region any phenomenon calculated to provoke or sustain the belief that the supply is intermittent, limited, or likely to rapidly come to an end.

Various reasons contributed in ancient times to draw the attention of the eastern world to the marvellous deposits of petroleum in the Apsheron peninsula, of which Baku is the principal centre. Baku, in the first place, boasts of the best harbour in the Caspian Sea. Practically speaking, it is almost the only good natural harbour of any size on the Caucasus coast, and it is situated opposite what was once the outlet of the river Oxus into the Caspian, or of some partial waterway from Central Asia formed by the Balkan bay running inland a considerable distance further than at present, and by the Oxus pursuing a more westerly course than to-day to meet it. The Indian trade in Pliny's time made its way to Europe by this route, and there is hardly a doubt that Baku rendered considerable service as a transit port. Such advantages of position naturally attracted the ancients to the place; but, apart from Baku bay, the peninsula of Apsheron was calculated to thrust itself upon the notice of the world by a phenomenon which excites wonder even to-day. The peninsula juts far into the Caspian. At its extremity, and on the islands which stretch beyond it, petroleum gas has flared for countless ages, arresting the attention of navigators at sea, as well as of people travelling by caravan on land, by its lurid glare at night. Such a phenomenon could not but excite the wonder of the superstitious East, and it is probable that the "Eternal Fire" on the peninsula was an object of devotion on the part of the natives, even before the worship of fire became the religion of the Persians. According to Jonas Hanway, the fire-worshippers from India, who flocked in his day to Baku, had a tradition that the Eternal Fire had flamed ever since the Flood, and that it would last to the end of the world.

Speaking on the subject of its antiquity, Mr. Arthur

Arnold, M.P. for Salford, who visited Baku in 1875, says:—" Twelve versts from Baku we came upon one of the oldest altars in the world, erect and flaming with its natural burnt-offering to this day. Surakhani is the ancient seat of probably one of the most ancient forms of worship. For unnumbered ages the gas which is generated by the subterranean store of oil has escaped from the fissures in the limestone crag, and the fire of this gas has lighted the prayers of generations of priests, as it blazed and flared away to the heavens. Fire-worship in Persia, of which, until the eighteenth century, Baku formed a part, is older than history. It may be that the fire in this temple at Surakhani has been unextinguished for a period extending from before the time of Cyrus (about B.C. 600), the fire-worshipping period being older than Cyrus."*

Dr. Haag, a celebrated professor of Sanscrit at Munich, says that "under no circumstances can we assign Zoroaster, the founder of fire-worship, a later date than B.C. 1000, and one may even make him a contemporary of Moses." If this were correct it would indeed give Baku petroleum an antiquity; but the generality of English and German scholars concur in fixing the commencement of the Zoroastrian period about B.C. 600, or nearly 2,500 years ago. The petroleum fires of the Apsheron peninsula being well known to the people of Persia, and the district forming part of the Persian dominions, and being easy to get at, the assumption is fair that from the earliest years of the Zoroastrian period the worshippers of fire resorted to Baku, to pay their devotions to the petroleum flames springing naturally from the soil.

"Baku," says Kinneir,† "was a celebrated city of the

* "Through Persia by Karavan." London. Tinsley Brothers, 1875. Page 131.

† "Geographical Memoir of the Persian Empire." By J. M. Kinneir, Political Assistan to Brigadier-General Sir John Malcolm in his Mission to the Court of Persia. London, 1813. Page 359.

ancient worshippers of fire, and before the conquest of the Saracens" (A.D. 636) "was annually visited by thousands of pilgrims."

"The peninsula of Apsheron," says another authority,* "has been celebrated for many centuries, in all eastern countries, as a sacred soil, and the fire-worshippers still make pilgrimages to adore the fires which there issue from the earth, arising from the ignition of the naturally formed naphtha. In ancient times Baku was held in the highest veneration by the Guebers, or Parsees, and was frequented by thousands of pilgrims."

"On the site of the modern town," states the Hon. George Keppel, who visited Baku in 1824,† "once stood a city celebrated in the times of the Guebers for its sacred temple, on the altars of which blazed perpetual flames of fire produced by ignited naphtha. To this place thousands of pilgrims paid their annual visits, till the second expedition of Heraclius against the Persians, when he wintered in these plains and destroyed the temples of the magi"—the priests of the Zoroastrian sect.

The naphtha or petroleum fires of Baku were thus in the zenith of their fame, when the mighty military sway of the Persians, extending to Constantinople, was shattered by the Emperor Heraclius. In A.D. 624, according to Gibbon, Heraclius wintered in the Mogon steppes, at the mouth of the river Kura, 70 miles south of Baku. There, says Gibbon, "he signalized the zeal and revenge of a christian emperor. At his command, the soldiers extinguished the fire and destroyed the temples of the magi."‡

* "Imperial Gazetteer," vol. i. Articles "Apsheron" and "Baku." London, 1855.

† "Personal Narrative of a Journey from India to England by Persia, the Western Shore of the Caspian, &c., in the year 1824." Vol. ii. page 214.

‡ "Decline and Fall of the Roman Empire," vol. iv. chap. xlvi.

Twelve years after this (A.D. 636), Persia was vanquished a second time by the Arabs, who, at the edge of the sword, converted the people from fire-worship to the Mussulman faith. Here and there, however, remnants of the ancient sect secretly performed their rites in South-East Persia, and large numbers fled to the island of Ormuz and thence to India, and gave origin to what are now the Parsees of Bombay. Although Mahomedan Persia intervened between the survivors and the Eternal Fire, many still continued to make their way annually to Baku. "Even as late as the 12th century pilgrimages were made to Baku, that Mecca of the Guebers, the purest fount of their sacred element."*

While we have historical evidence that petroleum gases have been flaring away for more than 2,500 years on the Apsheron peninsula, we have no direct testimony that the petroleum was exported as an article of commerce earlier than the 10th century, although there is no reason to disbelieve that it was used before then as light and fuel by surrounding nations. In the year 950 the Arab writer Masudi wrote a brief description of the fire-breathing mountains of "Baki"; and then we have a gap until the time of Marco Polo.

"On the confines towards Georgine," wrote that traveller, in the 13th century, "there is a fountain from which oil springs in great abundance, inasmuch as a hundred shiploads might be taken from it at one time. This oil is not good to use with food, but 'tis good to burn, and is also used to annoint camels that have the mange. People come from vast distances to fetch it, for in all countries round there is no other oil."†

Referring to this in a note, Colonel Yule, who is

---

* "A Journey through the Caucasus and Persia." By Augustus Mounsey. London, 1872. Page 329.

† "The Book of Ser Marco Polo, the Venetian," edited by Colonel Henry Yule, C.B. London: Murray, 1871, book i. page 4.

regarded as one of the foremost scholars of the day in matters appertaining to ancient Oriental geography, says:—"Though Mr. Khanikoff (the celebrated Russian traveller) points out that springs of naphtha are abundant in the vicinity of Tiflis, the mention of *shiploads* (in Ramusis indeed, altered, probably by the editor, to *camel-loads*) and the vast quantities spoken of point to the naphtha wells of the Baku peninsula on the Caspian. Ricold speaks of their supplying the old country as far as Bagdad, and Barbaro speaks of their practice of anointing camels with oil." This view is taken also by the "Encyclopædia Britannica" (vol. iii. page 259).

By the 13th century, therefore, crude petroleum was already an extensive article of Export from Baku. Persia, which had formerly prized the place on account of its petroleum gas, creating the phenomenon of the Eternal Fire, now began to value it on account of its oil. "Previous to its incorporation in the Russian Empire, Baku and its naphtha springs were long an apple of discord between the Persian shahs and the Armenian emperors."*

When Peter the Great commenced his series of conquests, having in view the conversion of the Caspian into a Russian lake, he took particular pains to secure Baku, on account of the valuable trade in petroleum it carried on with Persia. On finally annexing it in 1723, he gave special instructions for extracting the oil and exporting it up the Volga to Russia.

After his death, Nadir Shah recovered a deal of the Caspian littoral, and, to put an end to the costly struggle with him, Russia restored Baku to Persia in 1735. A few years later the Caspian Sea was invaded by a number of English pioneers of commerce, and one of them has

---

* "Russia; Past and Present." Adapted from the German of Laukenau and Oelnitz by H. M. Chester. London, 1881. Page 337.

furnished us with a work containing a valuable description of the petroleum industry under Persian rule.

This was penned by Jonas Hanway in 1754, under the title of "An account of British Trade over the Caspian Sea," a work which is still a standard one on the Caspian region. In his time, the reign of George II., the merchants of England were excited by the prospect of opening up trade with India and the East *via* the Caspian Sea. A number of schemes were broached; the all-powerful Turkey and Russia Companies fought for the concession of the trade; the matter was made the subject of diplomatic discussion between England and Russia; and finally, in 1741, Parliament gave the monopoly to the Russia Company. Captain Elton, who had long been in the Russian service, and had explored the Caspian three years earlier, was sent with a consignment of goods to the Persian ports of the sea, with Captain Woodroffe as commander. These officers neglecting the interests of the Company for those of Nadir Shah, one of the most intelligent and sagacious of the partners, Mr. Jonas Hanway, was deputed to proceed to Persia to investigate affairs. On his return he published a bulky work, in which he not only embodied his own experiences in the Caspian Sea, but also the surveys of Elton and Woodroffe, and a mass of historical data taken from the archives of the Company to which he belonged.

"What the Guebers, or Fire-worshippers, call the Everlasting Fire," he says, "is a phenomenon of a very extraordinary nature. This object of devotion lies about ten English miles north-east by east from the city of Baku, on a dry rocky land. There are several ancient temples built with stone, supposed to have been all dedicated to fire. Amongst others is a little temple, at which the Indians now worship. Here are generally forty or fifty of these poor devotees, who come on a pilgrimage from their own country. A little way from the temple is a low cleft of a rock, in which there is a horizontal gap, two feet from the ground, nearly six long, and about three broad, out of which issues a constant flame, in colour and gentleness not unlike a lamp that burns with spirits, only more pure. When the wind blows, it rises sometimes eight feet high, but much lower in still weather. They do not perceive that the flame makes any impression on the rock. This also the Indians worship, and say it cannot be resisted, but, if extinguished, will rise in another place.

"The earth round the place, for above two miles, has this surprising property, that by taking up two or three inches of the surface, and applying a live coal, the part which is so uncovered immediately takes fire, almost before the coal touches the earth; the flame makes the soil hot, but does not consume it, nor affect what is near it with any degree of heat. Any quantity of this earth carried to another place does not produce this effect. Not long since eight horses were consumed by this fire, being under a roof where the surface of the ground was turned up, and by some accident took flame. If a cane or tube, even of paper, be set about two inches in the ground, confined and close with earth below, and the top of it touched with a live coal, and blown upon, immediately a flame issues without hurting either the cane or paper, provided the edges be covered with clay; and this method they use for light in their houses, which have only the earth for the floor; three or four of these lighted canes will boil water in a pot, and thus they dress their victuals. The flame may be extinguished in the same manner as spirits of wine. The ground is dry and stony, and the more stony any particular part is, the stronger and clearer is the flame; it smells sulphurous, like naphtha, but not very offensive.

"Lime is burnt to great perfection by means of this phenomenon, the flame communicating itself to any distance where the earth is uncovered to receive it. The stones must be laid on one another, and in three days the lime is completed. Near this place brimstone is dug, and naphtha springs are found."

"Baku," he continues, "supplies Ghilan and Mazanderan, and other countries contiguous with naphtha." In his days, "the chief place for the black or dark-grey naphtha" was "the small island Wetoy, now uninhabited, except at such times as they take naphtha from thence." By Wetoy he meant Sviatoi, or Holy Island, off the extremity of the peninsula of Apsheron. Describing the operations of the petroleum exporters, he says:—"The Persians load it in bulk in their wretched vessels, so that sometimes the sea is covered with it for leagues together. When the weather is thick and hazy, the springs boil up the higher, and the naphtha often takes fire on the surface of the earth, and runs in a flame into the sea, in great quantities, to a distance almost incredible. In clear weather the springs do not boil up above two or three feet: in boiling over, the oily substance makes so strong a consistency as by degrees almost to close the mouth of the spring: sometimes it is quite closed, and forms hillocks that look as black as pitch, but the spring, which is resisted in one place, breaks out in another. Some of the springs, which have not been long open, form a mouth of eight or ten feet in diameter.

"The people carry the naphtha by troughs into pits or reservoirs, drawing it off from one to another, leaving in the first reservoir the water, or the heavier part with which it is mixed when it issues from the spring. It is unpleasant to the smell, and used mostly amongst the poorer sorts of the Persians, and other neighbouring people, as we use oil in lamps, or to boil their victuals; but it communicates a disagreeable taste. They find it burns best with a small mixture of ashes. As they obtain it in great abundance, every family is well supplied.

They keep it, at a small distance from their houses, in earthen vessels underground, to prevent any accident by fire, of which it is extremely susceptible."*

Sviatoi, or Holy Island, seems to have been selected by the Persians as the principal place for extracting the oil, because the beds were close to the shore and on a level with the sea. The island, however, has the drawback of indifferent harbour accommodation, so that once the petroleum trade assumed considerable proportions, it became obviously better to extract the oil from the mainland close to the splendid port of Baku. There is no reason to believe that the supply on the island has in any way diminished since Jonas Hanway's time. The only European traveller who appears to have visited it since is John Osmaston, an English tourist, who landed there in 1861 with a German, who was putting up a refinery. "The naphtha beds," he says, "lie on the west of the island, and are of very considerable extent. They are nearly all on a level with the sea, and of a uniform black colour, nothing growing upon them, and the surface flat, with pools of black-coloured water upon it. In several places gas was bubbling up through the water, and on a calm day it will easily ignite. Stones had been piled round one of these bubblings, forming a little chimney round it. On applying a lighted stick the whole chimney was filled with a pale yellow flame, which would continue burning for any length of time, if not extinguished by wind or rain. The depth of the bitumen beds is unknown."† Baron Thielmann, in describing his journey along the Caspian to Baku in 1874, speaks of passing through a number of islands impregnated with naphtha in

---

* "An Historical Account of the British Trade over the Caspian Sea." By Jonas Hanway, Merchant. London, 1754. Vol. i. page 264.

† "Old Ali, or Travels Long Ago: An Account of a Journey to Persia in 1861," by John Osmaston. London, 1881. Page 231.

approaching the Shakoff point of the Apsheron peninsula.

Besides getting black naphtha from Sviatoi Island, the Persians also in the last century obtained white naphtha from the peninsula of Apsheron.

This is a sort of natural kerosine, found even at the present day. Jonas Hanway describes it as "of a much thinner consistency than black naphtha. The Russians drink it both as a cordial and medicine; but it does not intoxicate. If taken internally, it is said to be good for the stone, as also for disorders of the breast, and in venereal cases, and sore heads; to both the last the Persians are very subject. Externally applied, it is of great use in scorbutic pains, gouts, cramps, &c., but it must be put to the part affected only; it penetrates instantaneously into the blood, and is apt, for a short time, to create great pain. It has also the property of spirits of wine to take out greasy spots in silks or woollens, but the remedy is worse than the disease, for it leaves an abominable odour. They say it is carried into India as a great rarity, and being prepared as a japan, is the most beautiful and lasting of any that has been yet found."*

Petroleum was also exported in Hanway's time from the island of Tcheleken, on the opposite coast of the Caspian. Woodroffe was sent by Nadir Shah to survey the place. In his diary is the following record:—"Sep. 14, 1743.—We weighed and came in close under the east side of Naphtonia, as the Russians call it. The Persians call it Cherriken. The coast is difficult of access, being high. It contains about 36 families, who have 28 large boats, with several wells of naphtha. The people subsist entirely by piracy. To remedy this evil, Nadir Shah some years ago offered to forgive all that was past, and to receive them into his favour, if they would come and settle about Astrabad Bay, where they might have lands

* "British Trade over the Caspian Sea." Vol. i. page 265.

and sell their naphtha to the inhabitants of that quarter. This they accepted, and carried on a brisk trade for about two years, selling their naphtha to the Persians, Turcomans, &c.; but getting tired of this way of living, returned to their trade of piracy."* O'Donovan described it in 1879 as "teeming with petroleum."

In 1801 Baku was re-annexed to Russia. J. M. Kinneir, who shortly afterwards accompanied Sir John Malcolm's mission to Persia in the capacity of political assistant, gives us the next description of Baku, in a well-known geographical memoir published in 1813:—
"The quantity of naphtha produced in the plain to the south-east of the city is enormous. The oil is drawn from wells, some of which have been found by a computation of the inhabitants to yield from 1,000 to 1,500 lbs. a day. These wells are, to a certain degree, inexhaustible, as they are no sooner emptied than they again begin to fill, and the naphtha continues gradually to increase until it has attained its former level. It is used by the natives as a substitute for lamp-oil, and when ignited emits a clear light, with much smoke and a disagreeable smell. . . . The whole country around Baku has at times the appearance of being enveloped in flames. It often seems as if the fire rolled down from the mountains in large masses with incredible velocity; and during the clear moonshine nights of November and December a bright blue light is observed at times to cover the whole western range. This fire does not consume, and if a person finds himself in the middle of it, no warmth is felt."†

The Hon. George Keppel, who visited Baku in 1824, during an overland journey from India to England, viâ Persia and the Caspian, observes that "the principal productions of Baku are black and white naphtha, which are found in such abundance that the wells are said to

---

* "British Trade over the Caspian Sea." Vol. i. page 89.
† "Geographical Memoir of the Persian Empire," page 359.

produce 1,500 lbs. a day." According to Colonel Yule, "the quantity of naphtha collected from the springs about Baku was in 1819 estimated at 241,000 poods, or nearly 4,000 tons, the greater part of which went to Persia."*

Shortly before the Crimean War, Dr. F. Wagner and F. Bodenstedt visited the Caucasus, and published a work in which they thus referred to Baku:—" In the neighbourhood of Baku large quantities of naphtha are found. It is burnt instead of candles, but the smell is very unpleasant. The whitish-yellow flame worshipped by the Indians exudes from the ground, and appears to be alimented by hydrogen gas."†

In McCulloch's works, and indeed in all others of the period, stress is laid upon the extensive character of the Baku petroleum deposits and the importance of the trade.

In October, 1860, Baku was visited by Mr. Osmaston. As he approached Baku at night he saw from the steamer " a bright light reflected behind the town, proceeding from the naphtha fires about seven versts off in the mountains." This was the same phenomenon which, centuries earlier, had awed the navigators of the Caspian Sea. " The soil all round for two or three miles exudes this gas, for if the earth be loosened, or a small hole made, gas immediately bubbles up, which can easily be ignited."

Describing the fire-worshippers, he speaks of a naphtha manufactory at Surakhani, and another "not far from Baku, where 117,000 roubles is its annual rent to the Crown, which shows of itself the magnitude of the undertaking." As in Jonas Hanway's time, a hundred years earlier, the people still used the gas exuding from the ground to burn their lime. While staying at Baku

* "The Book of Marco Polo.' Book i. page 4.
† "Schamyl." Translated from the German of Dr. F. Wagner and F. Bodenstedt by Lascelles Wraxall. London, 1854. Page 27.

he was taken to witness what has since become a notorious sight of the place—the sea on fire. This has been described by Mr. Arnold, Mr. Mounsey, Mr. O'Donovan, and many others. Osmaston thus records what occurred:—

"In the evening I made an expedition with Colonel Fragank to see the naphtha fires on the sea. Fragank had his long boat manned with ten men, and he and several of his friends and myself left the quay just as the sun went down. We were soon out far in the open bay, and then rounding a long promontory, entered another, and in half an hour more we reached the spot. Gas was bubbling up in several places near the boat, the water looking as if it were boiling. The distance from land is about half a mile, and the depth of the water full three and a half fathoms. A strong odour of naphtha pervaded the air. One of the sailors then threw out a piece of lighted tow, and after one or two ineffectual attempts, the waves were wrapt for several yards in flame. It was quite dusk, so we saw it beautifully. It was a most extraordinary sight; the sea as though it were on fire; a patch of bright flame burning upon its cold bosom. Setting the Thames on fire one had heard of, but I never thought I should really witness the sea in a blaze. We rowed round it, and then away, but the flame could be seen dancing up and down with the waves till we had gone nearly a mile distant. The wind then blew stronger and extinguished it, for it suddenly disappeared. There are several other spots in the Caspian where naphtha gas bubbles up in the same way."*

In 1866 Baku was visited by Mr. Augustus Mounsey, Second Secretary to Her Majesty's Embassy at Vienna, on his way home from Persia. "The whole country for several miles round Baku," he writes, "would seem to be

* "Old Ali, or Travels Long Ago." London: Hatchards, 1881. Pages 233-250.

underlaid by reservoirs of petroleum. Close to the Indian temple there is a large manufactory for the purification of it. The naphtha spurts like gas from a gas-pipe, and burns in like fashion wherever a hole is driven two or three fathoms into the soil."*

In his book on "Russian Metallurgical Works," published in 1870, by Herbert Barry, for many years engineer in Russia, he says (page 70):—"Petroleum exists in great quantities on the borders of the Caspian near Baku. Its quality is considered equal, or even superior, to the American oil."

Major Marsh, who rode through Persia and Afghanistan to India in 1872, tarried on his way at Baku. "The afternoon" (September 14th, 1872), he writes, "was devoted to the great natural wonders of Baku—petroleum and the everlasting fires. At Surakhani the whole country is saturated with petroleum; on making a hole in the ground the gas escapes, on lighting which it burns for a very long while—one of the few spots on earth where this extraordinary phenomenon can be seen. When there is no wind the flame is dull and small, but in a gale it roars and leaps up eight to ten feet. There are two naphtha refining establishments at Surakhani, the furnaces of which are entirely heated by the natural gas, which is collected as it rises out of the ground in iron tanks, and laid on by pipes. At night the whole place is lighted in the same manner, by ordinary gas-burners attached to the walls. On returning home in the evening we saw the silent waste lit up by various fires, each surrounded by a group of wild Tartars, cooking their food by its heat. The naphtha springs or wells are about five miles off, and the oil is brought in casks, in the crude state as it is pumped out of the wells—a thick, black fluid. The engine that works the Government

* "A Journey through the Caucasus and the Interior of Persia." London: Smith, Elder & Co., 1872. Page 330.

patent 'slip' uses this naphtha, instead of coal, for fuel. The oil is brought out of a tank by pipes and is blown into the grate by the force of steam, the heat and flame being regulated with the same ease as a gas-lamp, and steam can be got up in the large furnaces in a quarter of an hour. It is cheap, and has the advantage of being clean and easy to manage."*

A month later Baku received a fresh visitor in the person of Lieutenant Baron Max Von Thielmann, Secretary of the Imperial German Embassy at St. Petersburg. "The whole of the soil of the peninsula of Apsheron," he observes, "is saturated with naphtha. The most powerful spring lies near Balakhani, and rises to a height of 35 feet. Other less important springs are utilised by the Tartars, who collect the naphtha in jugs, which they bring to the distilleries. Besides the Kokereff distillery there are other large establishments, those of Meerzoeff, &c. The supply of gases is so abundant, that in the Kokereff manufactory not only are the steam-boilers and distillery apparatus heated by them, but the jets used for lighting the courtyard are left burning in the daytime."†

The following year General Valentine Baker passed through Baku, in proceeding on a surveying expedition with Captain Gill to the Perso-Turcoman frontier. He speaks of the "apparently inexhaustible supply of naphtha which is found in the neighbourhood of Baku," and refers to "gas in extraordinary quantities bubbling up to the surface of the Caspian Sea." When proper steam machinery on a large scale was in working order, he predicted that the naphtha "would be produced from

---

* "A Ride through Islam." London: Tinsley Brothers, 1877. Pages 54 and 55.

† "A Journey in the Caucasus, Persia, &c," By Lieutenant Max Von Thielmann. Translated by C. Heneage. London: Murray, 1875. Vol. i. page 7.

the wells at an almost nominal cost." "It promises to have a great effect in facilitating steam communication on the Caspian. The discovery of the immense supplies of naphtha at Baku, and its simple application to steam purposes, has obviated the disadvantages which previously existed through the high price of coal. The pure naphtha, as drawn from the wells, is not used; it is the refuse after distillation which is found so valuable for steam purposes. This is not highly inflammable, and its use seems perfectly safe and thoroughly under control. Vessels originally fitted for burning coal can burn this naphtha with very little alteration. The naphtha is forced into the furnace in the form of spray mixed with a jet of steam. One stoker is sufficient for a large steamer. All the engineers of the vessels burning naphtha speak in the highest terms of this fuel."[*]

Here then, we have, a series of travellers, of different nationalities, concurring in representing the petroleum deposits at Baku as enormous and inexhaustible, at a period when it was to the interest of no one to extol the place for selfish reasons. Up to 1872 the extraction of the oil was a close monopoly. In 1873, about the time of Baker's visit, it was thrown open to the world; but it is a curious circumstance that, so far as I am aware, no Englishman has ever attempted to exploit the Baku petroleum riches. The task of doing so has been left to Russians and Swedes.

Mr. Arthur Arnold, M.P., called at Baku during a journey to Persia in 1875. "Baku," he wrote on his return home,[†] "has 'struck oil,' and before many years are past the world will hear much of this obscure town —this Petrolia in Asia. The engines of the *Constantine*, the ship in which the Shah traversed the Caspian, were

---
[*] " Clouds in the East." London, 1875. Page 351.
[†] Through Persia by Caravan." London: Tinsley Brothers, 1877. Vol. i. pages 128-131.

driven with petroleum. Coal, the captain told us, cost 18½ roubles per hour, while petroleum costs only 1½ roubles,—a reduction from fifty shillings to four shillings. In a few years Baku will be united by railway with Tiflis and the Black Sea, and then probably all the steamships on the Euxine will be supplied with the same inexpensive fuel. For two or three miles along the shore of the bay, the many buildings in which the oil is refined by itself as fuel, pour forth dense smoke, and at eight miles from the town are the springs. The average depth at which the oil is touched seems to be about 150 feet. The wells are, for the most part, nine inches to a foot in diameter. From the first well we visited, a small steam engine with most primitive gear was lifting about 400,000 lbs. of petroleum a day. The oil is of a greenish colour, and as it is drawn up is emptied into a square pit dug in the surface, from which men take it in buckets and pour it into skins or barrels, the charge at the wells being at the rate of 1½d. per 50 lbs. weight of oil."

Major-General Sir Frederic Goldsmid, C.B., K.C.S.I., British Commissioner for the settlement of the Perso-Baluch frontier in 1870, and the Seistan Boundary in 1873, visited Baku about the same time as Mr. Arnold. The natural petroleum gas fires, which, as I have pointed out, have been flaring more than 2,500 years, he describes as "marvellous, and worthy of classification among natural wonders. There is a large tract of ground near the sea, out of which gas issues in profusion. The whole soil appears to be impregnated here with naphtha. The fires of Baku have attracted much attention from Caspian and Caucasian travellers, and are really well worthy of more general discussion and intimate acquaintance by the scientific world."

Mr. O'Donovan, the special correspondent of the *Daily News*, spent some months at Baku between 1879 and 1881, and gave graphic descriptions of the place. "All

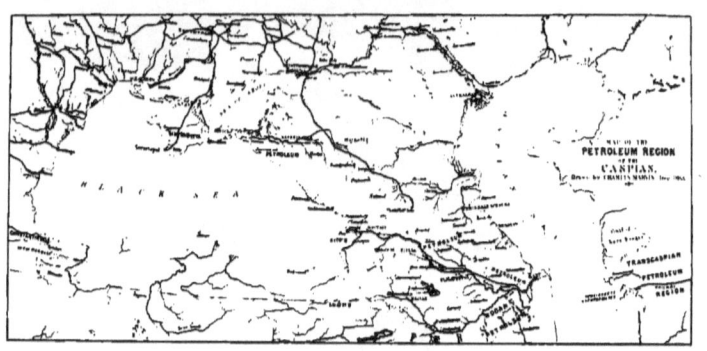

around Baku," he wrote, "the ground is sodden with natural issues of naphtha. In hundreds of places it exhales from the ground and burns freely when a light is applied. Only a couple of months before my visit its volatile products produced a remarkable effect a few miles from Baku. A large earth cliff fronting the sea was tumbled over as by an earthquake shock, and, as I myself saw, huge boulders and weighty ships' boilers were thrown a hundred yards. In view of the immense supply of natural petroleum, as yet only very slightly developed, and its application to the railway from Tiflis to Baku, I think this subject is worthy of every attention. Yet there are proprietors of large tracts of petroleum-bearing ground whose capital rests unproductive because of a want of demand."*

Mr. Edward Stack, of the Indian Civil Service was at Baku in August 1881. "The out-turn of the naphtha springs at Baku," he says, "was about 160,000 tons last year, and is increasing yearly. Difficulties of transport hinder this trade to a certain extent, but these will be largely surmounted if the American plan be adopted. . . . At present the naphtha is transported chiefly by water. A hundred and fifty vessels lie in the harbour, mostly schooners of 90 to 200 tons; but some three-masted steamers belong to the port, the largest being of 1,000 tons burden. Nobody can spend half-an-hour in Baku without seeing that it is a very rich and flourishing place. I envied it for India."†

Another well-known special correspondent, Mr. Gallenga, of the *Times*, made a journey through the Caucasus in 1881. Describing Baku, he observes:—
"What is said of the capabilities of the country in

---

* "The Merv Oasis." By Edmond O'Donovan. London: Smith, Elder & Co., 1882. Vol. i. pages 32-39.

† "Six Months in Persia." London: Sampson Low & Co., 1882. Vol. ii. page 209.

petroleum seems almost to exceed all credibility. Petroleum, it is asserted, in enormous subterranean lakes and reservoirs, underlies the Caucasian region from sea to sea. It is largely found beneath the steppes, both north and south of the mountain chain. At Baku, and the peninsula of Apsheron, at the end of the chain on the Caspian, naphtha has its main sources. The princess with whom I parted at Petrovsk, was not indulging her poetic fancy when she told me that ' Naphtha bursts forth in copious springs, sending up tall liquid columns not unlike the geysers in Iceland.' Up to this time the difficulty of conveying the material has stood in the way of the full development of this marvellous source of wealth." Referring to the scheme to convey the oil through a pipe from Baku to Batoum, he continues:—" But, by whatever means the liquid may be conveyed from Baku to the various seaports and railway stations of the world, it seems likely to effect little less than an economic revolution. There is scarcely any use, domestic or social, that naphtha cannot be put to. Could the liquid be made to travel so cheaply as to undersell English and other coal in countries like Italy, Spain, and other Mediterranean regions, where coal sells at three guineas a ton, it would be hardly possible to reckon what enormous wealth would accrue to the people of the Caucasus."*

It is particularly worthy of notice that none of the travellers who have visited Baku since the time of Peter the Great have expressed any doubts as to the durability of the petroleum supply. So far as I am aware, neither in Russia nor out of it has any person familiar with the region questioned either the unlimited character of the supply or its excellence. The geographers are at one with the travellers on this point. Reclus, the foremost geographer of the time, calls Baku a "great natural

* "A Summer Tour in Russia." London: Chapman & Hall, 1883. Pages 318-320.

workshop. The flames from the petroleum gases of the peninsula at times burst forth spontaneously, and during boisterous nights the hillsides are swept by sheets of phosphorescent light. Even in the middle of the sea the naphtha streams dribble up, clothing the ripples far and near with a thin irridescent coating. The legend of Prometheus, who stole fire from heaven, may in the popular fancy be possibly associated with the flaming hills and waters of the region. To the internal pressure of the gases is due the rising of the naphtha, which is forced upwards through the sands and shingly layers below the superficial tertiary strata. . . . So far, the 700 naphtha wells sunk in the neighbourhood of Baku show no sign of exhaustion. But immense loss is caused by the ignorance of those engaged in the trade. Thus a well at Balakhani, yielding 4,800 tons of naphtha daily, ran waste for four weeks before a reservoir could be prepared to receive the oil."*

In Stanford's "Compendium of Geography," the volume of which on Asia was compiled by the eminent geographer Professor A. H. Keane, and edited by Sir Richard Temple, the opinion is expressed that, "the inexhaustible naphtha springs promise to prove a future source of permanent wealth to the country" (page 362). "Baku is the centre of the most productive naphtha district in Asia" (page 381).

John Geddie, another geographer, writes† :—"The whole peninsula is saturated with naphtha, and the oil which exudes freely from the soil at various spots forms the chief riches of Baku. One of these naphtha wells has sometimes been known to catch fire by accident and to continue to burn for years, throwing up its pillar

* "The Earth and its Inhabitants." London : J. S. Virtue & Co., 1883. Vol. vi. page 108.
† "The Russian Empire : Historical and Descriptive." By John Geddie, F.R.G.S., London : Nelson & Sons, 1882. Page 378.

of flame to mark the furthest outpost of the Caucasus."

Two more opinions may be cited to clench the case. "The potential productiveness of the Baku oil region is incomparably superior to that of Pennsylvania," said Professor Mendalaieff, the celebrated Russian scientist, after a visit to Baku in 1882. "Comparing the results achieved in the two countries on one side, and the average depth and total number of wells on the other, it may be justly stated that the natural petroleum wells of Baku, as far as our knowledge goes, have no parallel in the world." Such was the opinion expressed by the British Vice-Consul at Batoum, Mr. Peacock, in a consular trade report published the same year.

I have been at pains to quote a large number of English authorities, even at the risk of being called a compiler, because commercial men are invariably so incredulous and suspicious in their attitude towards new ideas, that my assertions unsupported might have failed to have carried weight. In this chapter I have given almost all that has been published in English works on Baku petroleum. In the succeeding ones the matter will be original and derived from innumerable Russian sources. But even before proceeding to examine this mass of modern Russian data, the conviction should have taken root in the reader's mind that the old deposits of Baku are of a very extraordinary and wonderful character.

CHAPTER XII.

THE PETROLEUM DISTRICTS OF RUSSIA.

Official Estimate of the Area of the Petroleum Region of Russia—Localities where the Oil Abounds—The Crimean Deposits—The Supply in the Taman Peninsula—Operations at Novorossisk, in the Ter and Tiflis Districts, and near Petrovsk—The Caspian Deposits—Setting the Sea on Fire—The Transcaspian Oil Fields—Enough to Supply the whole Russian Empire—A Modest Annexation—Description of the Baku Oil Region—The Surakhani and Balakhani Plateaux—Quantity of Petroleum Extracted up to now—Geological Characteristics of the Caspian Petroleum Region—Erroneous Deductions of Scientific Men—Ludwig Nobel's Theory of the Petroleum Deposits—Instances of Variations in the Supply of Oil from Contiguous Wells—The Vastness of the Baku Supply beyond the reach of Controversy—Its Inexhaustibility—Relative Positions of the Baku and Pennsylvanian Supplies from Ports Accessible to European Shipping.

THE compiler of Spon's "Encyclopædia of the Industrial Arts," an authoritative work of reference, speaks of the Russian official estimate of 14,000 square miles composing the area of the petroleum territory of the Russian Empire, as "obviously exaggerated." I do not see what grounds exist for such a sweeping statement. Petroleum abounds in the Vistula province, in the Governments of Samara and Saratoff on the Volga, in the Petchora region of the distant North, and in the territory of Ferghana, on the confines of Afghanistan. But, excluding all these, and restricting ourselves entirely to the Caucasus and Caspian, we have there oil strata running direct from the Crimea, across the Caucasus, and under the

Caspian, to the Balkan Hills beyond—a distance of 1,500 miles, which, with a hypothetical breadth of ten miles, would alone give more than the area referred to.

The petroleum springs in the Crimea have never been worked or investigated to any extent, and I am told they are too far from the coast to pay at present the speculator. Crossing the sea of Azoff, we come to the Taman Peninsula, famous even in classical times for its petroleum springs. These are described as most resembling those of Pennsylvania, the oil, compared with the Baku supply, being meagre and soaking into the wells, rather than forming huge cellular reservoirs, or underground ponds, as in the case of Caspian petroleum. But, as a matter of fact, the petroleum fields of the Kuban region have never been thoroughly explored, and it is not improbable that the supply may be more copious than is generally imagined. It was in this district that the first spouting-well, or oil-fountain, made its appearance in the Caucasus, forming, in 1866, on Novoseltseff's estate an immense lake, which overflowing, penetrated to a branch of the river Kudako and ran out to sea. Ten years ago there were twenty-two wells and tubes in operation, producing 1,500 tons of oil annually. In 1875 there were forty-two wells, producing 4,000 tons. Latterly, as I have already stated, a French company has successfully bored for oil sixty miles inland of Novorossisk, and pumped it through pipes to a kerosine refinery on Novorossisk bay. Except for Baku, this petroleum region would probably have undergone considerable development, but while crude petroleum can be delivered at the Baku railway station for transport to Batoum for a few pence the ton, it will not pay to exploit the oil in the rocky, woody, roadless region of Kuban.

Proceeding further east, the next place where the petroleum is extracted to any extent is in the Ter and Tiflis districts, where also the oil has been used for ages.

In 1874 there were 113 wells in the former, producing 400 tons, and in the latter fourteen producing nearly 2,000 tons. Later statistics I have not been able to obtain. Further east still, there are wells in Daghestan giving a few hundred tons of oil annually to the mountaineers, and then we come to the Apsheron peninsula, jutting into the Caspian, which, when its oil fountains are playing 200 or 300 feet high, might not unfitly be compared to a huge spermaceti whale. From the mouth of the Samur river at the north of the peninsula, to the mouth of the Kura in the south, a distance of 200 miles, the whole of the region may be regarded as oil producing country. In this manner the entire chain of the Caucasus, 720 miles long, possesses petroleum, scattered for the most part sporadically over the surface of the interior, but welling up in vast quantities at the two extremities—the Taman peninsula in the Black Sea, and the Apsheron peninsula in the Caspian. Between these two points the oil is found at an altitude of 9,000 feet above the sea level, and 600 feet below it.

Respecting the Apsheron peninsula and its chief oil producing districts near Baku, I shall say more directly. Let me, as briefly as possible, dismiss the Caspian. From the extremity of the Apsheron peninsula to Krasnovodsk, a distance of 200 miles, a mountain ridge runs under the sea, sustaining an old local tradition that ages ago, before it was depressed by some volcanic action, it divided the Caspian into two lakes. This ridge, there is every reason to believe, is full of oil. At any rate, whereever it juts up to the surface oil flows from the reef. Russian sailors call these projections "Oil Rocks." The extent to which they eject petroleum seems to depend upon the weather. Holy Island, which lies a few miles off the extremity of the Apsheron peninsula, abounds with petroleum, which was once regularly exploited by the Persians. Tcheleken Island, on the opposite side of the sea, was famous in classical times for its springs of oil, and, according to Russian surveys I have by me, is literally a soddened mass of petroleum and ozokerit. Between these two islands there are numerous spots, where oil floats up to the surface of the Caspian, and a still larger number where the petroleum gas bubbles to the top. In Baku bay, between the Bailoff and Shikhoff promontories, there was a spot, now converted into a well by extending an artificial peninsula to it, where the gas used to come to the surface with sufficient force to upset boats passing over the eddies. The well was won from the sea by Selim Khan, and is called the Selimkhanoff well. It is situated close to the village of Shikhoff. If a light be applied on a calm day to the gas bubbles in parts of Baku bay, acres of water become covered with flame, the size of the phenomenon being dependent, it is said, on the direction of the wind previously prevailing. The flames do not give out any very great heat, as Mr. Ludwig Nobel once found when, by way of experiment, he drove his steam launch right through the water while thus ignited.

The Caspian traversed, there is a brief interval of desert, followed by the Balkan hills, where, since the final annexation of the region by Russia in 1881, extraordinary deposits of petroleum have been discovered. That oil existed there was long known, for the Turcomans used to extract it from wells and convey it on camel-back to Khiva. But it was not until 1881, when a party of engineers, while searching for water for the new railway, suddenly alighted upon the "Naphtha Hill," that Russia became aware of the value of what the Duke of Argyll used to designate her "barren and costly acquisitions." This hill lies sixteen and a half miles southwest of the Tageer wells, and fifty-three from the railway, with which it is connected by a Decauville miniature railroad. Shortly after it was discovered, a Baku oil exploiter—Prince Eristoff—quietly staked the whole property as his own, and began to make preparations for working it. The Governor of the Transcaspian region, General Röhrberg, however, heard of this annexation, and sent a geological engineer to the spot to survey it, when an estimate was made that the ozokerit and oil in the hill thus coolly appropriated were worth £35,000,000 sterling. Upon receipt of this news the Governor had Eristoff's stakes pulled up, and the Decauville railroad removed from Bami to the spot, so as to enable the locomotives to obtain their own supply of petroleum fuel from the locality, instead of importing it from Baku. At present there is only one well bored, giving ten tons of petroleum daily, which is amply sufficient for the wants of the railway. Konshin, the mining engineer in charge, reported last year that there were 20,000 acres of petroleum land round about the hill, which could easily furnish 1,000,000 tons of oil annually; that is to say, enough to light every lamp, grease every machine, and drive every locomotive in the Russian empire. Other deposits exist in the neighbourhood, which have not yet been surveyed. When the Transcaspian railway is extended further in the direction of India, as it will some day be, this "Black California," as the Russians call the place, will not only provide fuel for the line, but also fuel and kerosine for the people of Khorassan, Afghanistan, and Central Asia, who experience much suffering and inconvenience from a deficiency of both. The deposits will thus acquire immense importance. At present, while Baku is giving such a copious supply, we may regard the Transcaspian deposits as a reserve.

In this manner there are three great outlets for the Caucasus-Caspian petroleum deposits—the Taman and Apsheron peninsulas at the two extremities of the chain, and the districts of Tcheleken and Black California, which we may couple together, on the east side of the

Caspian. The latter constitute the extremity of the strata, no more petroleum being found further in that direction, so far as my knowledge of Central Asia extends, until Ferghana is reached, quite 1,000 miles beyond.

Returning to the Apsheron peninsula, a glance at the map will show that it extends 60 or 70 miles into the Caspian Sea. Baku is situated where the projection begins to break away from the coast line of the Caucasus. The peninsula there is about 20 miles broad from sea to sea. The oil plateau under exploitation lies midway between the two flanks of the peninsula, at a height of 175 ft. above the level of the Caspian Sea. The wells are thus sufficiently elevated to almost allow of the oil finding its way by gravity to the refineries situated on Baku bay, six or eight miles from them. There are two great groups of wells, the Surakhani and the Balakhani. The former exist on the site of the old Fire-Worshippers' temples, where the petroleum gas has been issuing from the ground from the pre-historic period. Only two or three companies carry on operations here. The majority are gathered at Balakhani, or, more correctly, on the Balakhani-Saboontchi plateau. Formerly all the oil was extracted at Surakhani; then a start was made at Balakhani, six miles to the west, where a more copious supply was discovered, and drilling operations were found to be more easily carried on. By degrees the oil fields grew till they encroached upon, and covered the Saboontchi plateau also. The collective area of the two plateaux under exploitation is now about a couple of square miles. Most of the 400 drilled wells of the Apsheron peninsula are collected on this small patch of ground, the properties being mingled together in apparently inextricable confusion. The wells are most inconveniently crowded, but the Russians and Armenians prefer to continue working the plateau to seeking oil elsewhere beyond its limits. On the plateau they are sure to get oil, but they are not so sure of oil outside it, and when the price of crude petroleum rules at 3d. or 4d. per ton there is no temptation for speculators to go sinking wells on virgin ground. If it be remembered that none of the wells have yet got lower than 825 ft., in spite of the terrific outbursts of oil, and that this lowest distance is the distance when American borers only begin to think of finding a supply of oil, it will be seen that the Balakhani well-owners have no temptation whatever to resign their sites, however crowded they may be, for others elsewhere. This policy does not imply any disbelief in the existence of rich oil-lands outside the present boundary. On the contrary, there is plenty of evidence to support the opposite view. Thus, there was a time when the Balakhani plateau alone was exploited; the same overcrowding existed in it; but although land could be had very much cheaper on the contiguous Saboontchi plateau, no one attempted to avail himself of the opportunity. At length, step by step, the Balakhani oil fields encroached upon the Saboontchi plateau, and it was found that it had a richer supply than Balakhani. Since then the biggest fountains have occurred in this neglected locality, and land which might have been bought for a trifle a few years ago is now literally worth its weight in gold.

Six miles to the west, across the Boyook salines, are several wells at the village of Binagadi, at the foot of the mountain Boyook Dagh; and a couple of miles south-west of these is a well or two close to an extinct mud volcano, alongside a lake of asphalte. When the market for petroleum increases, these latter, as well as other points undeveloped yet, will become as active as Balakhani. At present oil is such a drug that nobody has the heart to go boring for what no profitable sale can be found for, after it is got to the surface.

The peninsula, with its shoulders, possesses an area of

1,200 square miles of oil-bearing land. Of this area not more than three square miles have yet been developed. Were this oil extracted from strata, it might be affirmed that in working the three square miles the well-owners were exhausting the land lying outside the area. But the fact of the oil existing, not in beds or strata, but in countless cells, disposes of any such fear. The borers exhaust only the ground immediately below them; they do not interfere at all with the oil lying a short distance beyond. Throughout these three square miles the boring rods have never yet penetrated deeper than oil usually begins to be found in America. Yet the amount the wells have furnished since 1832 reaches the enormous total of 4,000,000 tons of petroleum. This quantity from 400 wells looks prodigious; yet, on the other hand, if spread over the three square miles, it would not represent a layer deeper than eighteen inches.

Geologically, little or nothing is known about the Caspian petroleum region. It has been ascertained that the oil rests in Tertiary beds overlying Miocene, but, beyond this simple fact, science is mute or at fault, and even the engineers working the wells confess themselves ignorant of the conditions regulating the supply of petroleum. Twenty years ago Baku was visited by a very eminent savant, Professor Abich, who possesses a wide celebrity on the Continent. Abich explored the Apsheron peninsula several times, and from his observations deduced certain theories, many of which have proved to be more or less wrong. He predicted, for instance, that no petroleum would be found after a depth of 60 or 70 feet, and counselled the Baku engineers to bore no lower. But practice has proved his prediction to be lamentably inaccurate. As far as 70 feet, wells give only from a few hundredweight to a couple of tons of oil per diem. Dissatisfied with this result, the Baku people disregarded Abich's advice, and boring 300 feet, found oil flowing at the rate of 150 tons a day. In Group XIV., at Balakhani, a fountain was struck at 250 feet, yielding 250 tons every twenty-four hours.

A few years later, in 1873, when more data were forthcoming to guide the *savant*, Trautschold visited Baku, and declared that no oil would be found of any value below 200 feet. After 140 feet, he held that the oil would lose its virtue. But events proved him to be altogether wrong. Crude petroleum has been obtained from a depth of 825 feet, quite as good as that exuding naturally from the surface.

Later on, Professor Mendelaieff made a journey to Baku. No Russian *savant* has a higher place in the esteem of English scientific men than Mendelaieff. In 1882, the Royal Society conferred upon him the Davey medal for his researches. On his return from Baku, Mendelaieff wrote a monograph upon the American and Caucasian petroleum fields; but there is nothing in that which has proved of any great value to the petroleum borer. He declared the region to be incomparably richer than that of America, which he also had visited,—but that was known beforehand, and was no new discovery; and he penned a brilliant essay on the origin of petroleum, which the Baku engineers and chemists, in common with a large number of scientific men, do not believe in, and which, whether right or wrong, has been of no service in accurately determining the conditions under which petroleum may infallibly be obtained. Receiving, thus, no aid from science, or, what is worse, repeatedly misled by exponents of it, the Baku people have had to bore for oil by guesswork. It has been quite a lottery. Oil has always been found, but it has been altogether a matter of luck whether at 100 feet, 200 feet, or 500 feet. With the exception of Nobel Brothers, none of the firms keep any record of the geology of their wells. There is consequently an absence of adequate data for the *savant* to work upon. Nobel Brothers have, I believe, geological records of the whole of their wells, and the theory held by Ludwig Nobel, deduced from them, seems to me the only one to meet the case. This theory is, that the oil-bearing strata, originally running regularly in an almost diagonal direction, became dislocated and thrust hither and thither horizontally during some volcanic disturbance, and a sort of irregular cellular character given to the petroleum deposits.

No other theory seems to me to satisfactorily explain how that the 400 wells and fountains existing at present at Baku should display, except in a few instances, no connection with one another, although most of them are disposed close together on less than a thousand square acres of ground. The independence of the wells shows unquestionably that although the subterranean fluids may at some time have been collected in one vast series of reservoirs, in regular strata, they must now be confined in innumerable sub-divided basins, having no connection between them. Let me give a few instances. Near the village of Strikhoff, at Bibi Aibat, a short time ago there were four wells giving oil within a few yards of one another—yet all at different depths, the first at 259 feet, the second at 560, the third at 280, and the fourth at 350. Close to them was a more striking instance. An old well existed, 70 feet deep, which for generations had furnished petroleum. The engineers set up a derrick a few yards from it, expecting to get oil readily at about the same depth, but did not strike any until they had penetrated 420 feet. At Surakhani, Meerzoeff sank a well 700 feet deep before reaching oil, although close by there were several pits giving oil at the depth of 100. If the oil were collected in a single reservoir, or in basins joined to one another, it is obvious that the fountains that often occur would exhaust the surrounding localities. The Droojba fountain, for example, which I saw in September spouting oil at the rate of two million gallons per diem from a depth of 574 feet, would have ruined all the neighbouring wells of a lesser depth had the reservoir been a general one. As a matter of fact, while it was shooting its oil 300 feet high, the wells a stone's throw off were giving their daily supply of petroleum, totally unaffected by it. Many pumping wells have been worked for years without the level of the oil being lowered in the slightest degree, or the wells in any way affected by discharges from adjoining fountains proceeding from greater or lesser depths. The peninsula of Apsheron is probably honey-combed with thousands of oil cells. One of these cells, belonging to Kokereff, has already given a million and a half of barrels of oil, and yet the pump draws the oil as freely and as readily to the surface as when the basin was first tapped by the boring bit years ago.

The subterranean basins vary considerably in size, but while well-filled cells are often found close to the surface, experience seems to show that the deeper the Baku people bore the more copious the supply. At any rate, the Baku firms are boring deeper every year, and every year the fountains become more terrific. The rule is, when a cell is tapped, to let the oil flow to the surface—if it does flow—until it ceases running, and then to pump it. When the cell is sucked dry, the engineers begin to bore again, and go on boring till another one is reached. This process goes on continually until some copious supply is reached, which is sufficient to last for years. This, as in the case of the Kokereff well, sometimes assumes a permanent character. In America, a depth of 1,000 feet is thought nothing of in boring for oil; a man is not particularly discouraged if he penetrates as far without discovering petroleum. In Baku, however, an engineer begins to look for it at 100 feet, and no well has yet got lower than 825. In 1883 two flowing wells in less than a month upheaved nearly 30,000,000 gallons of oil apiece from a depth of 700 feet, and when they were finally plugged, to "cork up" their supply for future use, they were still flowing at a rate of about 20,000 gallons of oil per diem. Nobel Brothers have got 14 such wells "corked up," because crude petroleum will not fetch more than a few pence a ton at Baku just now. Yet the deepest of these 14 basins, crammed with oil, is less than 800 feet from the surface. In America there are a number of wells in the Bradford region 2,000 or 3,000 feet deep, and one in West Virginia which will soon be 5,000.

That the Baku supply is immense is a point that is beyond the reach of controversy. Nobody has ever questioned it. It is therefore really unnecessary to defend what has never been attacked. As regards the inexhaustibility of the supply the case is different. One or two cavilling cries have been raised against Baku. But these have not proceeded from Russian experts at Baku, or from foreign experts who have visited the region. In a word, nobody who knows anything personally of Baku has ever entertained any doubts on the subject. The cry has simply been raised by importers of American oil, angry at the impending lowering of the market by the inrush of oil from Baku. I do not desire to carry conviction to these, but from the facts I have given, the public will shrewdly gather that if the petroleum cells in the three exploited square miles of Baku are sufficient to supply the whole of Europe with oil, there must be enough left in the basins lower than 825 feet, and in the untouched 1,197 square miles of the Apsheron peninsula, to stock the markets of the world for ages.

With regard to the accessibility of the supply, the Baku deposits lie about the same distance from the Black Sea coast that the American oil-fields do from the Atlantic littoral. If the Suram pass of the Lesser Caucasus acts as an impediment lacking in the case of America, it should be remembered that steps are already being taken to remove the obstacle; and that, further, Baku possesses in the Caspian and Volga a splendid water-way, close to the oil fields, surpassing the communications of Pennsylvania. To this should be added, that for the last four years the crude oil has been selling on the spot at Baku at the maximum rate 14 times cheaper than on the spot in Pennsylvania, while the minimum rate prevailing last autumn was 112 times cheaper than that of the American oil. It is obvious that such cheapness allows a very wide margin for profit.

CHAPTER XIII.

A DRIVE TO THE OIL WELLS.

The Phaetons at Baku—Driving to Balakhani—The Salines of the Apsheron Peninsula—Passing the Black Town—The Gardens and Vineyards of the Peninsula—Aspect of the Great Droojba Fountain from Baku—The Pipe-lines—Too Clever by Half—Baku Oil Transport before the Pipe-line Period—Grandiose Schemes for Pipe-lines to Europe—The Projected Oleoduct to the Persian Gulf—Duty on Iron Pipes—Capacity of the Pipe-lines—Aspect of the Balakhani Oil Plateau—How America Gained Upon and Beat the Old Baku Oil Supply—Statistics of the Monopoly Period—Present Free Trade Enjoyed by the Industry—The Excise Period—Recent Revolutions in the Trade—Stimulus Given by the Swedish Engineers—Robert and Ludwig Nobel—Prices of Crude Petroleum for the last Twenty Years—Number of Drilled Wells—Effect of the Batoum Railway upon the Industry.

THE petroleum wells lie eight or nine miles distant from Baku. The journey is mostly done by phaeton. It may also be accomplished by railway by means of the Petroleum Branch (Neftiani Ootchastok) of the Transcaucasian railroad; a train running from Baku Station to Surakhani at 11.45 A.M., arriving there at 12.28 P.M. and returning in the afternoon at 2.15. To Saboontchi and Balakhani two trains run daily, at 9.25 A.M. and 5.10 P.M., doing the distance in half an hour, and returning respectively at 10.25 A.M. and 6.25 P.M. But a phaeton drive is far preferable to the railroad. To get to Baku Station, in the first place, one must take a phaeton, the road being too bad for walking, and when the Saboontchi or Surakhani Station is reached another phaeton is needed to convey the traveller through the oil fields. The best plan, therefore, is for him to step out from the hotel, and, having selected a good phaeton, bargain with the driver for the trip. If the suburban streets in Baku are horribly paved, or rather not paved at all, consisting simply of jutting rock and shifting sand, there is an excellent set-off in the superiority of the vehicles. These "phaetons," as they are locally designated, are roomy and furnished with splendid springs; and in most instances are drawn by a pair of horses, which for vigour and endurance afford a marked contrast to the horseflesh we are accustomed to in our London streets. The drivers are Tartars, and a superior class of men compared with the *isvostchiks* usually met in Russian towns. The charge for driving to any part inside Baku is 15 copecks, or 4d.* The journey to Balakhani or Surakhani occupies more than two hours. For going there and back, and waiting at different points while his fare inspects the wells, the driver expects three or four roubles. As no refreshments are to be had on the road or at the wells, the traveller should take something with him, particularly something to assuage his thirst, the journey most of the year round being a warm and dusty one. In inspecting the derricks, he can hardly escape having his helmet and coat splashed with oil, and even if he turns up the bottom of his trousers he is sure to soil them in traversing the

* This is for two persons; for three or four the charge is 20 copecks. By the hour the charge is 50 copecks. To the Black Town, as far as Nobel's Works, the fare is 50 copecks, and 50 copecks back. To the railway station the fare is 20 copecks for two persons, and 30 copecks for four; to the goods' station 30 copecks for two persons, and 40 copecks for four; from the railway station to the town 30 copecks for two persons, and from the goods' station 40 copecks. Luggage, not carried in the hand, is charged 15 copecks extra at the end of the journey. The fares are fixed by the town authorities. After two o'clock in the morning the driver may charge double fare.

sand, ankle-deep, and moist with oil, round about the wells. It is a mistake, therefore, to go out to the wells too well dressed. Should he do so, however, and spoil his clothes, there are several tailors' shops opposite the Hôtel d'Europe where the grease will be extracted as cheaply and as thoroughly as in England.

If the weather be not too warm, the journey to the wells is not an unpleasant one, even for anybody unaccustomed to a good hard bit of travelling; the novelty of the drive provoking an interest rendering him insensible to the dust and the heat. The track, for there is no road, lies the whole way across sheer desert. The surface consists of rugged limestone, the ruts and the jagged projections being cased here and there by a layer of dust. Vegetation there is none, save the everlasting camel-thorn, which, when thick, imparts occasionally a green tint to the landscape. Now and again a black patch is seen; this is one of the numerous petroleum springs dotting the Apsheron peninsula. Close to Balakhani depressions are observed, covered with a dazzling white efflorescence; these are salt lakes, of which there are any number in this part of the Caucasus. When one gets into Balakhani itself, the white lakes are replaced by black ones—lakes of crude petroleum oil, in many of which there is plenty of room for boats to row. These lakes are often set on fire and burnt, to get rid of the oil, while millions pine for more light and fuel in Western Europe.

The town of Baku left behind, the traveller has on his right the *Tchorni Gorod*, or Black Town, where the 200 refineries are situated. These stretch along the bay, and belch forth smoke like a concentrated Birmingham. Afterwards the ground rises, and while the phaeton is crawling up it, there is a fine view of Baku Bay. If the wind be blowing from the sea, the breeze is pleasant, and moderates the intense heat of the sun, shining from a turquoise-blue firmament upon the rugged Apsheron peninsula. Further on, the railway is crossed, and then a whole bunch of pipe-lines are met running in a higgledy-piggledy fashion towards the Black Town, conveying the crude oil thither from the wells. The hills about are dotted with reservoirs, containing thousands of tons of oil. No villages or settlements exist between Baku and Balakhani, and not a structure is seen the whole distance, except a ruined stone watch-house at intervals, erected by Ludwig Nobel to protect his first pipe-line —the first in the country—from the infuriated Tartar carriers, whose lucrative pursuit was cut short when the pipe-line superseded the conveyance of oil in barrel. But although there are no habitations, there is plenty of traffic along the track. Crowds of donkey-boys are passed, with panniers crammed with grapes, going to Baku, or returning with empty ones from it. Most travellers describe the Apsheron peninsula as a total desert, but this is a mistake. On the northern side are many miles of gardens stretching along the shore, one strip—from the village of Gerodeel to Beelgia—having a length of twelve miles with a breadth in one place of five. This lies on the neck of the peninsula exactly opposite Baku, about twenty miles by road, and from it every day hundreds of camels and donkeys are sent to the town, laden with fruit and vegetables. For two or three copecks, the donkey boys will part with as many grapes as the greediest person could desire on a very hot day.

After driving a few miles, the traveller sees before him a whole series of wooden sentry-box looking structures, clustered together. These are the 400 derricks surmounting the wells of Balakhani. Should a fountain be spouting, a black cloud will be observed hanging over one of the derricks. The Droojba fountain, which during the first few days spouted 300 feet high, I saw easily without a glass from some rising ground near Baku eight miles distant. It had the aspect then of the conventional eruption of Vesuvius. The roar of the oil could be distinctly heard two or three miles before I got to the derrick.

Following the pipe-lines, the phaeton approaches closer to Shore Ozera—a saline lake five or six miles long by a mile and a half broad, flanking Balakhani, and then makes a sharp detour round it to the well-region on the other side. Only one pipe-line follows the road in this winding, the rest go straight across the lake on stone supports. With the exception of Meerzoeff's pipe, they sprawl across the ground anyhow; winding and twisting over the undulations of the desert, bridging chasms on the roughest of piers, and stretching stark across the road without any attempt to bury themselves in the surface out of the way of the traffic. But there is method in this apparent madness. While five of the lines run anyhow, the sixth is soberly laid on iron chairs on masonry supports the whole way from Balakhani to Baku town. For nine miles it is stretched as straight as a telegraph wire, and the level is sought to be maintained by cutting ditches through the hills and raising the ground in the depressions. "What a model to the rest!" exclaims the novice, as he views this elaborate piece of engineering, "it must sure belong to Nobel Brothers"—for one of the first things he learns when he arrives at Baku is, that Ludwig Nobel's organization is perfect in every respect. But, on the contrary, Nobel's lines run with the untidy ones, and when these are examined it is found that while none of them leak at all, or only to a trifling extent here and there, Meerzoeff's level pipe-line exudes oil at every joint. The cause is readily explained. The pipe is laid down too stiff and too straight to expand or contract, with the result that after costing twice as much to place in position as the other pipe-lines, it

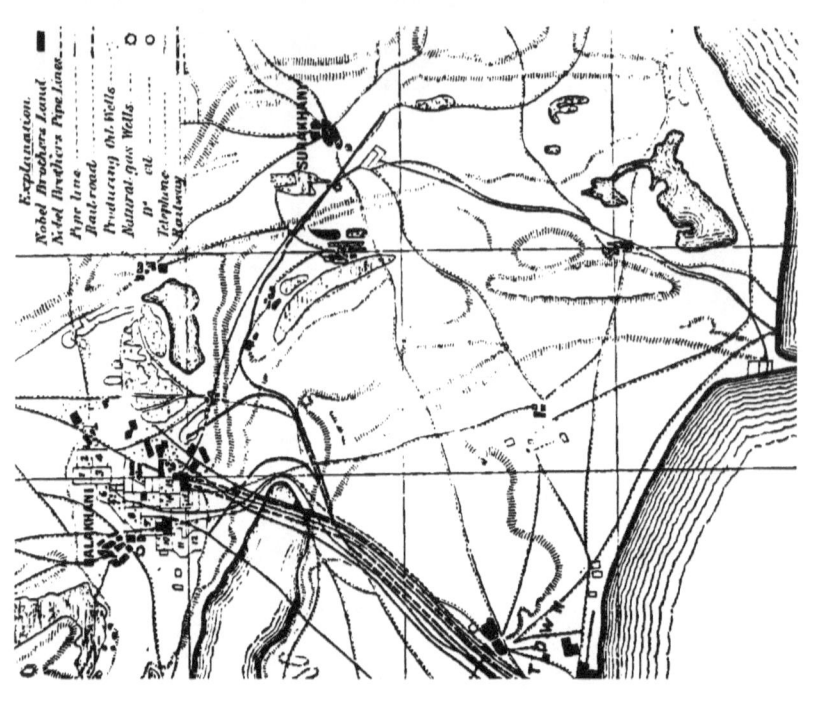

causes its owner ten times the loss in leakage. Meerzoeff's pipe-line was erected immediately after Nobel had demonstrated the system to be a financial success; but some ultra-technical Russian engineer thought he could improve on the lesson taught Baku by the practical Swede, and in his anxiety to construct a handsome and regular work forgot all about expansion.

Six pipe-lines run from Balakhani to the Black Town of Baku. Another extends from Balakhani to Surakhani, and thence to the outer part of Baku Bay, close to Sultan Point, to the kerosine refinery of the Zikhski Association. This belongs to the Baku Petroleum Company, and not being always required for oil, is often employed by Nobel Brothers for pumping water from the bay to their wells. The total length of the seven pipe-lines amounts to over 60 miles.

Pipe-lines are quite a modern institution at Baku, having only been introduced by Nobel Brothers during the last few years. Previous to that the oil used to be conveyed in barrels down to the coast. Mr. Arthur Arnold, M.P., who visited Baku in 1875, gives an interesting account in his " Through Persia by Caravan," of what the system was then :—"All day long petroleum rolls into Baku in carts of the most curious pattern imaginable. A Neapolitan single-horse two-wheeled carriage for fifteen people is unique, but it is commonplace in comparison with an oil cart of Baku. Few men would have the courage to import a Baku oil cart and drive it even for a very high wager through Regent Street or Pall Mall. Where is the man who would dare to pose himself there, perched and caged in a little rail cart big enough to hold one barrel of petroleum, and lifted so high on wheels seven feet in diameter, that another tub can be slung beneath the axle, the whole thing being painted with all the colours of the rainbow, and creaking loudly as it is drawn by a diminutive horse, the back of which is hardly up to a level with the axle? Yet the *exploiteurs* say that already they pay collectively not much less than £100,000 a year for the cartage of oil in carriages of this sort." When Nobel Brothers commenced refining operations in 1875, thousands of *arbas* or carts were employed in this operation. To diminish the expense, and insure a larger and more rapid supply, the Swedes endeavoured to persuade the Baku firms to combine and lay down a pipe. But jealousy and want of enterprise have always been the characteristics of the Russian and native firms of Baku. They refused. Thereupon the Swedes laid down the pipe-line themselves, at a cost of £10,000, and recovered the outlay the first year. This was the death knell of the *arbas*. Other lines were laid down in rapid succession by rival firms, or combinations of them, and the oil carts almost entirely disappeared from Baku. Pipe-lines have now become a recognized institution in the district. Not only is all the crude oil conveyed from the wells to the refineries by them, but they also join the 200 refineries one with the other and with the piers in the bay. Local feeling at present runs riot the other way. Grandiose schemes are constantly being discussed for conveying the oil to Europe. One of these, in favour several years ago, was a pipe-line a thousand miles long, running from Baku across the Caucasus to the railway system in South-East Russia. Another extended from Baku to the Black Sea at Poti or Batoum. This may be regarded as the most practicable, and if any pipe-line ever be laid down from Baku, this will inevitably be the one. At present there is a deal of talk of running a pipe-line from Baku to the Persian Gulf, with the idea of securing Baku the exclusive control of the markets of Asia. This would be 1,200 miles long, and could only be constructed with foreign capital.

Before ridiculing such schemes, it should be borne in

mind that in America the Standard Oil Company controls nearly 4,000 miles of pipe-line, or enough not only to pump the oil from Baku to the Persian Gulf, but beyond to the principal bazaars of India. A section of the Standard Oil Company's pipe-line, 2,500 miles long, would be sufficient to pump the oil from Baku to London.

The average diameter of the pipe-lines at Baku is six inches. The average cost of a six-inch pipe-line is reckoned at 8,000 roubles a verst, or £800 for two-thirds of a mile. Nobel Brothers' two pipe-lines, with pumping stations, cost collectively £76,000 to lay down. The pipes are made in Russia or Germany, and are conveyed by rail to the Volga, whence they are despatched by steamer to Baku. Now that the Batoum railroad is open, it ought to be cheaper to buy them in Western Europe and send them to Baku by that route. The duty on iron pipes of foreign manufacture however is very heavy, and an estimate has been made that the duty on pipes for a line 500 miles long, from Baku to the Black Sea would, amount to more than half a million sterling. A six-inch pipe should stand, I am told, a pressure of at least 1,000 lbs. to the inch, but none at Baku are worked above 200 lbs. Petroleum fuel is used in all the pumping stations; Blake's pumps have the preference, and many Tangye boilers are at work in the district. The Balakhani wells being situated 175 feet above the level of the sea, no intermediate stations are needed between the wells and the refineries. The total capacity of the seven pipe-lines is estimated at two million gallons of oil every twenty-four hours. The railway possesses two stations, east and west of the Balakhani wells, and a third at Surakhani, thus enabling it to convey crude oil in tank-cars from the wells to the refineries, or, if necessary, direct to the Black Sea. In 1882 the following quantity of crude oil was pumped through the pipe-line or conveyed by tank-car to Baku :—

Pipe-Lines.	Gallons.
2. Nobel Brothers, 2 pipes	77,254,324
3. Fedoroff and Pavloff	28,654,460
4. Lianozoff and Co.	15,312,484
5. Meerzoeff Sons	14,720,142
6. Baku Petroleum Company	13,426,240
7. Caspian Company	12,008,000
	161,375,640
Railway	50,544,180
Total	211,919,820

The two pipe-lines of Nobel Brothers have a united capacity for despatching annually 4,000,000 barrels of crude petroleum to the coast. The pipe-line owners not only pump their own oil from the wells, but also that of other persons who have no other means of transport. Apart from the seven principal pipe-lines, all the 200 refineries at Baku are interlaced between themselves, the 25 piers, and the reservoirs of the pipe-line proprietors, by a regular network of pipes, the aggregate length of which I have never seen stated, but which must run into some hundred of miles.

The detour round the salt lake of Shore Ozera effected, the traveller finds himself on the Balakhani-Saboontchi plateau, with a panorama spread before him of dingy tall derricks, low one-storey Persian stone buildings, log shanties, iron reservoirs in shape like gasometers, and greasy wooden engine sheds, mingled in groups in inextricable confusion, and having no visible mark or barrier to separate the one property from the other. Throughout the plateau, no intelligible road exists. In place of highways are innumerable paths and tracks, and these seam the oil-soddened surface in every direction, and with a network of pipe-lines, petroleum channels, and ponds and lakes of oil, utterly bewilder the stranger. To make confusion worse, many of the well-owners, and particularly Nobel Brothers, have not got their wells all in one spot, but possess several in different parts of the plateau, which for administrative purposes, is divided into about 20 "groups" of wells. To the west of the plateau is the village of Balakhani. This consists of several hundred white one-storey stone houses of the Persian style of architecture, and is large enough to claim the designation of town. A considerable number of people employed at the wells live there.

The first thought that strikes the observer as he surveys the lakes of oil before him is—Why Baku, having the richest supply of petroleum in the world, worked ages before the American oil was touched, should have nevertheless allowed the United States to take possession of the markets of both hemispheres, including for a time the very important one of Russia itself. The matter is susceptible of easy explanation. Until the Russians completed railway communication between the Black Sea and the Caspian, Baku was severed from the world. In summer it was not a very difficult undertaking to get to the place *viâ* the Volga; but when that river was frozen over in winter, Baku was practically cut off from the European system of communications. The only way to reach the place was to proceed to Vladikavkaz or Tiflis by rail, and post the rest of the distance through the Caucasus to Baku. This was not encouraging for capitalists, especially if it be remembered that it was not until 1878 that the last traces of independence were crushed out of the Caucasus, and the region delivered from further fear of tribal insurrection.

But there is another explanation which goes more deeply to the root of the matter. One of the first things the Russians did when they acquired Baku from the Persians in the early part of the century, was to make the extraction of the oil a crown monopoly, which they farmed out to a merchant named Meerzoeff.

Experience in all countries, in all ages has shown that

nothing is more fatal to the development of an industry, than for the State to render it a close monopoly. The petroleum industry at Baku was no exception to the general rule. The protective system of the Russians, following upon centuries of free trade under the Persians, stunted the growth of the petroleum trade. The industry grew, but its development was nothing like what it would have been, had there been no Government restriction.

The fatal monopoly check upon foreign and native enterprise was not removed until 1872, that is to say, twelve years after the American oil had already secured a foothold in the European market.

When the petroleum industry was at length emancipated from Meerzoeff, the Government instituted a fresh impediment in the shape of an excise duty. This latter obstacle was also removed in 1877, and now no tax is levied on the industry, nor is there any restriction in the shape of official supervision or disabilities in regard to foreigners. It would be impossible for a business to be less meddled with. The Russian Government has certainly made up for its past errors on this score. There is not an industry in Russia to-day where the *laisser faire* doctrine is carried to such lengths as in the Baku petroleum trade, and in this respect it will stand comparison not only with that of Galicia, but with the freest portion of the United States' oil-fields.

From 1821 to 1825, Meerzoeff paid the Government 131,000 roubles revenue, and afterwards, up to 1839, from 76,000 to 97,000 roubles a year, or, at the high rate of the silver rouble then prevailing (ranging between six and seven roubles to the pound sterling), on an average about £10,000 or £12,000 a year. During this period the production of crude petroleum rose steadily to more than a million gallons. Afterwards the output was as under:—

	Tons.	Revenue in Roubles.
1840	3,565	105,000
1841	3,421	117,000
1842	3,470	124,000
1843	3,434	119,000
1844	3,443	125,000
1845	3,432	100,000
1846	3,480	93,000
1847	3.490	94,000
1848	4,351	108,000
1849	3,340	100,178

During these ten years, it will be seen, there was scarcely any advance, and in the end an actual falling off. In 1849 there were about 130 pit wells in operation. Between 1850 and 1863, petroleum yielded a total revenue of 1,195,000 roubles. From then to 1867 the average revenue yearly was 162,000 roubles, and afterwards until the abolition of the monopoly in 1872, 136,000 roubles. The production in the meanwhile was as under:—

PRODUCTION OF CRUDE PETROLEUM DURING THE MONOPOLY PERIOD.

	Tons.		Tons.
1863	5,484	1868	11,900
1864	8,700	1869	27,180
1865	8,900	1870	27,500
1866	11,100	1871	22,200
1867	16,100	1872	24,800

While the production of Baku had thus been only slowly advancing, America had completely established her industry, and flooded not only Europe but the whole of Russia with her cheap burning oil. That an oil only recently discovered should gain upon and surpass in this prodigious manner an older oil, the existence of which had been known for 2,500 years, which had been regularly sold for 500 years, and for fifty years had been an exported commodity controlled by the State itself, was a most galling circumstance for Russia. Urged to action by the indignant clamour of the press, the Government appointed a commission to inquire into the petroleum industry, and at the end of 1872 the monopoly was abolished and the trade thrown open to the world.

A few figures will give an idea of the industry when this impediment was wisely removed. Total production of petroleum in 1872, 24,800 tons; number of pit wells, 415; number of drilled wells, 2; price of crude oil per pood, 45 copecks, or, at the rate of exchange then prevailing, about £3 10s. 0d. per ton—it is now a few pence per ton; Government revenue from the same £17,000 a year; number of refineries 50; quantity of oil refined 6,450 tons.

When the monopoly was abolished, there was at once a rush to acquire oil property and develop it. The ground belonged to the State, and was sold on a freehold or leasehold tenure, or was given to high officials as a reward for their services. Of the former 1,836 acres were sold in 1872 for £30,000; as much as £3,500 an acre being paid for some of the plots. The rent fixed for the leased land was on an average ten roubles the *desiatine*, or about 7s. 6d. the acre. Some of the Caucasus officials received large plots, General Lazareff, who stormed Kars, getting, for instance, ten acres of the best land, which is now worked by his son. Other officials sold their property for a trifling sum as soon as they received it. For a time fancy prices were paid for plots, but of late years, owing to the oil becoming a drug, it has been easy to obtain land on very favourable terms.

Meerzoeff, of course, stood at the head of the trade when the monopoly was abolished. He bought of the Government forty *desiatines*, or about 115 acres, for £130,000; and having two large kerosine refineries, retained for a moment the monopoly of the export market. But he did not hold this position long. In 1873 the Khalify Company, in boring for oil, struck the first fountain at Baku and became the possessors of the largest flow of oil. So fast grew the stock that the price dropped from forty-five copecks to five copecks per pood, above which it has only advanced occasionally since. A year later the Transcaspian Trading Company was established, with a capital of half a million sterling, to develop the resources of the Caspian region, and transforming itself into the Baku Petroleum Company, took the lead in the oil business. Finally, in 1875, Robert Nobel started a refinery at Baku, and, in conjunction with his brother Ludwig, organized in a few years a huge concern which overshadows not only Meerzoeff and the Baku Petroleum Company, but the whole of the well owners and oil refiners put together.

In most countries reforms are never so sweeping as they ought to be. In the case of that at Baku the monopoly was removed, but an excise duty was imposed, which involved a fresh check upon the industry. Still it rapidly advanced, and a considerable amount of capital was thrown by Russians into the undertaking.

PRODUCTION AND PRICE OF CRUDE PETROLEUM DURING THE EXCISE DUTY PERIOD.

	Tons.	Price per Ton.*
1873	64,000	7/9
1874	78,000	6/3
1875	94,000	15/6
1876	194,000	7/9
1877	242,000	12/6

It will be seen that there was a considerable fall in price from the £3 10s. exacted the last year of the

* Since the Crimean war the rouble has fluctuated so much in value that it is impossible to give the exact English equivalents throughout. I have reckoned the rouble from 1872 to 1877 at the average value of half a crown. The Russian prices were:—1872, forty-five copecks the pood ; 1873, five copecks ; 1874, four copecks ; 1875, ten copecks ; 1876, five copecks ; and 1877, eight copecks the pood.

monoply period. In 1877 the excise duty was abolished, at the recommendation of a special commission presided over by Prince Leuchtenburg, and the industry left without any tax or restriction. The following statistics will give an idea of the industry when this revolution was accomplished. Total production of crude oil in 1877, 242,000 tons; number of drilled wells 130; price of crude oil 12s. 6d. per ton; excise duty paid throughout the whole period from 1873 to 1877, 1,245,954 roubles or about £160,000; number of refineries 150; quantity of oil refined 74,000 tons.

Rid of the monoply and excise, the industry at once rapidly advanced with acclerated speed; but its progress would have never been so remarkable as it has been, but for the marvellous system of transport organized by two Swedish engineers, Robert and Ludwig Nobel.

These colossal exploiters had already commenced operations in 1875, anterior to the abrogation of the excise duty; but it was not until afterwards that their operations began to exercise any marked effect upon the output of oil. The revolution they accomplished inaugurated what Russians call the Nobelevski, or Nobel period, extending up to the present day.

PRODUCTION AND PRICE OF CRUDE PETROLEUM DURING THE NOBEL PERIOD.

	Tons.	Price per Ton.*
1878	320,000	8/8
1879	370,000	6/3
1880	420,000	3/8
1881	490,000	2/6
1882	680,000	2/6
1883	800,000	2/6 to 0/3½

* Since 1878 the rouble, on an average has been worth about 2s. The Russian prices for these years were:—1878, seven copecks the pood; 1879, five copecks; 1880, three copecks; 1881 and 1882, two copecks; and 1883, from two copecks to a quarter of a copeck the pood.

PRODUCTION OF REFINED PETROLEUM.

	Tons.		Tons.
1878	97,550	1881	183,000
1879	110,000	1882	202,000
1880	150,000	1883	206,000

The number of drilled wells has increased as under:—

	Wells.		Wells.
1871	1	1876	101
1872	2	1879	301
1873	17	1882	370
1874	50	1883	400
1875	65		

From the present year will probably date a fresh epoch in the petroleum industry—the Batoum period. Up to the summer of 1883 Caspian petroleum only found its way to Europe *viâ* the Volga and Western Russia, traversing more than 2,000 miles in steamers and tank-cars before reaching the holds of foreign vessels. The construction of the Batoum line reduced this distance to 560 miles at a stroke, and laid the industry open to the civilized world.

CHAPTER XIV.

THE OIL FOUNTAINS OF BAKU.

Number of Wells in Baku and America Compared—One Baku Well Yielding More than all the American Wells Put Together—A Million's worth of Oil from a Single Well—Description of a Baku Petroleum Fountain—The Droojba Spouting Well—Mode of Boring for Oil. The Balakhani Drilled and Pumping Wells—Cost of Sinking a Well—Price of Land at the Oil Fields—The Kalpah, or Well-stopper—Storing the Oil—The History of the Oil Fountains during the last Ten Years—Subterranean Explosions—Six Hundred Thousand Gallons of Oil in Twenty-Four Hours—Enormous Waste of Petroleum—The Fire at Krasilnikoff's Wells—A Sand Volcano 400 Feet High—Account of the Droojba Fountain—A Liquid Grindstone—Gagging the Wells at Baku—Statistical Account of the Oil Wasted by the Droojba Fountain—Science and the Oil Fountains at Baku—Their Effect on Commercial Men—Necessity of Placing the Fountains Under the Control of the State.

In America there are over 25,000 drilled petroleum wells. Baku possesses 400. But a single one of those 400 wells has thrown up as much oil in a day as nearly the whole of the 25,000 in America put together. This is very wonderful, but a more striking fact is, that the copiousness of the well should have ruined its owners, and broken the heart of the engineer who bored it, after having yielded enough oil in four months to have realized in America at least one million sterling.

"In Pennsylvania that fountain would have made its owner's fortune; there's £5,000 worth of oil flowing out

PLATE 13.—AN OIL FOUNTAIN AT BAKU. Noble Brothers' No. 25 Well.

of the well every day.* Here it has made the owner a bankrupt." These words were addressed to me by an American petroleum engineer, as I stood alongside a well that had burst the previous morning, and out of which the oil was flying twice the height of the Great Geyser in Iceland, with a roar that could be heard several miles round. The fountain was a splendid spectacle—it was the largest ever known at Baku. When the first outburst took place the oil had knocked off the roof and part of the sides of the derrick, but there was a beam left at the top, against which the oil broke with a roar in its upward course, and which served in a measure to check its velocity. The derrick itself was seventy feet high, and the oil and the sand, after bursting through the roof and sides, flowed fully three times higher, forming a greyish-black fountain, the column clearly defined on the southern side, but merging into a cloud of spray thirty yards broad on the other. A strong southerly wind enabled us to approach within a few yards of the crater on the former side, and to look down into the sandy basin formed round about the bottom of the derrick, where the oil was bubbling and seething round the stalk of the oil-shoot like a geyser. The diameter of the tube up which the oil was rushing was ten inches. On issuing from this the fountain formed a clearly-defined stem about eighteen inches thick, and shot up to the top of the derrick, where in striking against the beam, which was already worn half through by the friction, it got broadened out a little. Thence continuing its course more than 200 feet high, it curled over and fell in a dense cloud to the ground on the north side, forming a sand bank, over which the olive-coloured oil ran in innumerable channels towards

* This was a rough guess. The actual value was over £11,000. The quantity then flowing was 400,000 or 500,000 poods a day, which at 23 copecks a pood, the quotation price in Pennsylvania at the moment, would have realised from 112,000 to 140,000 roubles, or at the least £11,200 a day.

the lakes of petroleum that had been formed on the surrounding estates. Now and again the sand flowing up with the oil would obstruct the pipe, or a stone would clog the course; then the column would sink for a few seconds lower than 200 feet, to rise directly afterwards with a burst and a roar to 300. Throughout the previous day a north wind had been blowing, causing the oil and sand to fall in a contrary direction from that pursued while we were there. Some idea of the mass of matter thrown up from the well could be formed by a glance at the damage done on the south side in twenty-four hours —a vast shoal of sand having been formed, which had buried to the roof some magazines and shops, and had blocked to the height of six or seven feet all the neighbouring derricks within a distance of fifty yards. Some of the sand and oil had been carried by the wind nearly 100 yards from the fountain—the sand-drenched roofs of the adjacent buildings showing how far the cloud of matter had extended. From this outer boundary where the oil lay an inch or so deep on the ground, the sand-shoal rose gradually, until at the rim of the crater it was about twenty feet deep, the surface being hard and soddened, and intersected with small channels, along which the oil was draining off to the lakes. On the opposite side a new shoal was forming, and we could see the sand as it fell drifting round the neighbouring derricks and burying all the outhouses in the way. Here and there gangs of men were at work with wooden spades, digging and clearing channels round about the mouth of the well, to enable the oil to flow away. Their task was no easy or agreeable one. Upon their heads and shoulders oil and sand never ceased to fall, and they had to be careful to avoid being drawn into, and engulphed in the vortex round the base of the crater. Luckily no stones of any size were being thrown up with the oil. Sometimes blocks weighing several pounds are hurled up from the depths below, and then it becomes a dangerous matter to approach a petroleum fountain. Standing on the top of the sand-shoal we could see where the oil after flowing through a score of channels from the ooze, formed in the distance on lower ground a whole series of oil lakes, some broad enough and deep enough to row a boat in. Beyond this, the oil could be seen flowing away in a broad channel towards the sea.

It may be asked how a magnificent oil fountain of this description should be able to make its owner a millionnaire in one hemisphere and a bankrupt in another. The answer is simple enough. The fountain belonged to a small Armenian Company, the Droojba, having ground enough to establish the well upon, but nothing to spare for reservoirs. Consequently, all the oil was flowing away upon other people's property, and the amount subsequently caught and saved upon the waste lands afar off was being sold at such a low price, as to be altogether inadequate to meet the claims for compensation from those whose houses and shops had been engulphed, and their derricks hindered from working, by the sand thrown up from the well. Had the Droojba possessed plenty of land round about their well to store the oil, they would not have been so badly off, but their well happened to be in the midst of several hundred estates covering the Balakhani plateau, and hence the damage done ruined them.

Boring for petroleum is a simple and interesting process. A wooden derrick, of planks and boards, like a huge sentry-box, is erected over the spot selected for the well. This is about 20 feet square at the base, 60 to 80 feet high, and tapering upwards until the top is only 3 feet square. Here rests a heavy beam, to which the boring apparatus is rigged, much in the American fashion; an iron bit, gouge-shaped, being fitted to a boring bar about 10 feet long, and successively increased by other lengths as the depth of the boring increases. The Armenian companies usually bore by manual or horse, or use primitive machinery, but Nobel Brothers and other large firms employ engines heated by oil. In general, all the Baku firms model their operations upon those of the Nobels. Every innovation Ludwig Nobel makes is imitated more or less successfully by the Russians and Armenians. The latter make no effort to inaugurate anything fresh themselves, or even to keep themselves acquainted with what is being done in America. Ludwig Nobel, on the other hand, is always improving his mode of operations, either availing himself of his own engineering skill or that of his *employés*, or introducing fresh ideas from the United States. He is thus the connecting link between Baku and Pennsylvania; between, one might also say, Armenian and Russian backwardness and American progress and enlightment. Without going into technical particulars, Nobel Brothers' mode of working may be defined as the American system intelligently modified and adapted to the peculiarities of Baku. If the stranger visits Nobels' wells, accompanied by Mr. Sandgren, the very intelligent Swedish manager, and then goes the round of the remainder, he will find that while none come up to theirs in efficiency and simplicity of working, a large number are merely caricatures, or just emerging from the old primitive modes of exploitation. I am not saying this in a carping spirit. I am only stating an actual recognised fact. In justice to them all, I must observe that they display the utmost readiness to show the stranger over the wells, and give him any information he requires. It is only in the kerosine refineries that anxiety is evinced to safeguard technical secrets.

In America the bores often run small, but in Baku the tubes are invariably large—that is to say, from ten to fourteen inches. The thickness of the tubes runs from

$\frac{1}{8}$ inch to $\frac{3}{16}$ inch. The 400 pit wells do not exceed fifty feet in depth; the 400 drilled wells run from 300 to 800. The average depth of drilled well in 1882 was 350 feet. It increases every year. The deepest at Balakhani in 1883 was 825 feet. In America wells run from 600 to 1,800 feet in depth, and there are a number exceeding 2,000 feet. Packed together as the Balakhani wells are in such a small area, they naturally have an exhausting effect on the supply immediately below them, and have consequently to be constantly deepened. The deeper they go, the more prodigious the supply. The result is, as I have already said, that although every day they become more cramped for room, they have no inducement to go elsewhere.

Balakhani seems to have been selected as the principal place of operations, because the surface there, in the old shallow-pit days, was the easiest to work. The ground consists of mingled rock and sand, and curious enough the sand often occasions the greatest trouble and expense; containing small boulder stones which move aside when the boring-rod passes through the soil, and fall into and clog the channel on its being removed to insert the tubing. When the oil is touched there is usually a prolonged discharge of impure hydro-carbon gas. Sometimes this pours up the pipe with terrific force, roaring so loudly that nothing can be heard alongside the well. As often as not grit is carried up with it, and finally comes the oil. Directly the gas begins to blow, all haste is made to withdraw the boring rod and fasten a *Kalpak*, or iron cap, over the orifice. This is fitted with a sliding valve to regulate the passage of the gas and oil. Should the well be successfully capped over, the chief danger of an irrepressible fountain is removed, but it often happens that the oil follows too fast, and then nothing can be done to check the outburst of petroleum until its force moderates. A well of this character, which shoots its own oil to the surface and requires no pumping, is known in America as a "spouting" or "flowing" well; in Baku it is called a *fontan*, or "fountain." Last year, when the engineers at Nobels' No. 25 Well struck oil, the gas exploded and blew into the air 500 feet of boring rod before it could be removed. Formerly the tubes were sunk without any packing round the top. The consequence was that when they were capped the pipes burst. To obviate this, it has been the custom for some years past to dig down twenty or thirty feet round about the mouth of the well, and fill the hole up with a concrete or asphalte setting. If this be well done, it will resist the strongest pressure, in spite of a filtration through it, as occurred when the Droojba fountain was stopped last December. With but a few exceptions, every care is taken by the well borers to prevent the wells becoming fountains beyond control. The Droojba catastrophe was due to an accident. The well was properly capped over, and it was while improving and strengthening the cap that the oil suddenly blew it off, and spouted 300 feet high. It then became, of course, beyond control. In a few days the grit carried up with the oil ground to pieces the huge and massive beams at the top of the derrick.

When a good supply of oil is tapped, and properly placed under restraint, it usually flows for a considerable period without requiring any pumping. As soon as it ceases to do this, tubes are used to raise the oil to the surface. These are of a cylindrical shape, about ten feet long and ten inches broad, and have at the bottom a valve which opens on touching the ground, and closes when the tube is lifted. About two minutes are required to lower and lift the tubes, which bring about fifty gallons of oil to the surface each stroke. When the supply begins to show signs of exhaustion, the cylinder is removed, and the engineer recommences boring. The process of "torpedoing," common in America when a well gives evidences of sterility, is never resorted to at Baku. The owners know they have only to bore a little lower to find a good supply afresh.

To sink a well costs from £1,000 to £3,000, according to the depth and difficulties encountered. The people employed at the wells are mostly natives—Tartars and Armenians—and receive about £2 a month wages. The foremen get £10 a month, and a commission of 3s. upon every foot bored. Most of the *employés* live at Balakhani village, but Nobel Brothers lodge theirs in extensive stone barracks, close to their work, where they enjoy more comfort than they would elsewhere. All the same, a more dreary place than the oil fields it would be difficult to find. Round about it the country is an arid desert, without a tree, shrub, or blade of grass. The landscape on which these *employés* have, many of them, looked for years, is made up of an undulating tract of rock and sand, with a conglomeration of several hundred dingy black derricks in the middle, interspersed with sand mounds marking the sites of extinct fountains, inky-looking petroleum lakes, and huge iron reservoirs. But for the ever-beautiful sky above, existence would be intolerable.

Having no well-defined boundaries, and sub-divided as the ground is into innumerable small plots, many of which plots belong to associations of shareholders, the complications arising from the tenure of the land are fruitful of lawsuits. The seventy derricks owned or leased by Nobel Brothers are scattered throughout the entire area of the Balakhani plateau. Within this area it is difficult to get cheap land, and impossible to purchase plots of any size. Ground at present sells at from 10s. to £2 the square *sajine*, or Russian fathom (seven feet). The proximity of the land to a good well or fountain naturally enhances its price. Outside the area under exploitation, where no wells have yet been bored, large plots of ground can be had for 10s. the square fathom. No great difficulty is experienced just now in leasing wells or buying them outright.

When the oil reaches the surface, it is allowed to run along wooden pipes to channels outside the derrick, whence it makes its way to ponds, or reservoirs, as they are called. These are little more than hollows scraped in the ground, or natural depressions with banks of sand around them. A certain amount of oil is wasted by absorption in the sand, but once the soil becomes saturated it acts like clay, and opposes a further passage to the petroleum. There are any number of these ponds of petroleum scattered over the Balakhani plateau; some so large as to merit the designation of lakes. Many are the product of the terrific fountains of the last five years. In the aggregate they contain many million gallons of oil, spoilt for want of a buyer. When the oil has stood a while in the ponds and cleared itself of the sand and water brought up with it from the well, it is sucked through pipes into iron reservoirs, and thence pumped through the pipe-lines to the refineries on the coast. Nobel Brothers possess the largest iron cisterns on the Balakhani plateau. One of them holds 1½ million gallons of crude oil.

A feature of the American oil supply is, that while there are many wells yielding thousands of gallons of petroleum daily, the larger proportion give only hundreds. The richest well on record, I believe, has not exceeded 200,000 gallons a day. At Baku the wells are nearly all of them what Americans would consider extremely copious ones. A well yielding only a few hundred gallons of oil a day, a Baku firm would not consider worth working. This is not remarkable, seeing that the richest of the Baku wells has yielded 2,000,000 gallons, or ten times the largest yield in America, in twenty-four hours.

It is difficult to convince people of such extraordinary copiousness, and I have come across one or two Americans who have declared it to be impossible. But the facts of the Baku petroleum industry are too clearly defined, and the evidence to support them too substantial, to admit of their accuracy being impugned. There is not a statement about the industry which I have not carefully tested, both on the spot and by light of the materials that have reached me since. Since I returned from Baku in September, there have been conferences of oil well proprietors to discuss how to extend their transport, open up fresh markets, and, above all, to frame regulations for putting a stop to the fearful waste caused by fountains. If I mention that all the Baku well proprietors hate one another, and that the only sentiment they have in common is a general hatred of Nobel Brothers, it may be inferred that during these discussions—the reports of which now lie before me—the facts of the industry have been exposed to a very close sifting, and all exaggerations corrected either by jealous rivals or by the local press. In connection with the fountains, the Mayor of Baku invited all the proprietors to furnish an account of what had occurred to each of them, and these reports, with the discussions upon them, I have found of great value in guiding my remarks upon these remarkable oil geysers, which are causing so much talk just now in the English scientific world.

Flowing wells yielding from 40,000 to 160,000 gallons of oil every day, of rare occurrence in America, are quite common at Baku. The ordinary yield of the pumping wells is from 10,000 to 25,000 gallons. It is common for these pumping wells to be worked for years, without the supply diminishing. Gospodin Kokereff has one which has already produced 60,000,000 gallons of oil, and still continues to yield at the same rate as at the outset. In Group VIII. is a flowing well belonging to the Baku

Petroleum Company, which for two years has given a regular supply of 40,000 gallons daily from a depth of 252 feet, without showing signs of exhaustion.

Owing to the low price of crude petroleum, which such an abundant supply has occasioned, Nobel Brothers have plugged up fourteen fountains at Balakhani, until the oil rises in value, preferring in the meanwhile to buy what they require from neighbouring well proprietors. One of these fountains spouted 112,000 tons of petroleum in about four weeks on the oil being struck. Occasionally, a fountain is opened to examine its condition, when it is always found that the supply is as prodigious as when capped over.

The first fountain at Baku occurred in July, 1873, when the Khalify Company, an Armenian concern, in boring for oil, suddenly penetrated a reservoir, from which the liquid spouted with a fury nothing could restrain. Mr. Arthur Arnold, M.P., who visited Baku two years after, says the stalk of the fountain was nine feet in diameter, and the fountain itself forty feet high. This fountain caused the price of crude oil to fall from forty-five to five copecks the pood. Since then it has never risen higher than ten copecks. For want of storage room a large quantity of oil from the Khalify fountain was lost.

In 1874 there was another fountain, in Group XIV., spouting from a nine-inch well. Commencing on the 25th July it continued playing until the end of the year. It then became an intermittent spouter for six months, and finally decayed into a pumping well. Every effort to stop the outflow of oil failed, and millions of gallons were wasted.

In 1875 there was a third fountain, in Group XIII., which spouted 600,000 gallons of oil every twenty-four hours. This belonged to the Company of Petroleum Participators, which has had a number of fountains in the course of its career. In 1874 the well, which was 196 feet deep, and had been giving 8,000 gallons a day for some time, began to diminish. Boormeister, the German engineer, thereupon began to bore deeper to obtain a fresh supply. At 280 feet he lost oil altogether, although plenty of gas came to the surface. At 315 feet he reached a bed of rock. This was so hard that he had to put on eight men to drill through it. Suddenly, on the 26th of October, the boring tool broke through the roof of the subterranean reservoir, and only one man was then needed instead of eight. To ascertain the cause of this sudden facility of working, the tool was withdrawn, when a small fountain of oil began to spout. This ceased after a few minutes, and then the gas began to roar, accompanied by a sort of explosion below, producing perceptible tremblings of the earth round about the well. Afterwards oil and gas spouted at intervals. To keep both down a cap of half-inch boiler plate was placed over the tube; but in the night the oil suddenly broke it off, and began to spout forty feet high. The next day oil flowed at the rate of 600,000 gallons in twenty-four hours. Four huge lakes of oil were formed in the course of a month, the fountain not being closed over until the 23rd of November.

The following year the same company had another fountain. This was 280 feet deep, the tube being $6\frac{1}{2}$ inches in diameter, and composed of $\frac{1}{8}$ inch iron. Directly the oil was touched it burst up into a fountain, with a force of four atmospheres, lasting three months, during which it formed a lake which still exists to this day. None of the oil was sold, there being no market for it. The fountain spouted about 270,000 gallons of oil daily for ninety days, and it was estimated the lake contained twenty-four million gallons of crude petroleum. In common with most of the wells bored up to this time, the tube was passed through the surface without anything being done to strengthen it at the top. Hence it was impossible to close the fountain, because directly this was attempted, the oil burst through the sides of the tube. Taught by experience, Lentz, an expert in sinking wells, dug down twenty-five feet round the top of the tube, and packed the hole with cement, clay, stones, &c., well stamped down, to resist the pressure. After this an iron cap was successfully fitted over the top of the tube, which did not burst.

In 1877 Orbelovi Brothers had a great fountain from a well 210 feet deep, with a bore of $10\frac{1}{2}$ inches. The oil spouted slightly a few days, and was then capped, but in making some improvements afterwards to the cap the pressure below burst it off the tube, and the petroleum issued with a fury nothing could check. In half an hour a reservoir holding 40,000 gallons was filled, and then the oil ran all over the place, forming a series of lakes. This fountain never spouted less than 40,000 gallons of oil a day, and sometimes attained 1,200,000 gallons. The total quantity of oil lost before the fountain was subdued was forty million gallons.

A less striking but more valuable fountain in 1877, was Meerzoeff's No. 5, in Group IX. The oil was first touched in 1876. The following spring, in deepening the well to 340 feet, the oil began to spout at the rate of 80,000 gallons daily; the gravity being 0·865. After a while it was successfully capped, and has since then given a permanent supply, amounting up to the end of 1883 to 16,000,000 gallons.

In 1878 the Caspian Company had a fountain from a depth of 462 feet, giving 160,000 gallons daily. Altogether the well spouted nearly ten million gallons of oil, of which six millions were sold for liquid fuel, and the remainder lost. Several remarkable fountains occurred the following year. One of these was in Group V., and belonged to Gospodin Mnatsakanoff. The well was 294 feet deep, with a tube of No. 12 iron, ten inches in diameter. The first month water and gas issued, then the sand started to spout, and played for four hours, followed by petroleum, bursting off the cap that had been successfully fixed. For 120 days the oil spouted without cessation day and night, the average flow being 120,000 gallons daily—a record which the most copious well in America has never been able to maintain beyond two or three weeks. The total quantity of oil thrown up was fifteen million gallons, of 0·868 specific gravity. Of this, 2,000,000 gallons were sold at half a copeck the pood, or between 7d. and 8d. the ton; 600,000 gallons were sold to the Caspian Company for 800 roubles (£80) for the entire quantity!—being used for fuel; and the remainder was burnt or allowed to sink into the soil. The tube, costing £500, was completely worn to pieces.

In the same group another well also spouted throughout the latter part of 1879. This belonged to the Ararat Company, and was 280 feet deep, with a $10\frac{1}{2}$-inch bore of $\frac{3}{16}$ iron. On reaching petroleum-sand the boring tool was withdrawn, but the oil refused to rise. Boring was then resumed, and pierced 15 inches of rock, when oil started to spout. With some difficulty the boring rod was extricated, and a Benkston cap fixed on, but the pipe cracked under the pressure, and the oil shot through the orifices in a sufficient quantity to supply all the requirements of the firm. The well spouted for a year and a half, the highest level maintained being 40,000 gallons. The total quantity of oil ejected was 40 million gallons. Of this quantity 16 million gallons were sold at 7d. or 8d. the ton; 8 million gallons given gratis to Kolesnikoff, as a set-off for damage done by the oil flowing on to his land; and 16 millions penetrated to Lake Zabratsky, and was lost. Beginning at a gravity of 0·867, the oil ceased at a gravity of 0·872.

Still in the same Group V., a third fountain occurred

the following year, 1880. This belonged to the Sun Company, which had a plot next to that of the Ararat Company, and, undisturbed by the fountain owned by the latter, began boring a new well, 12 inches in diameter, of ⅜ inch iron. Infusing energy into the operations, the engineers reached oil sand at 266 feet. Clay followed this, and then water-sand. Believing they would next reach the stratum of the Ararat fountain and suck the oil from it, they suspended operations while they got ready the top of the well for the anticipated outburst. Digging out the soil for a depth of 20 feet round about the head of the tube, they filled the hole with concrete, well packed and tightly rammed round the tubing. This done, they started working night and day, and on the eighth night suddenly struck oil. It was then at once seen that the well had penetrated the reservoir feeding the Ararat fountain, for the latter immediately ceased playing. When the valve of the cap over the Sun well was closed the Ararat fountain started afresh; when it was withdrawn the latter left off spouting. An effort was made to get the two companies to combine, but without success, and the wells were worked against each other for two months, when the Sun well burst off its cap one day, and all control over it was lost. During these two months from 60,000 gallons to 160,000 gallons were sold daily; the total thus disposed of being 4,800,000 gallons, at two copecks a pood (2s. 6d. the ton). The third month 8,000,000 gallons flowed to Lake Zabratsky, and was lost. Afterwards, both it and the Ararat well ceased to spout; the two together having thrown up nearly 53 million gallons of oil. Since then, both have been regularly used as pumping wells, giving 24,000 gallons apiece daily.

In 1881 Gospodin Mnatsakanoff began deepening a 12-inch well, which had exhausted the oil at 294 feet. Having reached 434 feet, oil was touched again. Great pains were taken to pack round about the tube, and fix a good cap to resist the pressure, but after a few days the oil broke through all impediments, and spouted. From September 13 to November 1 a total of 3,320,000 gallons issued, which was sold for 18,000 roubles (£1,800). The fountain was then placed under control. The following year, from Feb. 19 to the end of the navigation season, the well was allowed to spout, and ejected 18,000,000 gallons, which was sold for 86,000 roubles (£8,600). The fountain began to lose its force then, but in February, 1883, it played a third time for a fortnight. Very little of the oil was lost. When first struck the oil showed gravity of 0·876, but from April, 1882, it stood at 0·881.

The same year Krasilnikoff had two fountains. One was at Shaitan Bazaar, where a well was completed his engineers had been working upon at intervals since 1877. At a depth of 378 feet sand began to shoot up the tube, and after a time oil flowed at the rate of 160,000 gallons a day; the gravity being 0·850-51. Eleven days elapsed before a cap could be fitted; the loss during the interval being 800,000 gallons. After the well was capped it gave an abundant supply under firm control from the same depth for 15 months. In the case of the second fountain the depth of the bore was 504 feet, and the well gave 80,000 gallons a day. The total outflow was 4,800,000 gallons, of which 1,600,000 were sold as fuel and the rest allowed to run to waste in Lake Saboontchi. On the 3rd September the fountain caught fire, and flared with terrific fury for ten days, when it was extinguished. Afterwards the well spouted afresh.

The same year Lianozoff Brothers' No. 9 well became a fountain. The depth the oil was touched at was 329 feet; the tube was 12 inches thick, of $\frac{3}{16}$-inch iron. The fountain played three months, and threw up 7,200,000 gallons, of 0·860 specific gravity. The greater proportion was caught in reservoirs.

At Shaitan Bazaar Orbelovi Brothers had an enormous fountain at their No. 2 well. The engineers began boring it by hand in 1877, and completed it in 1881. The tube was 12 inches in diameter, diminishing to 10½. At a depth of 490 feet oil was struck, and spouted 4,000,000 gallons in a week. The stem of the fountain was over 200 feet high, and a strong wind blowing at the time carried the oil spray 500 yards to the office of the Baku Petroleum Company, the manager of which lodged a complaint against Orbelovi Brothers, affirming that there was a serious danger of the establishment being set on fire. The oil flowed into a saline depression, and was there burnt to get rid of it. When the fountain ceased playing, the tube was found to be choked and ruined. Since then the well has remained unworked.

In the case of Nobel Brothers' No. 25 well, which during the summer spouted sand over 200 feet high, on the oil being tapped at 582 feet the gush carried away the whole of the boring gear, weighing more than a ton. When the engineers proceeded to clear the tube of sand, the oil spouted so furiously, that not wishing to have a fountain and waste the oil the engineers capped it over. Since then it has been left untouched as a reserve.

In 1882 the Company of Petroleum Participators had a fountain at their No. 9 well, from a depth of 476 feet. The tube was 10 inches in diameter, and was composed of $\frac{3}{16}$-inch iron. Its installation was effected under the supervision of Lentz, whose system of concreting round about the upper part of the well had proved so successful on a previous occasion. The fountain lasted twenty days, during which it carried to the surface 8,000,000 gallons. The average was 400,000 gallons a day. Of this 1,600,000 gallons were sold, and 5,200,000 gallons lost. A cap was fixed on the sixth day. The well has since proved one of the most productive at Balakhani.

The same year the Baku Mining Company had a fountain from a well 450 feet deep. The tube was 14 inches in diameter. In September it spouted 400,000 gallons in 12 days; in December, 1,200,000 gallons in 6 days; and early in January, 1883, 400,000 gallons in 2½ days. Of the total of 2,000,000 gallons, only 640,000 gallons were sold, at ¾ copeck the pood (about 11d. the ton). The specific gravity of the oil was 0·867.

The Baku Petroleum Company struck a fountain the same season at a depth of 305 feet, the tube being of ⅛ inch iron, 14 inches in diameter as far as 217 feet, and 12 inches the remainder of the distance. Eight million gallons of oil, of a gravity of 0·870, came to the surface, and most of it was sold for 3s. 8d. the ton.

Last year was remarkable for the size of the fountains. The firm of Lionozoff had two on their estate. The first occurred in connection with their No. 15 well, which was begun in November, 1882, and completed in May, 1883. The tube was 12 inches in diameter. At 420 feet there was a terrific outburst of gas, which was repeated at 490 feet; the oil each time mounting to the surface, but disappearing after the cap was fixed. The third time, at 546 feet, the explosion of gas was terrific, hurling the pumping cylinder into the air, and smashing the top of the derrick to pieces. Afterwards dry sand began to spout with terrible force, forming a fountain of grit from 350 to 400 feet high. Bits of rock were hurled so high as to be lost to sight. All the windows of the neighbouring engine-houses were smashed, and the metal roof of a boiler-house was broken through by a falling stone. This "sand-volcano" lasted 45 minutes, and was succeeded by a blast of gas which poisoned the atmosphere at Balakhani the rest of the day. After considerable time a cap was fixed on the tube, and directly afterwards the oil began to spout. There being no demand for crude petroleum just then, Lionozoff stopped the flow, and left the well capped over. The pressure of the oil and gas below was subsequently relieved by a second 10-inch well; which was completed about the same time, and at 560 feet penetrated the reservoir of No. 15 and gave another outlet for the gas. Both wells are now full of oil, and spout whenever the caps are opened; but there is no extensive sale for petroleum, and the owner benefits little by his success.

The Nazareth, or Nazaret, fountain was a curious instance of the uncertainties attending well boring. The well was commenced by Abayantz and Co. in 1879, only manual power being used, and by the end of 1881 a depth of 581 feet had been attained without any signs of oil. Despairing of success, the owners left the well untouched for a couple of years, when they leased it to one Nazaret, the head of a private company, consisting of Toomacff and several other Armenians, on the condition that he was to bore at his own expense and share with Abayantz and Co. half the profits whenever he reaped oil. Nazaret only bored seven feet deeper, when he touched a reservoir, and the sand began to spout. The tube was a 10-inch one, diminishing to seven and a half inches in diameter, and soon got clogged up. After a fortnight spent in digging away the sand-shoal round about the mouth of the tube he cleared the latter and the oil spouted freely. The gravity of the oil was 0·862 at first, increasing to 0·870. About 3,200,000 gallons of oil were ejected, of which a deal was sold for fuel. The pipe was ruined, however, and the well is now useless.

A considerably larger one than this was Meerzoeff's, occurring at their No. 14 well. The tube was 14 inches in diameter. Oil was reached at 441 feet, and spouted from 20,000 to 40,000 gallons a day at first, increasing to 400,000 gallons, and then diminishing to 40,000 again. Altogether it spouted during the summer 10,000,000 gallons, of which 6,000,000 gallons were despatched to Meerzoeff's refinery at Baku, and the rest stored in a lake, where it is now sold for fuel. The well is still full of oil, and spouts whenever wanted.

A very remarkable fountain was Nobels' No. 9 well, which spouted from a depth of 642 feet 112,000 tons, or nearly 30 million gallons of oil in four weeks. The height of the fountain was 200 feet, and it threw the oil and sand for a distance of 200 feet round about the derrick. Thanks to the extensive means of the company, only 1,000,000 gallons were lost out of the 30 millions spouted, and of the latter 20 million gallons were at once converted into kerosine and other products, and the remainder stored in reservoirs. After the pressure in the well had fallen, so that the orifice could be conveniently plugged by mechanical means sufficiently tight to resist the force below, the delivery of oil was still at the rate of 600 barrels per hour. Another fountain at their No. 25 well threw up nearly two million gallons of oil daily from a depth of 582 feet. The pressure on the tube, ascertained by scientific instruments, was about 200 pounds to the square inch. The well now yields a million gallons of crude oil per diem.

But the great fountain of the year, and one whose renown penetrated to every part of Europe, was the Droojba. The maximum pressure of gas in previous fountains had not exceeded four atmospheres, but in the case of Nobels' No. 9 fountain and the Droojba it exceeded thirteen. I have already described in the opening part of this chapter what a magnificent spectacle it was. Had the well been situated at the bottom of the Monument it would have spouted higher than the golden ball at the top. The "oil-volcano" threw up, according to the estimate of the local experts, Mr. B., an American petroleum engineer, who chanced to be at Baku, the semi-official newspaper *Baku Isvestie*, and a number of other authorities, 400,000 or 500,000 poods, or from 1,600,000 to 2,000,000 gallons of oil every day for some time after the first outburst, which occurred on the 1st of September. In the middle of November it was still spouting 240,000 gallons a day, and a three-inch iron boiler plate was ground to pieces in an attempt to divert the stalk of the fountain.

This was not the first case of the kind at Baku, although exaggerated reports of the incident penetrated even to England. When the oil is projected, it carries with it grit with such force as to convert its volume into a sort of liquid grindstone. If an iron plate be placed in contact with the stream the sand in the oil literally grinds it to pieces in a few hours. The first caps that were used at Balakhani were completely destroyed in this manner. Nobel Brothers have one at their office in Baku, preserved as a curiosity, which was worn into holes in a few hours, although three inches thick. It was this circumstance that led to the invention of a special kind of cap fitted with sliding valves, which is capable of gagging the strongest fountain, if only it can be fitted on the tube in time.

A gagged fountain has now become one of the sights of Baku. The visitor is shown a deserted derrick, in which, he is told, a *kalpak* keeps down, with the grip of a vice, millions of gallons of oil in the cellular basin 600 or 700 feet below. On removing the slide of the cap there is a furious blast of gas, followed by an out-rush of petroleum a considerable height; which is suppressed with equal ease by gradually closing the slide again. When Admiral Shestakoff, the Minister of Marine, visited Baku last autumn, he was taken to see one of Nobel Brothers' gagged fountains. For ten minutes the gas roared so loudly that nobody could hear each other speak, and then the oil spouted higher than the derrick. When the Minister's curiosity was gratified the oil fountain was turned off as easily as the water fountains of Trafalgar Square.

With regard to the Droojba, in consequence of the prodigious outflow of oil, the crude article lost its value for the moment. Fedoroff filled his reservoirs with 2,800,000 gallons of oil for 300 roubles, or £30. No one would give more than ¼ copeck the pood for what had previously fetched 2 or 3 copecks. Thousands of tons were burnt outside the district to get rid of it; thousands were led towards the Caspian; huge lakes of oil were formed near the well, and on one occasion the liquid suddenly flowed into a distant engine-house, and, but for the promptness of the engineer in extinguishing his petroleum furnace, the whole locality would have been ablaze. Houses were completely buried by the sand cast up by the oil; all efforts to stop the fountain on the part of Baku experts were fruitless. The indignation in Russia at the waste of oil was unbounded; at Baku all the well-owners formed themselves into a congress to decide upon means for checking the fountain. Finally, the Government at St. Petersburg was appealed to, and 2,000 roubles were assigned to equip two engineers to Baku. On the 10th of December the fountain suddenly stopped of its own accord—the pipe had got blocked— but after three hours it burst out afresh with increased violence. At length, on the 29th of December, Zorgé, a neighbouring well-owner, succeeded in fixing a cap, and, in spite of a strong filtration round the tube, the oil remained under control the whole winter. Directly the outburst was stopped a great disturbance took place in Nobels' No. 14 well, showing a connection of both with the same reservoir. The depth of the Droojba well was 574 feet. The quantity of oil spouted is reckoned to have ranged between 220,000 and 500,000 tons; which in America would have yielded from £616,000 to £1,400,000 sterling.*

* The following is the calculation made by Zorgé and Stchastlivtseff two neighbouring well-proprietors, of the quantity ejected :—

Such a prodigious outflow of oil was without parallel, not only in the annals of commerce, but in the records of science. The old Eternal Fire, and the blazing water at Baku, sink into insignificance compared with such a marvel. To the man of science the oil fountains of the Apsheron peninsula promise to become a source of permanent interest. Now the oil fields are more developed there are plenty of curious facts that need elucidation. One of the most striking of these is, that the fountains always play the fiercer after a north wind. Why this should be the case no one has yet satisfactorily explained.

But if the oil fountains of Baku are likely to prove a magnet to the *savants* of Europe, they may be expected to exercise a more powerful influence upon commercial men. Ten thousand pounds a day wasting itself on the desert air, and a railway close by to take the oil to the ships of Europe—what a tempting bait to the cupidity of the world! The owners of the Droojba, for want of capital to grip their good fortune, let a million sterling slip through their fingers. Gariboff the engineer, appalled by the havoc, and vainly trying to check it, broke his heart. But had the Armenian firm been a rich European company, with the engineering resources of the West at its command, the result would have been very different.

					Poods.
Aug. and Sept. (O.S.),	43 days at	200,000	poods a day =	8,600,000
October	31	„	100,000	„	3,100,000
November	30	„	50,000	„	1,500,000
December	11	„	40,000	„	440,000
	115			Poods	13,640,000

Or, about 55,000,000 gallons, or 220,000 tons of crude oil. This was the lowest estimate, and avowedly fell short of the reality. The quantity spouted varied. Thus, in November it frequently rose to 80,000 gallons a day. The average for that month was struck by basing calculations on the quantity pumped away from the well by the Baku Mining Company.

The Droojba oil well would have been more valuable than many a gold mine.

These are the scientific and commercial aspects, but there is another and a higher one. Such a waste of the world's resources ought not to be tolerated for a moment. Oil fountains promise to become a permanent feature of Baku; in fact, they are that already, for with the commencement of the season of 1884 several fountains have had their caps removed, and are spouting afresh as lustily as ever. Among them is the irrepressible Droojba, which recommenced playing on the 22nd of March. Bureaucratic supervision is always to be deprecated: officials in every country are a nuisance. Were there any guarantee that the oil would be as little wasted as in the case of Nobels' wells I should be the last to support the agitation that has been set on foot at Baku to place the fountains under Government supervision. But when a single man pricks the earth and wastes for ever 50,000,000 or 100,000,000 gallons of good oil—enough to supply London for years—then there is an end to the common sense of the *laisser faire* doctrine, and the State ought to step in and suppress the outburst at the owner's cost, even though that cost be confiscation.

CHAPTER XV.

THE CASPIAN OIL REFINERIES.

The Black Town of Baku—The 200 Refineries of the Caspian—The Smokelessness of Petroleum Fuel depends upon the Apparatus, and Care in Using it—A Lesson in Geography for English Statesmen—The Refinery of Nobel Brothers—Consumption of Kerosine in America—The Growth of the Trade—Qualities of the Various Kinds of Refined Petroleum Manufactured at Baku—Agitation for a Uniform Standard—Mode of Refining Petroleum—Table Showing the Productibility of 100 Gallons of Russian Crude Petroleum—The American and Baku Oil Compared—Mr. Boverton Redwood's Analysis of Russian Kerosine—Condition of the Industry at Baku—The Fittings of a Refinery at Baku—Russian Lubricating Oil—Export of Kerosine to Europe—Future of the Lubricating Oil Trade—Medical Properties of Petroleum—Ozokerit Deposits East of the Caspian—Barbarous Waste of the Lighter Oils—Petroleum Dyes and Colours—Hydro-Carbon Gas at Surakhani—Natural Gas Stoves.

ONE of the most striking portions of Baku is the district lying on the bay to the north of it, called the Black Town (*Tchorni Gorod*). It is here that the crude petroleum, sucked up or allowed to spout from the bowels of the earth at Balakhani, and pumped thence from reservoirs through pipes to the shore of the bay, is distilled into burning oil and other products for the markets of Europe. Altogether there are nearly 200 refineries in the Black Town, and as almost all of them, except Nobels' Works, emit vast volumes of oil-smoke, life in that locality is as bad as confinement in a chimney-pot. All day long dense clouds of smoke, possessing the well-known attributes of oil-smoke, rise from hundreds of sources in the Black Town, and either hang like a pall overhead, fouling the fair sky, or drift lazily with the breeze backwards or forwards, inland or out to the sea. A more noisome town than the Black Town it would be difficult to find. The factories cover several square miles of ground. For the most part they consist of low stone buildings of the heavy Persian style of architecture, enclosed or connected one with the other by grim stone walls. The buildings are black and greasy, the walls are black and greasy; the roads between consist of jutting rock and drifting sand, interspersed with huge pools of oil-refuse, and forming a vast morass of mud and oil in wet weather. Inside the greasy entrances to the refineries gangs of natives may be seen at work, half naked; their bodies and their ragged clothes saturated with oil. Not a tree, not a shrub, not a flower or a blade of grass, not a single object to raise or refine a man is to be found in this wretched hole, where Russians and Swedes, Armenians and Persians, distil the oil that burns in the lamps of Russia. Along the shore for a mile or two are a line of jetties, stretching far out into the bay, at the head or at the sides of which huge steamers may be seen receiving aboard the oil to convey it to the Volga. Here the piers and the steamers are dirty and greasy, the sea is covered with oil-scum, the strand contains more pools of oil than of water, and stretching along it are huge embanked reservoirs holding millions of gallons of oil refuse. For Mr. Coxon, who penetrates to this infernal region as a change to the monotony of buying beautiful Persian carpets in the bazaar, it is a new and practical lesson in geography to observe in the Caspian Sea steamers from his own native river; and as he realizes it, I cannot help wishing I had in his place the Duke of Argyll and other disbelievers in Russia's growing power in Asia, to press home to them the conviction that a country which in a few years can despatch a score or two of steamers—150 to 250 feet long, from the Tyne and from Stockholm to the Caspian Sea, by means of a magnificent canal system, is not likely to be much hampered in transporting the largest army across that sea for an attack upon India. For Mr. Coxon, as a representative of Newcastle, there is also another lesson to carry back to his fellow-townsmen. The steamers of the Caspian once burnt wood or coal. They burn now nothing but oil, and there are fifty of them constantly running between Baku and the Volga. In the Black Sea the steamers at present burn chiefly English coal. But the time is not far distant when the millions of tons of crude petroleum and petroleum refuse, wasting uselessly amidst the rocks and sands of Baku and Balakhani, will be cheaply conveyed to Poti and Batoum, and drive English coal out of the Euxine. The Black Sea steamers and towns and factories will get their fuel from Baku, instead of from Newcastle, and another market will be closed to the coal trade of England.

To the blackness and smoke, and to the dirt and disorder of the Black Town, there is one very notable exception. This is the refinery of Nobel Brothers. The two hundred other refineries are buried in smoke; the atmosphere above Nobels' place is not polluted by a single whiff. The squalor of the 200 is appalling—Nobels' establishment is kept as clean and as bright, considering the nature of the business, as any English barracks. Yet Nobel Brothers refine more kerosine than all the other firms put together, and can now furnish a sufficient supply to equip all the year round half the lamps in Russia. The difference is simply due to good appliances and good discipline. A badly-constructed lamp or a good lamp turned up too high will inevitably smoke; but when an apparatus is used like that of Nobel Brothers' at Baku not a particle of smoke need issue from petroleum fuel, and, as a matter of fact, does not. Hence, while all the Black Town fussily perspires and smokes, Nobels' place at the uttermost extremity is as calm and as bright as any part of old Baku itself; and misled by the absence of sooty clouds, a stranger might travel past without being aware that inside the stone walls a band of Swedes were quietly "turning out" a larger quantity of kerosine than any other refinery in the world.

The present consumption of refined petroleum, or kerosine, in Russia is about 250,000 tons a year. The first refinery was established in 1859. At the time of the abolition of the monopoly in 1872 there were fifty at work. Now there are about 200, the number constantly changing with the opening, closing, or amalgamation of establishments. The following has been the growth of the refining trade during the last twelve years:—

	Tons.		Tons.
1872	16,400	1878	97,550
1873	24,500	1879	110,000
1874	23,600	1880	150,000
1875	32,600	1881	183,000
1876	57,100	1882	202,000
1877	77,600	1883	206,000

Most of the oil refined at Baku has a gravity of 0·822. The following is a list, showing the differences in the gravity of the kerosine refined by the different firms. The flashing point is determined by Abel's apparatus.

BAKU REFINED PETROLEUM.

Firm.	Gravity.	Flashing Point.
Nobel Brothers	0·8200	32 deg. C.
Meerzoeff Sons	0·8201	28 ,,
Fedoroff	0.8222	28 ,,
Vagiroff, No. 1 sort	3.8230	36 ,,
,, 2 ,,	0·8203	27 ,,
Taraeff	0·8228	23 ,,

Firm.	Gravity.	Flashing Point.
Pasha Beg	0·8214	33 deg. C.
Palashkovsy, No. 2 sort	0·8244	33 ,,
,, 1 ,,	0·8155	28 ,,
Caspian Company, No. 1 sort	0·8180	27 ,,
,, ,, 2 ,,	0·8207	26 ,,
Baku Petroleum Co., No. 1 ,,	0·8190	26 ,,
, ,, 2 ,,	0·8194	26 ,,
Nagieff	0·8130	12 ,,
Toomaeff	0·8199	23 ,,
Tagieff, No. 1 sort	0·8198	34 ,,
,, 2 ,,	0·7965	12 ,,

It will be seen from the above that the flashing point ranges from twelve degrees to thirty-six degrees Celsius. The first is obviously a dangerous, inflammable oil, but the last is fit for the hottest climate. Taking the entire quantity of Baku petroleum refined, the average of the flashing point is thirty degrees. This will explain why it has attained such a rapid success in the German market. Nobel Brothers are sending Baku oil sustaining a flashing test of thirty-two degrees, whereas the average American oil breaks into flame at twenty-one degrees Celsius. Measures are now being taken by the Russian steamboat and railway companies, in conjunction with the principal Baku firms, to secure a uniform high standard in the refined petroleum exported from Baku; and there is very little doubt that the inferior kerosine, which, it should be strictly borne in mind, is but a trifling fraction of the entire quantity manufactured, will before long be entirely eliminated from the market, or confined to local consumption at Baku. The Technical Society at Baku recommends that the standard for the best Baku burning oil should be fixed at not higher than 0·821, with a flashing point not lower than twenty-five degrees Celsius (Abel test), and that further, it should be water-white and have a pleasant smell. At present the adoption of a uniform standard is under discussion, and there is a disposition in some quarters to refuse to follow any rule laid down; but this feeling simply prevails among the smaller firms. The larger ones, who have dealings with foreign countries, recognize the necessity for a standard, and as their oil is already within the limits suggested they have no reason for opposing the plan.

I have already said that the crude petroleum, after standing awhile in ponds on the surface, to rid itself of the sand, is sucked into reservoirs and pumped through the pipe-lines to the Black Town, where it enters fresh iron reservoirs. One of these, belonging to Nobel Brothers, holds 1,200,000 gallons of oil. On issuing from them the petroleum is heated, and then passes into the retorts to be distilled. The process of distillation varies in most refineries, and is attended with trade secrets which the firms are very loth to have exposed. Meerzoeff Sons exclude strangers from their refinery, but in the case of Nobel Brothers, although their system is simpler and more perfect, no restrictions are enforced. The distillation is conducted at a temperature commencing at 140 deg. When no more oil comes over at this heat the result is withdrawn, and the temperature increased by ten degrees. This second result is also laid aside, and the heat being again increased, a third distillation is carried on, until no further easily-evaporated liquid remains. This last constitutes the best quality burning oil. In the case of the large firms it is this oil which finds its way to the market; Nobel Brothers, who supply the greater part of Russia with lamp-oil, vend no other; but nearly all the small firms, while distilling perhaps an excellent oil originally, largely adulterate it with the lighter product. It is said even that a large quantity of bad oil is sent to Russia and sold to merchants there to mix with Nobel's kerosine. It is to check these malpractices that some sort of restriction on the export of dangerous oil is advocated.

The gravity of Baku crude petroleum varies from 0·780 to 0·890. According to Gospodin Gulishambaroff, the following are the component parts of it, and the theoretical evaporative power per pound of fuel.

Petroleum.	Specific Gravity at 0 deg. Cels.	Carbon.	Hydrogen.	Oxygen.	Heating Power, British Thermal Units.	Theoretical Evaporation per 1lb. Fuel at Eight Atmospheres.
						lb.
Russian light oil	0·884	86·3	13·6	0·1	22·628	17·4
,, heavy oil	0·938	86.6	12·3	1·1	19·440	16·4
,, petroleum refuse	0·928	87·1	11·7	1·2	19·260	16·2
Pennsylvanian crude heavy	0·886	84.8	13·7	1·4	19·210	16·2

Some time ago Mr. Ludwig Nobel gave the subjoined analysis as indicating the various products obtainable from Russian crude petroleum. The Table was a practical, not a theoretical one, and was intended to give a general idea of the results derived from refining Baku oil.

Productibility of 100 *Gallons of Russian Crude Petroleum.*

	Gallons.	Gravity.	Flashing Point.
			deg.
Benzine, light oil	1	0·725	− 10
Gasoline, ,,	3	0·775	+ 0
Kerosine, burning oil	27	0·822	+ 25
Soliarovi, lubricating oil	12	0·870	+100
Veregenni, ,, ,,	10	0·890	+150
Lubricating, ,, ,,	17	0·905	+175
Cylinder, ,, ,,	5	0·915	+200
Vaseline,	1	0·925	
Liquid fuel	14		
Lost in refining	10		
Total	100		

It will be seen from this that the Baku oil gives only 27 per cent. of kerosine, as compared with the 70 to 75 per cent. obtained from the American product. Theoretically 30 per cent. should be obtained, but 27 per cent. represents the practical working. It is an obvious disadvantage that Baku petroleum should give less than half the quantity of kerosine obtainable from the American oil; but, on the other hand, this is counterbalanced by the prodigious quantities of the crude article to be had for a few pence per ton, the circumstance of double the quantity of the more valuable lubricating oil being derivable from it, and the advantage of the burning oil being in many respects better than that imported into Europe from America.

Respecting the yearly deteriorating quality of this, there have been universal complaints of late, resulting, in effect, in such a clamour that the Standard Oil Company has been compelled to send a commissioner to Europe to investigate the charges. The importers in England declare the American oil is becoming every year worse; the Standard Oil Company throw the blame upon the deterioration in the quality of the wicks. Wherever the truth may lie, the fact certainly remains that there is a widespread feeling against the American oil, and a general desire for a superior article. That article is to be found in the kerosine exported from Baku, which, apart from the individual merits of the different firms in the Caspian region, possesses in general peculiar advantages of its own over the American refined petroleum. With a view to putting this matter on a clear basis, Mr. Boverton Redwood, Chemist to the London Petroleum Association, instituted tests a short time ago with some refined petroleum of Nobels' brand, which had found its way to this country from Baku. In a report he afterwards drew up he says: "In colour and odour the oil compares favourably with the ordinary oil refined in the

United States, the colour being, in fact, but little darker than that of many parcels of so-called water-white American petroleum. The flashing point usually ranges from 86 deg. to 88 deg. Fahr. (Abel test), which is considerably higher than that of the ordinary American oil. The high specific gravity (in some cases as much as 0·822) is a characteristic feature of the product, and arguing from experience gained in relation to American petroleum, it has been erroneously asserted that such oil would require a special form of lamp for its satisfactory consumption. These experiments were therefore directed to the determination of the burning quality of the oil in such lamps as are commonly used in this country. As a preliminary step the oil was first tested roughly by burning it for lengthened periods in various forms of lamps, both cheap and costly, including those with single flat wicks, two parallel flat wicks (Duplex), and circular wicks (Argand). No difficulty was experienced in obtaining a flame of good size and character in each form of lamp, and the flame preserved those features until the whole of the oil contained in the lamp reservoir had been consumed. Ordinary American oil, in fact, exhibited marked inferiority to the Russian oil in the size of the flame after some hours' burning, the most noticeable features being that the Russian oil was consumed with remarkably little diminution in the size and illuminating power of the flame, and that the wick exhibited a very small amount of charring. To the unaided eye of the ordinary observer there was, on the whole, little, if any, difference in the light-giving power of similar lamps, charged with Russian and American oil respectively, burning side by side. The practised eye could, however, with some of the lamps detect somewhat less brilliancy in the flame of the Russian oil during the earlier hours of the burning, but at a later period, when much of the oil had been consumed, these conditions became reversed. In the cheap form of lamp, with a single flat wick, so largely used by the poorer classes constituting the bulk of the consumers, the Russian oil gave, on an average, the same amount of light as was yielded by the American oil."

Summing up his prolonged and exhaustive experiments, Mr. Redwood came to the conclusion that: "1. The Russian oil possesses advantages over the ordinary American petroleum oil of commerce, in respect to colour and odour. 2. Although the photometer indicates that the ordinary American oil is capable of yielding in the test-lamp a greater amount of light, irrespective of the quantity of oil burned (especially when the lamp has been recently filled and trimmed), than the Russian oil affords in the same lamp; yet the latter gives (A) what the consumer would call a good light, not only at first, but also after several hours' burning, and actually furnishes (B) more light per gallon of oil than is afforded in the combustion, under similar circumstances, of three out of five samples of ordinary American oil examined, and (C) but little less light than is yielded by an equal quantity of the American water-white oil tested."

The result of these experiments, without touching upon those that have been made at the instance of the German Government, and which have led to an almost identical opinion, is sufficient to put beyond cavil the merits of Baku kerosine, even apart from the fact that it is the principal lamp oil now burnt in the Russian Empire, and is rapidly taking a hold upon the German market. The testimony of a large number of scientific experts, of European celebrity, is unanimous in affirming the crude-petroleum to be a first-class product, having many qualities superior to the American oil, or in which the American oil is quite deficient. This cardinal point satisfactorily determined, the question of the quality of the oil refined from it is simply one of manufacture, the standard of which can be readily raised by introducing improved modes of distillation and refining. If the Baku kerosine, which is in its infancy, can stand such a favourable comparison with the American refined oil, it is clear that there is a great future before it; since it is a matter of fact that the quality of the oil has been improving every year, owing to improvements in manufacturing it. In Nobel Brothers' refinery, where there are forty-two retorts constantly at work, nothing that the engineering or chemical skill of the world can offer is treated with indifference. The Swedish manager, Mr. Törnudd, is an engineer of comprehensive mind as well as of practical skill. Now that the refinery, after piecemeal construction ranging over several years, has reached completion, every effort is being made to simplify the process of refining, and turn out the finest oil. The other firms show less readiness to march with events and improve their processes, although several of them have skilled German engineers and chemists. This want of enterprise is one of the causes that contributed to the success of the Americans years ago in establishing a monopoly in Russia, and which in more recent times has enabled Nobel Brothers, more vigorous and energetic, to replace that monopoly with one of their own. Their refinery is situated on rising ground occupying an area of more than a square mile. The establishment is very compactly arranged, and thoroughly organized in every detail. It is able to turn out nearly a quarter of a million gallons of the best refined petroleum per diem.

Kerosine is the principal product to which Baku at present devotes its attention. A large demand for the burning oil exists, and as the distillation and purification of it can be conducted on a small scale with relatively trifling capital, the Russians and Armenians readily go into business. The appliances needed are very simple.

They comprise a gasometer-like iron reservoir to receive the oil, a still heated by liquid fuel obtained in distilling the oil itself, an iron cooling tank, and purifying tanks to cleanse the refined fluid with sulphuric acid and caustic potash. After these come an iron reservoir to store the kerosine, and another the dregs or liquid fuel. All the reservoirs and tanks are connected by a network of pipes, and the oil is pumped through them by small pumping-engines. Such are the simple fittings of an ordinary Baku kerosine refinery, differing from the large ones simply in point of size. The list is completed with two more pipes, varying in length from a hundred yards to two or three miles, to carry away the kerosine and the liquid fuel to the piers or the establishments of other firms stretching along the bay.

When a Baku refinery simply distils kerosine it has on its hands afterwards two products—a large quantity of the light oil, evaporated during the first distillation, and comprising benzine, gasoline, &c., and a large quantity of heavy oil, fit for extracting lubricants from, remaining after the kerosine has been secured. For the former there is very little demand, and it is therefore in most instances allowed to run into the sea. In the case of the second it is pumped with the rest of the dregs through a pipe to the manufactories devoted to the extraction of lubricating oil, or else is simply sold as liquid fuel. The extraction of lubricating oil requires more extensive appliances, and greater skill, than the ordinary firms are willing to devote; hence it remains in the hands of a few firms. Such firms, and particularly a large firm like Nobel Brothers, have thus an immense advantage over the smaller ones. Besides being able, owing to superior organization, to extract the kerosine more cheaply, they utilize in various forms the light oil the refiners cast into the sea, and reap a considerable profit from the lubricating oil, which latter they extract from their own oil or else buy from the small firms in a condition fit for extraction at a price ranging from 1s. 6d. to 3s. a ton. Thanks to these circumstances, they are enabled to sell their kerosine at a lower price than the small firms, and their quality usually being better they are rapidly reducing the number of the latter. Every year the kerosine trade of Baku displays a greater tendency to pass into the hands of a few great firms, and even these to disappear before the colossal competition of Nobel Brothers. After allowing for a fair profit, and general charges, the refiners are able at the present moment to sell the finest kerosine at Baku for a penny per gallon.

The total production of refined petroleum at Baku in 1883 was 206,000 tons, or double that of 1879, and nearly ten times as much as the output of 1873. Now that such a vast system of transport is being established, the production, in response to the demand, cannot but increase very rapidly, the output being restricted of late years by the low prices prevailing on the spot. Thanks to Nobel Brothers' widespread system of distribution, the Russian refined oil finds its way to-day to every town in European Russia touched by a railway, and west of the Polish frontier as far as Vienna and Berlin. East of Baku the kerosine is exported to Askabad; south of it as far as Teheran; south-west to Van in Turkish Kurdistan; and west of the Caucasus, *viâ* Batoum, to Alexandria (where a shipload was delivered a few weeks ago), Constantinople, Trieste, and Marseilles. If it can be conveyed 2,500 miles by river and railway, and undersell the American oil in the Berlin and Stettin market, it clearly has a grand future in the south of Europe—a railway run of little more than 500 miles being all that is needed to convey the oil to the shipside at Batoum. The Batoum line was opened in June, 1883. From then to the end of the year 3,356,298 gallons were conveyed to Batoum to be shipped abroad, and 3,715,992 gallons to be despatched to the Black Sea ports of Russia. There were also large shipments from Poti.

If the crude petroleum of Baku gives less kerosine than the American oil, it affords a very much larger quantity of lubricating oil, and of a quality throwing the American article completely into the shade. Being a highly viscous fluid, completely free from any tendency to freeze within wide ranges of temperature, or to oxidise, it has already become highly appreciated in many countries, particularly in France, to which there is a large export from Baku. It is almost unnecessary to point out its very abundance renders it extremely cheap, and makes it a serious competitor to the American article. At present it is produced only by the larger firms at Baku, Nobel Brothers, Meerzoeff Sons, Shibaeff, &c., all of whom are now exporting considerable quantities to Europe *viâ* Batoum and Libau. Much of it is sent abroad in a crude condition, to be there worked up into the various varieties of lubricants needed in the arts and manufactures. In this manner there is a large anonymous sale of the oil, unsuspected by the general public. Of late years the production of lubricating oil has assumed large dimensions, and it must be expected to rapidly increase from two causes: the opening up of a great export trade *viâ* Batoum, and the establishment at Baku of factories by European capitalists to manufacture on the spot refined lubricants. Messrs. Nobel Brothers, who are able to turn out 27,000 tons of lubricating oil annually, have already devoted their attention to this branch, and may be expected to secure a large trade for it before long.

In 1883 over 4,000,000 gallons of lubricating oil were exported from Baku. During the period the Batoum Railway was opened last year the export of crude lubricating oil was 418,410 gallons, and refined 788,211 gallons. If Baku kerosine is destined to compete severely with American refined petroleum in Southern Europe and on the Continent, a future may be said to await the lubricating oil throughout the world. An immense foreign trade is anticipated for this article, once it becomes generally known that Baku can produce a better series of lubricants than Pennsylvania, at a price rendering American competition hopeless.

The heavy oils terminate in vaseline, which has the consistency of jelly. I saw some beautiful samples of it at Baku, although at present the demand for the article is not very great. The discovery of the medicinal properties of petroleum is by no means so recent as the advocates of vaseline, or petroleum jelly, wanted the world to believe a few years ago. Marco Polo wrote in the thirteenth century that it was "used to anoint camels that have the mange," and 140 years ago Jonas Hanway found the Russians drinking the white petroleum—a kind of natural kerosine found in certain parts of the Apsheron peninsula—both as a "cordial and medicine."

In America, also, the medical properties of petroleum seem to have been known to the Indians, who were in the habit of resorting to the springs to cure themselves of skin diseases.

On the opposite side of the Caspian, on the island of Tcheleken and in the Balkan hills, there are whole cliffs of ozokerit, or earth-wax, of which so much is used nowadays in the manufacture of paraffin candles. At present there is only a limited demand from abroad, but this may be expected to increase when the existence of the deposits and the excellent facilities for transporting the product are better known. A purer form of solid paraffin is also obtainable from ordinary petroleum, and already preparations are being made for despatching large consignments to this country. Factories for making kerosine candles are projected at Baku and at St. Petersburg.

Of the lighter oils a deal is either barbarously allowed

to run to waste or is used to adulterate good kerosine. All the small firms at Baku are more or less addicted to this practice. At one native manufactory I saw as much as 17 per cent. of the light oil running away like water to the Caspian, the firm having no means of utilizing it. About a quarter of a million gallons of benzine were sent up the Volga in 1883. There is also an export to Persia. At Nobel Brothers' works large forgings are made by means of gasoline. The property possessed by benzoline to take out greasy spots in cloth was noted so long ago as 1745 by Jonas Hanway. He also says: "They say it is carried into India as a great rarity, and being prepared as a japan, is the most beautiful and lasting of any that has been yet found."

This trade would seem to have ceased some time ago, for I could find no traces of it; but, none the less, Baku petroleum has a great future before it in the manufacture of dyes and colours. The tars, at present wasted, contain volatile benzole, from which the beautiful aniline colours, mauve and magenta, can be made, and also the solids, naphthaline and anthracene, from which can be prepared the alizarin, the red colour of madder, and also indigo, the staple blue dye. At present no dyes are manufactured in Russia, although the country imports 3,240,000 lbs. of alizarin yearly from Germany, and 648,000 lbs. of anthracene, paying the Germans £200,000 a-year for them. When the petroleum trade at Baku becomes a little more developed Russia will probably drive these dies out of her market, and prove a serious rival in turn to the madder industry of Holland and Turkey, and the indigo trade of India. In the Kura Valley, south of Baku, immense quantities of madder grow wild, but no attempt has been made to utilize the plant, as there would be no chances of success against the petroleum product.

Except at Surakhani, no use is made of the petroleum

or hydro-carbon gas, which escapes to the extent of millions of cubic feet from various parts of the peninsula. At Surakhani, as has been the custom for centuries, tubes are stuck into the ground, and the gas passes up them to any part of the building a light is wanted, where it flares away night and day. Lime is still burnt by taking off the crust of the ground and piling the stones upon one another in the hole. A light is then applied to the gas issuing naturally from the earth, and in a few days the lime is ready for use. The workmen cook victuals by sticking two or three tubes in the ground and placing an iron pot over them, after the manner of a gas stove. At some of the factories at Surakhani the hydro-carbon gas is conducted in a like manner to the furnaces and employed instead of oil refuse for fuel. Finally, after the crude petroleum has given mankind hydro-carbon gas, kerosine, lubricating oil, vaseline, candles, dyes, and colours, a valuable product still remains in the dregs, which is used as fuel by all the steamers and locomotives in the Caspian region; but this is such an important article that it deserves a chapter to itself.

CHAPTER XVI.

LIQUID FUEL.

Petroleum Furnaces no Novelty—Use of Oil Fuel in Ancient Times—Enormous Supply Available at Baku—The Early Use of Hydro-Carbon Gas—Bricks of Oil—Invention of Oil-Burning Appliances in America—Aydon's Furnace—Shpakovsky's Discovery of the Value of Steam as a Pulverizer—Why Liquid Fuel has not been Adopted in England and America. The Piracy of English Inventions by Russian Engineers in the Caspian Region—The First Liquid Fuel Steamer in the Caspian—Shpakovsky's Success—Improvements Effected by Lenz, the Inventor of the Apparatus now Generally in Use on Board the Caspian Steamers—Flat flame Pulverizers—Account of the Vessels Using Lenz's Apparatus—The Oil-burning Locomotives on the Transcaucasian Railway—Brandt and Karapetoff's Pulverizers—The Rival Advantages of Oil and Coal—Experience in the Caspian—Crude Petroleum may be Safely Used as well as Oil Refuse—Extension of the Use of Petroleum-burning Locomotives on Russian Railways—The Discovery of Oil in Beluchistan, and its Effect on the Russian Railway to India—Liquid Fuel in the Black Sea—Summary of its Merits—Prospects of Petroleum Fuel in the East—Satisfactory Results Already Achieved.

IF it be true that one half the world does not know how the other half lives, it is still truer that one half the world is ignorant of what the other half does. In Western Europe engineers are constantly peddling with petroleum furnaces, and putting forth liquid fuel as a novelty. In India the authorities undertake experiments with amateur squirts of oil and steam, with a view to proving whether oil will burn in furnaces or not, and treat the whole question *de novo*. If a London newspaper publishes a leading article on the substitution of petroleum refuse for wood or coal, it regards the matter as a purely speculative idea; feasible enough maybe, but still for the moment merely an interesting topic for *dilettante* writing. Yet liquid fuel for heating furnaces has been for years an established institution, and the barbarous distant Caspian region, associated in the public mind with Turcomans, scorpions, shifting deserts, and slow-paced caravans, is able to act through it the part of instructor to the engineers of the world.

In the Caspian basin petroleum refuse is the only fuel used in the furnaces of steamers, locomotives, and factory engines. Liquid fuel has throughout this region replaced wood and coal, and the use of it is now extending as far as Moscow to the north, Teheran to the south, Merv and Khiva to the east, and Batoum to the west. Baku is the centre of the liquid fuel system. It is the Newcastle of the Caspian. Ere long it promises to become the fuel source of the Euxine also; in which case there will be an end to the export trade of English coal to the Black Sea.

From the account given of the fountains of Baku it will have been seen that enormous quantities of crude oil are wasted every year. But it is not the original petroleum that is most advantageous for fuel, although it can be readily utilized; but the residue after the refining operations. This is called by the Russians *astatki*, which is simply the word for "dregs." In Baku the Tartar word *mazoot* is more commonly used. It means the same thing. *Astatki*, or *neftiani astatki*, however, is the term that has become adopted by commercial men throughout Russia, and is evidently destined to be the permanent designation. Of this *astatki*, countless millions of gallons have been wasted during the last ten years. In 1883 the aggregate export of *astatki* to Russia by all the Baku firms was 281,000 tons. On the other hand, the production was estimated as exceeding half a million tons; leaving, after making allowance for the consumption in the refineries, perhaps as much as 200,000 tons, or 50 million gallons, undisposed of. Owing to this glut the price for years has fluctuated between a few pence and half-a-crown a ton, varying according to the demand and the distance of the product from the coast; while enormous quantities have been allowed to run away to waste. During the last few months Nobel Brothers have completed the organization of their refinery, and for the future expect to turn out oil refuse at the rate of 1,300 tons a day, or 450,000 tons in the course of a year. As in a good hydro-carbon furnace one ton of oil-dregs goes as far as three tons of mineral fuel, it follows that this single establishment alone will produce annually the equivalent of 1,350,000 tons of coal.

From time immemorial petroleum has been used as fuel in the Caspian region. The earliest Persian records refer to its utilization for heating purposes. The works of travel of Arabs of the eighth century constantly mention this fact. In Marco Polo's time Baku exported petroleum for fuel as far as Bagdad. When the Russians first burst their way into the Caspian they found the extraction and shipment of the oil a regular branch of Persian commerce. But it must be admitted that the use of the liquid fuel was on a very limited scale. In the Apsheron peninsula it was never employed when hydrocarbon or petroleum gas, issuing naturally from the ground, could be more easily obtained; nor did the natives possess any apparatus for burning the liquid fuel. They simply mixed it with dirt and ashes. When the Transcaspian Trading Company established a kerosine factory at Baku, in 1858, they did not do what is the regular custom to-day—construct the refinery on the coast at the Black Town, and use crude petroleum or oil refuse in the furnaces—but chose Surakhani as the site, on account of the supply of hydro-carbon gas afforded spontaneously by the soil. This gas was allowed to accumulate in gasometers, placed over the crevices in the limestone, and was then conducted to the furnace. It was not until three years afterwards that the refuse oil was used instead. The first to introduce this innovation at Baku was a mechanic named Werser, employed at a refinery which a German, Herr Witte, had established on Holy Island. He adopted various contrivances for burning the oil, but ultimately settled upon an apparatus, consisting of a series of grates or griddles, amidst which the liquid trickled and burnt. In 1867 he took out a patent for this, and many firms adopted the apparatus, but it was so wasteful that they relinquished it the moment better contrivances came into use.

In the meanwhile a whole series of eminent men, in various countries of Western Europe, had advocated the utilization of oil refuse as liquid fuel. Cochrane urged its employment in this country quite fifty years ago. But it was not until about the sixth decade of the present century that the inventor came to the aid of the man of science; the occasion being created by the opening up of the petroleum deposits of America by Drake's new system of boring wells for oil. John Bidley took out a patent in the United States for an oil furnace for steamers in 1862, and Shaw and Linton six months later. The first was a very unsatisfactory invention, and nothing practical seems to have come of it; but in the case of the second, the United States Government appointed a commission to examine its merits. Their report was distinctly favourable to the employment of liquid fuel, and the interest excited penetrated even to Russia; where, at the time, the naval authorities in the Caspian region were trying to use in the furnaces petroleum bricks—the oil worked into masses of pitch-like consistency, and thrown into the furnaces in the same manner as ordinary coal. In

1864 the Scientific Committee of the Russian Admiralty recommended that the Russian consular agent in America should be instructed to furnish reports of the progress of liquid fuel, and send home drawings of any appliances that might come into use there. The same year experiments were also carried on at Woolwich Dockyard with the Richardson apparatus, invented in this country, and of which much was expected; but directly it became apparent that a demand might arise for waste oil, the latter, which up to then had possessed no value, rose to a price that placed competition with coal completely out of the question.

In this simple fact may be detected the principal cause of the ill-success that attended the advocacy of liquid fuel in England and America. In both countries coal was abundant and cheap, and the advantages of oil fuel were less apparent than in the Caspian region, where the Russian territory bordering on the sea contained neither wood nor coal, and where as much as £5 a ton was sometimes paid for anthracite. The difficulties attending the dispatch of coal from the Don valley to the Caspian region compelled Russia to resort to the use of liquid fuel, and this explains its rapid development once a good apparatus had been invented to consume it.

The honour of inventing this must be divided between two persons, Aydon, an Englishman, and Shpakovsky, a Russian. Both hit upon the idea about the same time, of making an apparatus to pulverize the oil, and blow it into the furnace in the form of spray. This principle is the main feature of all the appliances in use in the Caspian region to-day. But the utility of the idea rested upon the means adopted to carry it into practice, and when we come to examine this point we see at once how the two inventors assisted one another. Professor Mendelaieff has claimed, I believe, that Aydon copied his invention from Shpakovsky's, and supports this view by stating that the latter had the precedence of three and a half months in registration.* But during this period Shpakovsky's drawings were deposited in the Patent Office, where Aydon had no access to them; while further, Shpakovsky simply put in a sketch, and Aydon a complete and elaborate set of practical designs. Then, again, Shpakovsky used a blast of hot air in his pulverizer, while Aydon employed a better agent—superheated steam. Afterwards, Shpakovsky certainly improved upon the latter by adopting ordinary steam, but still the idea of using steam at all rested with Aydon. Apart from this, Aydon's apparatus was the first of the kind to be shown in a working condition, and in this manner first placed the employment of pulverized petroleum on a satisfactory basis. In his appliance the oil was allowed to run through a small orifice, about $\frac{1}{8}$ inch in diameter, in a continuous stream at the rate of about three gallons per hour. As the oil fell vertically it was met by a jet of superheated steam, which forced it into the furnace in the form of a cloud of exceedingly fine spray, at the same time converting it into vapour, which took fire and was consumed.

Gospodin Gulishambaroff, after examining the claims of the two inventors, says:—"Aydon's was the first attempt at a steam pulverizer for petroleum, which gives such brilliant results to-day; only the apparatus has undergone considerable modifications, and is still in a state of transition. One of its greatest defects was the employment of superheated steam, which was a source of inconvenience, and the heat was not maintained at a regular temperature." But for the moment it was not a question of a pulverizer so much as of the agent used to inject the oil into the furnace. In replacing the hot blast and superheated steam with ordinary steam, Shpakovsky hit upon the best solution of the problem.

* Shpakovsky's pulverizer was registered in England June 27, 1865 (No. 1,711).

But here we see what an important effect a real demand for an invention exercises upon its development. In England there was no pressing need for liquid fuel furnaces, and Aydon's apparatus simply remained a curiosity. This may be said to have been the case with most English patents of the kind. New ideas were constantly being registered in England, but for want of means of applying them they simply stagnated and died out. On the other hand, those same ideas, which in Western Europe were bringing their inventors no profit, were being adopted and improved upon in the Caspian region, and gradually conducing to the development of the apparatus now in use.

The first liquid fuel furnace of the pulverizer description employed in the Caspian region was the Kamensky furnace, in the early part of 1869. Kamensky was the government engineer of Baku port. The petroleum fields had not been greatly developed then, and Baku owed its importance mainly to the presence of the dockyard there, the head-quarters of the Caspian fleet having been shifted to the place a couple of years earlier from Astrakhan. Kamensky obtained plans of the apparatus which Henri Deville had brought out in 1868, and fitted to the 60 horse-power engines of the *Le Pouebla*, one of the yachts of the Emperor of the French; and making one or two alterations, passed off the invention as his own. In France Deville obtained a great reputation by the energetic and elaborate manner he dealt with the subject of liquid fuel; but his apparatus was a failure. Kamensky, on his part, was equally unsuccessful with his copy of it, and the Baku naval authorities after a while refused to sanction any more experiments with the thing.

In the meanwhile, the Caucasus and Mercury Company, the State-aided steamboat company running vessels on the Caspian, had been making equally unsatisfactory trials with liquid fuel at their dockyard at Astrakhan. At

s

the close of these the directors thought the best thing to do would be to send their principal engineer on a tour through Europe, to pick up all the ideas he could on the subject. Gospodin Lenz accordingly repaired to England in 1869, and saw Aydon and Dorsett, and afterwards to France, where he made the acquaintance of Deville. The French apparatus pleased him the most, and he brought back with him to Russia drawings prepared by Deville for the *Derjavin*, one of the Company's steamers. This proving a failure Lenz grafted the best features of Aydon's apparatus upon it. The composite apparatus worked for a couple of months and gave the *Derjavin* the right of being regarded as the first steamer worked with liquid fuel in Russia; but the experiment was none the less a failure, and the apparatus was not used after the close of the season of 1870.

All this while Shpakovsky, Aydon's rival, had not been idle. For several years he had been improving his apparatus, and within a day or two of the stoppage of the *Derjavin* a steamer appeared on the Volga fitted with it. This was the *Alexai*, belonging to the Lebed Company, an unsubsidized steamboat corporation competing with the Caucasus and Mercury Company on the Caspian Sea. The experiment with the *Alexai* was sufficiently successful to justify its more extended application, and in May 1870 the first petroleum-burning steamer appeared on the Caspian—the *Iran*, of 45 horse-power, engined by Penn. This had low pressure engines, with a couple of furnaces. Shpakovsky fitted each of the latter with three pulverizers, and replaced the coal bunkers with six oil reservoirs, each holding seven or eight tons apiece, and two extra ones in the bow, containing ten tons apiece. The expenditure of oil fuel was found to be not more than seventy pounds an hour. The apparatus was a great success, and to Shpakovsky must certainly be assigned the honour of having solved the problem of employing liquid fuel, since, apart from his early discovery of the advantages of steam as a pulverizer, his apparatus was the first to stand the test of permanent practical use. The *Iran* has been running now with Shpakovsky's apparatus fifteen years, during which period she has made on an average sixteen trips annually from Baku to the Volga and back. Two hundred and forty voyages constitute a prolonged experiment, placing all cavil against the employment of liquid fuel completely out of the question, especially when I add that the fire bars of the *Iran* have only been changed three times during the whole period, and the boilers cleaned once a year.

In 1871 the Company had the *Russia* fitted with Shpakovsky's apparatus, in 1873 the *Helma*, and finally in 1879 the *Daghestan* and *Pir-Bazaar*—the latter having engines of 80 horse-power. To diminish the intensity of the flame jutting to the extremity of the furnace, the inventor lined the end of it with bricks—not fire-bricks, but made of the ordinary clay at Baku. As these last a long time, Gulishambaroff is of opinion that the alleged ruinous effects of the heat upon the boilers in using the Shpakovsky apparatus are exaggerated; but, all the same, the Lebed is the only company using it. The apparatus is obviously a good one, or it would not have been retained so long in use by that pushing company; but it is admittedly not the best. The most perfect appliance, and the one most generally used in the Caspian Sea, is the invention of Mr. Lenz.

We have seen that Lenz had failed completely with his combined Deville-Aydon apparatus. This so discouraged him that he dropped the matter for several months. The success of Shpakovsky's *Alexai* however, revived his energies. In the Shpakovsky furnace the oil was injected with steam; to do this, it was necessary to first get up a certain amount of steam in the boiler—a task accomplished by burning a little wood. An examination of this arrangement suggested to Lenz the idea of replacing Deville's patent furnace with an ordinary wood-burning furnace, as adopted by Shpakovsky. When the Deville pulverizer still continued to give unsatisfactory results he replaced it with the Aydon pulverizer, which worked very much better. After this he set to work to improve upon the latter, and finally in 1872 produced the apparatus which is now commonly employed in the steamboats of the Volga and Caspian.

This is a copy of Aydon's apparatus, but with many advantages. It consists of two horizontal pipes, thrust a little way inside the furnace. The upper one is fed with oil, and the lower one with steam; each pipe being regulated by a cock by which the supply can be cut off. The two fluids enter the pulverizer, but are prevented from mingling by a diaphragm. This contains notches filed in the lip of it, through which the petroleum trickles, to be blown off by the steam escaping from the under side. Besides following Shpakovsky instead of Aydon in using ordinary steam in lieu of superheated steam, Lenz introduced an improvement in regulating the flow of oil and steam—placing the check, not previous to the passage of the fluid into the pulverizer, but where it issued from it, which led to easier and steadier working. The pulverizer was also subjected to numerous alterations, and after many experiments he adopted a flat flame, instead of the conical flare or the ring of jets common to most other appliances.

Lenz's apparatus having become the most generally adopted, may be said to have experienced the severest test of all. It was first fitted to the *Turcoman*, belonging to the Caucasus and Mercury Company, in 1873; and soon afterwards to the *Bariatinsky*, of 120 horse-power; the *Michael*, of 100 horse-power; the *Volga*, of 70 horse-power; and the *Armenian*, *Caspian*, and other vessels belonging to the same company. In 1874 the Russian Government decided to adopt it for the Caspian Fleet, and gradually fitted the whole of the vessels with it.

Year Adopted.	Name of War-vessel.	Engine-power.
1874	Khivenets	60 horse-power.
,, ...	Araxes	40 ,,
1875	Nasr-Eddin Shah	160 ,,
1876	Sekeera	70 ,,
1878	Ural	100 ,,
,, ...	Persianin	60 ,,
,, ...	Lotsman	22 ,,
1879	Griboyadoff, Pestchal & Legki. Various.	

Other vessels have been fitted with it since.

Besides the Caspian Fleet, there are over forty steamers belonging to the Caspian mercantile marine using this pulverizer, or close imitations of it, and upwards of 100 steamers on the Volga. These steamers are not trifling ones. The *Spinoza*, 245 feet long, carrying 750 tons of oil cargo, and having engines of 120 nominal horse-power, will give an idea of the dozen steamers possessed by Nobel Brothers alone, without touching upon the flotillas of other companies.

As soon as his apparatus proved a success Lenz left the Caucasus and Mercury Company, and set up as an engineer on his own account at Baku. Recently he has endeavoured to apply his apparatus to locomotives, but has been less fortunate in this; the alleged objections being that it destroys the tube sheet, starts the tube ends, and does not heat the fire box equally all over. But he is continually experimenting, and may yet in course of time overcome these defects.

Since Lenz achieved his original triumph a number of rival appliances have been invented, and every year sees fresh additions to their numbers. Benkston, an engineer in the employ of the Caucasus and Mercury Company, brought out a pulverizer a few years ago, on the Shpakovsky principle, which is now used in the engineering establishment he subsequently started at Baku. Sandgren, another engineer of the same company, who succeeded Lenz, patented in 1878 a pulverizer which has been fitted to several vessels. Brandt, the head of an engineering firm at Baku, has devoted himself chiefly to locomotives, and his pulverizer has been adopted for the Transcaspian railway, and is now being introduced on the Transcaucasian line.

This is described as a very ingenious arrangement, distinguished from all the preceding ones by having an all-round discharge, so that it gives a tubular flame. The petroleum enters through the central pipe, and overflowing on to the diaphragm, trickles down to the lip, where it meets the steam, and is driven off in spray. The regulation is effected by cocks from the foot-plate, while the burner stands in the centre of the fire-box, and delivers a sheet of flame, which is carried upwards by the draught, and impinges upon all the plates very equally.

Some time ago it was tried on the Transcaucasian railway, but Karapetoff, the engineer of the line, reported unfavourably of it. But the fact of Karapetoff himself having his own appliance in use largely accounts for this, the more independent and less biassed Baku Technical Society having declared in its favour. In the steamers of the Caucasus and Mercury Company, and in the stationary engines of the Baku refineries, Brandt's pulverizer has proved a great success; and lately the Transcaucasian Railway Company, in spite of Karapetoff's report, has ordered a number of locomotives to be fitted with it.

Karapetoff's arrangement, which is in use in the locomotives running between the Caspian and the Black Sea, is simply an imitation of Lenz's. The pulverizer is fixed in the fire-box door in such a way as to throw a flat flame on to a refractory brick bottom, which soon attains a high temperature, and thus aids in inflaming the small bubbles of petroleum which may reach it unconsumed. Were Lenz's pulverizer placed in an inclined position over a brick bottom the result would be the same.

The year before last Ludwig Nobel brought out a pulverizer, reminding one at first sight of Brandt's, but containing several improvements upon it. By cutting one or more spiral grooves in the conical head he gives the flame a rolling motion, which sweeps it along the inner surface of the cylindrical boiler flue. Various other modifications render it one of the most economical appliances in use at Baku. Not that this is a special recommendation in the Caspian region. Oil refuse is so cheap that it is almost a matter of indifference whether an apparatus is wasteful or not. The further the distance from Baku, however, the more important becomes the feature of economy. Lenz reckons that his apparatus ought not to consume more than six pounds of oil an hour to each horse-power; but the furnaces of the different steamers vary considerably in point of consumption, and the actual practice with Lenz's apparatus is said to range from eleven to seventeen pounds. Ludwig Nobel estimates the expenditure of his apparatus at from five to seven pounds per horse-power per hour.

Quite as much seems to depend upon the engines and boilers of the vessel as upon the apparatus itself, and even when both are satisfactory the mechanic may waste the fuel. Some instances will show how diverse the results are, and the perfection that may, in spite of them, be attained by liquid fuel. The war vessel *Ural*, of 100 horse-power, used to burn thirty poods of anthracite an hour; on being fitted with a Lenz's apparatus it burn: twenty-eight poods of liquid fuel. The gunboat *Sekeera*, of seventy horse-power, consumed exactly as much liquid fuel as it had previously done coal. The same was the case with the *Khivenets*. The war steamer *Tchikishlar* was allowed by the regulations to burn fourteen pounds of coal per horse-power every hour; its consumption of *astatki* was eleven and three quarter pounds. This was a little better. In the case of the schooner *Pistchal* the proportion was fourteen and a half pounds of liquid fuel to fourteen pounds of coal. But in most of these cases the engines and boilers were of ancient construction, the pulverizers were of early make, and there was no check placed upon the consumption of fuel, so long as it did not exceed the regulation quantity of coal. On the merchant steamers of the Volga, where a restriction was imposed by the enhanced cost of the fuel in conveying it to that river from Baku, the results were of a very different character. The *Constantine Kaufmann* burns only five and one-third pounds per horse-power per hour; the *Alexander Jandre* burns six and a half pounds; and the *Peter the Great*, a large passenger steamer of 200 horse-power, has the reputation of burning least of all. Its consumption is only four and three-quarters pounds of liquid fuel per horse-power per hour.

Theoretically a ton of liquid fuel ought to go as far as two tons of coal, and as a matter-of-fact, in the more economical furnaces a proportion of one to three is often attained. This feature is of extreme importance away from Baku; but at Baku itself the firms, like the Government, are quite content if a ton of *astatki* goes as far as a ton of coal. It is easy to understand this, when it is remembered that a ton of *astatki* is thirty or forty times cheaper than a ton of coal, and never exceeds in the dearest times the price of half-a-crown a ton.

Practice has demonstrated that petroleum refuse is a perfectly safe fuel; being, indeed, safer even than coal. One or two scientific men, among them Professor Lisenko, of St. Petersburg, have declared the crude oil to be dangerous, but Gulishambaroff proves this to be a fallacy. Says Lisenko:—"Petroleum dregs constitute, owing to the difficulty of setting fire to them, a material perfectly safe for river steamers. This, however, cannot be said of crude petroleum, which ignites more readily, and hence, owing to its dangerous qualities and the irrationality of making use of it when dregs will do as well, its use ought to be prohibited on rivers." Gulishambaroff, arguing from practice, combats both these opinions. He asserts it is quite safe, after standing a little while in the air, and he rightly opines that if there is a strong demand for the article as fuel, and the crude oil is forthcoming in large quantities, the question of "irrationality" ought not to be made a cause for official prohibition.

"Crude petroleum," he says, "only needs to stand in the open air for a few days, and then a firebrand may be safely thrust into it; men may be often seen doing this in the oil lakes of Balakhani. In summer it clears itself of its inflammable qualities very rapidly, which is proved by the fact that oil thrown up by the Baku fountains, and forming lakes, loses in a few days ten to fifteen per cent. of its gravity. This operation may be accomplished in winter by heating the oil in open receptacles. The flashing point of crude petroleum, fresh from the well, and having a gravity of 0·870, is 40 degrees Celsius; the flashing point of petroleum refuse ranges between 80 and 170 degrees Celsius. But the same crude oil that flashed at 40 degrees on issuing from the well will not flash under 60 degrees if allowed to remain in the open air a week; while after a fortnight the temperature must be 70 degrees for it to ignite."

Abundant proof might also be cited from the experience of the last ten years at Baku. Thousands of tons of crude petroleum, thrown up by the fountains and allowed to spoil in the surface lakes, have been used as fuel, without any mishaps. For years also the locomotives of the Petroleum Branch of the Transcaucasian Railway have been running daily from Balakhani to Baku, with trainloads of crude oil freshly drawn from the wells, without a single case of explosion. So much for the crude article. As for the safety with which the dregs may be carried and used on any kind of steamer, there should be sufficient proof afforded by the fifteen years' practice in the Caspian to set all fears at rest. What test could be severer than its employment on steamers loaded from head to stern with hundreds of tons of inflammable kerosine? Yet hundreds of voyages have been performed by the floating oil-cisterns of the Caspian, without a single case of destruction from the ignition of the vessel by its liquid fuel, or its refined petroleum cargo.*

To-day not a single steamer or locomotive in the Caspian region burns wood or coal. *Astatki* is the exclusive fuel employed. Having established itself thoroughly in the Caspian Sea, the product is rapidly pushing its way up the Volga and along the south-east Russian railways. Experiments conducted in 1883 on the Griazi-Tsaritzin Railway showed that the cost per verst of a train driven by a petroleum-burning locomotive was 11·64 copecks, as

* Petroleum refuse is so safe that the municipal authorities at Baku use it to "water" the streets with. The latter liquid is both scarce and dear at Baku, and even if otherwise it would be of little use to allay the dust during the hot season, most of the streets containing shoals a foot or more thick. The ordinary watering cart would only mitigate the evil for a few minutes, whereas a dressing of petroleum refuse soddens the sand and renders it too heavy to rise for a month or so. In April this year Meerzoeff Sons made a present to the town of 400 barrels of petroleum refuse, to "water" the streets with in this manner. It answers the purpose capitally; but it has one drawback: when any dust at Baku settles on one's clothes the heat of the sun causes the oil to penetrate into them, and no amount of brushing will remove the stain.

compared with 26·35 copecks expended on anthracite coal. The effect of this upon the company is displayed in a letter which Mr. Thomas Urquhart, M.I.M.E., locomotive superintendent to the railway, addressed to *Engineering* in March this year, with reference to an article of mine in that paper upon petroleum. I may state that I know nothing of Mr. Urquhart personally, and was quite unaware that there was any English engineer on the railway.

"Out of 131 locomotives on the Griazi-Tsaritzin Railway, 72 are now altered and burning petroleum refuse as fuel, and by October this year the whole of the locomotives on the line (465 miles) will be burning petroleum. From fully a year's experience with petroleum as a fuel on a large scale with passenger and goods' engines of various types, I venture to state that petroleum refuse is the best and most convenient form of fuel ever used for locomotives or marine purposes. Space will not admit of enumerating the many advantages this fuel possesses, but a few will suffice to show the saving in time and money which is possible by its use, on sea or land; certainly only in countries where it abounds in large quantities, and at prices favourably compared with other forms of fuel. A practical evaporation of from 12 to $13\frac{1}{2}$ pounds per pound of petroleum is quite possible in locomotives under ordinary conditions. A cold locomotive can be fired up to eight atmospheres in from 50 to 55 minutes; and in engines in daily service where the water remains warm steam can be made to eight atmospheres in from 20 to 25 minutes. Water and fuel can be taken at the same time by simply having the water and petroleum tanks or columns conveniently arranged, the latter being required only at engine depôts, say from 100 to 150 miles apart. From three to four tons of petroleum carefully measured can be run into the tank on the tender in about four minutes, requiring the presence of only one fuel attendant. The combustion is smokelessly complete, leaving no soot or other residue in the tubes or furnace. A cast-iron plate, having simply a two-inch sight-hole, is fixed over the firing door, thus virtually having no door whatever. The main obstacles hitherto encountered when applying petroleum as a fuel for locomotives are completely obviated by new and improved appliances especially designed for the purpose, a saving of nearly fifty per cent. in weight as compared with coal being attained in regular practice. Besides locomotive consumption, petroleum has become quite general as a fuel for pumping and other engines at the several stations and works on the line."

Tsaritzin is the first railway point touched at on the river Volga, and is 318 miles higher up than Astrakhan. Sailing vessels are chiefly used to convey the oil refuse to the mouth of the river, where it is pumped into barges, and thence tugged north as far even as Nijni-Novgorod. The following is the average cost of a ton of *astatki* delivered at Tsaritzin.

	s.	d.	
Price delivered on board ship at Baku 4 copecks the pood or	2	6	the ton.
Freight to mouth of the Volga 3 copecks the pood or	1	11	,,
Freight to Astrakhan at 2 copecks the pood or	1	3	,,
Freight to Tsaritzin at 4 copecks the pood or	2	6	,,

Total 13 copecks the pood, or 8s. 2d. the ton.

The maximum cost last year was sixteen copecks, or ten shillings the ton, but the increase of shipping lowered freights in the autumn. Some experts at Baku are of opinion that the price will fall lower than eight shillings per ton; but it is obvious that there is a point below which it would not be worth while to carry it, and if the complaints of the shippers have any real basis, that point is already almost reached. Thanks to its cheapness, it is a severe competitor of Russian coal, which had begun to be developed in the Donetz valley. Most of the South Russian railways are experimenting with petroleum-burning locomotives, and there is hardly a doubt that the example of the Tsaritzin line will exercise an important effect on them. The total quantity of coal at present used yearly on all the Russian railways is about a million and a quarter tons; which is chiefly absorbed by the southern and western lines, and is for the most part imported from abroad. Baku could readily supply the equivalent of this in liquid fuel. The amount of wood used on the railways is 650,000 cubic *sajines*, or seven-foot fathoms. Where wood is abundant and cheap the competition with *astatki* is severe; but such localities are becoming rarer every year. In Moscow English coal was the only fuel used on a considerable scale a few years ago, in excess of the native wood. Now petroleum refuse has been adopted by a considerable number of firms.

The Caspian is thus rapidly becoming a fuel provider for Russia proper. South of the Caspian Sea the use of *astatki* extends as far as the Persian capital. Fifteen hundred tons of *astatki* and crude petroleum are despatched from Baku to the Persian ports yearly, and this supply will develop enormously with the extension of the Russian railway system in the direction of Teheran. East of the Caspian it is the exclusive fuel used on the Transcaspian railway, and in the forts and barracks of the newly-annexed Turcoman region. I have already referred to the immense demand that will spring up when that railway extends to India. At present the gap between Kizil Arvat, the Russian terminus, and Sibi, the English terminus, is 1,122 miles. This will be reduced to 1,037 miles with the completion of the Quetta section, and again to 902 miles with the extension of the Russian line to Askabad, which is simply a question of a year or two. When these two sections are finished there will only remain 900 miles of line to construct to join India with Europe by railway, and no power on earth can prevent the ultimate junction of the two systems in this direction. When this is brought about the railway will use nothing but liquid fuel—no other is available in Central Asia; and it is a remarkable circumstance that not only do enormous deposits of oil exist at the starting-point of the Russian railway from the Caspian, but a great quantity has also been discovered recently in proximity to Quetta. How large the Beluchistan deposits are has not yet transpired, but, for the moment, it is satisfactory to know that this great railway of the future is amply secured in point of fuel. Further eastward an extensive supply has been found in the Punjab, covering an area of 102 miles long by 88 miles broad. What has been achieved by the marine of the Caspian and the railways of the Caucasus and South Russia in replacing coal with oil may yet be repeated in the immediate future on board the steamers of the river Indus and the locomotives of North-west India.

As for the European outlets in the Black Sea, by means of the present one, *viâ* Batoum and Poti, and the future additional one when Baku is connected with Novorossisk, *viâ* Petrovsk and Vladikavkaz, the prospect is equally encouraging. The Transcaucasian Railway Company charges, I believe, the same rate for *astatki* as the more valuable burning oil; which renders its cost delivered at Batoum for the moment not much under twenty-six shillings the ton. Russia imports yearly to the Black Sea about 300,000 tons of coal, chiefly from England. The price of this ranges from £2 to £3 a ton. Petroleum fuel is thus two or three times cheaper than English coal, or, if we reckon that it goes two or three times as far, a ton of petroleum fuel, costing at Batoum twenty-six shillings, is equal to £4—£9 worth of coal; £4 being the minimum and £9 the maximum. The price of English coal long ago reached its lowest price in the Black Sea; it is unsusceptible of further reduction. The present price of petroleum refuse, however, is only at its maximum point, and as the Transcaucasian railway develops its resources, and the ramifications extend to Novorossisk, the charge at Batoum may gradually fall to ten shillings a ton. This is apart from any question of a pipe-line to pump the residue to the Black Sea. Some persons at Baku hold this scheme to be impossible: the sediment would be too great, they say; but I have been assured by an American engineer, thoroughly conversant with pipe-lines in the Pennsylvanian region, that this difficulty could be easily overcome by the employment of electricity and other means.

The Russian Government has recently been conducting experiments with liquid fuel at Sevastopol, with a view to using it instead of English coal for the men-of-war of the Black Sea fleet. It is contemplated to reduce the Caspian fleet to the proportions of a police flotilla, and place it under the control of the naval authorities of the Black Sea. This will render Baku dockyard a branch of the Black Sea naval establishment, and the Caspian will certainly prove a nearer source of fuel supply than either Newcastle-on-Tyne or Cardiff. When petroleum fuel has spread to the Black Sea its extension to the Mediterranean is but a mere matter of time. The expensive English coal will be hardly able to compete with it there. But it is through the Suez Canal, along the Eastern trade routes, that the greatest triumph of liquid fuel may be expected. Every mile adds to the cost of English coal in that direction, and renders competition with *astatki* shipped from Batoum more difficult. From Malta to Singapore Baku will be able before long to keep every coaling station abundantly supplied with inexpensive oil refuse. From Singapore to China the task of maintaining the cheap oil supply could be undertaken by British Burmah, which possesses enormous deposits of petroleum gradually being opened up. Baku and Rangoon could readily furnish enough petroleum fuel for all the trade routes of the East, and may, in fact, be expected some day to do so, once its advantages are generally recognized.

Those advantages are more important than is commonly imagined. The fuel is perfectly smokeless, which is a very great merit on board cruisers and men-of-war. Burned in locomotives on the Metropolitan Railway it would put an end at once to the greatest difficulty experienced in working the line—the annoyance to the passengers caused by the smoke. If petroleum-burning engines ran on the Underground line, as they run on the Transcaucasian railway, there would be no need for hideous smoke holes; and if employed in the projected Channel Tunnel, the necessity for using an elaborate and problematical system of ventilation would be done away with at once.

Another great advantage is the absence of any stoking, and the ease with which the fire can be lighted or suppressed at a moment's notice. Few people realize the miserable life led by stokers afloat, particularly during the passage through the Suez Canal and Red Sea. The sufferings of thousands of unfortunates would be suspended at a stroke by using liquid fuel, which, being burned in the form of a huge gas jet, requires no stoking or personal attendance of any kind, and maintains what is impossible to secure with coal—a steady even temperature. The fire can be manipulated to any degree of intensity by simply touching the cock of the feeding pipes; and the sole bit of trouble—burning a few handfuls of cotton waste or wood in the first instance to get up a little steam to start pulverizing the oil (the work of ten minutes or a quarter of an hour)—is abolished in the recently perfected Walker furnace, in which some hydro-carbon gas is kept stored for this purpose. Instead of there being a stoker or two to each furnace, a single man can look after a dozen or twenty furnaces, and as a matter of fact, does so in the Caspian oil refineries. This is a very important economy. So simple is the fuel to use, and so reliable is the action of the pulverizer, that the English and the Russian engineers running the steamers from Baku to the mouth of the Volga told me that having turned on and adjusted the flame at starting, they concern themselves no more about their fires until they reach their destination, in a couple of days' time. The fuel is clean to use, and there is none of the dust arising from coal or wood, which is a great nuisance on board passenger steamers.

Equally important is the economy gained in storage room. A ton of liquid fuel can do the work of two or three tons of coal; thus a steamer can either take two or three times less fuel, and utilize the bunker space for cargo purposes, or it can go two or three times as far without stopping to coal. But there is an additional economy beyond even this. A ton of oil refuse, I believe, takes up very little more than half the space of a ton of coal. In this manner, in the more economical liquid fuel furnaces, 1,000 tons of oil refuse not only goes as far as 3,000 tons of coal, but takes up only the bunker space of 500 or 600 tons of coal and allows the balance of 2,500 tons to be applied to passenger or cargo purposes.*

* General Valentine Baker, Mr. Arthur Arnold, M.P., and other eminent travellers who saw the petroleum-burning steamers of the Caspian when the use of oil was in its infancy, speak in the warmest terms of the advantages of liquid fuel. In America, where there has not yet been anything like the development observable in the Caspian, and the use of the fuel is still in a crude experimental stage, the following are the advantages claimed by Chief Engineer Isherwood, of

T

Altogether, therefore, without touching upon minor advantages, liquid fuel compares so favourably with wood or coal that Baku would appear to be fully justified in anticipating such a great future for her inexhaustible stores of the article. If it be remembered that during the last two centuries upwards of 2,000 improvements have been registered in bringing the present oil lamp in use to perfection, the progress achieved by fifty inventors, in England and Russia, France and the United States, in creating in the course of a little more than twenty years a furnace capable of satisfactorily burning liquid fuel in steamers and locomotives, cannot but be regarded as remarkable; and affords grounds for sanguine expectations of further advances in the mode of utilizing the product. Such advances will not only be to the advantage of Russia, but of India also; for there is little doubt that some day liquid fuel will be extensively used throughout the peninsula. Progress at Baku is thus calculated to react favourably on the development of the petroleum deposits of British Burmah, the Punjab, and Beluchistan, and add to the prosperity and comfort of the people of India.

the United States Navy, for liquid over solid fuel :—" 1. Reduction of 40·5 per cent. in weight of fuel. 2. Reduction of 36·5 per cent. in bulk. 3. Greater facilities in storage. 4. Reduction of number of stokers to a quarter. 5. Greater speed in raising steam. 6. Fires can be extinguished instantly. 7. No smoke, no ashes, no waste. 8. No loss of heat from opening furnace doors to feed with coal. 9. Ability to command increased temperature without forced draught." The Russian authorities are beginning to use it instead of wood to heat the public buildings and barracks in the Caucasus.

PLATE 14.—PORTRAIT OF LUDWIG NOBEL.

CHAPTER XVII.

THE OIL KING OF BAKU.

The Most Important Factor of the Baku Oil Trade—"Beyond the Sea a Chicken may be Bought for a Farthing, but it Costs a Pound to Bring it Home"—Career of Ludwig Nobel—Origin of the Nobels—Invention of the Torpedo by Emmanuel Nobel, and of Dynamite by Alfred Nobel—How Ludwig Nobel Acquired the Fortune with which he Started Operations in Petroleum—Commencement of the Enterprise at Baku—Laying Down the First Pipe-line—Replacing Barrels with Cistern Steamers—Account of the Oil Fleet—The "Nine-Foot" Shallows of the Volga—Transporting the Oil from Baku to Tsaritzin—Inaugurating the Tank-Car System—Establishment of the Petroleum Network of Depots Throughout Russia—Mode of Distributing the Oil in the Provinces—Not a Drop Sold except for Cash—Baku Kerosine in Germany—Prospects of the Trade Abroad—Statistical Description of the Present Position of Nobel Brothers' Petroleum Production Company—The World Does Not know its Greatest Men—Russian Hatred of Foreigners—Character of Ludwig Nobel—His Remarkable Talents as an Engineer.

THE factor exercising the greatest influence on the past, present, and future of the Caspian petroleum industry is that of transport. Baku controls a larger supply of crude petroleum than America. It can turn out a cheaper kerosine and a better lubricating oil, while possessing in addition an enormous quantity of liquid fuel. For all these products there is a great and growing demand. This is particularly the case with kerosine. If the reader lives in London, where refined petroleum is only used as a casual substitute for gas, this fact may not be sufficiently realized by him; but he can hardly go away

T 2

from that great city without observing the demand for good cheap lamp oil that prevails in the village, the roadside cottage, and the country railway station. In many parts of the Continent, where gas-lighting is less developed, the demand for burning oil is still greater. Out of the total of 101 millions composing the present population of the Russian Empire, probably ninety-five millions are dependent on other light than of gas. In the suburbs of all Russian towns lamps are used—Moscow, one of the best lit cities in the Empire, having no less than 8,000 kerosine lamps in use in the streets. Consequently in Russia alone there is a great home demand for Baku petroleum oil, without touching upon foreign markets. But a cheap and abundant supply of good kerosine in the Caspian is of no use to Russia, unless it can be placed in the lamps of the people at a price accessible to all. That price is entirely dependent upon the cost of the transport. The Russian people have a proverb that "beyond the sea a chicken can be bought for a farthing, but it costs a pound to bring it home." Applying this to kerosine, it is no source of satisfaction for Russia to have kerosine at a penny a gallon at Baku, if its carriage to Moscow adds three or four shillings per gallon to the cost.

There was a time, however, when this condition of things existed, and when it was cheaper for the merchants of the upper course of the Volga to get their oil from America than from the Caspian Sea. Even so recently as last year, Tiflis, up to within a few weeks of the opening of the Baku railway, drew her supply of lamp-oil from America, a distance of more than 8,000 miles, in spite of countless millions of gallons of petroleum running to waste 341 miles from her doors. For years America literally controlled the entire petroleum market of Russia. How at length her sway was overthrown, and her power attacked in turn in Austria and Germany, forms one of the most interesting episodes of modern industrial progress. The revolution was due to Ludwig Nobel, the Baku oil king. The manner in which it was effected can be best described by giving an account of himself and his brothers.

The father was a Swede of great ingenuity and skill, thoroughly devoted to his profession, who, in the hope of finding wider scope for his talents, proceeded to Russia in 1838, carrying with him the models of two torpedoes of his own invention—one for naval and the other for land purposes. These so impressed the Russian Government that it gave him a sum of money for the patent, and assisted him in establishing a workshop to manufacture them. As he spoke no Russian, a young Finnish engineer, speaking Swedish and Russian, was placed at his disposition by the authorities. This individual, General Baron Standertskjöld (pronounced Standertsheld), is now head of the Government Small Arms Factory at Toula, and in subsequent years proved a staunch friend to Emmanuel Nobel's sons in assisting them in the petroleum enterprise. In 1842 Ludwig Nobel, then a boy of twelve, proceeded with the rest of the family to St. Petersburg—his elder brother Robert had already preceded him and entered the business. Seven years later Ludwig also became an apprentice; and it can be well understood that under the guidance of a father who possessed the characteristics which have made the Stephensons a proverbial type, he had every opportunity of becoming a clear-headed, ingenious, hardworking, practical engineer. Ere long the Crimean war broke out; and the father and the sons had their hands full of making submarine mines for Cronstadt and Sveaborg. The task of placing them in the water to hamper the Allied Fleets also devolved upon them, and involved a constant exercise of ingenuity.* It would be

* The mines occasioned more annoyance than injury to the Allied Fleets, but this was due to causes beyond Emmanuel Nobel's control.

interesting to describe these operations more fully, but they are hardly relevant to the present work; and what I have already said on the subject will be sufficient to indicate the genius of the Nobel family:—Emmanuel Nobel, the father, was the inventor of the torpedo, and of his sons, Alfred Nobel discovered dynamite, and Robert and Ludwig Nobel became the twin organizers of the Russian petroleum industry.

In the second year of the Crimean war the Government built a powerful fleet of gunboats and floating batteries, and Emmanuel Nobel was encouraged to construct engines for them. This was a very onerous undertaking, as there was no skilled labour forthcoming, and the Swedes had to train the workmen as well as supervise them. For a whole year Ludwig Nobel worked as a blacksmith with the men to get out the large forgings required. This necessity for practically creating an organization out of the most unpromising materials gave both Robert and Ludwig Nobel a mobility of mind, energy, readiness of resource, knowledge of human nature, and patience in elaborating success in face of ignorance, prejudice, and stupidity, of immense use to them in after years. Between 1855 and 1858 the Swedes built three pairs of engines of 500 H.P., and five of 200 H.P.; from 1857 to 1862 they constructed fifty steamers, for the most part for the Volga, many of which are running to-day. By the year 1860 the engineering

---

At Sveaborg, for instance, he wanted to lay them down sufficiently far from the forts to prevent the Allied Fleets approaching near enough to bombard the latter. The Russian authorities, however, thought that if this were done our sailors would fish them up and steal them. They, therefore, had them placed close under the guns of the forts, so that the artillery might protect the torpedoes. The result was what might have been expected. The Allied Fleets approached near enough to the forts to bombard them, without advancing sufficiently close to experience injury from the strings of mines placed across the channel. The latter, consequently, proved of no use.

works had developed into an extensive establishment—one of the largest in Russia—and in anticipation of lucrative Government contracts Emmanuel Nobel sank a considerable amount of capital in still further extending it. But a period of retrenchment ensued, the promises of orders were not realized, and in the end the firm suspended operations. The father retired with broken fortunes and broken health to Sweden, to die there, and the prospect seemed black indeed for the three sons, although two of them are now millionnaires. But if their capital was gone, they had what was ultimately destined to rebuild their fortunes — an exceptionally vigorous and practical engineering training. The manufacture of the submarine mines, and the laying of them down in the roadsteads of Cronstadt and Sveaborg, had taxed the ingenuity of the Nobels for months together. After the war, for years they had been engaged making steamers and machinery at a period when improvements were out-racing one another, and it was no easy matter to keep pace with the times. Ludwig Nobel, in particular, enjoyed a great reputation for engineering skill, and when the firm became bankrupt he was asked by the creditors to continue carrying on the works for a while as manager. Robert Nobel went to Germany, and in course of time began to take an interest in the petroleum industry, the rapid development of which in America was then the talk of Europe. Alfred Nobel applied himself entirely to chemical pursuits, and after a while discovered dynamite, the explosive that has since revolutionized warfare and shaken thrones, and rendered him a millionnaire.

Ludwig Nobel carried on the business for the creditors for a couple of years, and then, with £500 saved during the interval, began life on his own account. In little more than twenty years that simple sum of money has developed into a princely fortune, bringing in £500 a-day!

Establishing a small engineering works, he took a series of contracts from the Government for casting shot and shell, converting guns, and manufacturing rifle stocks, which rapidly carried him on to affluence. It has been said that he rendered himself a millionnaire exclusively through Baku petroleum. This is a mistake. When his brother Robert, enamoured at what he had seen of the oil industry during a journey to the Caucasus in 1874 in search of walnut wood for the rifle stocks manufactured by him, urged him to co-operate in the enterprise, he was already worth £400,000, realized during his twelve years' operations. Aided with capital by his brother, Robert Nobel began operations as a petroleum refiner in a small way at Baku in 1875. At that time there were more than 120 refineries at work there, and hence he started in face of as severe a competition as any pessimist capitalist might expect to find to-day. The Swede did not concern himself, however, with concessions, subsidies, and other similar crutches dear to the heart of the company promoter. He simply settled down in an ordinary way at Baku, as any quiet plodding capitalist might from England to-morrow; and commenced the campaign, conscious that success lay in replacing the desultory, primitive, and wasteful operations of the native firms with the resources of engineering, chemistry, and commercial organization.

As soon as Robert Nobel began to refine the crude oil from the wells at Balakhani he revolted against the practice of carrying the oil in barrels as being slow, wasteful, and costly. But the other firms would not consent to co-operate in placing a pipe-line, and Ludwig Nobel therefore had to be applied to. For £10,000 a pipe was laid down eight miles long, from Balakhani to the Black town of Baku, and paid its expenses the first season. This gave Robert and Ludwig Nobel a widespread reputation, and by inciting other firms to do the same, laid the basis of the modern activity and enterprise at Baku. As for the thousands of carriers who had made £150,000 a year in conveying the oil in barrels to the refineries on the coast, a death-blow was struck at their trade, and to protect the pipe-line from their fury watch-houses had to be built the whole distance every few hundred yards. To-day all the oil is pumped through pipes to the coast, and a carrier's cart is scarcely ever seen. This was the first revolution in the industry effected by the brothers.

Having got their refinery in working order and a pipe-line laid down, the Nobels began to think of securing their own oil supply. Ground was purchased, and the Swedes at once decided to improve upon the primitive Baku system of boring for oil. Six petroleum borers were brought over from America, and Robert Nobel set them to work boring in the Pennsylvania fashion. This was not found to be altogether suited to the requirements of the Apsheron region, and a number of modifications were introduced by the brothers, and the "composite system" adopted, such as is in general use to-day throughout Balakhani. For some time the Nobels were very unlucky with their wells, and even began boring for a cheaper oil in the island of Tcheleken; but at length they triumphed over difficulties, and for years have had more oil than they have known what to do with. The improved system of boring, resulting in an unprecedented copious supply of cheap oil, was the second revolution effected by the Nobels.

In the meanwhile a fresh problem had arisen, requiring to be solved. The Nobels had got a good supply of crude oil at Balakhani, a pipe-line of their own to convey it to the Black Town of Baku, and a well-organized little refinery there to convert it into kerosine. What was now needed was an improved means of conveying the refined oil thence to the consumer in Russia. The system in vogue at the time was to put it in barrels, and convey it by steamer and railway to the home market, 1,000 to 2,000 miles distant. This was a very inconvenient and costly mode of transport. In the first place, there was no wood in the locality to make barrels of, and to bring it from the Volga occasioned a serious expense. Barrels were so expensive that many firms purchased the empty American ones for Baku, and even then the barrel was considerably dearer and more valuable than the oil it conveyed to market. In the second place, owing to the extreme dryness of the Caspian region half the year round, the leakage from the barrels was very great; and in the third, the steamboat and railway companies exacted heavy freights for conveying such inconvenient cargo to Russia. To do away with them altogether, Nobel Brothers suggested to the Directors of the Caucasus and Mercury Company that they should fit up a steamer or two with a cistern, so that the oil might be conveyed in an unbarrelled form to the river Volga. In return for doing this they offered them a lucrative contract for carrying oil for a term of years. The Caucasus and Mercury Company, however, has always been notorious for want of enterprise. Making a handsome percentage yearly by means of the State subsidy, no incentive exists to exertion. The offer, therefore, was refused, and Nobel Brothers were compelled, in default of any other means, to decide upon constructing a fleet of steamers themselves.

And now were displayed the advantages they possessed over other Baku firms in having an engineering establishment on the Neva, where steamers could be planned and built, machinery manufactured, and apparatus and appliances tested by skilled engineers before being sent to the Caspian. With the engineer, Robert Nobel, on the spot, the engineer and financier, Ludwig Nobel, controlling operations at St. Petersburg, and the talented scientific investigator, Alred Nobel, to refer to in chemical matters, the firm possessed advantages which rendered serious

PLATE 15.—CASPIAN BASE OF OPERATIONS AGAINST INDIA: ONE OF THE FORTY OIL-STEAMERS.

rivalry from ill-educated and apathetic Russians or Armenians impossible. In making the first steamer, one or two difficulties of no mean order were encountered. The Caspian Sea is liable to sudden tempests, and it was necessary to take every precaution against the insecurity of such a shifting cargo as oil. Wiseacres in Russia asserted, that as the gifted Americans had never deemed it feasible to bring oil to Europe in cistern-steamers, it was sheer folly for any one to attempt it in the Caspian region. However, Ludwig Nobel was by birth an inventor, and he schemed out a steamer, after a considerable amount of thought, in which the cargo was kept under control by an elaborate and peculiar system of water-tight compartments, without in any way interfering with the rapid loading or unloading of the vessel. The trial steamer proved a complete success. As might have been expected, it paid for itself the first season. Having got the start, the Nobels kept it up. They added to their fleet as fast as they could, getting the steamers cheaply constructed in Sweden. The profits were relatively enormous. With their steamers they beat the barrel transport so completely that the other firms had no chance against them, and as the profits were swiftly applied to extending the business, the company in a few years became a gigantic concern.

The first "liquid transport" or "cistern-steamer" appeared on the Caspian in 1879. There is now a regular fleet of them. Nobel Brothers possess twelve—the *Mahomet, Tatarin, Bramah, Spinoza, Darwin, Talmud, Koran, Calmuck, Zoroaster*, &c. The dimensions of the *Spinoza* will give some idea of the class of steamer composing the fleet. The vessel is steel-built, 245 ft. long, $27\frac{3}{4}$ ft. broad, and when laden with kerosine has a draught of 11 ft. The engines are of 120 nominal horse-power, steaming at ten knots an hour. They burn petroleum fuel, the bunkers containing a supply calculated to last six days, *i.e.*, sufficient for the journey from Baku to the mouth of the Volga and back. The cistern-hold accommodates 750 tons of kerosine each trip. Some of the other vessels vary slightly from these dimensions. The *Koran* and *Talmud* are each $252\frac{1}{3}$ ft. long, and $28\frac{1}{2}$ ft. broad, and carry passengers as well as oil.

Owing to the splendid canal system connecting the Neva with the Volga comparatively little trouble was experienced in conveying the Swedish steamers to the Caspian. In the case of the larger ones they were cut amidships to facilitate the passage; the open extremities being filled with iron bulkheads before entering the canals, and the vessel being put together again at Astrakhan. Altogether Nobel Brother have sunk over £400,000 in establishing their petroleum fleet, and possess a regular dockyard at Astrakhan to repair the Caspian transports and the flotilla of smaller steamers on the Volga.

Directly Ludwig Nobel's cistern-steamers proved a success other firms hastened to purchase similar ones for the Caspian, most of them ranging from 150 to 250 ft. in length. Some of these were built by Mitchell & Co., on the Tyne. Up to now about forty or fifty have been added to the Caspian marine, and twenty more are to arrive at Baku this season. The creation of such a fleet is an exploit of which any engineer might be proud, and Ludwig Nobel may certainly claim credit for having, by the substitution of the steam-propelled 200,000-gallon-floating-oil-tank for the 40 gallon wooden barrel, effected the third great revolution in the Caspian petroleum industry.

The mouth of the Volga is too shallow to allow of the passage of vessels of deep draught, and the large steamers were therefore restricted to service in the Caspian. The transhipment of passengers and cargo is usually effected at a locality 80 miles below Astrakhan, known as "Daivet Foot"—"Nine Feet," from the depth of water at the spot. This is not an ordinary river bar, but a fan-like shoal extending for miles beyond the delta of the Volga. Here, twenty miles or so from land, the transhipment staff of the various steam boat companies live on hulks for eight months out of the twelve, retiring to Astrakhan in the winter. Following the general practice, Ludwig Nobel arranged that the oil should be pumped into light draught cistern-steamers or large barges at Daivet Foot, and tugged up the river. This involved the formation of a second flotilla.

The vessels of this range in size from 60 feet to 150 feet, and convey the oil from the Nine Foot shallows to Tsaritzin, the first railway point on the river Volga, 400 miles distant. Nobel Brothers have about a dozen such vessels, costing £6,000 or so apiece, besides eleven iron tank-barges for kerosine, four wooden ones fitted with 128 iron tanks, and twenty-eight wooden barges for the liquid fuel. Thanks to these vessels, the oil can be conveyed from Baku to Tsaritzin with wonderful rapidity. From the storage reservoirs at the refinery at Baku the kerosine descends by its own gravity through an eight-inch pipe to the head of the pier on the bay, and pours into the cistern-steamers at the rate of 100 to 200 tons per hour. Nobels' large steamers, containing 750 tons of oil, can be loaded in this manner in four and a half hours. The cistern full, the steamer proceeds to the mouth of the Volga, pumps the oil into the barges, and returns again with water ballast, the journey there and back being done in four and a half days. Water being scarce at Baku, and in fact more precious than oil, it is pumped from the steamer into reservoirs, and is either used at the refinery, or for irrigating the park at Villa Petrolia which Ludwig Nobel is having laid out for his employés on the shore of the bay a short distance north-east of it. In the meanwhile, the smaller steamers run oil up the

Volga to Tsaritzin in a couple of days, and pump it into reservoirs for storage alongside the railway, from which it is ultimately sent to every part of the Russian railway system, and to Middle and Western Europe.

In all there are twenty-five piers for loading oil at Baku, most of them large enough to accommodate several vessels at a time. Only the best steamers are employed to carry the kerosine, the conveyance of liquid fuel being confided to wooden sailing vessels, or any kind of craft. These latter, however, are now being rapidly replaced by steamers. Thanks to the tank-steamer service between Baku and Tsaritzin, kerosine, which in the barrel days of the industry could not be sold at the latter place under ninepence a gallon, now realizes a profit at 1¾d.

It was a great achievement for Nobel Brothers to have covered the Caspian and Volga with a fleet of steamers, conveying the oil in floating cisterns instead of barrels to the starting point of the Russian railway system at Tsaritzin, but a deal more remained to be done. At first the oil, on reaching Tsaritzin, was barrelled and sent in that form to various parts of Russia; but after a while Nobel Brothers sought to replace the truck loads of inconvenient and leaky barrels with regular oil-waggons, or tank-cars. As with the Caucasus and Mercury Steamboat Company, so with the Griazi-Tsaritzin Railway Company, the directors pooh-poohed the idea of carrying the oil in a "liquid" form; they refused to add a single tank-car to their rolling stock, in spite of the offer of an advantageous contract. Thereupon the courageous Swedes set to work to make hundreds of these tank-cars themselves, and before long had 1,500 in operation, conveying kerosine to every part of Russia at a price rendering competition on the part of the barrelled oil impossible. This was the fourth revolution effected.

When the tank-cars began to run Nobel Brothers found they needed depôts, and here again the Russian railway companies refused to give any assistance. If Nobel Brothers required oil sidings, they must build them themselves. So, besides placing their own oil trains on the line, they had to purchase lands at various commercial points and build stations for themselves. That they should have never been discouraged by the opposition they met at every step they took, from Baku firms, steamboat companies, and railway companies, is a remarkable testimony to the unflinching courage and irrepressible perseverance of Ludwig Nobel. By this time the firm had undergone considerable changes. Stricken in health, Robert Nobel had quitted Baku and Russia, after firmly laying the foundations of the oil industry, and Ludwig Nobel, from merely taking a sleeping interest in the speculation, had embarked in it a considerable portion of his wealth and become the soul of the enterprise. In 1879 the business became a joint-stock concern, under the title of Nobel Brothers' Petroleum Production Company ("Tovarishchestvo Nephtanavo Proïsvodstva Bratieff Nobel"); the chairman being Mr. Ludwig Nobel, and the directors General Bilderling, Count Tatischeff, and Mr. Beliamin, of St. Petersburg, and Mr. Alfred Nobel, of Paris. Henceforth, the control of the organization centred in Ludwig Nobel at St. Petersburg, who devoted himself entirely to the development of the concern from the Russian capital, while Mr. Törnudd, the manager, armed with autocratic power, supervised the operations in the Caspian region. In Russia "Nobel Brothers" is only the official designation; the public always evinces its recognition of the master mind controlling the firm by ascribing every movement or innovation to Ludwig Nobel.

We have seen that the firm sunk, between 1879 and the close of last year, over £400,000 in placing "floating cisterns" on the Caspian and Volga. A further sum of £275,000 was also sunk between those two periods in placing 1,500 tank-cars, or sixty trains of twenty-five cars each, on the Russian railways. Tsaritzin was made the starting point. Here wharves and reservoirs were built, numerous sidings constructed, barracks erected for the employés, and a factory fitted with barrel-making machinery for casking lubricating oil. To facilitate operations at night, the whole of the area from the wharves at the water-side to the rearmost reservoirs on the lofty bank of the Volga was furnished with the electric light. The united capacity of the storage tanks is now 5,000,000 gallons. That of the other depôts and stations is as follows:—

		Gallons.
Central depôt and station at Orel ...	Tanks for	18,000,000
Depôt and station at St. Petersburg ...	,,	2,300,000
Two depôts and stations at Moscow ...	,,	2,300,000
Depôt and station at Warsaw	,,	1,800,000
,, ,, Saratoff	,,	3,600,000
Twenty-one various smaller stations and depôts	,,	2,800,000
Total storage capacity, including Tsaritzin	,,	35,800,000

The construction of this ramification of depôts has involved an outlay of more than a quarter of a million sterling.

The organization of the petroleum network, the extent of which will be appreciated by a glance at the map I have given, has occasioned an enormous amount of thought and care, and only a man of the Lesseps or Ludwig Nobel order, possessing peculiar and rare talents, could have ever carried it out. In winter the Volga is frozen over, and no oil can be carried for four months from Baku to Tsaritzin. In summer, on the other hand, when the boats can run freely, twilight prevails all night long, and the public needs no kerosine. As a result of this, it was necessary to form in different parts of Russia great storage depôts, where the oil could be collected in

PLATE 16.—Map showing Nobel Brothers' Network of Petroleum Depôts in Russia

summer, and from whence it could be distributed in winter. The central place chosen for this operation was Orel, which is conveniently situated in Middle Russia for distribution in the most populous districts. Here the reservoirs were made to hold 18,000,000 gallons of burning oil at the time, and with the oil station, the sidings, and the repairing shops for the tank-cars, cover several hundred acres of ground. Four other large depôts were erected at Moscow, St. Petersburg, Warsaw, and Saratoff. Scattered between these, and between the Baltic and Black Sea on the one side and Germany and the Volga on the other, were twenty-four smaller depôts. In this manner, in the summer the sixty oil trains run from the Volga to the twenty-six depôts in every part of European Russia, including Poland and Finland, filling up the reservoirs; and in winter they change their base of operations from Tsaritzin to those depôts, and convey the oil to the various intermediate railway stations where a demand exists for kerosine. No barrelling is carried on by the firm. They sell the oil by the train-load to the petroleum dealers in provincial Russia, who bring their own barrels to the railway station, and carry it away in this form to their stores. A fortnight is allowed for this operation. A remarkable fact is, that although Nobel Brothers are able to send to Russia over 200,000 tons, or more than 54,000,000 gallons of kerosine every year, not a drop is sold except for ready cash! By arrangement, the railway companies undertake to receive payment for oil consigned to any station, receiving a small commission for their trouble, and until the money is paid to the booking clerk the petroleum dealer is not allowed to touch the oil. At St. Petersburg large scale maps are kept in the central office of Nobel Brothers, and a clerk is posted in charge, whose duty is to receive telegrams from the guards of the various trains, and note with flags on the maps their whereabouts. All the year round the sixty oil trains of Nobel Brothers are continuing running over an area twenty times larger than Great Britain, yet at any moment of the day Ludwig Nobel can go into the office and see at a glance the actual whereabouts of every one of them.

The tank-cars hold about ten tons of oil apiece. Twenty-five make a train, which thus conveys 250 tons of oil each trip. A tank-car can be filled in three and a half minutes, and the whole train in a little more than an hour. The cost of a tank-car is about £200. None of the other firms at Baku possess tank-cars of their own. Recently the Griazi-Tsaritzin Railway has added 300 to its rolling stock and about a couple of hundred are running on the Transcaucasian Railway. None of the other lines have any.

Thanks to their petroleum network, Nobel Brothers have practically secured a monopoly of the Russian kerosine trade. Refined petroleum conveyed by railway in barrel from the Volga has no chance whatever against them. Possessing vast resources, they can raise or depress prices in that quarter, and not only drive the American oil completely out of the market, but undersell all Russian competitors likewise. It is but fair to say, however, that up to now they have never abused their position, and have always displayed generosity towards rivals, seeking of their own accord to enter into friendly arrangements with them rather than ruthlessly expel them from the field.

Stimulated by the profits Nobel Brothers have realized from their tank-cars, the railways have been discussing of late the expediency of adding them to their regular rolling stock. A short time ago the Griazi-Tsaritzin Railway applied to the Minister of Ways of Communication for permission to increase its capital to purchase tank-cars, but for some reason or other the proposition fell through. The Baku firms, on their part, have raised an agitation that the transport of oil should be undertaken by the State, and rendered a Crown monopoly. But, although the authorities have responded to the clamour and discussed the idea, nothing has come of their deliberations, nor is any action apprehended. As a matter of fact, the cheap and expeditious transport of oil is not a task that can be efficiently undertaken either by a railway or by the State. The market needs to be carefully watched, so as to concentrate oil on a particular spot at a given advantageous moment, and this is a matter which is not likely to be well performed by a Government official or the traffic manager of a railway. A railway, in fine, can only properly look after the oil on its own line, which is but a fraction of the entire Russian network; and besides, only two or three railways, situated close to the Volga, have evinced any inclination to supplement Nobels' transport with a service of their own. In this manner it is very improbable that the Russian Government will burden itself with oil transport, or that the Russian railways will do more for the moment than add a few trucks to their rolling stock. In the meanwhile Nobel Brothers, having established their organization and got the start, may be expected to develop into a Russian Standard Oil Company, if, indeed, they are not that already; and, stimulated by the new trade they are opening up with Austria, and Germany, and England, assume proportions which will render rivalry of any kind in Russia completely out of the question.

Until last year Nobel Brothers confined themselves to Russia; they were fully occupied completing their organization, and, further, the home market was a better one for kerosine than Western Europe, where the American oil was less handicapped by a duty and the trade was more thoroughly developed. However, last summer a train-load of Baku kerosine successfully undersold American refined petroleum at Bromberg, and out of the sensation created by this new invasion has sprung up what is daily becoming a larger trade. At first the German buyers held aloof, but, practice revealing Nobels' brand of kerosine to be as good as the best American, a company was formed with a capital of 1,500,000 marks (£75,000), in 300 shares of 5,000 marks each, to import the oil. The Deutsch-Russische Naphtha Import Gesellschaft in November last concluded an arrangement with Nobel Brothers for distributing Baku kerosine, and preparations were made for erecting at the various railway points on the German frontier large barrelling depôts, the German regulations forbidding the transport of the oil in tank-cars. However, these regulations have since been abolished, and arrangements are now in progress for running oil trains on the German railways. As the oil can be pumped from a Russian oil train into a German one (the difference of gauge rendering the circulation of the Russian trains on German lines impossible) in a little more than an hour, the expense of transfer will be a mere nothing, and render the Russian article able to evict the American oil from the German market. If a similar arrangement can be entered into with Austria, where there is already a considerable trade in Russian oil, and if no obstacles be raised against the "liquid" form of oil transport by other States, we may see, in the course of a year or two, trains laden with Baku petroleum circulating from one end of Europe to the other, and carrying consignments from Tsaritzin, Saratoff, Samara, and other railway points on the Volga to the leading cities of Germany, Austria, France, Switzerland, Belgium and other States. While the Continent is thus being opened up by railway, Nobel Brothers and one or two other firms are shipping oil products from Libau to German and French ports, and to England. Libau is likely to become a great outlet for Baku oil, and it is said that Nobel Brothers contemplate running a cistern-steamer service between it and Western Europe. They have also purchased land at Batoum, and project similar operations there. In this manner, while the tank-car trains running from the Volga will attack American oil in every country on the Continent, flotillas of cistern-steamers issuing from the Baltic on the one flank, and from the Black Sea on the other, will do battle in the northern and southern ports.

Such a prospect is most alluring to Russia; although I must admit that many unenterprising and dim-visioned firms at Baku—sighing for State aid, increased duty on imported kerosine, and other crutches—do not yet realize it. The remarkable growth of Nobel Brothers' business may be cited against those who consider the picture overdrawn. Nine years ago Nobel Brothers had not devoted any attention to petroleum; they were simply engineers. They began in a very small way, simply with a view to giving Robert Nobel a chance to make a fortune, Ludwig and Alfred having already in other spheres of life accumulated wealth; and it was not for three or four years that Ludwig Nobel began to take a direct interest in the industry. They never had any support from the State, they received every discouragement from the people at Baku, from the shipping and railway companies and the transport trade generally, and they were constantly being assailed by the Panslavist Press because they were foreigners. Yet these two Swedes, Robert and Ludwig Nobel, have as completely revolutionized the Russian petroleum industry, and the Russian industrial and political position in the Caspian, as Alfred Nobel has transformed mining operations and the art of war, and given incalculable power to democracy, by his discovery of dynamite.

Nobel Brothers' Petroleum Production Company now control a capital of £1,500,000 sterling, paying on an average a dividend of twenty per cent. At the oil fields of Balakhani they have over forty wells, of which fourteen are "fountains." One of the latter, as I have already said, yielded last year 112,000 tons of crude oil in a month. Two pipe-lines, each eight miles long, and able to convey 4,000,000 barrels yearly, connect the wells with the refinery in the Black Town of Baku. These cost, with the branches and pumping stations, over £75,000 to lay down. The refinery covers more than a mile of ground, and is able to turn out daily in the busy season 220,000 gallons of burning oil, 80 tons of lubricating oil, and 1,300 tons of liquid fuel; equal to a yearly production of 65,000,000 gallons of illuminating oil, 27,000 tons of lubricating oil, and 450,000 tons of liquid fuel. Each of its large refuse reservoirs holds 4,000,000 gallons of liquid fuel at a time. On the Caspian the firm have twelve large cistern-steamers, costing over £250,000 sterling; twelve steamers and forty barges on the Volga, and a dockyard at Astrakhan, costing collectively £180,000; besides which they charter a large number of schooners and barges every season from other owners. At Tsaritzin, and twenty-six other points in Russia, they have established depots for 35,000,000 gallons of kerosine, at a cost of nearly £300,000, and have placed on the railways 1,500 tank-cars, at a cost of more than £275,000. The railway freight alone they pay yearly exceeds a quarter of a million sterling. Altogether their organization gives employment to no less than 5,000 people, and at times this has been raised to double the number. If it be borne clearly in mind that Robert and Ludwig Nobel came quite fresh to the petroleum trade in 1875, and that the growth of all this vast organization practically dates from the close of the Turkish war, I think my readers will agree with me that few enterprises will compare with what has been so successfully accomplished in such an amazingly short space of time by these talented Swedes.

It is often said that the world does not know its greatest men. To my view, if Mr. Smiles were to examine the story of Ludwig Nobel's achievements, he would find that in far-off Russia a practical example had been furnished of engineering genius, inventive talent, capacity for organization, power of patiently pressing down obstacles, and by sheer force of character commanding success, such as he would readily give honourable prominence to in a revised edition of his "Self Help."

In that popular work Mr. Smiles gives many remarkable instances of industrial enterprise and success, but it seems to me that there are few that surpass what Robert and Ludwig Nobel have achieved. The story of their career would make a most interesting book—I have simply been able to give a silhouette of their achievements. And in connection with their success there is a very striking fact. Russia is notoriously a corrupt country. There are few commercial fortunes made there that would bear a public examination. The Nobels have amassed their fortune by an honesty and broadness of principle rare even in England to-day.* Their generosity towards their employés is remarkable. Outside Baku a handsome suburb is rising on the coast of the bay. It is really a walled park, to contain when complete fifteen beautifully designed stone bungalow-villas, with lodgings for several hundred persons. These are surrounded by hundreds of trees brought from the Volga, and irrigated by fresh water conveyed thence by the oil steamers on their return journey. This suburb is Villa Petrolia, where Nobels' chief employés will form a colony and live under conditions of comfort which many an English

* As an instance of this, I may mention that the moment Ludwig Nobel acquired sufficient money he paid off all the liabilities his father had contracted when he became bankrupt, a duty which was certainly not incumbent upon him, and which only a man with a rare, chivalrous sense of honour would have thought of discharging.

capitalist might copy with benefit to those beneath him. A public library is being built for them, billiard-tables have been sent to amuse them, and a sort of co-operative principle has been introduced enabling the employés to invest their money in and participate in the profits of the firm.

The feeling of enmity and jealousy of the Baku rival firms towards the Nobels is easily understood, but I could never get at the bottom of the hostile attitude of the Russian Press. Probed to the depths, the only reason I could discover was an ultra-Slavonic foreign-hating spirit. It is a feeling Englishmen cannot understand. A short time ago Sir William Siemens, a German located in this country, died, but the circumstances of his nationality, and the fact of a large proportion of his employés at Charlton—several hundred I believe—being Germans, did not prevent England honouring him with a funeral service in Westminster Abbey. Not a word was uttered against him on the score of nationality. Ludwig Nobel holds a position similar to that of Sir William Siemens. He found the Russians unfitted for his enterprise, and employed Swedes instead. The fact of his being a naturalized Russian, speaking Russian like a native, and having a sincere sympathy for Russia, has been no excuse for this crime. While I was at Baku a Russian special correspondent visited the petroleum district. Nobels' manager gave him every assistance, and at the end of his investigations asked him what he thought of the industry. The Russian replied: "Your organization is splendid—it is perfect; but there is one thing that provokes my regret—what a pity it is not Russian." The reply was characteristic. "Russian or Swede, what does it matter, so long as Russia gets good cheap oil? You say the Baku firms dislike us. We cannot help that: but if you can find in Baku any man who can prove we are dishonest, cheat, adulterate, or refuse to redress substantial grievances, we will confront an inquiry in your presence; and, if guilty, make amends."

Generally speaking, there is very little that is attractive in the careers of millionnaires. Giants in their own narrow money-grubbing domain, they are insignificant, and too often contemptible out of it. Men enriched by shoddy, by patent pills, by sharp practice on the Stock Exchange, and other modes of spoiling the public, are not worthy of much notice, and the less literature has to say about them the better. But there are millionnaires and millionnaires. No shoddy feature is to be found in Ludwig Nobel's career. His wealth is due not to speculations favoured by the exceptional cheapness of oil in the purchasing market, and the exceptional dearness in the selling one—if that had been the case, hundreds of Russians and Armenians already in the trade when Robert Nobel started operations in 1875 would have stood an equal chance of becoming millionnaires—but to the genius that planned a vast transport organization, the engineering skill that carried it into effect, and the integrity that raised the quality of the product transported from a debased and despised condition, crushed by foreign superiority, to a position fit to compete in turn with that superiority and overcome it. Only a man of rare and remarkable talents could have done what Ludwig Nobel has achieved; and if his success has brought him immense wealth, he has the proud consciousness that not a voice can be raised against the genuine ring of every penny of it. But without dwelling any further on his character—the facts I have given chant their own praise, and need no additional eulogy from my pen; there are one or two more points connected with his success, which possess considerable interest. Times are very bad, we are daily told, and for years past the opportunities are alleged to have been few for piling up a fortune. Yet Ludwig Nobel's wealth has been chiefly formed since the

Russo-Turkish war, during the severest period of commercial depression Russia has experienced for generations. Again, most fortunes are of slow growth, and are the outcome, as it were, of a man's whole existence. This cannot be said of the fortune Ludwig Nobel has realized from Baku petroleum. Up to 1874 he had never taken the slightest interest in the product; until 1879 the attention he gave was only of a casual and intermittent character; and when at length he took in hand the organization of the industry, ninety-nine out of a hundred people would have said that the development of the petroleum trade was more the task for a city man, a clever financier, than for an engineer whose life had been spent amidst machinery. Yet it was the engineer, and not the trader, who was destined to reap in five or six years such a fortune from oil that the most covetous or sanguine merchant might be elated with.

CHAPTER XVIII.

THE FUTURE OF THE CASPIAN PETROLEUM TRADE.

Repeated Crises of Late Years at Baku—Their Cause—Production of Russian Refined Petroleum by Nobel Brothers and Other Firms—Russia Beginning to Push the Petroleum Industry—New Combinations on the Volga—Statistics of the Import of American Oil into Russia—The Russian Petroleum Trade and the Markets of Germany and Austria—Prospects of Rivalry with America—Projected Railways to Transport the Oil to Europe—Petroleum Traffic on the Transcaucasian Railway in 1883—Export from Batoum and Poti—Progress of the Various Branches of the Trade—New Markets in Southern Europe and the East that may be Expected to Fall to Russia Once the Batoum Route is Developed—The Cheaper the Oil the Larger the Consumption—English Enterprise of the Past and the Present—Whether we participate or not the Baku Petroleum Region is sure to be developed.

THE success of Nobel Brothers has not been unmarked with suffering on the part of other interests at Baku. There are always two aspects to a victory—the radiant triumph of the conquerors, and the groans and grief of the vanquished. The success of George Stephenson's locomotive meant ruin to hundreds interested in stage-coaches, and in a like manner the improved methods introduced by the Swedes have reacted adversely upon the fortunes of those wedded to old ways. Thus, the introduction of the pipe-lines at Baku caused the collapse of hundreds of carriers who conveyed the oil in barrels from the wells to the refineries. When cistern-steamers were introduced many coopers at Baku found the demand for barrels gone, and with it a very lucrative business. Before the petroleum fleet reached its present proportions Nobel Brothers gave handsome freights for the carriage of oil products to the Volga. This led to over speculation in the construction of oil schooners, and when the steamers arrived the former were left anchoring idle at Baku, their occupation gone. The success of the

Nobels in boring for oil also, accompanied with a succession of extraordinary spouting wells, brought down the price of crude petroleum to a few pence a ton, and reduced to insignificant proportions the income of those who had lived exclusively upon the money realized from the sale of the produce of the wells. Worse than all, however, was the crushing competition which the 200 other refiners experienced at the hands of the Nobels. The cheap transport of the Swedes brought down prices everywhere in Russia, while the 200 firms having no organized transport of their own, and having to rely upon the careless, shiftless, exacting railway and steamboat companies, could not possibly deliver oil at a price that would enable them to compete with the Nobels. It is true that after a while they bought steamers of their own, but in the meantime they had lost their hold upon the market. Besides, Nobel Brothers not only delivered oil cheaply, but the quality was unfailingly good, and improved every year, while the supplies of less organized and scrupulous firms could not be relied upon. The subjoined table of the production of Russian refined petroleum during the last twelve years will show how severely the battle has gone against the non-Nobel Baku firms.

PRODUCTION OF RUSSIAN REFINED PETROLEUM.

Years.	Nobel Brothers.	All other Firms.	Total.
	Tons.	Tons.	Tons.
1872	—	16,100	16,400
1873	—	24,500	24,500
1874	—	23,600	23,600
1875	—	32,600	32,600
1876	100	57,000	57,100
1877	2,500	75,100	77,600
1878	4,550	93,000	97,550
1879	9,000	101,000	110,000
1880	24,000	126,000	150,000
1881	50,000	133,000	183,000
1882	72,000	130,000	202,000
1883	106,000	100,000	206,000

Thus in a few short years Nobel Brothers' production has progressed until it has completely surpassed that of the 200 other oil refiners at Baku put together. By further additions to their refinery they have rendered themselves able to turn out this year 232,000 tons of refined oil, or nearly enough to supply the whole Russian market. All this will explain why for several years past there have been several so-called crises in the Baku petroleum trade, and a considerable amount of outcry at times about the industry going to the dogs. As I have already pointed out, the industry, generally speaking, has been prosperous and progressive enough, but this improvement has been mainly due to the enterprising Swedes, whose rapid and unprecedented success has been the innocent cause of stagnation, arrested growth, and even ruin in individual cases. There has been nothing whatever during this period to warrant any pessimist views with regard to the general future of Baku petroleum. Baku contains enough oil to supply the whole world. The markets of that world lie open to it, and the success of Nobel Brothers in the limited sphere of Russia is a sufficient demonstration of what may be done by other foreign capitalists in the hundreds of other markets in Europe, Africa, and the East.

Already Russia herself is beginning to participate in the extension of the enterprise. The Caucasus and Mercury Company is arranging for the conversion of old steamers to oil-carrying purposes, and the construction of new ones, with a sufficient aggregate capacity to convey 120,000 tons of oil during the season. The company will build its own reservoirs at Baku, and convey oil of a uniform quality to Tsaritzin. Here a newly-formed Russian company, called the "Neft," or "Petroleum," with a capital of £200,000, will receive it in reservoirs and convey it in tank-cars to different parts of Russia; the Caucasus and Mercury Company, the "Neft," and the Griazi-Tsaritzin Railway worked a through traffic in oil by a mutual arrangement with each other. This combination will not oppose very serious rivalry to Nobel Brothers, because its rates are high, and the management divided; but it will enable other Baku firms to send oil to Russia under more favourable conditions than hitherto, and probably result in the complete expulsion of the American oil from it.

The following shows the import of American oil into Russia, compared with the growth of the refined petroleum trade from 1871 to 1880, beyond which year no official statistics are forthcoming. It is known, however, that the import of American oil has still further decreased of late years. The figures are in poods, each containing $4\frac{1}{2}$ gallons :—

	Imported from America.	Produced at Baku.	Total Quantity used in Russia.
1871	1,720,418	380,000	2,100,418
1872	1,790,334	400,000	2,190,334
1873	2,701,093	832,800	3,533,893
1874	2,524,160	1,336,675	3,860,835
1875	2,653,126	1,990,045	4,643,171
1876	2,662,486	3,145,075	5,807,561
1877	1,701,502	4,594,766	6,296,268
1878	1,989,034	6,255,910	8,244,944
1879	1,711,811	6,963,658	8,675,469
1880	1,445,558	7,858,750	9,304,308
Total	20,899,522	33,757,679	54,657,201

Now that Baku kerosine is from 80 to 100 per cent. cheaper than American refined petroleum at St. Petersburg the latter product can hardly be imported into Russia much longer, especially as it is weighted with a duty of 40 copecks the pood. Besides the new transport service just mentioned, a large number of barges and steamers are to be added this year to the Volga flotilla as well as to the Caspian marine, and consequently the Volga outlet for Baku petroleum will rapidly attain its fullest development. When this is accomplished, and cheap oil floods the Russian market, there will naturally be an overflow into Germany, Austria, and other states. At Berlin Baku petroleum is being sold for one rouble twenty-four copecks the pood, as compared with one rouble forty-three copecks asked for the American oil. At Stettin it can be sold for sixpence per gallon, while the price of the American oil is 7½d. per gallon.* Germany imports over 100,000,000 gallons of oil from America every year, and Austria at least half that quantity. In Austria for some time past the Russian oil has been gaining ground, having been conveyed thither by sea, from Batoum to Fiume, as well as overland viâ the Volga. Without going further west, the reader will see at once that an extensive market for the oil exists immediately outside the confines of Russia. From Libau large quantities of lubricating oil are being shipped to London. As already stated, this port promises to be the Baltic outlet of the Caspian petroleum trade, Nobel Brothers

* Cost of the refined petroleum delivered at Tsaritzin on the Volga, including general charges and a reasonable profit, per gallon ... ... 1⅜d.
Railway freight for conveyance in Nobel Brothers' tank-cars from Tsaritzin to Libau, per gallon ... ... 1⅝d.
Extra charge for wear and tear of the tank-cars ... ... ½d.
Freight from Libau to Stettin ... ... ⅝d.
Proportionate cost of barrel at Stettin, with storage, discharging, leakage ... ... 1⅜d.

Total cost per gallon ... ... 6d.

Actual selling price of American petroleum per gallon at Stettin ... ... 7½d.
Selling price of Baku petroleum .. .. 6d.

Difference in favour of Baku ... ... 1½d.

having already established an exporting depôt there, and other firms beginning to follow their example.

Summing up the Volga route, we may expect to see during the next few years not only a continual development of the steamer service at the same remarkable rate that has characterized its growth since Robert and Ludwig Nobel showed how cheaply oil could be conveyed in floating cisterns, but also a rapid increase of the rolling stock of the railways; the result being a large export of Baku oil from the Baltic ports, in excess of the inrush of the article across the frontier into Germany and Austria.

To overcome the disadvantage occasioned by the freezing of the Volga four months out of the twelve, a proposal has been put forward by the Minister of Railways to extend the Russian railway system from Vladikavkaz to Petrovsk, on the Caspian. Petrovsk is only a day's run by steamer from Baku, and once railway communication established vessels could carry the oil thither, and tank-cars convey it thence to every part of Russia, including Rostoff-on-the-Don, where it could be shipped to South Europe. It would thus compete with the Tsaritzin route on the one hand, and with the Batoum route on the other; giving facilities, as a third route, for the additional export of from 50,000,000 to 100,000,000 gallons of oil from Baku every year.

During the autumn of 1883 a party of Government engineers surveyed the ground for this undertaking. The length of the line was found to be about 160 miles, and the cost estimated at a little over one and a half millions sterling. The strategical value of the railway has been so often insisted on by military experts that the Baku refiners entertain reasonable hopes that the line will be early taken in hand. In connection with this scheme there is another, to which I referred in my description of Novorossisk, for extending the Vladikavkaz Railway to the Black Sea at that point. This would give the oil a better European outlet than Rostoff-on-the-Don, which is frozen up in winter. There is also a third scheme for extending the railway from Petrovsk to Baku, and link that place with the Russian railway system. When this is carried out the tank-cars will convey the oil direct from Baku to every part of Europe.

In the meanwhile, pending the constitution of these lines, the Baku-Batoum railway is the most accessible outlet for Europe. The opening of this line is calculated to exercise a remarkable effect upon the development of the trade, bringing the oil at a stroke into a region where the American article can only be sold at a high price, and whence it can be readily despatched to the Mediterranean for the southern European ports, and, *viâ* the Suez Canal, to India and China. The markets most advantageously situated for Baku, and the least open to American competition, by this new route, are as follow: appending thereto the quantity of fine petroleum they imported from America in 1882:—

	Tons.
Austria (Trieste and Fiume)	42,592
Italy	52,340
Algeria	4,903
Malta	775
Greece	2,920
Constantinople	9,912
Other Turkish ports	13,829
Egypt	10,181
Gibraltar	4,276
African Coast	11,718
British India	93,967
China	82,410
Japan	55,717
Bangkok	1,230
Indian Archipelago	44,763
Australia and New Zealand	47,173
Total	478,706 tons.

Or about 3,500,000 barrels.

With the advent of a cheaper oil the consumption in these countries would rapidly increase, as in the case of Russia, where in the days of dear petroleum in 1871 only 9,000,000 gallons of kerosine were burnt, while last year the amount exceeded 40,000,000 gallons.

Nobel Brothers have already secured the monopoly of the Volga oil route, and there is very little probability of foreign capitalists interfering with them there, but the Batoum oil route still remains to be developed. Although no organization has yet been established, an encouraging trade has already sprung up, as the kerosine oil traffic returns of the Transcaucasian Railway for last year will show.

REFINED PETROLEUM TRAFFIC ON THE TRANSCAUCASIAN RAILWAY, 1883.

	In Barrel.	In Tank-car.	Total.
	Gallons.	Gallons.	Gallons.
January	—	—	275,962
February	—	—	297,293
March	—	—	97,452
April	—	—	117,710
May	453,335	337,500	790,835
June	397,386	480,870	878,256
July	427,928	496,913	924,841
August	515,601	365,175	880,776
September	718,227	695,340	1,413,567
October	505,993	613,800	1,119,793
November	1,000,940	248,525	1,249,465
December	1,790,725	943,200	2,733,925
Total	5,810,135	4,181,323	10,839,875

These returns do not include the exports of Messrs. Bungé and Palashkovsky, the constructors of the Baku Railway, who for some reason have kept their traffic a secret, and have been allowed to do so by the Government. Of the kerosine exported between August and December 80 per cent. went to Batoum, and 5 per cent.

to Poti; the remaining 15 [per cent. was absorbed in its passage over the line, 7 per cent. being taken by Tiflis, and the rest by other towns and stations *en route*. From August to December 1,300 tons of lubricating oil were also transported from Baku, of which 450 tons went to Batoum and 650 tons to Poti; the remainder being delivered at Tiflis and Shamkhor. During the same period 1,200 tons of liquid oil were transported; 350 tons to Batoum, 250 tons to Poti, 450 tons to Tiflis, and the rest to intermediate stations. As regards crude petroleum, only 140 tons were carried by the railway, and of this only half a ton penetrated to Batoum. These figures, which Gospodin Gulishambaroff has been at great pains to collect, are not put forward by him as perfectly accurate. The Customs' returns at Baku, as well as the traffic returns on the Transcaucasian Railway, are not kept with sufficient care to be treated as altogether reliable; but they give an approximate idea of what has been done in the way of the export of oil from Baku, *viâ* the Black Sea ports, since the railway was opened. The returns of the Batoum Custom House supplement the above figures by including the products sent abroad by Palashkovsky, and making good other omissions.

EXPORT OF BAKU OIL PRODUCTS FROM BATOUM TO FOREIGN COUNTRIES FROM MAY, 1883, TO JANUARY 1, 1884.

	Gallons.
Refined petroleum	3,356,298
Crude lubricating oil	418,410
Refined lubricating oil	788,211

EXPORT OF BAKU OIL PRODUCTS FROM BATOUM TO RUSSIAN BLACK SEA PORTS DURING THE SAME PERIOD.

	Gallons.
Refined petroleum	3,715,992
Crude lubricating oil	22,378

Throughout the autumn of 1883 great dissatisfaction

existed at Baku at the inadequate transport service of the new railway, and the slowness in despatching oil to the Black Sea. A consignment of oil rarely reached Batoum under three weeks. In reply to a deputation, the traffic manager of the Transcaucasian Railway excused himself on the grounds that no reservoirs existed at Batoum, thus preventing the despatch of oil in large quantities, while no organization had been yet established to ship the oil regularly to Europe. He did not think it was the duty of the company to construct reservoirs or to provide tank-cars; although he admitted that the despatch of the oil in barrels was detrimental to the trade. The following, in his opinion, were the measures needed to establish the export trade on a proper basis :—

1. To build a port at Batoum.
2. To establish a large tank-car service between Baku and Batoum.
3. To form a fleet of cistern-steamers to convey the oil from Batoum to Europe.
4. To reconstruct the Suram section of the railway, so as to do away with the congestion occasioned by that pass.
5. To enforce a uniform standard in the kerosine exported from Baku.

Shortly afterwards General Possiet, Minister of Railways, visited Baku and Batoum, followed by General Ostrovsky, Minister of Crown Domains, and Admiral Shestakoff, Minister of Marine. All held conferences with the Baku petroleum firms, and one of the results was the decision of the Government to construct at once a port at Batoum. The formation of a tank-car service and a fleet of steamers was left to European enterprise, but a promise was made to construct a tunnel under the Suram pass as soon as circumstances would allow.

Since the beginning of the year there has been a rapid increase in the export of oil from Poti and Batoum. From the former port no less than five vessels were sent away with cargoes of kerosine during the first ten days of February. Already the trade has increased beyond the limits of convenient shipment at Batoum, but this is being remedied by the steps taken to create a great commercial port there, to accommodate the traffic. In the meantime, it is stated that a number of temporary jetties are to be erected to provide for the shipment of oil. When a pipe-line is laid down between Baku and Batoum, to carry the kerosine to the Black Sea coast, as is confidently anticipated will be the case in the course of a few years, the oil trade of the Caspian will assume vast proportions. Such a pipe-line would not seriously interfere with the traffic of the railway, as the tank-cars would still be needed to convey the lubricating oil and the liquid fuel to the Black Sea.

For the crude petroleum a large export is neither expected nor desired. To utilize this, refineries would have to be erected in Western Europe, and as the principal products can be more cheaply extracted on the spot, the present disinclination of the European petroleum trade to make use of it may be expected to continue. A curious instance of this occurred a short time ago. Instructions were given by a Russian export house to despatch a shipload of petroleum refuse to Western Europe for the use of lubricant manufacturers. The Baku agents, having no dregs on hand, concluded that crude oil would do as well, and consigned a shipload as directed, with a result that the vessel had to go begging from one country to another before a purchaser could be found for the article. But there is no need for this mistake to be repeated, or for the inference to be drawn from it that the market for Baku petroleum products is in any way restricted.* For

---

* America only exports 2 per cent. of crude petroleum. A strong feeling prevails in Russia against allowing the oil to be exported except in a manufactured form, so as to retain for Russia the profit of refining it.

the kerosine there is an immense future, particularly in the East, its high flashing point rendering it superior to the American oil in hot climates. The crude lubricating oil has already found large purchasers in France and this country, and for this product and the refined article there is likely to be a very large sale in England, owing to its extreme cheapness and excellence. The oil refuse is also in great request, and apart from its employment in various manufactures there must be an immense export of it, at no distant date, from Baku to the Black Sea and the Mediterranean, for purposes of liquid fuel. The establishment, on a large scale, of kerosine candle manufactories and dye-extract works at Baku is only to be expected when the industry has become more mature.

Nobel Brothers have taken the lead in the opening up of the Baku oil supply, and, excited by their success, capitalists in other parts of Europe are turning their gaze towards the Caspian Sea. Some have already done the wisest thing under the circumstances—gone direct to Baku to see the state of affairs with their own eyes, and are no doubt now reaping the benefit of their journey. Up to the present moment England is the only country that has held aloof from participating in the enterprise. This is a very curious circumstance, since the English were the first to open up and survey the Caspian for Russia, and sought for many years in the reign of Elizabeth, and again in the time of George II., to establish a trade *viâ* the Caspian Sea with India. Of late English enterprise has withered in that corner of Asia, but there is no reason why it should not revive, once the importance of the Baku petroleum trade is realised. Mr. Peacock, the British Consul at Batoum, wrote to me early this year:—" The petroleum riches near the Caspian are so great, and the wells yield so much more than the Baku traders are in a position to work or send raw to market, that the question of exhaustion for at least many years to come need create no fear among people directly or indirectly connected with the Baku petroleum industry. It is almost painful to observe the total absence of English merchants at Baku. I know the drawbacks of the country very well, but I daresay they were as numerous and perhaps more aggravating in the time of Jonas Hanway, described in your pamphlet on Baku, and still our merchants risked penetrating to the wildest corners of the world." If we do not act as the carriers of petroleum from Batoum the future fleets of cistern-steamers will be in other nations' hands. A regular line of steamers has already been established by the Germans between Hamburg and Batoum. We cannot retard the development of the industry by holding aloof, nor is the industry, like problematical mines, of such a character as to involve serious risk to those who participate in pushing it. Whether the lucrative export trade of Baku oil *viâ* Batoum shall be taken up by English merchants, or revert to Continental rivals, depends entirely upon ourselves. I have done my best to describe the industry impartially, and the option of acting upon my information rests with the community at large.

CHAPTER XIX.

OLD PERSIA—NEW RUSSIA.

Sermons Preached by the Rocks at Baku—The Slovenly Persians of To-day—Will the English Some Day become Pariahs in India?—Russia Growing Towards Our Eastern Empire—We are Only Sojourners in India, the Russians are Settlers in the Caspian—The Material Growth of Russia More Fraught with Danger to Our Rule than her Military Operations in Central Asia—Russia becoming More Unassailable in Central Asia, while We continue as Vulnerable as Ever in India—The Shortsightedness of English Statesmen—The Caspian now a European Lake—The Widening of the Boundaries of Europe—Its Significance—The Waterway between London and Baku—The Population of Baku; Remarkable Growth—Tchernayeff's New Road to Central Asia *viâ* the Mertvi Kultuk and Khiva—Discovery of Petroleum along it—The Traffic on the Volga—Russia's Progress towards the Persian Gulf—Fate of Persia—The Baku Road to India—Statistics of it—Disappearing Obstacles—The Cossack Approach to India—Impossible to Prevent an Approximation of the Two Empires—The Duty of all Englishmen.

OLD Persia—New Russia: what deep meaning exists in those words! What visions they conjure up of the extension of the White Tsar's dominions towards our Eastern Empire! Twenty-five centuries of Persian priests mumbling their prayers at the Surakhani altars, day after day, year after year, and in the interval the great Persian Empire expanding to its fullest—stretching from the Indus in India to the Bosphorus in Europe, and embracing at times Afghanistan, modern Persia, the Caucasus, and Asia Minor—and then contracting, breaking up, and becoming bit by bit what we see it to-day—a mere Khanate, dependent for its existence upon the nod of the Emperor of Russia. If the rocks at Baku could speak, what tales they could tell the slovenly slippered Persians, loafing about the bazaars under the eye of the bearded, heavy-booted Russian policeman, of the great creed and great empire of their ancestors. As they pass me chattering—a sapless, effeminate, dirty rabble—I regard them with curious interest. To think that these should be the children of men, proud citizens of a great and warlike empire—who once upon a time used to resort to the Surakhani altars, to thank the great Fire God that they were not as other people, poor cowardly oppressed creatures, but warriors and statesmen respected from Delhi to Constantinople. It is not the past, however, that engrosses all my thoughts. What if I could penetrate a few centuries into the future! I might then see some curious traveller watching with similar interest ragged loafers in the bazaars of Bombay and Calcutta, and asking himself—can these possibly be the children of the gifted English warriors who once possessed the most magnificent empire the universe had ever seen?

But the world rolls faster to-day than it used to do in olden times. Empires rise, ripen, and rot more rapidly. Our Eastern empire is growing towards Russia; Russia's empire is growing towards ours. In a few short years the two will touch, and then humanity will see whether the Russian empire will swell beyond the line of demarcation, and break up our empire as it has already broken up and sucked the sap out of the Persian empire; or whether the superior vitality of our empire will stem any further advance in the direction of India. More we cannot hope for. The Russians can break up our power in India—they can trip us off the backs of the natives: we cannot break up their empire in Asia. The English are only sojourners in India: the Russians are settlers in the Caspian region. Generations hence, unless the

character of our rule change, we shall still be merely
casual residents in the East, while the Caspian region,
from being on the outskirts of the Russian empire, will
be as much within its limits as Novgorod and Penza;
and the Russians dwelling there will exercise the influence attaching to numbers which we cannot hope for in
India. The English will be then, as now, but a drop in
the ocean of Indian humanity. The Russians, on the
other hand, will be the main element in the Caspian
region. While a mere handful of white faces will be all
that will represent English suzerainty at Benares and
Allahabad, Merv will be a busy Russian mart—another
Kazan or Orenburg—and Baku, with a population of
half a million or more Russians, the all-powerful metropolis of the Caspian.

Hence, the rocks of Baku have sermons to preach to
Englishmen as well as to the degenerate children of
Iran. We are citizens of a great Empire. The jewel of
that empire is India. We know, although there are
traitors in our midst, ever whispering suggestions to the
contrary, that the greatness of England is largely bound
up with the maintenance of her rule over that grand
dependency. We know it to be the set purpose of
Russia, who is already at the gates of India, to strive to
expel us from the peninsula next time we openly thwart
her ambitious plans in Europe. Yet though we see the
vigorous roots of Russia deriving sustenance from the
vitals of Tartary, Persia, and Turkey, and every year
thrusting out suckers further and further east, we make no
attempt to check that growth or set our empire in order.

To my view, the material growth of Russia is fraught
with more danger to our rule in the East than the extension of her armament towards Herat and Candahar.
We are developing India enormously. I do not know
anything more calculated to make an Englishman proud
of his empire than the rapidity with which we are open-

ing up the resources of that splendid country. But while commerce grows and wealth accumulates the number of Englishmen ruling and defending India shows no sign of increase. Excluding women and children, and including the army, administration, and mercantile classes, there cannot be more than 150,000 English in the country. All these regard themselves as strangers in a foreign land, and look to some day returning home; none are encouraged to settle in India. Quite the reverse is the case with Russia. The Caspian Sea, which not so long ago was a purely Persian expanse, is now becoming as much a Russian lake as Ilmen or Ladoga. The peasants of Middle Russia are colonizing the steppes at the foot of the Caucasus. Soldiers are settling down in colonies in Transcaucasia. Baku, Tiflis, Batoum—once strongholds of Persia, Georgia and Turkey—are assuming the aspect of Russian towns. Officials, soldiers, and traders come and go, but there is always a proportion, and a significant proportion, that permanently settles down in the country. Twenty years hence the 150,000 English in India will have received only solitary additions to their numbers; they will still be strangers in Kurachee and Calcutta, Delhi and Madras. On the other hand, by that time Baku will have become as thoroughly Russian as Odessa, and the Persian element will have disappeared from the Caspian as completely as the Turkish element from the Sea of Azoff. In plainer language, while we shall be still as liable as now to be shaken off the surface of the 250 millions of India, by means of a judicious manipulation of the discontented elements there, it will be beyond the power of any mortal man to expel Russia from the Caspian. Therein lies the great significance of the Russian advance. Russia, as she settles down in Central Asia, becomes more and more unassailable. England, on the contrary, remains just as vulnerable as ever.

Our statesmen have neither imagination nor memory. Their foreign policy always reminds me of the classical imbecile, who sat down by the waterside, and deferred crossing until the river should run dry. They are always expecting that the Russian advance shall some day cease. The expansion of Russia has never halted from the time of Ivan the Terrible, and never can arrest its course until the Sepoy-guarded frontier of India be reached; but with a persistent foolishness, indifference, stupidity, or any other epithet the exasperated reader may choose to apply to it, the larger proportion of English statesmen have always treated an approximation of the two empires as impossible in our generation. Although their views of Russian progress have always been falsified by events, they have never allowed themselves to be influenced by the teachings of history. Lord Salisbury used to think that the Turcoman barrier would last his time. The Duke of Argyll ridiculed the notion of the Russians establishing a great base in the Caspian. The one was as short-sighted as the other. The Cossack is now far in front of the Turcomans, the Caspian has become the grandest military base in the world, and yet, although Merv is in the Postal Union, and Mr. Gladstone can send a penny post-card to Sarakhs, the day is still regarded as far distant when the Russians or the English will be ruling Herat and Candahar, and free communication will be established between Europe and India.

It is but the other day that the Caspian was a distant Asiatic Dead Sea. It is now a busy European lake. In maps published in the early part of the century the frontier of Europe is drawn along the Volga to Tsaritzin, and then down the Don to the Azoff and Black Sea. Orenburg and Astrakhan, the plains of Stavropol and the valleys of Transcaucasia, belonged to Asia. The Russians have changed all this. They have dealt as roughly with geographers' maps as with statesmen's treaties. Bit by bit the Asiatic border has been thrust back, until all these towns and districts have become included in the European system. And this removal of Asia from the Don to the Persian ports of the Caspian is not a mere academic freak, but a significant fact. The population of Russia has expanded with the frontier, until Astrakhan and Orenburg, and the towns of Cis- and Transcaucasia, have as much right to be regarded as members of the European system as Odessa and Sevastopol, .St. Petersburg and Cronstadt—all four cities founded by Russia long after we first made our appearance in India. Madras and Calcutta, Bombay and Kurachee, which have grown up under our fostering care, are admirable instances of Indian progress, but they are not English towns. On the other hand, Kars and Batoum, Tiflis and Baku, Merv and Samarcand will have become quite Russian in another lifetime. There are men living who remember when Odessa was a wretched Turkish fort. There are boys living who, long before their beards have grown, will see Afghanistan wiped out as completely as Tartary, and trains running from opposite Baku to the Burmese limits of India.

Fatuitous and frothy politicians of both parties will perhaps ridicule such a prediction, but the revolution that has taken place in Central Asian affairs since 1880 should put the reader on his guard against such traitors to his interests. There was a time when similar men tended the Eternal Fires at Surakhani. Did they ever tell the crowds of prosperous Persian devotees that their Empire would some day succumb to the forces from within and without, and their sacred altars be ultimately turned into greasy stills for stewing lamp oil? For years, fatuitous and frothy priests, Conservative as well as Liberal, have been tending the sacred flame of Gabble at St. Stephen's, assuring their infatuated admirers that all was well and ever would be well with the Empire; and even now that the Russians have left the Caspian far behind them, and are posted at Merv and Sarakhs, we have them still asserting, in solemn chant, that Russia will never meddle with India.

As I rested against the newly-erected stone embankment at Baku, which always reminded me of the Thames Embankment, and looked over into the water splashing against its base—water stretching in never ending ripples all the way from the one embankment to the other, from Baku Bay to the River Thames—I used to wish I could take one of the fleet of Caspian steamers, and proceeding direct *viâ* the Volga, the Neva, and the Baltic to Westminster Bridge, turn on a steam [roarer and roar a few facts into the ears of the chatterers.

One of which facts would have been this: Growth of the population of Baku, the future metropolis of the Caspian region:—

1870	... ...	12,191 people
1879	... ...	15,105 ,,
1883	... ...	**50,000** ,,

Baku, which ten years ago an English diplomatist passed through and "saw nothing of interest" (English diplomatists, by the way, never do seem to see, or say anything of interest), now possesses 5,000 houses and 1,500 shops, and an immediate prospect of rapid and indefinite extension. When we contrast Russia's industrial and mercantile development in the Caspian with our mud-pie progress at Quetta, it is impossible not to feel that we are being beaten out and out in every factor of the great game of Central Asia.

Even Russians themselves are only now finding out the resources they possess in the Caspian region. They have looked so far ahead in the direction of India that many advantages existing under their very noses have remained unseen. It is only the other day that the expedition took place against Khiva. We all remember what difficulties beset the march of the various converging columns, and how that one succumbed miserably in the Kara Kum sands, and two others were only saved by a miracle. Yet all the while there was a simple easy road from the Mertvi Kultuk Bay, opposite the mouth of the Volga, to the oasis of Khiva, which, if it had been known, would have saved Russia hundreds of lives and millions of roubles. This road merits a few words of description, because since I began to write this chapter petroleum has been discovered at the starting point.

When General Lomakin was deservedly thrashed by the Turcomans at Geok Tepé, in 1879, the whole of the Transcaspian steppes became exposed to their raids, and Vaniushin, a Russian merchant, accustomed yearly to despatch caravans of goods from Khiva to Krasnovodsk for the Great Fair at Nijni-Novgorod, was obliged either to suspend his operations, or else strike out for a safer point further north. He had some idea of making for Fort Alexandrovsky; but the Kirghiz were restless, and the route thither long and arduous, and so at last he determined he would attempt a short cut direct from the oasis to the Caspian, immediately opposite the mouth of the Volga. To his surprise the road proved to be the best he had ever traversed; it was tolerably level most of the way; it had plenty of water, fuel, and forage; and at its extremity the Dead Bay was found to yield a very accessible harbour to the Volga steamers.

Tidings of the new road penetrated to Orenburg, and Gospodin Rajeff, agent for the Russian Transport Company, who had hitherto conveyed goods from Bokhara and Turkestan to Orenburg, viâ the Kirghiz deserts north and south of the Syr Daria, decided to despatch a consignment in that direction from the upper part of the Oxus. He also, in his turn, found the road as superior to the Khazala-Orenburg road as Vaniushin had found it to be to the Krasnovodsk one, and adopted it as the regular caravan route for his Company. This decision got known in time at Tashkent, and General Tchernayeff, to ascertain whether the road would be equally practicable for troops, despatched Colonel Alexandroff to survey it. Alexandroff's report was eminently satisfactory, and led Tchernayeff himself to adopt it when he proceeded to the Tsar's coronation last year. Tchernayeff, finally, was delighted with the route, and had a scheme drawn up for running a railway to Khiva, so as to render it the chief highway to Turkestan.

A few months ago he fell in disfavour, and his enemies at once seized the opportunity to ridicule his Kultuk-Khivan railway scheme. "Tchernayeff's road to Central Asia," as it was called, although it was really Vaniushin's, was pitilessly assailed by the innumerable enemies he had made by his reforming zeal in Turkestan. However, roads with a destiny, like men with a destiny, can never be killed by ridicule. The traders stuck to the road they had opened up (and such unbiassed preference was worth a bushel of staff officers' reports), and now a peculiar importance has been given to it by the discovery of petroleum springs near the Mertvi Kultuk Bay. Should these prove to be of a copious character, the railway to Khiva (an inevitable undertaking of the future) will possess its own fuel supply, and another reserve will be afforded for Russia, should in distant ages the Baku oil supply begin to fail.* It is not improbable, indeed,

---

* A few particulars, condensed from reports by Vsevolod Krestovsky (Tchernayeff's private secretary), Vaniushin, Rajeff, and others, may not be without interest to experts. The new highway runs from Bokhara to Ustik Kurgan, on the Oxus, 60 miles, with crowded settlements and cultivated fields all the way, except one break of 18 miles of sands. Ustik Kurgan is a small Bokharan fortress; has a good descent to the river, and plenty of ferry boats. The journey thence to Kungrad, 443 miles, occupies six or seven days going down the river, and a fortnight or three weeks ascending the stream. This

that other discoveries of petroleum may be made when the mining engineer investigates more closely the Transcaspian Steppes. Only so recently as the winter of 1883 Konshin, in one of his surveys, came across a hill fifty feet high, amidst the Kara Kum sands, containing at least eight million tons of the finest brimstone.

Such discoveries of new routes and fresh resources bid us to anticipate a wide development of Russia's power in the Caspian in the immediate future. Besides yielding inexhaustible quantities of petroleum, the Caspian is the seat of the most flourishing of Russian fisheries. Excluding the thousands of tons of sturgeon, over 200 million herrings are caught off the mouth of the Volga every year. Then there is the increasing trade with Persia, between £300,000 or £400,000 of goods being conveyed from the Persian ports to the Great Fair every season.* Afterwards we may glance at busy Astrakhan,

---

would be lessened when the steamers arrive of the state-aided Oxus Navigation Company, which is now being formed at Moscow, with a capital of £100,000, to work the river traffic. The water has a minimum depth of 4½ feet as far as Kabakli, and 9 feet to Kungrad. From Kungrad to Port Yaman Arakti is a distance of 292 miles, occupying ten or twelve days; a wheeled transport service already exists along it. A pier at Yaman Arakti, erected by the Russian Transport Company, runs out into 5 feet of water. There is a house for travellers; saksaoul fuel abounds; the Kirghiz are settling down round about; and a detachment of troops has been located there (May 1884). The minimum depth of water in the Mertvi Kultuk bay is 6½ feet in summer and 9 in spring. The distance from Astrakhan is three days for a tug, and forty-eight hours for a passenger steamer. Using the Kultuk-Kungrad route, troops from Fort Petro-Alexandrovsky, in Khiva, can reach Astrakhan in fifteen to seventeen days; by the old route the journey to Kazala occupied twenty-eight days, and to Orenburg thirty days, or in all, fifty-eight days. Troops were sent to Khiva by the route in May this year, and 3,000 tons of cotton despatched by it from Khiva to Astrakhan.

* In 1883 the total was 3,763,225 roubles or £376,323. Among the articles were: raisins and kishmish, £126,525; lambskins, £51,400; cotton, £48,500; millet, £33,090; nuts, £25,625; almonds, £18,750;

that great emporium at the mouth of the Volga. In 1882 the trade of this port was estimated at £5,350,000 sterling. Formerly vessels of more than three or four feet of water could not pass between Astrakhan and the Caspian, owing to the shoals in the outlets of the Volga. During the last two or three years, however, the Bakhtemir channel has been deepened to eight feet, and now a large number of steamers run regularly between the upper Volga and lower Caspian, without transferring goods at the mouth of the river.

Finally, the Caspian is the receptacle of the Volga itself—that grand waterway, wholly enclosed in the Russian dominions, draining with its affluents and the Caspian an area of 6,823,000 square versts populated by 32,364,000 people. The traffic on the Volga amounts to over 10 million tons annually, conducted by 650 cargo steamers, and 3,000 barges with a united capacity of nearly 3,000,000 tons. The value of these steamers and barges is estimated at 8 millions sterling. In excess of the 3,000 permanent barges of 1,000 tons capacity each, there are hundreds of temporary ones constructed to convey cargoes to Nijni-Novgorod or other destinations, and then broken up. On the Volga and Kama 100 such barges are yearly constructed, with a cargo capacity each of from 300 to 500 tons, and 200 with a capacity of from 5,000 to 8,000 tons. These huge vessels, and the 300-foot permanent barges, are too large to pass through the canal system to the river Neva, the locks and shallows of which do not admit of the passage of craft exceeding in length 147 feet, and in breadth 27½ feet; hence 1,000 smaller barges, 100 feet long, and having a capacity of 200 or 300 tons apiece, are yearly constructed simply for the transport of goods from Rybinsk on the Volga, to St.

silk, £1,860. The Persian merchants remitted home 15,000 gold half-imperials and £3,000 in paper roubles; the remainder was expended in Russian goods for the Persian market.

Petersburg on the Neva. Steps are now being taken to improve the canal system, which, as will be observed, is already on a magnificent scale, and ultimately vessels 300 feet long will be able to float from the Neva to the Volga. Besides the extensive shipbuilding referred to above, 4,000 barges, wherries, fishing boats, and other craft are annually built on the Volga for the lower course of the river and the Caspian Sea. The central point of the traffic on the Volga is Nijni-Novgorod, where there is an annual turnover at the Great Fair of from twenty to twenty-five millions sterling. The traffic passing through the mouth of the Volga amounted to a million tons in 1882.

These, then, are some of the resources which could be directed upon the Caspian through the new eight-foot channel with the greatest ease, the flowing stream bearing them swiftly down the river to the great outlet-basin, with the magnificent concentrating point of Baku Bay on one side of the sea, and the equally splendid harbour of Krasnovodsk on the other. The great trade-route between Baku and St. Petersburg is already well organized —there is a water-channel the whole way. The trade-route from Europe to Baku *viâ* Batoum I have already dwelt upon. Two others are now left to be examined: from Baku to India, and from Baku to the Persian Gulf. Let me deal with the latter first.

Bearing in mind the high pitch of organization the trade on the Volga has already attained, and the rapid development of Russia's commerce in the Caspian Sea, I think that there can be hardly a doubt that ere many years are over our heads the Russian traders will be pushing their way to the Persian Gulf. The distance between the Caspian and that gulf is altogether insignificant compared with average distances in Russia. From Baku to Rybinsk, where vessels leave the Volga for the canal journey to the Neva, is over 2,100 miles. On the other hand, from the decks of the Russian steamers in the southern Caspian, to the Persian Gulf, is only a matter of 900 odd miles.

The recently published opinion of a Russian official is not without interest on this subject.* In describing the ultimate extension of Russia's trade to the Persian Gulf, Gospodin Yogel observes:—

"A mere glance will be sufficient to show that the newly-opened Baku-Batoum railway does not fulfil the requirements of Transcaucasia, and that another line must be built to run down the Aras valley from Erivan to some port in Lenkoran. The Caspian is a natural extension of the river Volga: the Persian Gulf is a natural continuation of the line of communication running from north to south viâ the Volga, the Caspian, Persia, and the Persian Gulf to the Indian Sea. From the Caspian to the Persian Gulf all that would be needed would be a railway 700 or 800 miles long† to complete this highway of communication with India. In course of time there is very little doubt that such a line will be constructed, and it is indispensable that Russia should take timely measures to secure the control of the branches that converge upon the Caspian."

If we bear in mind the fascination which the trade of the East exercises over Russia, and the growing ambition of the officials in the Caspian region, we can hardly consider Persia's independence destined to be long lived. Persia is assailable at a hundred different points, and the prestige Russia enjoys throughout the country is such that a heavy blow swiftly struck at Teheran would lay in

* An Investigation of the Volga and the waters of its riverine territory, founded on official and local data. By N. B. Yogel, ex-Chief of the Kazan Circle of Ways of Communication. St. Petersburg, 1884.

† By the existing caravan road the distance from Resht to Bushire is 933 miles.

dust for ever the rotten remnants of the old Persian monarchy. Seven million people, scattered over desert or mountain-severed provinces, susceptible of being easily broken off the Shahdom in detail, and possessing neither national vitality nor ardent love of liberty, do not constitute a very formidable community for a power to crush and annex, which has already robbed it of the Caucasus and Caspian. To go into the past and present of the rival politics of Russia and England in Persia is beyond my province on this occasion, but two short opinions may be expressed. As regards the past, I do not think that any Englishman can carefully read the history of Persia for the last thirty years without being amazed at the persistent imbecility of English diplomacy, and the credulity of a large proportion of English political writers in imagining that Persia could offer any check to the material and military progress of Russia. As regards the present, although the coast of the Persian Gulf lies to-day as closely under the English guns as the shore of the Caspian does under the cannon of Russia, yet there is one very essential difference. A great Russian colony is growing in the Caspian, which will spread its roots southwards, finding nothing to check their course till they touch the ports of the Persian Gulf. We have no such colony or settlement developing in the Persian Gulf, nor are we striving to create one with the resources of India. Hence, when the ramifications of Russia reach the Persian Gulf, I cannot see any other prospect for English influence than that it should droop and die.*

* Such a development need not imply a costly conquest of Persia, although Russia is quite willing to pay a good price for territorial extensions or predominant influence in the Shahdom. In March, 1884, died at Shusha an uncle of the Shah, Bahmen Meerza, who fled from Teheran during the troubles of 1848, and had never left his place of exile in the Caucasus. Russia maintained him as a convenient pretender to the throne in case of necessity, and allowed him a pension of 36,800 roubles a year. Altogether, from the time he arrived from

If Baku is destined to play an important part in the opening up of direct relations between the Caspian and the Persian Gulf, still greater is her future in connection with the Russian Cossack and Caravan advance upon India. Russia's present policy of seeking to attain the Indian confines for political and commercial purposes from the Caspian basis is sometimes spoken of as a new and novel movement. In reality, it is only the revival of an old one. I have already referred to the time when the wares of India used to make their way to Europe *viâ* the Caspian and Transcaucasia; and to the mania that possessed English merchants a hundred years ago to despatch goods from London to India *viâ* the Baltic ports of Russia, the Volga, the Caspian, and across Persia or the Khanates of Central Asia. Ignoring both these movements, English statesmen when they evacuated Candahar treated intercourse between the Caspian and India as a matter that would never ripen in their time. Since then, most of the obstacles, geographical and political (the greater portion existing only in the fancy of English statesmen), have disappeared; and Russians are talking freely of the time when the great trade-route of the past will be re-established.

In effecting this re-establishment, Russia will doubtless be largely aided by the enterprise and public spirit of her merchants. Russian caravans followed immediately in the track of the Cossack when Merv was occupied in the early part of the year. And this energetic action was accompanied by a circumstance which deserves to be recorded in these pages. The oasis of Merv is peculiarly well adapted for the cultivation of cotton, of which there has always been a slight export to Bokhara. Moscow draws several thousand tons of cotton yearly from

Persian until his death he received £135,000 from the Russian Government. He was very fond of marrying, and bequeathed to Russia 15 wives and nearly 100 children.

Central Asia, and has long advocated an extension of its cultivation. But Russian merchants are not like many English ones—continually talking of public spirit, and never displaying it. When the occupation of Merv had been effected, the first act of the Moscow cotton spinners, Konshin and Morozoff, was to distribute gratis several tons of American cotton seed among the Turkomans, knowing that this was the most effective way of realizing the wishes of Moscow. Savva Morozoff did not rest content with Russian subjects, but adopted a similar course with those of Persia, distributing a ton and a half of seed gratis at Meshed and 900 pounds in Deregez. Such enterprise will make short work of the trifling obstacles to trade existing between the Caspian and India.

How slight these are we may realize by examining a few hard facts. From Calcutta to Quetta is about 2,000 miles. When the Quetta railway, now in course of construction, is complete, there will be railway communication the entire distance between the two places. From St. Petersburg to Baku is a little over 2,000 miles, with steam communication complete almost the whole way. Baku and Quetta are thus about the same distance from the respective Capitals of Russia and India. Now, crossing the Caspian Sea from Baku to Port Michaelovsk, we find that the distance thence to Quetta is as follows:—

	Miles.
Michaelovsk to Sarakhs	464½
Sarakhs to Herat	202½
Herat to Candahar	369
Candahar to Quetta	145
Total distance from the Caspian to Quetta	1,181 miles.

That is to say, it is only about half as far from the Caspian to Quetta as from Baku to St. Petersburg. This is not calculated to damp the ardour of Russian traders very much. But if we uncoil this fact further, we find other points of greater significance wrapped inside it. From Michaelovsk to Kizil Arvat there is a railway to facilitate intercourse; hence we may knock off 144 miles. From Kizil Arvat to Askabad is a wagon service along an easy, safe, and well supplied road; hence we may reduce the figure further by 135 miles. From Askabad to Sarakhs the distance of 185½ miles is similar to the last in characteristics, and will be organized for trade in a few months' time. We may therefore eliminate from the general total this section also. Thus, from Sarakhs to Quetta all the distance the Russian trader has to traverse is 716½ miles, or a trifle further than from St. Petersburg to Nijni-Novgorod. Perhaps I lack the penetration of statesmen of the Gladstone school; but I certainly cannot detect in this insignificant distance any bar to the almost immediate establishment of commercial intercourse between the 101 millions of the Russian empire on the one side of the vanishing Afghan zone, and the 250 millions of the Indian empire on the other, especially if it be borne in mind that only two slightly fortified towns bar the intervening high road the whole way—Herat with 50,000 people, and Candahar with a population of 60,000 souls.

Should the Russian trader put off direct intercourse with India for a while, and confine his operations to Afghanistan, five easy marches will take his caravan from Sarakhs to Herat, and if he goes beyond, the distance from Herat to Candahar is less than from Tiflis to Baku. From Sarakhs all the way to Candahar is only ten miles longer than from Baku to Batoum.

Hence, apparently the time is not far distant when the Parsees will be back again at Baku, not to worship the Everlasting Fire, but for the purpose of buying lamp oil for the bazaars of India, and other commonplace objects. What will be the effects of such intercourse I have no space to discuss in this work, but some suggestions as to their character may be found in the Appendix. We cannot prevent this intercourse. The past and present policy of Mr. Gladstone's Government, of making a Chinese wall of Afghanistan to keep out the Russian trader and Russian tchinovnik, is so appallingly stupid that one cannot wonder at the statesmen of St. Petersburg holding our ministers in such high esteem. Even now that Russia is upsetting things right and left in Central Asia, they still continue to hope that a couple of towns held by a rabble will indefinitely separate the two empires. Yet nothing on earth and nothing in heaven can prevent the approximation of Russia and India. If we do not secure at once a strong frontier to defend India, Russia will organize a strong frontier to assail it. And when she gets that strong frontier, England will have to be on her good behaviour in the East.

On this account, with the Cossack entrenching himself at Merv and Sarakhs, and Kerosine revolutionizing affairs in the Caspian, the time has arrived when we should leave off being, like the Guebers of old—mute devotees before the Altar of Everlasting Talk—and ourselves fashion and impress a sound patriotic policy upon our rulers. The Empire first, Party afterwards—this should be our motto; nor can I conceive a loftier aim than that all should combine to uphold that Empire against those forces which have made Old Persia a prey to New Russia, and given over to the sway of the Cossack the magnificent resources of the Region of the Eternal Fire.

CHAPTER XX.

1884-1887.

Rapid Development of Baku since 1884—Apathy of the British Petroleum Trade—"The New Wonder of the World"—Fountains at Baku of Late Years—The 11,000-Ton Gusher—Tagieff's Fountain—The Great Fountain of 1887—Production of Crude Oil—New Pipe-lines—Growth of Traffic on the Transcaucasian Railway—Trade at Batoum—The Conflict between the Crude Pipe-line and the Kerosine Pipe-line—The Pipe-line over the Suram Pass—Policy of the Russian Government—The Burmese Oil Fields—One Thousand Million gallons of Lamp Oil manufactured every Year—The "Moloch of Paraffin"—Growth of Russian Power in the Caspian—The Afghan Boundary Settlement—"A Clerk in Epaulettes"—Russia and the Helmund.

THREE eventful years have elapsed since I penned the foregoing chapters on the condition and prospects of Russia's power in the Caspian region, and there is hardly a forecast I made in 1884 that has not been realized in a manner not only amazing to the world at large, but to myself also. To-day every petroleum merchant knows something of Baku, and Russian oil maintains its place side by side with the American article in every market in Europe. Yet only three years ago Baku was practically unknown, and I had to argue and prove over and over again in the press that a large supply existed there at all. The copiousness of the wells I had seen was ascribed to ephemeral volcanic agency, and prophets hastened to declare that Baku would be played out long before she became a rival of Pennsylvania. That a single Baku well should spout more oil in a day than all the wells of America put together, was a statement smilingly described as a "traveller's tale," and my appeal that England should take a prominent part in the development of the new industry, in advance of foreign rivals, apparently fell dead upon the public ear.

Had Baku been situated in some inaccessible and isolated region, my fate might have been that of Bruce, Marco Polo, and other travellers, but being placed midway between England and India, and occupying a central position on the Euro-Indian railway system—a system of which only a few hundred miles, from Merv to Quetta, remain to be constructed to complete railway communication between London and Calcutta—it came into prominence as soon as Russia began breaking down the sole remaining obstacles to a re-opening of the great highway of commerce of the past between Europe and India, *viâ* Poti, Baku, and Herat. In a couple of years Baku was visited by more Englishmen than during the whole of its previous history. The Lumsden Mission, after passing through it, on its way to the Afghan frontier, maintained communication with London by means of couriers and detached officials, who constantly halted at Baku. Gaze and Cook, adopting my suggestion, escorted thither bodies of tourists. Of military officers anxious to see (at their own expense, *à la* Burnaby) what Russia was doing in the Caspian, at least a dozen must have paid a visit to Baku. The accounts these and other visitors gave of the wonderful oil deposits of the Apsheron Peninsula, fully confirmed all I had said, and England began to think that, really, after all, there must be some money lying latent in Baku oil. Then the English and the United States' Governments sent consuls thither to report, and the scientific bodies of this country set a good example to somnolent Chambers of Commerce by promoting discussions on the future of Russian petroleum. Finally, the importation of Baku oil into Austria led to an acute ministerial crisis at Vienna, which secured a wide advertisement for Baku, and revealed to England that while she had been sleeping the Germans, Austrians, and French had been going largely into the trade, and making money out of it.

In 1884 the Swedes were the only non-Russians exploiting Baku, and it is no secret that they would have welcomed the co-operation of Englishmen. To-day the industry is attracting the attention of every country in Europe, and, unless England displays promptness and energy, the Petroleum trade, not simply of Baku, but of the whole world, will slip through her fingers. All along I have hoped, and continue to hope still, that England would shake off her lethargy, and make up for the decadence of old branches of commerce by developing new ones. A business into which the proverbially cautious Rothschilds have thrown themselves with vigour, investing nearly £2,000,000 in the Baku industry since 1884, surely cannot be considered unsafe for Englishmen.

The copiousness of the Baku oil supply is now a point thoroughly established, and my views in regard to it have been confirmed over and over again, by fountains pouring forth prodigious quantities of oil, in a manner that renders Baku, to quote the expression used by Professor Tyndall in a letter to me on the subject, "the new wonder of the world." The Droojba fountain, spouting in 1883 upwards of 3,400 tons of oil a day, or more than all the 25,000 wells of America put together, had been looked upon as a phenomenon that would never occur again. However, in subsequent years, there were numerous other fountains, although not so prodigious, and then, in 1886, a climax was reached with one that spouted the almost incredible quantity of 11,000 tons of Petroleum per diem. In other words, from a single orifice, ten inches wide, there spouted more oil than was being produced throughout the whole world, including therein the 25,000 wells of America, the thousands of wells in Galicia, Roumania, Burma, and other countries, and the shale oil distilleries of Scotland and New South Wales. On the 6th of October 1886, the Russian official newspapers published the following telegram :—" Baku, October 5.—At Tagieff's wells a fountain has commenced playing at the rate of 500 tons an hour. Its height is 224 feet. In spite of its being five versts from the town, the Petroleum sand is pouring upon the buildings and streets." The news was all the more interesting, because the Tagieff spouter was the offspring of quite a new locality. As described in this volume, most of the great fountains had occurred in the Balakhani district. The new one, however, was situated three miles to the south of Baku, and eleven or twelve from Balakhani, on the promontory of Bybyibat, forming one of the jaws of Baku bay. Here Gospodin Tagieff had commenced boring in 1884. Petroleum was reached in due course, but after a while the flow subsided, and the oil had to be pumped to the surface. Later on, the yield diminishing, Tagieff resumed boring operations. At its best the well had never yielded more than 16,000 gallons a day, which is not enough to excite competition at Baku, and hence Tagieff had no rivals to speak of at Bybyibat. On the 27th September the boring tool found oil at 714 feet, and the oil began to spout with a force unparalleled in the annals of Baku.

"From the town," said the *Baku Isvestie*, "the fountain had the appearance of a colossal pillar of smoke, from the crest of which clouds of oil sand detached themselves and floated away a great distance without touching the ground. Owing to the prevalence of southerly winds, the oil was blown in the direction of Bailoff Point" (on which Baku dockyard is situated), "covering hill and dale with sand and oil, and drenching the houses of Bailoff, a mile and a half away. Nothing could be done to stop the outflow. The whole district of Bybyibat was covered with oil, which filled up the cavities, formed a lake, and on the fifth day began pouring into the sea. The outflow during three days was estimated at 5,000 or 6,000 tons daily. On the sixth day the wind freshened, and the oil spray began flying all over the town. The square in front of the Town Hall of Baku was drenched with petroleum, which even fell on houses in the outskirts to the north. The loss of oil was prodigious. On the eighth day the maximum was reached, the oil then spouting at the rate of 11,000 tons, or $2\frac{3}{4}$ million gallons a day. To prevent the petroleum being totally lost, attempts were made to divert the stream flowing into the sea into some old wells. After the tenth day it began to diminish, and by the fifteenth day the engineers had so far got it under control that the outflow was only a quarter of a million gallons a day. Altogether over 10 million gallons of oil came to the surface, and most of this was lost for want of storage accommodation. Had the owner had a cap ready in time he might have saved the whole until wanted. As it was, the oil simply poured itself uselessly into the Caspian Sea, and was lost for ever to mankind."

In the spring of this year the copiousness of the new locality was attested by another "gusher," known as the Zubaloff Fountain. This occurred on ground belonging to the Crown, and denominated "Group 20." It had been leased to the firm of Jakelli and Co., who in turn sublet it to Zubaloff. The latter started boring in 1885, and penetrated to 567 feet, when from discouragement and other causes he suspended operations. The success of Tagieff, however, whose 11,000-ton spouter was situated close to his own, caused him to start boring afresh in November, 1886. The depth reached when the fountain burst forth was 672 feet, the 16-inch diameter tube reaching 196 feet, the 14-inch to 392 feet, the 12-inch to 623 feet, and finally the 10-inch to 672 feet. The Tagieff Fountain had not spouted until a depth of 714 feet had been attained.

At seven o'clock on Sunday morning, March 20, petroleum began to spout freely, and soon attained a height of 350 feet. Stones were thrown up in great abundance, some weighing over 20lbs. The wind being light and blowing from Baku, the sand and stones fell on and round about the well and did no great damage. At eleven o'clock in the day there was a perceptible falling off in the strength of the fountain, the height of the stalk being only 200 feet. Gangs of men were set to work and directed the stream in the direction of some reservoirs Zubaloff had been constructing. These the oil filled in course of time, broke down the earth walls, and forced its way into the Caspian. From the 20th to the 24th the oil spouted without intermission, when it suddenly ceased for four days, the tube becoming clogged with stones and sand. On the 28th the fountain began playing afresh, and gushed with great violence for several days, after which the tube became completely blocked. Nearly the whole of the oil was lost.

This year, the Balakhani plateau, as if to revive its dimmed prestige sprung a fountain which for weeks excited the wonder of Russia. The well belonged to the Baku Mining Company, and on the 13th of August began spouting at the rate of 7,000 or 8,000 tons daily. In a couple of days it had already formed a crater of sand 14 feet high. The force exercised was prodigious, the oil shooting 400 feet high at times, and the spray falling, when the wind blew fresh, 12 versts (8 miles) away. In other words, the oil spouted twice as high as the Monument, and sprayed from it as far as Woolwich Arsenal is from the City. All the holes and depressions near were filled with oil, which finally flowed away for miles. The sand buried houses two or three hundred yards off. The gas emitted was so powerful that it was dangerous to approach the fountain, and not a fire could be lit for miles round about. Yet one day a heedless sightseer from Baku nearly provoked a universal catastrophe by attempting to strike a match to light a cigarette. The fool, very luckily, was seen by some workmen, who knocked the match from his fingers, and would have lynched him on the spot by hurling him into the oil lake but for the opportune arrival of the manager. After this the fountain was surrounded by Cossacks to keep off idiotic intruders. Day after day the fountain played for more than six weeks, the volume gradually decreasing to about 2,000 tons a day. At last the patience of the Russian Government was exhausted, and permission was given to the rest of the firms at Baku to seize and lynch the well. Availing themselves of the power given, Messrs. Nobel, the Rothschilds, &c., assembled their best engineers on the spot, and after a few days managed to fix a cap on the well and throttle the fountain. The amount of oil wasted was almost as great as that of the Droojba—50 million gallons.

These three fountains completely falsified the prediction of those who, after the Droojba Fountain of 1883, had argued on the flimsiest grounds that Baku would speedily play itself out. "See," these pessimists said, "they have to bore deeper for oil every year." Of course they did, for it is the inevitable experience everywhere. There is, however, this all-important difference between Baku and America—the deeper Baku bores the greater the gush of oil, which is not the case with her Transatlantic rival. Then the margin is altogether in favour of Baku. In America it is quite common to bore 2,000 feet for oil, and many wells attain a depth of very much more than this. At Baku a well 700 or 800 feet deep is considered by croakers a deep one, and last year the average depth of all the wells was only 462 feet. Considering that the Apsheron Peninsula has been bleeding oil 2,500 years, and that every season is characterized by gushers of a more and more extraordinary description, it is difficult to believe that 500 prickings in an area of three or four square miles should cause the entire oil area of 1,600 square miles to dry up in a few years. Of the two it is rather America that is becoming exhausted than Baku.

As a result of the copiousness of the fountains, the crude oil has been selling at times at the rate of fifty gallons for a penny, and there is every reason to believe low prices will be maintained for many years to come. Of course the development of the industry has been accompanied by numerous crises, and ignorant observers have mistaken these "growing pains" for symptoms of a collapse. But, although this collapse has been "going to occur" several times it has never yet come off, while at the end of every year the industry has been found to have forged ahead considerably. The growth of large firms usually means the ruin of many little ones, and Baku has been no exception to the general rule. In 1884 there were about 200 refineries at Baku, now there are 121, comprising 36 large ones and 85 small. On the other hand the output of oil has immensely increased, demonstrating that although many of the small Asiatic refiners have been driven from the field, the industry generally has developed.

PRODUCTION OF CRUDE PETROLEUM.

	Tons.		Tons.
1883	800,000	1885	1,780,000
1884	1,435,000	1886	2,000,000

In 1883 the quantity of kerosine, or refined oil, manufactured, was under 60 million gallons. In 1886 the quantity exceeded 150 millions.

As might be imagined, the bulk was produced by Nobel Brothers; after them coming Messrs. Rothschilds, who own large refineries in the new suburb that has grown up beyond Villa Petrolia. This has been dubbed White Town, in contradistinction to Black Town. The latter in time may become white also, since the Baku authorities now rigorously prosecute any refiner who fails to consume his own smoke. The firm of Meerzoeff has disappeared altogether.

The six pipe-lines running to the refineries from the oil fields in 1884 have developed to fifteen, having a total length of 100 miles, and valued at £400,000. It is encouraging to note that many miles of these iron pipes have been supplied by the firm of Messrs. A. and J. Stewart, of Glasgow. The unexpected benefits that proceed from pushing business in new markets is strikingly illustrated in the operations of this enterprising firm. The reputation which it obtained in supplying Baku with oil pipes led the Russian Government to order at a stroke 23 miles of pipes, to be laid down as a water pipe-line along the Transcaspian Railway in the direction of Kizil Arvat. The idea of piping water across the desert being adopted by the British Government also, the same firm received an order for 55 miles of pipes, to be laid down along the Suakin-Berber Railway. This order was executed at the rate of a mile a day, without interfering at all with the ordinary business of the firm, and the quantity might have been doubled or trebled per diem, if necessary, without unduly straining the resources of the establishment. People sometimes talk of the proposed pipe-line between Baku and Batoum, 600 miles long, as an undertaking of extraordinary difficulty; but from the foregoing it will be obvious that the whole of the pipes needed could be manufactured by a single British firm in a little more than six months. As in the future many ramifications of pipe-lines will extend from Baku, it is to be hoped that the good name Glasgow has secured there as a producer of iron pipes will cause the bulk of the orders to fall into British hands. At any rate it will pay us to keep a sharp eye upon Baku.

The great drawback the petroleum trade of the Caspian has all along had to contend with has been a deficiency of transport. Every year the means of exporting the oil have improved, but on the other hand the production has always kept ahead of the improvement. In 1883 there were forty tank steamers plying on the Caspian Sea; the number is now 100, and is yearly increasing.

In 1883 the export of refined oil from Baku to Russia *viâ* the Caspian Sea was under 60 million gallons. In 1885 it exceeded 87 million gallons. In 1883 the export of *astatki* by the same route amounted to 281,000 tons; the total in 1885 was 460,000 tons.

When I described the Transcaucasian route in 1884 there were only a few hundred tank cars running on the line from Baku to Batoum. There are now several thousands. In the interval the transport of oil by the railway has developed as under:—

TOTAL OF PETROLEUM PRODUCTS CONVEYED BY THE TRANSCAUCASIAN RAILWAY.

	Gallons.	Traffic Receipts.
1883	14,000,000	£50,600
1884	25,500,000	£108,200
1885	41,000,000	£163,800
1886	71,000,000	£241,200

Most of the oil conveyed consisted of kerosine.

	Kerosine Gallons.	Lubricating Oil. Gallons.
1883	11,700,000	812,000
1884	20,200,000	2,268,000
1885	34,600,000	3,092,000
1886	62,500,000	3,868,000

As the limit to traffic imposed by the clogging in the Suram Pass is estimated at 80 million gallons, it is clear that the traffic in 1886—71 million gallons—almost reached this margin. To improve matters the Russian Government in the summer of 1887 decided to allow a kerosine pipe-line to be laid over the pass, the idea being that tank cars should run the Baku oil to one side

of the Lesser Caucasus ridge, and tank cars take it on to
Batoum from the other, the intermediate stage of about
40 miles across the pass being done in pipes. As the
pipe line will increase the traffic power of the railway
from 80 to 130 million gallons at a stroke, this decision
gave great satisfaction, and before long will exercise a
favourable influence on the export from Batoum.

Baku oil was only just beginning to percolate through
that port to Europe when I visited it in 1883. By 1885
the export had so far grown that it comprised 24 million
gallons of kerosine, 330,000 gallons of lubricating oil,
and 532,000 gallons of *astatki*, making a total of 25 million gallons of petroleum products altogether. Last year
the total exceeded 45 million gallons. This did not include oil shipped from Batoum to Odessa and other
Russian ports.

In 1883 the oil was shipped from Batoum solely in
barrels, and there was not a single tank-reservoir in
the place. Now there are forty-five, capable of holding
20 million gallons of oil. Instead of being conveyed to
Europe in barrels, the oil is shipped in tank or cistern
steamers, of which there are now more than a dozen running regularly to various European ports. At Odessa,
Smyrna, Fiume, Trieste, Genoa, Marseilles, Antwerp,
Bremen, Libau, and other European ports, iron reservoirs
have also been erected to store the oil in bulk.

When I published "The Region of the Eternal Fire" in
1884, many pooh-poohed my prediction that in a few
years tank-steamers would be plying in European waters
and running oil in bulk across the Atlantic. Such
steamers, I was assured by naval men, could not stand
the huge Atlantic waves, or the rough waters of the Bay
of Biscay, although they had weathered many a squall in
the Caspian; while the members of the petroleum trade
of this country, who, almost to a man, are as devoid of
general intelligence as they are of enterprise. assailed me

with abuse as a dreamer. However, while they were still declaring, with all the vehemence of Podsnaps, that tank-steamers never could come into use in Europe, the Russian tank-steamer *Sviet* brought a cargo of 1,700 tons of kerosine across the Bay of Biscay from Batoum to London, and directly afterwards the English-built, but German owned, tank-steamer *Glückauf* arrived at Bremen with 2,600 tons of oil from New York. After this, tank-steamer succeeded tank-steamer—Messrs. Sir William Armstrong, Mitchell and Co. constructing half a dozen in a year, and now the conveyance of oil in bulk is regarded as a matter of course. It is true that what I chiefly aimed at—that the revolution from barrels to tanks should be accomplished by England, and the bulk transport of oil on the ocean highways of the world pass wholly into her hands—has not come to pass, but England cannot complain that she was not warned in time. While English merchants have been sleeping, or lecturing to workmen on the advisability of removing the existing depression of trade by the universal adoption of technical education, the revolution has been allowed to be accomplished mainly by the Germans, and these enterprising rivals promise to control the whole of the petroleum carrying trade at no distant date.*

It is not simply that English merchants refuse to open up new markets of their own accord, but they assail with abuse those travellers and consuls who attempt to point out the advantages to them. In the autumn of 1886 I drew attention in the press to the fact that the Russian Government contemplated giving permission to home or foreign capitalists to lay down a pipe-line, 600 miles

* A pamphlet I published in 1886 on this movement, entitled "The Coming Deluge of Petroleum," was twice translated into German; my views eagerly discussed and acted upon by German merchants; yet, notwithstanding several hundred favourable reviews in the English press, the petroleum trade of London did nothing.

long, between Baku and the Black Sea. For merely describing this, I was attacked as a "secret agent of the Russian Government" by one of the City Podsnaps. Yet it was surely to the interest of the petroleum trade to know every movement that was taking place in the Russian industry. This question of the pipe-line to the Black Sea was one that had attracted a good deal of attention just then, and it may be useful if I say a few words about it for the benefit of those who, like the more cultured merchants of Germany, consult this work for the purpose of assisting them in their business.

To overcome at a stroke the difficulties of transport, the proposal has frequently been made that a pipe-line should be laid down from Baku to Batoum, or some other point on the Black Sea, through which the oil would be piped direct to the piers of the sea-going steamers. The engineering difficulties are of no great importance, for there are several pipe-lines 300 miles long in America, where, in all, 9,000 miles of pipe-lines are in use; so that 600 miles of line from Baku to Batoum would not in the least be very wonderful. As I have already said, a single British firm, such as Messrs. A. and J. Stewart, of Glasgow, could manufacture all the pipes for this line in little more than six months. A pipe-line of the capacity sanctioned by a committee appointed by the Russian Government, would allow of the passage of 160 million gallons of oil yearly, and enable Baku to completely beat the American oil supply.

Up to 1886 the Russian Government opposed all pipe-lines, on the ground that, having to meet the guarantee on the Transcaucasian railway, it could not allow the traffic on it to be destroyed. Towards the summer of that year, however, it became clear that the traffic provided by Eastern goods, and corn, wine, manganese ore, and other local products, was ample enough to occupy the energies of the railway, and a committee of officials from the different ministries was appointed to formulate a general scheme for a concession. This was accordingly done; but before the Russian Government could even adopt the scheme, fresh considerations arose which involved another investigation. The chief of these was the question, whether the line laid down should be reserved for the passage of crude oil or for that of the refined product. Not so important, but still serious enough, was the demand of the Tiflis authorities that the terminal point of the line should not be Batoum, but Poti; to which port they recommended the whole of the petroleum export trade should be shifted.

Messrs. Nobel and other large refiners at Baku opposed the proposed crude pipe-line scheme, because they feared that rival refineries would spring up on the Black Sea coast, which, being able to dispose of all their residual products, and thereby make a larger profit, would be able to seriously compete with, and perhaps ruin, the refining industry at Baku. This probability was admitted by those who advocated the crude pipe-line scheme; but they urged that national interests were more precious than private ones, and that it was intolerable for Russia that millions of gallons of residual products (30 millions in 1886) should be barbarously wasted in the Caspian region every year, for want of a market, when, if the refineries were situated at Poti or Batoum, the bulk could be sold to European consumers. To construct a kerosine pipe-line meant a rapid increase to the refinery development of Baku, but, at the same time, a proportionate increase of the waste, which already excites the indignation of the scientific men of Russia.

It is difficult at present to say which side will win. If anything, the chances are rather in favour of the kerosine pipe-line. The promoters of it, at any rate, have secured a start. Until the spring of this year the Transcaucasian Railway Company enjoyed the right of running only its own tank-cars on the line. In consequence of the constant complaints of Baku respecting the deficiency of rolling-stock, the Government then gave permission to any refiner to run tank-cars. The principal refiners immediately availed themselves of this privilege, and the natural, and perhaps anticipated result was, that in a few months there were so many tank-cars running that it was impossible for the whole of them to circulate over the Suram Pass. A fresh clamour thereupon arose, and the Government had to give permission to the refiners to lay down 40 miles of piping over the Pass.

When this kerosine pipe-line is in working order the oil pumped to the top of the ridge from the tank-cars on the Baku side of the Lesser Caucasus will be able to flow by its own gravity much of the distance towards Poti and Batoum, the former of which is only 78 miles from Quirill. It is already foreseen, therefore, that the question will soon arise—why not allow the Suram kerosine pipe-line to run on to Poti or Batoum, instead of transferring the oil a second time to tank-cars at Quirill? If the Government yield to this agitation, the refiners will then demand—why, seeing that one-third the distance from Baku to Batoum is traversed by a pipe-line, not allow the remaining two-thirds to be put down? In this manner, by degrees, it is hoped that the kerosine pipe-line will win the race.

Such is the state of affairs in regard to the pipe-lines. The financial side of the question—the expenditure of two millions sterling on the crude pipe-line scheme—on which stress has been laid by ignorant persons, is really the least difficult part of the affair; for a Government which has already sanctioned the expenditure of a million sterling on the Suram tunnel, and finds millions to make lines to the heart of Central Asia, would not stop short of giving financial support to the pipe-line scheme, if the problem were not confused by a variety of distracting issues. A wrong policy might ruin Baku without giving proper compensation in the shape of another refinery town on the Black Sea, or it might place the industry under the control of a few firms, who might check its development, as Meerzoeff did during the monopoly period. The Russian Government, therefore, wisely maintains an expectant attitude, and it is really only persons ignorant of the historical march of events who mistake this for financial impotence.

As the construction of the pipe-lines would involve large orders for pipes, pumping-machinery, and reservoirs, I have always maintained that England should keep a vigilant watch upon the Russian petroleum industry. Years ago, when the first tank-steamers were appearing in the Caspian Sea, I urged that England should compete with the Swedes in supplying them. My recommendation, repeated time after time, fell on deaf ears, and ultimately not only were nearly the whole of the 100 steamers now there built by Sweden, but when an English firm sent an agent to Baku a year ago it was found that the Swedes had too firm a control over the market to be dislodged.

I am well aware that a disinclination exists to invest money in Russia, but trading is a very different thing from investing, and my charge against the petroleum trade of this country is, that not only has it held aloof from the Russian market, and allowed the foreigner to lay the basis of a future monopoly of trade, but has also ignored advantages existing within the limits of the Empire. Upper Burma, annexed two years ago, contains in the valley of the Irrawady and elsewhere enormous deposits of petroleum, potentially as copious as those of America, and, perhaps, as those of Baku. Yet, although situated alongside the river, and within 60 miles of the Rangoon-Prome railway, and although possessing a reputation as old as that of Baku, if not older, no attempt has been made to open up the deposits by the merchants and capitalists of this country. In this volume I have described the wonders that the development of the petroleum industry have achieved at Baku. There is no reason why similar wonders should not be repeated in Burma.*

Every year the petroleum industry becomes more and more important. The world now consumes nearly one thousand million gallons of petroleum lamp oil every year, and the consumption is rapidly on the increase.† Liquid fuel, a novelty when described in 1884, is now largely used on steamers, on railways, and in manufactories in the United States, and has become one of the commonplaces of engineering. That it will supersede coal in countries where coal is cheap and oil is dear, may be doubted, but a wide sphere of usefulness may be predicted for it whereever the reverse is the case.

Simultaneously with the progress of Russian petroleum in the Caspian, the political and military power of our rival in that region has developed in a manner fully foreshadowed in this work, but which at the time was as much unheeded as my forecasts regarding the future of Baku oil. So long ago as 1881, I published maps in my "Merv the Queen of the World" in which, in large type,

---

* For an account of the Burmese oil fields, see "England as a Petroleum Power." (London, R. Anderson & Co., 14, Cockspur Street, price One Shilling.)

† Unfortunately this increase is accompanied by an increase of fatalities, arising from the use of the oil in dangerous lamps. In the United Kingdom nearly 200 people meet an agonizing death, and several thousands are injured through lamp accidents every year. To check this evil I issued in 1886 a pamphlet, entitled "The Moloch of Paraffin" (R. Anderson & Co., 14, Cockspur Street), in which I specified the conditions of danger and safety in lamps, and described those that should be avoided. Only one lamp—the Defries Safety Lamp—reached the standard of safety I established. Now that public opinion is aroused, I trust the time will not be far distant when the ravages of the Moloch of Paraffin will be stayed, either by law, or by people resolutely refusing to use any other lamps than those which can be proved to be in every essential absolutely safe.

I indicated that the "annexation of Merv would infallibly lead Russia to Penjdeh"—Penjdeh being then a point heard of for the first time in this country—and recommended that the frontier line should be drawn from the Oxus to Sarakhs while there was yet time for England and the Ameer to arrange their interests on the Murghab, in advance of the Russian occupation of Merv. This and other recommendations fell on deaf ears, and in due course Russia annexed Merv, occupied the "no man's land" I indicated, and a conflict occurred for Penjdeh which no really patriotic and impartial Englishman can look back upon without a feeling of humiliation and shame. The Afghan frontier delimitation must ever remain a stain on two administrations—on that of Mr. Gladstone, which for years made no attempt to anticipate the clearly foreshadowed movement, and finally, after swallowing humiliation after humiliation during the seizure of Merv, Sarakhs, Pul-i-Khatun, and Ak Robat, submitted to the expulsion from Penjdeh; and on that of Lord Salisbury, which, after a show of firmness, suddenly surrendered to Russia the district of Badghis. The latter act, in many respects, transcended in pusillanimity and perfidy the surrender of Penjdeh; because Sir West Ridgeway quitted the ranks of those brave military men—General Sir Charles MacGregor, General Valentine Baker, Colonel Burnaby, and others who had made every sacrifice to stem the Russian advance, and, for the paltry credit of having successfully negotiated a paper treaty, supported the concession to Russia of a camping ground within 80 miles of Herat. For the first time in my writings on Central Asia, I had to brand a British officer as a traitor to the Empire. It is hard to be deceived by a Russian; but to be deceived by one's own countryman is a miserable ending to the gallant efforts made by a host of military men to keep back the Russians from laying their hands upon Herat. As a soldier himself, Sir West Ridgeway might have left it to some poltroon of a party politician to betray to Russia the Key of India.

But there are soldiers and soldiers. One cannot examine the lives of Skobeleff in Russia and General Sir Charles MacGregor in India, without feeling that both men were patriots in the truest sense of the term, since they were ever ready to sacrifice their career to promote the interests of the country, and resolutely refused to truckle to time-serving officials and ministers when those interests were in danger. Speaking of one of these to me once, Skobeleff, in reply to my remark that the person under discussion was a "general," exclaimed, with withering contempt, "phoof, a clerk in epaulettes." Burke has finely said that "great empires and little minds go ill together." If England sends little minds to represent her Imperial interests, whenever such matters as the Afghan frontier question are under discussion, she must not be surprised if the envoy fails as miserably in safeguarding them as Sir West Ridgeway did in the present year of grace.

Year after year Russian power is extending in the Caspian region at a pace which is fraught with serious danger to our rule in India. Already her ability to attack is so far ahead of our ability to defend, that she can place her home troops in front of the fighting position of Candahar, *i.e.*, on the river Helmund, in advance of any home troops we may send there to assist our Quetta garrison, and it is not easy to see how the counterpoise can be re-established. Still, the problem is one that will have to be faced, and faced resolutely by the statesmen of this country; and no evasion of our duties as citizens to-day will save us or our children from the ruin that will befall England should ever our Eastern Empire succumb to the forces that menace it from within and without.

APPENDIX.

1.—SKOBELEFF'S PROJECT FOR INVADING INDIA.
2.—SKOBELEFF ON THE RUSSIAN POSITION IN CENTRAL ASIA
3.—THE RUSSIAN INVASION OF INDIA IN 1877 AND 1874.
4.—RUSSIA'S POWER OF SEIZING HERAT.
5.—THE RUSSIAN ANNEXATION OF MERV.
6.—WHAT THE ANNEXATION OF MERV MEANS.
7.—THE CAUCASUS VIEW OF THE INVASION OF INDIA.

SKOBELEFF'S PROJECT FOR INVADING INDIA.

AT various times small extracts have been given from the correspondence of the late General Skobeleff, containing his views of the practicability of a Russian invasion of India. The subjoined is the first complete document, however, that has yet been published on the subject. Its authenticity is beyond question. The italicised passages exist in the original:—

Letter from General Skobeleff to a near relative, on the invasion of India, recently found among the papers of the late Prince Tcherkassky.

"I thank you heartily for your unchanging remembrance of me. I am thankful, but not surprised; it was by your co-operation that I began life in the military arena, and I am indebted to you for the first impressions of independent military service. To a certain degree I boldly express my conviction that you will henceforth take an interest in me, and assist me to continue to serve exclusively for war, which (after the success I have achieved it has now become manifest) is for me in life not a means but an end; and, moreover, the only one which causes me to value life. In this is really included the exclusiveness of my ambition, not always intelligible to everybody. You, who with discernment supported me more than twelve years ago, will probably now not refuse my petition, it being of a perfectly identical character; of course, conformably with fresh circumstances and position, as that with which Cornet Skobeleff, of the Horse Guards, stood before you. However, my petition is not altogether of an unconditional character. If I have decided to trouble you, it is because I am firmly persuaded that we have nothing to expect of a *decidedly serious* nature on the part of the inhabitants of Turkestan in the event of a war with Turkey, and that if we are going to fight exclusively with Turkey, or that the idea of the *terrible, offensive, decisive, significance* of Turkestan in the event of hostilities with England has not yet come to maturity in the highest spheres, it would be too severe a trial to remain here during the war.

"The object of this letter is to partly remind you of myself and my recent responsible fighting, but chiefly to express to you with the fullest frankness what in my opinion ought to be and could be undertaken by Turkestan for the glory and greatness of Russia, in the event of a decisive rupture with England. The aim to which I point possesses a great, a world-wide significance. Every Russian, acknowledging the possibility of success, and placed by fate near the affair, cannot fail to display the very significant means which, I allow myself to say, our authorities have accidentally amassed in this country, and with which, with corresponding decision and timely preparations, we could strike not only an effective blow at England in India, but also crush her in Europe. All this I repeat *in the presence of the full control we have over the Turkestan region, and its perfect security as a base of operations.* In the latter I firmly believe, and I have too many facts not to be convinced of the absolute character of our strength and prestige here, of course subject to the condition, more essential in Asia than elsewhere, 'not to waste words where force should be employed.' Impressed with the indispensability of fulfilling my duty to Russia at such a critical moment, I gave in my notice to the Governor-General on the 27th of December, 1876, wrote to Uncle Sasha, and now write to you, without thought of the consequences to me of what I have done, but only praying God that attention may be given to that terrible offensive power which we possess in Central Asia.

"I was appointed Governor of the Namangan district on the 22nd of September, 1875. A detachment was confided to me which had been assigned for defensive operations in the expectation of the reinforcements that were to arrive from the Empire in the spring of 1876. The condition of affairs on our frontier at that time was very serious—very unfavourable for us; in proof of which may be cited the fact that eighteen companies, eight sotnyas of Cossacks, and fourteen field guns, not reckoning the cannon for the fortifications, were assigned to defend the department.

"Directly after the departure of the main body for Khodjent on 16th of October, 1875, under the command of the head of the troops of the district, the whole of the seriousness of the position of the detachment confided to me became at once apparent. The enemy in all his strength burst upon the unfinished fortifications of Namangan on the 23rd of October, and from that time commenced a series of incessant conflicts with him. The results were at first the storming of Namangan and the purging of the Namangan district of the presence of hostile bands, and afterwards, when the troops had secured supplies, a period of active operations, comprising the routing of all the available forces of the former Khanate of Kokand, in number more than 40,000 men, at Baluiktche, on the 12th of November, 1875, and a whole series of more or less bloody conflicts (I will name those of Goor-tiube on the 28th of November, and Uladjibai on December 2, as being the more important of them), after which the Namangan active force stormed Andijan for a second time on the 8th of January, 1876, crushing at Assaké the remaining forces furnished by the war party, compelling the surrender of the leader of that party, Avtobachi, and laying, after a six months' compaign, the whole of the Khanate of Kokand at the feet of the Emperor. All this happened a year ago, and with this period coincides my appointment as military governor of the province of Ferghana. As may be imagined, there remained many unsettled elements in the province. With a view to finally pacifying them, the troops were directed upon the Alai, where, resigning myself to exclusively peaceful aims, I acted quite in a different manner from before. The Alai expedition did not cost Russia a single drop of blood, and the rebels were compelled to throw up the inaccessible positions they had occupied by the exclusive employment of strategy, by which I consider was fulfilled to the utmost degree the will of an Emperor who values so much the blood of his subjects. What was done under orders you had an opportunity of seeing from the announcement of the Governor-General after his inspection of the province of Ferghana. By rights I ought not to concern myself at such a time with my fate, but leave it to my superiors to decide where it is best I should serve. I reveal to you my heart on every occasion, and announce to you beforehand my desire to go on active service, at any moment, and in any position whatever. I can still less, I repeat, unconditionally beg leave to quit this region, *firmly believing* in its mighty offensive significance in solving the Eastern Question.

"More than once has the warning been uttered that Russia can menace from Central Asia the dominions of the English in India, and that it is indispensable in consequence to take measures to check the advances of the Russians in Turkestan. In reality, if we look around, we shall see that our position in Turkestan is extremely threatening, and the apprehensions of the English not without foundation. We have formed a strong base in Central Asia, with an army of about 40,000 men, from which we can always set apart for operations beyond Turkestan not less than 10,000 or 12,000. Besides, we can rely on the tranquillity of the country, the more so, since up to now there have been no serious indications whatever of any connection between the Mussulmans of Turkey and those of Central Asia at the present political moment. If the military means of Turkestan could be reinforced from Western Siberia by say six companies, with as large a number of Cossacks possible of the Siberian army, and a battery and three regiments of Cossacks could be sent from Orenberg, a corps could be formed, the approximate strength of which would be from 14,000 to 15,000 men. Such a corps, thrown across the Hindoo Koosh, might achieve a good deal. Everybody who has ever concerned himself with the question of the position of the English in India has declared it to be unsteady, that it is only maintained by absolute force of arms, that the European troops are only sufficient to keep the country quiet, and that the native soldiers are not to be depended upon at all. Everybody who has concerned himself with the question of the possibility of a Russian invasion of India would declare that it is only necessary to penetrate to a single point of the Indian frontier to bring about a general rising.

"It may be said that an enterprise against the English in India is a hazardous one; that it might end in the destruction of the Russian force. I imagine it to be only right that I should admit that the undertaking is a hazardous one. It is only necessary to remember, however, that in the event of the complete success of our enterprise we might crush the British Empire in India, the results of which it would be impossible to estimate even in England itself. Competent people in England acknowledge that a defeat on the Indian frontier might drag in its train a social revolution in the metropolis itself; since for the last twenty years identical causes and effects in all the relations with France (including unfitness for war) have bound England of to-day more than any previous period of her Indian possessions. In a word, the fall of the British power in India would be the *beginning of the fall of England*. In the event of an incomplete success on our part, *i.e.*, should a mutiny not take place in India, and we should not be in a condition to invade her territory, we should, nevertheless, tie the whole India army to Hindustan, and prevent the English transporting any part of it to Europe; nay, we should even compel England to send some portion of her European troops to India. In a word, we should, to a considerable extent, paralyze the land forces of England for a war in Europe, or for creating a new theatre of hostilities from the Persian Gulf to Tabreez, and on to Tiflis, which has been the aim of English military men ever since the Crimean war. The indispensability of the participation of Turkestan in the impending events is demonstrated by the fact that we should be compelled, in the event of ill-success in war, to evacuate the country or restrict our position there. If we, even in the event of a complete failure of our undertaking in Europe as well as in Asia, displayed,

A A

through an unfortunate spirit of enterprise, all the possible menace of our present position in Central Asia, we might have the alternative, should we be compelled to conclude an unfortunate peace, of buying ourselves off with Turkestan, which would have risen in value. There can be no comparison between what we should risk, in deciding to make a demonstration against the English in India, and those universal consequences that would be the outcome in the event of the success of our demonstration. The vast difference in the results of success between ourselves and the enemy should urge us to go boldly forward.

"On the declaration of war with England, operations ought to commence by sending immediately an embassy to Cabul, and by the formation of an active detachment (to give it more prestige I would call it an *army*) at Samarcand, consisting of ten battalions, fourteen sotnyas, and about forty guns; in all from 10,000 to 12,000 men. This to be the *minimum*, and to consist, moreover, of our very best combative forces. The object of the mission would be to draw Shere Ali into alliance with us, and enter into league with the disaffected elements in India; and in order to enable the negotiations to attain their end it would be indispensable, after forming the detachment, to march it without delay *viâ* Bamian to Cabul. If Shere Ali, in spite of all this, remained the ally of England (not very likely; the invitation of him *among the vassals* to Delhi to the festivities on the occasion of the proclamation of the title of 'Empress of India' was not accepted, and in general he expressed his dissatisfaction at the insult he considered was done him by this invitation)— if he remained the ally of England, then the pretender to the Afghan throne, Abdur Rahman Khan, who lives at Samarcand, should be sent forward, and through him a civil war sown in the country—Persia in the meanwhile being secretly encouraged to renew her pretensions to Herat. By turning Persia's attention towards Afghanistan we should draw her away from the Caucasus: and since the movement of Persian troops towards Herat would demand supplies and transport on a vast scale, this, among other things, would paralyze in the most effective manner the English plan of marching from the Persian Gulf upon Tiflis. The active force having left Samarcand, a fresh detachment should be formed there, comprising two battalions of infantry, a battery, and sixteen sotnyas of Cossacks, to occupy supporting points on the line of communications, and in general for service in the rear. Without going into details, the campaign, in my opinion, ought to fall into two periods—first, that of swift action and diplomatic negotiations with Afghanistan, the latter to be supported by pushing forward our active corps towards Cabul. The second period after the occupation of Cabul would be one of waiting, when we should have to enter into relations with all the disaffected elements in India, and convert them to our interests. The main cause of the failure of the rebellion of 1857 was the fact that the insurgents were not properly organized and led. And, finally, it would be our chief duty to organize masses of Asiatic cavalry, and, hurling them on India as our vanguard, under the banner of Blood and Rapine, *thus bring back the times of Tamerlane.*

"To define the further operations of the Russian column from Cabul in the plan of the campaign would be sheer guess work. If circumstances favoured us, our operations might end with planting the Russian banner on the walls of Benares. If the contrary were the case, the column might with honour retreat upon Herat, and meet troops pushed forward from the Caucasus. Such an operation would involve several battalions and about six guns to every 1,000 men. An Asiatic enemy, above all, the Turcomans—is not very terrible in the open, and even the victorious English army would melt away to a considerable extent in marching upon Herat.* In the present condition of the British army, the English could not move beyond the borders of India more than 25,000 men, of whom a considerable number would have to be left at the supporting points. Besides, it must not be forgotten that Turkestan would lie on the enemy's flank, and that our means would increase in proportion as we approached the Caspian. I have already said that the whole undertaking would be a risky one, but it is justified by the greatness of the aim and the immensity of the results. If the results be kept in view, there can be no talk on the part

* It is a fact beyond dispute that the acclimatized troops of Russia are better fitted to endure the hardships of a Central Asian campaign than the English. (See " History of the War in Afghanistan." By John William Kaye. London : 1851.) – SKOBELEFF.

of Russia of risk, and nothing at all is worth while saying about Turkestan. From the troops that would be fortunate enough to participate in such an expedition more should be exacted than self-sacrifice, even in the highest sense of the term among military men. The Hindoo Koosh once crossed, I believe the conviction would be kindled in the breast of each combatant that he had come to Afghanistan to conquer or die. This the Emperor demands of him, and there would be no reproaches made if our banners remained in the hands of the foe beyond the Hindoo Koosh after every Russian soldier had fallen.

"Such consciousness, such a decision on the part of the entire corps, could only be brought about in the Russian army, in my opinion, by the undoubted feeling of all of boundless attachment and love for their Sovereign. The difficult task of animating a corps to a degree proportionate with the character of the enterprise might be best accomplished by sending one of the Emperor's sons with the expedition, who, when the proper time arrived, would proclaim to the troops what their Tsar and Russia expected from them. I firmly believe that a corps made happy by the presence of a son of the Emperor would not under any circumstances soil the name of a Russian. During our ten years' stay in this region the Turkestan troops have worked out for themselves an entire system of military operations (founded on the knowledge of local conditions, of the character of the enemy, always the same in Mussulman Asia, but chiefly on the consciousness of its own aptitude for fighting) which enables them to clearly define military undertakings corresponding with the present military means of Turkestan. It may be said that there exists no longer any invincible barrier in Central Asia if we go on acting with our Turkestan force as we have done up to now. Masses of Asiatics can only disturb us; they cannot prevent us in the least from carrying out our intentions. We have now reached a point, thanks to which defined and systematic operations can be carried on by a corps, possessing arms and supplies relatively far exceeding the requirements of any European campaign, against almost any enemy in Central Asia, in the open as well as behind walls, and this, I repeat, with scarcely anything like the losses in the past. In fine, with our present experience, our plucky troops, and in my opinion our *very considerable* military resources, there is nothing in Asia that could really prevent us from carrying out the broadest strategical schemes.

"Our policy during the last ten years has given a world-wide importance to Russia. The sublime activity of our Government in the opinion of Englishmen and Asiatics has no bounds in Asia. This *prestige* serves in a principal degree to render our position secure. Not long ago, while reading Lieutenant-Colonel Cory's work—'Shadows of Coming Events; or, the Eastern Menace. London: 1876'—I was struck at his not imagining to himself the power of Turkestan, otherwise than connected by a railway running from Tchardjui on the Oxus to Moscow. Asiatics believe to this very moment that our troops spit fire when they rush with hurrahs upon them.

"An acquaintance with the country and its resources infallibly leads to the conclusion that our presence in Turkestan in the name of Russian interests can only be justified *by hastening to our own benefit the solution of the Eastern Question. Otherwise the Asiatic fleece is not worth the tanning*, and all our efforts in Turkestan will have been in vain. To prevent this it is very essential for us to take care lest by our inactivity here in Central Asia at the decisive moment in the West we display to the enemy all the casualness of our conquests. This would infallibly lead in its train the diminution of our prestige, and demand in the future still greater fruitless sacrifices. I repeat, that with a minimum army of 40,000 men, knowing how to operate, it would be possible not only to keep the Turkestan region in order, with Kashgaria and Bokhara acting against us, but also, I dare to affirm, enable us to evacuate Turkestan and conquer it over again. In case of need we could draw into Turkestan six Siberian Cossack cavalry regiments (thirty-six sotnyas), several companies from West Siberia, a battery of eight guns, and perhaps three regiments (eighteen sotuyas) from Orenburg. It must not be forgotten that, even after throwing from 16,000 to 20,000 men across the Hindoo Koosh, with proportionate artillery, of which there is any amount in Turkestan, there would still remain with the above-mentioned reinforcements 31,800 men for the defence of Turkestan, and this without touching the effective forces of the Amu Darya district (two battalions, four sotnyas, eight field guns), and without reckoning the forces in the Transcaspian region.

"There are no doubt many trials in store for us in Central Asia, but for them to attain a head it is necessary for the Mussulman race to first come to maturity, and that a whole class of influential men should rise knowing us well, and thoroughly realizing the mainsprings of our power and success. The well-known Nana Sahib was brought up in the midst of Europeans, and he was admitted into the highest English circles, and for that reason alone was able to be such a menace to the English. Elements of that sort have not yet formed among us. Therein lies one of our absolute advantages over the English, and when once events in the West attain a culminating point, this fact, together with many others, should impel us to get from Turkestan the whole of the benefit it is in a condition to accord.

"En Asie, là où cessent les triomphes commencent les difficultés (Lettre du duc de Wellington à lord Auckland, gouv. des Indes, 1839). This is indisputably true—in a political sense we are outliving the epoch of triumph, and must therefore make the utmost use of it. You see how much I anticipate from our might in Central Asia. It can be easily understood that having had the fortune for a long time of sharing the trials of war with the Turkestan forces, I cannot wish to exchange my fighting services here for any other; but it would be rather hard to be here doing nothing when the greater part of our army was shedding blood in the West for the fatherland. Hence I beg you again not to forget me in the event of any declaration of war.—Your affectionate and grateful,

"MICHAEL SKOBELEFF.

"P.S.—A few orders of the day to the troops of the Ferghana District to give you an idea how we live here. Read them through, and do not refuse to share with me your impressions, which I prize so much."

"I have just received the *Golos*, No. 358, of December 29, 1876. On reading the leading article I see that a declaration of war on the part of Russia against the Ottoman Porte constitutes the desired event of our enemies, that Europe has made a muddle of the question, and trusts to the precipitancy of Russia, so unfavourable for her (Russia); and, finally, that events have got in such a tangle that a decided and speedy unravelling of them is altogether out of the question for the moment. Already in the third decade of the present century Field-Marshal Count von Moltke pointed out the impossibility of obtaining rapid and decisive results in European Turkey, and acknowledged it would be exceedingly difficult to carry on war there without having a powerful fleet and the absolute dominion of the Black Sea. As is well known, even Field-Marshal Prince Varshavsky in 1829 expressed a doubt respecting the significance of aggressive operations in Asia Minor, on account of the lack of a decisive objective point. The only advantageous one he could see was the trade route joining Bagdad with Scutari; but this has now lost its importance with the opening of the Suez Canal. And thus one might almost decide on saying that, however happily a campaign might be carried on in European and Asiatic Turkey, it would be *difficult to find in those seats of war a solution of the Eastern Question.* A frank behaviour on the part of England, conformable with the views of our Government, would, of course, so far as I understand the question, lead to the satisfaction of our legitimate requirements. However, we ought not to lose sight of the chance of a war with England. That country might not declare war formally against us, but by sending her officers to the ranks of the Turkish army, and by helping Turkey with means, would virtually be at war with us.

"Would it not be better to make use of our *new, powerful, strategical position* in Central Asia, our better acquaintance than before with the routes and means in the extended sense of the term, in order to strike at our real enemy a deadly blow in the event (doubtful) of the evident signs of our *determination to operate against the line of operations most sensitive to the English* failing to cause them to entirely give way to us? This state of affairs is, obviously, very serious, and therefore we might, having resolved to remain on the defensive on the Danube and in Asiatic Turkey, place a corps of 30,000 men at Astrabad to co-operate with the troops of the Turkestan military district against Cabul. By doing this we might spare our Russian army in Europe and Asia Minor those insuperable difficulties it has had to contend against unsuccessfully several times every century. It is, of course, not for me to decide by what means Transcaucasia should be defended against an invasion of a Turkish army, or how far the helpless condition of the Christian inhabitants of Turkey would allow the Danube army to maintain a purely defensive attitude, in the event of war being proclaimed; but in any case I will presume to put on record my convictions.

"1. That if an invasion of India with a force of 18,000 men, in the present condition of the English power in Asia, is a rather hazardous feat, but all the same a possible and desirable one, then such an invasion with 50,000 troops would be without any risk whatever.

"2. That in the Caspian Sea, from the early spring, we possess all the means for the rapid concentration at Astrabad of a body of 30,000 men, and the furnishing of them with supplies.

"3. That the country from Astrabad to Herat and Cabul is in every respect favourable for the passage of considerable forces. By exercising adequate political pressure on Persia, Khorassan might be rendered a base for supplies—Transcaucasia, Transcaspia, and Persia furnishing the transport.

"4. That the Turkestan military district having been reinforced with six regiments of Siberian Cossacks, three regiments of Orenburg troops, six companies of infantry, and one battery from Western Siberia (the troops might arrive in Turkestan—*i.e.*, Tashkent, towards the spring), it could push forward 18,000 men with corresponding artillery to march upon Cabul.

"5. That it is possible to march from Samarcand to the foot of the Hindoo Koosh, and that the passage from Khoolum, across Khebek, Kurem, Bamian, and the passes of Kara Kotel, Dentan-Sheken, Ak-Robat, Kalui, Hadjikak, and Unna, into the valley of the river Cabul, is likewise feasible. Although it has been shown that field artillery (battery guns) could be conveyed across these passes without special appliances, still, all the same, *in order to be prepared for the worst,* I have occupied myself with the question of those appliances necessary to ensure the complete success of the passage of field artillery over mountain tracks.

"Already I can confidently say that the simplest method

has been discovered, a new conveyance, with a four-pounder slung underneath, having proved on experiment yesterday a success. However, a final judgment as to its merits, and consequently as to its being able to cross any kind of mountain, can only be given after a practical march with two trial guns across the snowy mountains on the confines of the province, which we have decided shall take place in February.

"6. That Shere Ali, the successor of Dost Mahommed, cannot but long for the possession of Peshawur, and that in general it would not be difficult to raise all Asia against India, in the name of blood and rapine, and revive the times of Tamerlane.

"7. That Shere Ali is dissatisfied at the present moment with the English.

"8. That the English troops in India do not exceed 60,000 men, with corresponding artillery, and that the native army is more a menace than a support to its rulers.

"9. That even the contact of an insignificant force with the frontier of India might lead to a general insurrection throughout the country and the *collapse* of the British Empire.

"It would appear to be opportune at the present moment to give heed to all that has been written above.

"Kokand, Jan. 27 (O.S.), 1877, 12.50 A.M."

GENERAL SKOBELEFF ON THE RUSSIAN POSITION IN CENTRAL ASIA.

THE preceding letter of General Skobeleff's was written before the Russo-Turkish war of 1877-78. The subjoined was penned afterwards, in 1879. It was published this year in the *Russ* by Gospodin Aksakoff, the well-known Panslavist.

Letter from General Skobeleff to a Russian Diplomatist abroad in 1879 :—

"In accordance with your wishes, I venture to communicate to you an abridgment of my Report to General Kaufmann on the question, 'What to do in Turkestan in the event of war between Russia and England?' written in Kokand, Dec. 25, 1876, and afterwards completed from data furnished by the unpublished 'Manuscript Magazine' compiled by Colonel Soboleff in 1870.

"You yourself are good enough to observe that current events in Central Asia are in no way a surprise to those of us in both camps—Russian and English—who have followed the question of the probable conflict between Russia and England, in its decisive phase, which can only take place on the eastern and western slopes of the Indian Hindoo Khoosh. The chief aim of the policy which is called by the party of action in England 'Imperial' consists mainly in employing every effort to turn the balance of chances, in view of a war in Asia Minor and Central Asia, decidedly in favour of England. The near future will show us, I believe, that England is about to make in this direction a series of attempts and efforts, bearing at first a purely commercial character, but which will eventually result in our borders being threatened by a mighty offensive force of Mussulman elements, armed and organized in European fashion, but none the less inspired by that spirit of religious fanaticism so characteristic of the people of Asia, and so dangerous in fighting them.

"The occupation of Cyprus on June 4, 1878, the Expedition to Afghanistan—taken together and coupled with the consideration of the great strategical importance of the points occupied—constitutes more than the prologue to the first part of the British programme. This advance will be finally completed when English influence is confirmed by the establishment of military General-Consulships and other such-like institutions in Erzeroum, Diarbekir, Mossul, Bagdad, Bussora, Candahar, Cabul, and even Herat, if, unhappily, we allow the latter to be thus controlled—and when the railroads which are already being surveyed for, join the Gulf of Iskanderoon with the Euphrates (the waters of which will be cut by thousands of steamers), with Kurachee a! large naval port, and with Bombay; when railroads stretch far away to the north from Kurachee through Candahar to Ghuznee and Cabul in one direction, and to Herat in another.

"All these suppositions, fictitious and fantastic as they seem—and the realization of which would indeed be beyond the power of any other State—will, unhappily for us, only too soon enter the domain of fact, unless England meets on her way serious obstacles. The gigantic works undertaken after the terrible Mutiny of 1857 to establish the network of Indian railways may be cited as convincing evidence. The result will be the weakening of our influence and diminution of the security of our Asiatic frontiers, the extent of which is so enormous.

"When once these results, attained by the fulfilment of this first part of the programme, are sufficiently established, I am convinced that even with the most peaceable —if such an expression is permissible—with the most Gladstonian Ministry, England will be drawn into the paths of invasive action—at first, perhaps, indirectly— against our possessions in the Caucasus and in Central Asia, and also against the preponderating influence which guaranteed the observance of the Treaty of Turkmentchai for us both at the Court of Teheran and throughout Persia, and which neither our reverses in the Crimea nor the victorious campaign of England in 1857 could shake.

"At the same time, our position in Central Asia can

only be considered comparatively secure so long as our influence meets no rival. Our uninterrupted successes during ten years in this country have been attained not merely by numbers and the strength of our battalions, but mainly by the unquestioned nature of our influence. When General Romanoffsky took Oura-Tioube by storm in October, 1866, the elders of the town who were brought before him kept asking, 'But where are the giants who breathed out fire?' The General wisely answered them that he had sent the giants back to Russia, but would recall them at the first necessity. At the present moment, after General Kaufmann's abortive attempt of last year, when the natives have found out that there are fire-breathing giants on the other side, too, of the Hindoo Khoosh, who might even compel us to turn tail, our influence must inevitably be shaken, and may even be transferred to the English. From the moment that this occurs, security within our own boundaries is at an end. The Mussulman population of those districts, mastered by us, but still quivering feverishly, will remain submissive to us only in proportion as it believes that might is still on our side.

"If we have hitherto been able to encounter and suppress the outbursts of Mussulman fanaticism amongst the population of the conquered provinces with our extremely limited fighting means, we are indebted for this success, in the first place, to the state of dependence on us in which we have placed the Khan of Khiva, the leaders of the Turcoman tribes (except the Akkal Tekkés), the Emir of Bokhara, the Begs of Shahrisiab, Karategin, and of the Kara Kirghiz of Alai, and the consequent impossibility of making these districts the centres of political and religious opposition. How clearly the danger of such a turn of affairs was evident to all persons standing at the head of our Central Asian administration is shown by the fact that when Kashgar, under Yakoob Beg, tried to raise the standard of the Prophet, it was understood in Tashkent it was absolutely necessary either to conquer Kashgar by force of Russian arms, or give it over to the Chinese hordes. As is well known, the last alternative was chosen. In the second place, we were much assisted by the dissensions existing between all these petty Mussulman princes, who out of selfishness, envy, and fear of our arms, quietly looked on when we attacked their neighbours (in 1866, war with Bokhara alone; in 1868, war with Bokhara, when the Ambassador of the Khan of Khokand, Khudoiar-Mirza-Khakim-Parmanatsky, as representative of the Khan, was present at the battle of Tchupan-ata and Zerabulak, and at the capture of Samarcand; in 1873, war with Khiva, when the Emir of Bokhara, Musafar-Edin-Khan, allowed our troops to cross his territory, and furnished them with provisions; finally in 1875–6, war with Khokand, when Kashgar, Bokhara, and Khiva displayed a calm neutrality).

"One man alone in Central Asia understood then that unity was the pledge of power, and that was Yakoob Khan. When, in January, 1876, I was driven to hazard the storming of Andijan by the fact that the position of affairs had become doubtful, at the beginning of our advance my spies brought word that Yakoob Khan had sent emissaries to the Emir of Bokhara with the object of inducing him to enter into an alliance for maintaining the independence of the Khanate of Khokand.

"Some time afterwards General Kaufmann warned me to the same effect. It was affirmed then that troops were already concentrating on our frontiers. The successful storming of Andijan put an end to all these attempts. But even now, when Yakoob Khan is dead, the danger continues to exist. The eldest son of the Emir of Bokhara, Katta-Tiura, exiled from Bokhara and shut out by our influence from successive dreams of revenge, finds for his restless energy a field not only in Afghanistan, but even beyond the Indian frontier. Personal bravery and a life full of adventure have made him in some sort the unquestioned leader of the Mussulman Party and representative of Mussulman fanaticism. In the hands of the English such a man may become a powerful and dangerous weapon. The idea of an alliance of the Mussulman rulers and peoples in Central Asia, destroyed, apparently, by our military successes, may spring up once again, and with greater vitality, under English influence, which will certainly make itself felt after the conquest of Afghanistan, thanks to the financial and military power of England. The treaty of 4th June, 1878, giving the Sultan into the hands of England, by that also gave the latter influence over all the orthodox Mussulmans of Central Asia.

"What must not we Russians fear in Central Asia, seeing that England has succeeded in entangling with a thousand snares him whom the orthodox of Central Asia consider to this day their leader in war, and the representative of the Prophet?

"What position ought we to take up in view of English intrigues, which have already placed us on the defensive? Ought we to oppose force to force, and answer the English invasion of Afghanistan by a movement of Russian troops in the same direction? Although our military forces in Turkestan have remained untouched, and the army of the Caucasus has recovered its freedom of action, I believe that at present it would be enough:—1. To oppose to the future English base of operations (Cyprus, Iskanderoon, the Euphrates, the Persian Gulf, the Arabian Sea, Kurachee, the railroad, Kandahar), a Russian base of proportionate dimensions, and also furnished with steam. Moscow, the Volga, the Caucasus, the Caspian, Krasnovodsk, a railroad (or at least a tramway) uniting the Caspian and the Aral, and navigation on the Oxus about as far as Kerki.

"2. To lean this base against a fortress able to resist present means of attack. In choosing the locality the preference might be given to Samarcand, on account not only of its strategic position as available for defence as for offence, but of its spiritual and religious significance in the eyes of all the Mussulman peoples of Asia.

"3. To the advance of the English, who will very soon endeavour to turn our present vassals into open enemies, and will threaten the security of our own frontiers, we ought to oppose at any cost a point whence we could (a) sever the independent Khanates on our frontiers from Afghanistan (under British influence), by the exercise of material force and moral influence; and (b) secure Herat from sudden seizure—the "Key of India," as the English call it, and the possession of which would bring with it inevitably a complete predominance of English influence at Teheran, and—more important still—a military organization of the Turcoman hordes. This point should be Merv."

THE RUSSIAN INVASION OF INDIA IN 1877 AND 1884.*

BY CHARLES MARVIN.

WE recently gave a translation of a project drawn up by General Skobeleff in 1877 for a Russian invasion of India, and pointed out that the Russian position had completely changed since then, rendering the enterprise incomparably more feasible. On this occasion, we can hardly do better than illustrate this change by showing what would have probably been Skobeleff's scheme of operations to-day had he been still living. We should remark beforehand that extreme historical significance attaches to the project of 1877. It was not simply a bit of military speculation, interesting only on account of being the production of a gifted and popular general, but it was the basis of those operations against India which marked the following year. Skobeleff advised that an envoy should be first sent to Cabul, followed by an army, and that a supporting column should operate from the Caspian to divert the Turcomans and Persians from the force, and sustain it if it fell back by way of Herat. It is not generally known that directly after the Russians invested Constantinople in 1878 a council of war was held in camp to arrange a scheme for attacking India, at which Skobeleff was present, and that his project of 1877 was accepted without any vital alteration. Even two of the officers were sent from this Council of War—Stolietoff and Grodekoff, the former being accredited envoy to the Ameer and the latter receiving the post of the chief of Kaufmann's staff. Russian diplomatists constantly represent Skobeleff as a hot-brained general, whose projects exercised no influence on the Russian Government and were unworthy of the notoriety they excited in England. Here we have a clear

* *Morning Post*, April 17, 1884.

illustration to the contrary, the march of Kaufmann's column to Djam in 1878, *en route* for India, and Lomakin's expedition to Khoja Kala against the Turcomans, being the practical outcome of the brilliant general's scheming while acting as Governor of Ferghana. Up to the moment that Stolietoff appeared at Cabul and Kaufmann set off from Tashkent towards India, there were two cardinal points Liberal politicians always adhered to—one that Russia would never meddle with Afghanistan, the other that she would never undertake such a foolhardy enterprise as an invasion of India. After the military and diplomatic operations of 1878, the public were able to judge who had been wiser—Conservative or Liberal statesmen; and their perception has increased a hundredfold since with the rapid unfolding of events in Central Asia. To be plain, it is only fools or fanatics who hold to-day that Russia will never seek to upset our sway or otherwise injure our rule in India. In 1877 the Turcomans constituted an effective barrier to a Russian advance from the Caspian at Krasnovodsk; further, the road by way of Askabad to Herat was believed to be impracticable for an army. Hence, what is now known to be the easiest and the shortest road to India does not figure at all in Skobeleff's project. Napoleon's highway of invasion, from Astrabad on the Caspian to Meshed and Herat, running parallel with the above, passed through the territory of a Power which was undoubtedly more hostile to Russia than England in 1877. A Russian army could not have landed at Astrabad in that year without running the risk of rendering Persia a foe; and this was a more serious matter than appears at first sight, since in 1877 the Caucasian tribes were not quite pacified, and attacked the rear of the Russian forces located on the Perso-Turkish border in 1878, while an advance to Herat parallel with the Turcoman region would have brought down the Tekkés on the Russian flank. To-day Persia is virtually the vassal of Russia, the city of Astrabad could be occupied without fear of displeasure and with every probability of active co-operation; and finally, there would be no Turcomans to worry the flanks of the invading force. Skobeleff was so impressed with the difficulties existing in this direction in 1877, that he limited the Russian operations from the Caspian base to simply the movement of an auxiliary column. Placed as

Russia was in 1877, Turkestan was her best base of operations, and Skobeleff's project was accepted by the Russian Government, although it would have taken six months for reinforcements to have reached Samarcand from Orenburg; and the army of invasion, besides having to march 700 miles over desert and mountains, would have had to cross the broad and rapid Oxus, ill-provided with boats, and the passes, 15,000 or 20,000 feet high, of the Hindoo Koosh. Skobeleff's project contains frequent admissions of the difficulty and risk of the enterprise. It was bad enough to march troops to the Turkestan outposts without taking in hand any operations beyond. There was even a fear that Turkestan itself might rise against Russia. Despite all these drawbacks, the Russian Government authorised Skobeleff's project to be practically tested, and enough was done to indicate the outlines of the proposed attack. Had the Congress at Berlin been a failure, Stolietoff's arrival at Cabul would have been followed by Kaufmann's army, and there can be no doubt that the Afghan conflict in consequence would have worn a very different complexion. Whether active or passive, the Russians at Cabul would have been a serious menace to India. If active, their attacks, in conjunction with the Afghan tribes upon the forces disposed along the Indian frontier, would have been extremely harassing; if passive, the intrigues they would have fomented in the rear of those forces in India itself would have been still more disagreeable. Our Government would have been in constant fear of a mutiny. How far Skobeleff carried his hatred of England in time of peace is shown in Grodekoff's recently published history of his last Turcoman campaign, in which it is stated that after the fall of Geok Tepé, Skobeleff, in order to raise Russian prestige in Central Asia, sent emissaries to the bazaars of Khorassan to spread about the report that it was Russia who had caused England to evacuate Afghanistan. This is a mild specimen of the intrigues the Russians would have resorted to in India in 1878 after occupying Cabul, and which there is every probability they will carry on from their new outposts at Merv and Sarakhs. In the event of defeat Kaufmann would have evacuated Cabul and fallen back, not on Turkestan, where a rising was to be apprehended, but on Herat, to join on the way a succouring force from the Caspian.

Every step the Russians took would have brought them closer to fresh resources, while the English column of pursuit, weakened every march by the extension of the line of communications, must in the end have given up the chase. Even if the Russians had simply caused us to concentrate our military efforts to protect India, the disablement to our power of offence in Europe this would have occasioned would have been worth the defeat, nay, even the annihilation of the Turkestan force. Were Russia to reopen the Eastern Question again this year in the some sudden manner she has recently reopened the Central Asian Question by the totally unprovoked annexation of Merv, General Kuropatkin (who is looked upon as the best disciple of Skobeleff in the Russian army, and is a noted Turkestan officer) would have to draw up quite a totally different plan of operations against India. The road would lie, not *via* Orenburg, Samarcand, and Bokhara to Cabul and the Khyber; but from the Caspian, through Krasnovodsk, Askabad, Sarakhs, and Herat, to Candahar and the Bolan, with perhaps an auxiliary force operating along the Astrabad and Meshed track. The road would be different, the resources different, and the diplomatic campaign would have to be waged in a different manner. Let us discuss them a little in detail.

The Russian Empire may be compared to an octopus, with feelers stretching out to the various seas encompassing the great plain of Europe inhabited by the Slavs. Moscow and the adjacent governments form the body, with a solid mass of orthodox Russians, 60,000,000 in number; and these control the rivers running to the White and Black Seas, the Caspian, and the Baltic. The Russians first pushed their way out from this central position to the Baltic, then south-east along the great river Volga to the Caspian. This was in Peter the Great's time. Catherine the Great pushed down the Don and Dnieper to the Black Sea; and Alexander I. and then Nicholas, working round the south of the Caucasus to Tiflis from the Caspian and the Black Sea, incorporated the Caucasus and laid the foundations of that great base of operations in Asia. Alexander II. started a fresh advance from Orenburg, and thrust out a large wedge into Central Asia to Khiva and Bokhara. This gave Russia her second base in Asia, the one Skobeleff meant to have utilized against India. More recently the present Emperor, who evidently possesses all the ambition of his predecessor, caused the Turkestan and Caucasus bases to be joined by the annexation of the Turcoman region, and this incorporated territory is now to be formed into a separate administrative centre, and constitute a third base against our Eastern Empire. This new province will comprise the country from the Atrek mouth in the Caspian Sea to Askabad, Old Sarakhs, Merv, and Khoja Sala on the Oxus, thence along that river to Khiva, and back again in a straight line to the Caspian, opposite the mouth of the river Volga. The new base is thus situated at the head of the great Volga highway, and can be nourished by the resources of that river, without drawing in the least on the strength of the Turkestan base on the one hand and the Caucasus base on the other.

All these resources are available for despatch to the very extremity of the Volga waterway at Port Michaelovsk, where commences the railway to the Turcoman outposts. Skobeleff's base in 1877 was distant from four to six months' steppe marching from Orenburg, the extremity of Russia's resources in that direction. The resources of the new base are only six days distant from Askabad. The result is, that instead of Russia having to commence a campaign with a large force concentrated beforehand in Turkestan, with a gap of nearly half a year separating it from its reinforcements, she can start operations with a small force severed only a few days from the mammoth resources of the Volga basin, and pour those resources in a continuous stream in the direction of India. In 1877 it was a question whether 18,000 men could be despatched from Turkestan to India. With 50,000 Skobeleff thought there could be no doubt of a successful Russian invasion, but he admitted that Turkestan could only manage to send 18,000. In 1884, however, it would be possible to despatch not merely 18,000 or 50,000 from the Caspian base, but 180,000; and provide it with sufficient food and transport to carry it to the Herat valley, where enough supplies could be had for a further advance upon Candahar.

In the event of the advance of such a force upon Herat, Candahar, and India, by the easy road through the Turcoman region, the waiting game Shobeleff proposed playing at Cabul could be carried on in the first instance at Herat, and afterwards at Cabul or Candahar. Herat, on the showing of the best Russian and English experts, contains ample sustenance for an army of at least 100,000 troops. Such a force Russia, even in her present condition, when she has not yet completed the organization of the Merv oasis, could concentrate at Herat with far greater ease than we could concentrate 100,000 men at Quetta. And even if we did succeed in gathering such a force on the Indian border, we should have one serious disadvantage to contend with. Russia, with the head of her army protruding to Herat, would be absolutely free from any attack, and having her troops massed in a single district could strike with concentrated force at any point along the border line, several hundred miles long, of the Indian frontier, to defend which frontier our force of 100,000 troops would have to be broken up and scattered. It is a popular delusion, shared, we regret to say, by many politicians even, that there are only two cracks in the Indian frontier by which Russians can enter India—the Bolan and the Khyber; instead of which the Intelligence Department possesses a list, we believe, of 298 passes, all fit for the passage of camels, and many capable of being readily adapted for vehicular traffic. With a Russian force of 100,000 troops posted at Herat, and able to move upon Candahar in one direction and Cabul in another, and from either of these points force a passage of the border by a score of passes, aided by the Afghans, the position of the English army on the present frontier would not be a very enviable one, and most probably, indeed, would prove disastrous. Herein really lies the significance of Herat as a place at arms and basis of operations. There is no place near where Russia could concentrate such a large army as we have referred to. By keeping her out of Herat we restrict her initial advance to 40,000 or 50,000 troops. By letting her have it, or by leaving it open to capture by a *coup de main*, as is the case at present, we place it in her power to mature there a huge army to attack and expel us from India.

To sum up, while Skobeleff would have used only the Turkestan base for the principal attack in 1877, he would have chosen the Transcaspian one to-day, but drawn more largely upon Turkestan and the Caucasus. What he said about Turkestan's power of offence possesses just as much force as ever. Turkestan could easily send 18,000 troops in the direction of Cabul, and carry out Skobeleff's plan of operations from that point. Bokhara, in 1877 an unreliable feudatory, has since become so friendly that the Russian General, no longer fearing any rising in Turkestan, could even still further reduce his garrisons and enlarge his force, or take with him 10,000 or 20,000 Bokharan levies. Such would be the fighting capacity of the Turkestan base. As regards the Transcaspian, Russia could concentrate in the Caspian and despatch to Herat a force of 100,000 or more troops, brought *viâ* the Volga from the depôts of Middle Russia; and finally, the Caucasus base could send at least 50,000, and could readily add to their strength if necessary. Such troops might be despatched from Baku to Astrabad, and thence to Meshed and Herat, feeding themselves on the resources of Khorassan, and giving Russia, on their arrival at Herat, an overwhelming force for operations in Afghanistan. If the Ameer refused to co-operate or remain neutral, the Russian tactics would be the same Skobeleff proposed availing himself of in 1877—setting up a pretender against Abdurrahman Khan, and, under the threat of civil war, coercing him into becoming an ally. Diplomatic operations of any kind would be all the more easy with Abdurrahman Khan, because he has a great personal liking for the Russians, who treated him well when a refugee; and, further, because he is loyally regarded by only a small portion of his father's subjects. With three bases to operate from instead of one, 180,000 troops to manipulate instead of 18,000, and a starting point six days ahead of the resources instead of six months, Russia possesses advantages to-day over her position in 1877 which gives a significance to Skobeleff's project English statesmen cannot lay too closely to heart.

RUSSIA'S POWER OF SEIZING HERAT, AND CONCENTRATING AN ARMY THERE TO THREATEN INDIA.*

BY CHARLES MARVIN.

LADIES AND GENTLEMEN,

I am going to demonstrate to you to-night the importance of the annexation of Merv, not by elaborately describing Merv itself, which I have sufficiently done in my works already, but by imitating General Tchernayeff, and giving you a realistic sketch of a Russian invasion of India. You will remember that, during the last war in the East, Russia concentrated vast forces on the Turkish frontier, overran the Balkan peninsula, and finally, after a series of bloody struggles, settled down in front of the defences of Constantinople. This great army of Russians moved along the western side of the Black Sea. Their total number was nearly half a million men. Another army moved along its east side, besieged and conquered Kars, occupied Erzeroum, and was ready to march on to Constantinople when peace was concluded. The strength of this second army was 100,000 men.

Now, I want you to imagine a condition of politics in which Russia should declare war against England, without previously undertaking any operations against Turkey. It was an opinion held by the late General Skobeleff, and it is shared by many generals now in power in Russia, that the simplest way to finally accomplish the conquest

---

* Lecture delivered before the Balloon Society, February 29, 1884. Although hastily prepared, it was the first attempt that had been made since the evacuation of Afghanistan to analyze the effects of the new annexations beyond the Caspian upon the Russian military position in Central Asia.

of Turkey is to upset our sway in India. The idea is, not that Russia should take over the control of India, but that, posing as a benevolent Power, she should help shake off from the backs of 250,000,000 natives 150,000 tyrannical, money-grubbing Englishmen, of whom those oppressed natives are heartily sick. You probably imagine that you are doing India a real service by ruling the country. It is a view I myself share. But Russians in power consider that you are an unmitigated set of blood-suckers, and that they would be rendering India a service by helping the people to get rid of you. They are persuaded the people would rise if they had a chance. To quote Skobeleff's words, "The main cause of the failure of the mutiny of 1857 was the fact that the insurgents were not properly organized and led." Russia would supply that deficiency. If she succeeded, she believes your commerce, and with it your power, would crumble to dust. She would then be left alone to work her sweet will upon Constantinople.

Let us imagine war declared, and Russia bent upon concentrating the whole of her efforts upon an expedition to India. Of course, England blockades the Baltic and Black Sea, but Russia takes up a passive attitude there, and our fleets are unable to effect much injury—at any rate, not sufficient to coerce Russia from her undertaking. Russia begins operations by concentrating her armaments in the Caspian, where, as you know, no power can get at them. In 1877 and 1878, 500,000 troops, with an enormous amount of military stores, were directed upon Constantinople—let us imagine only a fraction despatched to the Caspian, and the whole of Russia's efforts concentrated in giving them transport. The railway system touches the Volga at four great points—Nijni-Novgorod, Samara, Saratoff, and Tsaritzin. It would be an easy matter, therefore, to get the troops to that river—incomparably easier than getting them to the Danube in '77. On the Volga is abundance of transport: 700 steamers, and thousands of barges 100 to 300 feet long. The Volga is the great highway of Russia. It may be a new geographical fact for some of you to know, that if you were to set out in a steamer 150 feet long from London Bridge to-morrow—no, not to-morrow, but a little later on, when the Volga is free from ice again—you could go with that steamer all the way to the Caspian Sea. I saw, two or three months ago, a number of large oil-steamers at Baku that had made their way to the Caspian from the Tyne. The through voyage was accomplished by means of the magnificent canal system joining the Neva with the Caspian, thanks to which Russia could despatch any number of transports to the Caspian Sea. But these would not be needed. On the Caspian Russia has forty or fifty powerful steamers, and twenty more from 150 to 250 feet long are to be added this year. This rapid growth of the Caspian marine is due to the development of the Baku petroleum region, incomparably the richest in the world. I wish I had more time to describe Baku. That is the point I fix upon as the base of any operations against India. Ten years ago an English official passed through Baku, and saw nothing of interest. Ten years ago an English officer passed through and saw only one wooden jetty. The town that has risen there since has a frontage of six miles along the bay; 7,000 vessels enter and leave the port every year; the port owns twenty-five piers, with an aggregate accommodation for 100 steamers at one and the same time; the 200 oil refineries contain any amount of engineering skill —a valuable adjunct to an army; and a railway, opened a few months ago, enables any portion of the army of the Caucasus, 150,000 strong on a peace footing, to co-operate at Baku with the forces arriving from the Volga against India. Without experiencing anything like the difficulty she encountered in 1877, Russia could assemble at Baku an army quite as large as she invaded Turkey with then; it would have better transport, the troops would arrive at the base in better trim, and they would have the enormous food supply of the Volga basin to sustain them in their campaign.

So much for the concentration at Baku. From there across to Krasnovodsk is a sixteen hours' run. I have told you Baku possesses pier accommodation to load 100 steamers at the time. There would thus be no difficulty in ferrying the army across the Caspian, nor yet in conveying it in tugged barges to Michaelovsk, should the railway from Krasnovodsk to that point be not then finished. At Michaelovsk the army would come in contact, for the first time, with the immense deserts which the dressing-gown school of English politicians used to regard as a barrier to the Russian advance, and which even now, in these days of enlightenment, certain Rip van Winkles still believe in. Ladies and Gentlemen, will you believe me? You can take a third class ticket for 4s. 4d., and a second-class ticket for 8s. 8d., across this great desert barrier; and when you get to Kizil Arvat station, at the extremity of the Transcaspian railway, you have not got a bit more desert, in the strict sense of the word, all the way to India. From Kizil Arvat to Herat you have in the Akhal and Atak oases and in the valley of the Hari Rud a magnificent soil alongside the highway the whole distance, either producing extraordinary crops or capable of producing them when tilled by Russian peasants. Mr. Gladstone will tell you that many a year must elapse before the region between the Caspian and Herat will be peopled by Russian colonists. I retort, What about Baku? Look at Merv! Three years ago it was one of the most inaccessible spots in the world. Even Lord Salisbury regarded it as a barrier likely to last some years. Yet, in a few weeks' time, Merv will be in the Postal Union, and if any of my Russian friends go there I shall be able to send them a letter for 2½d. If you will turn up the Candahar debates and the Candahar speeches, you will find that there is hardly a prediction made by the present Government in regard to the Russian advance that has not been falsified by events, which ought to have been foreseen, and, as a matter of fact, were foreshadowed by more than one Conservative statesman.

The Russian railway system—for the Transcaspian railway is a natural extension of the Baku-Batoum railway—terminates at Kizil Arvat, 144 miles from the Caspian. Now, I should like you to remember a very great fact, and one which I hope you will never allow any gammon-monger to humbug out of your memories, and that is this. Russia's steam communication terminates at Kizil Arvat. From her home provinces she can send to that point as large an army as she invaded Turkey with, and an incomparably larger army than you can ever hope to send to India; but whereas—and please remember this—but whereas that army could be conveyed thither without any enemy being able to molest a single man, or even to report its movements, for in time of war the Russians would cut off all telegraphic communications with abroad, your army of defence would be open to attack the whole of the way to India, for a period of three weeks, by means of cruisers and disguised torpedo-boats. Now that the Merv Turcomans are annexed, Russia has no enemy to fear the whole way to Herat; and while you must guard every inch of your road to India—a serious drain on your resources—she need not detach a single Cossack to defend her forces the whole of the distance to Herat.

From Kizil Arvat to Askabad, 135 miles, there is a wagon service in operation. Turcoman settlements extend the entire distance, forage and food are plentiful, and travelling is as easy as in any part of Russia. The garrisons along the road at present number 7,000 troops, who are encouraged to settle down in the country on the expiration of their term of service. I wish I had with me, to show you, some photographs of Askabad I saw at Baku. Askabad, which was as troublesome to get as Merv three years ago, now possesses all the features of a prosperous Russian town. Before long the railway will be extended thither. To extend it the whole distance from Kizil Arvat to Herat will only cost Russia £2,192,000, or a quarter of the sum she has expended in connecting Batoum with Baku. The political and strategical effect of the Russians running a locomotive into the Key of India would be worth ten times, nay, twenty times, that outlay in hastening the solution of the Eastern Question, the existence of which exercises such a disastrous, such a paralyzing effect on Russian progress, Russian trade, and Russian finance.

At Askabad we first come face to face with Merv, distant 200 miles from it by a direct road across the desert, which is impracticable, or by another extending straight ahead to Kahka, and then striking off at right angles *viâ* the Tejend oasis. This is a little longer. You have recently been told over and over again by certain howling dervishes of Parliament and the Press, that Merv does not lie on the road to India. Well, it does not require one to be a Cabinet Minister to realize that fact. Merv was on the road to India when the Russian advance lay through Turkestan. As you are probably aware, and as General Tchernayeff has just found to his cost, there are two Russian advances towards India, two Russian movements—one from Turkestan managed from Tashkent, and the other from the Caspian controlled from Tiflis. Now,

I do not profess to know all the secrets of the Russian Government, but I believe I am not far wrong in ascribing the annexation of Merv and the downfall of General Tchernayeff to a large extent to the jealousy and the rivalry between these two administrations. Experts in Russia have long foreseen that whichever administration first hooked Merv would secure to itself all the good appointments connected with the encroachments proceeding from that base, and the opening up of relations with India. Bokhara was a barrier between Tashkent and Merv. While the Emir was alive it could not be decently annexed; so General Tchernayeff opened up a new road for his province from opposite the mouth of the Volga to Khiva, and thence up the Oxus, which completely turned the Bokhara impediment, and brought the Turkestan officials into direct contact with Merv and Afghanistan. This manœuvre was deeply resented by the Caucasus officials. I heard all manner of angry ridicule cast upon it while I was in the Caucasus. And, to be beforehand with Tchernayeff, General Komaroff, Governor of Askabad, set on foot those secret coercive measures which resulted in the Merv Tekké chiefs hurrying to his head-quarters and giving in their submission.

Here, then, you have an illustration of the dangers arising from the two rival Russian administrations in Central Asia, which, by the way, the Government jumbled up most confusedly in the House of Commons the other night. If Tchernayeff had annexed Merv, the oasis would certainly have been upon the road to India, either from opposite the mouth of the Volga or from Turkestan. That the road might not have been a good one is quite a different matter. We need not concern ourselves with that. All we need bear in mind is that Tchernayeff would have found Merv a splendid base for encroaching upon Afghanistan.

Merv fell to the Caucasus administration, and it does not require one to have the superlative genius of the Duke of Argyll to see that, to an army advancing from Askabad, Merv did not lie upon the road to India. In that narrow sense, as General Grodekoff—for whom I have the warmest personal esteem—explained to me before his brother-officers' two years ago, Merv is not the Key of Herat. Sarakhs is the stepping-stone to Herat to an army operating from the Caspian. But, until Merv was annexed, Russia could not turn the corner at Sarakhs and advance along the Hari Rud to Herat without exposing her flank to the attack of 50,000 of the finest horsemen in the world. And now you will begin to realize the importance of that annexation. Russia, instead of having to protect her army against those 50,000 Turcoman cavalry, will carry along with her that force to occupy Herat and fight you at Candahar or at Quetta. Russia has, in a word, broken down the only living barrier intervening between the Caspian and Herat, and she can now, thanks to the annexation of Merv, march an army all the way to Herat without meeting a single enemy to molest her scouts. I think you will, therefore, agree with me that the annexation of Merv is something more than the " mere annexation of a few mud huts," as the Duke of Argyll defined it a few years ago, and that England has been perfectly justified in regarding the annexation with unqualified resentment and alarm.

And now let us get back to our invading army, which we left at the railway station at Kizil Arvat. From this point runs an easy road, *viâ* Askabad, the Atak oasis, and round the corner at Sarakhs, all the way to Herat. The distance is 523 miles, and the only obstacle to be encountered the whole way is the passage of the Barkhut hills, near Herat, 900 feet above the surrounding level, or roughly, three times the height of St. Paul's Cathedral. This, ladies and gentlemen, is the terrific mountain barrier protecting India from the Russian—three times the height of St. Paul's Cathedral, and which even in its present condition is as easy to cross, for artillery and wagons, as Shooter's Hill. You have thus no living obstacle and no geographical obstacle to prevent a Russian army marching into Herat whenever it likes. The stages are three in number. The first is from Kizil Arvat to Askabad, 135 miles, along the oasis of Akhal, where the Russians have already established a vehicular postal service, and organized the road for the passage of an army. The second is from Askabad to Sarakhs, $185\frac{1}{2}$ miles, where Russia has to turn the corner. Of this $185\frac{1}{2}$ miles of road, 47 miles, from Askabad to Baba Durmaz, belong to Russia—the remainder, as far as Sarakhs, passes through what is called the Atak oasis. This is a fertile band of country running alongside the road, with plenty of settlements, and capable of considerable development. It belongs to Persia by rights, but Russia, in order to get to Merv *viâ* the Tejend, and to organize the road of invasion of Herat, has semi-officially declared she means to annex it with Merv. Here, then, you have another of the significant results attending the annexation of Merv; for what does the incorporation of the Atak mean but that the Cossack will be brought to within $202\frac{1}{2}$ miles of the Key of India—*i.e.*, within a week's march of Herat. Once the Russians occupy the Atak they will organize it as they have Akhal, and means will be established for the passage of the vast invading army we started with from the Volga.

And now for the last stage—from Sarakhs to Herat—$202\frac{1}{2}$ miles. Last week, on the day of the Merv debate, the *Pall Mall Gazette* published a map, with an article criticising a pamphlet I had issued to the House of Commons to give life to the discussion, in which it declared that the alarmist party consisted only of myself and Mr. Ashmead-Bartlett. My words, it declared, fell on deaf ears; nobody, it said, cared about Merv. Well, before that night was over, I had the pleasure of seeing both sides of the House of Commons, with my pamphlet in their hands, admitting that my words did not fall on deaf ears, and that both the Government and the Opposition really did entertain sincere alarm at the Russian advance. So much for the rash article of the *Pall Mall Gazette.* Now for its map. Sarakhs, as you know, is a Persian fortress, laying on the west side of the Hari Rud. Russia does not mean to touch it. She means to turn the corner on the opposite side of the river, and move along the east bank to Herat. By annexing Merv she is annexing the Atak and the Tejend oases, both leading up to this corner, and there for the moment lies the whole pivot of the Central Asian Question. On this map published by the *Pall Mall Gazette* you will find a most terrific barrier raised to the Russian advance. And that is this:—From the Murghab, or Merv river, a line is drawn across to Sarakhs, and all the country up to Herat is marked in awe-inspiring characters—" Afghanistan." The inference is, that if this great Russian army gets to Sarakhs, the mere fact of a line being drawn across the map, claiming the land south of the turning point as Afghan territory, will deter it from going any further. Well, such an obstacle may do for men whose life is spent in dressing-gown and slippers, but I do not think it would exercise much effect on the good-humoured, blustering, unscrupulous giants composing the Russian army. It is no use chalking a line on a bit of paper, and expecting the Russians, after occupying Merv, to scrupulously refrain from crossing it. Russians, as you know, have no scruples. From Sarakhs up to within a short distance of Herat there is not an Afghan to be seen. The country has been so harried by the Turcomans that it is quite depopulated. Such being the case, can you expect Russia, after getting to Sarakhs, to the point where the Persian and Afghan frontiers theoretically touch— can you expect Russia to refrain from sending her Cossacks roaming all over the country south of it? And can those Cossacks be prevented from dropping into Herat to get their vodky and tobacco. You must pay the Sepoy alongside Sarakhs if you want to keep the Cossack back.

To occupy Candahar from Quetta, hilly country, infested by fierce tribes, has to be traversed; but Russia can march from Sarakhs to Herat, over the plain, without exchanging a shot with an enemy; and when she gets to Herat she can bombard the town into submission in a few hours, in its present condition of defence. I do not see how England can possibly make Afghanistan swell out to Sarakhs so as to prevent the Russians turning the corner there. If the country is left as it is, unpopulated, the Russians will certainly overrun it, and, the land being well adapted for cultivation and colonization, they will organize it in a few years for the passage of an army. In this manner, the country from Askabad to Herat, 388 miles, which is already adapted for the passage of a powerful expedition, will be rendered fit for the passage of the largest army necessary for turning you out of India. A railway to Herat would render the preparations complete.

You do not need to be reminded that the valley of Herat contains resources for sustaining the largest army. No argument can make you believe that a Russian army cannot attack India from Herat; because only three years ago, Ayoob Khan, marching from Herat with artillery, thrashed you well at Candahar. If I can demonstrate that the Russians can occupy Herat whenever they like with a powerful army, I claim to have proved to you that India is susceptible of attack, if not invasion.

And every year this operation is becoming more simple for Russia to effect, more difficult for you to repel. You cannot appreciably quicken your steamboat communication with India. It will always occupy two or three weeks. I know plenty of Russians who would undertake to sever that communication altogether by secretly dynamiting the Suez Canal. On the other hand, every year Russia is growing stronger on her Asiatic confines, every step she advances with her railway renders her better able to shake your power in India. Take last year: by the completion of the Baku-Tiflis railway she reduced at a stroke the time needed to transport troops from the Tiflis to the Caspian from twenty-one days to twenty-two hours—in other words, she rendered available the 350,000 men of the Caucasus army on a war-footing for rapid operations against India. And what did England do as a counterpoise? England, ladies and gentlemen, showed her appreciation of the crisis by sending a few Sepoys to mend the caravan track in the Bolan Pass.

The other night, as I sat under the Gallery of the House of Commons, I was very much interested in the declaration the Government would make as to its measures for counteracting the effects of this new Russian annexation. I have only had time to-night to point out part of the significance of the annexation of Merv. You have seen that it brings the Cossack to Sarakhs, 202½ miles from Herat, beyond which there is nothing to prevent him securing the Key of India whenever he likes. Merv itself is 240 miles from Herat, and the annexation of the Sarik Turcoman tribe, which is practically confirmed by news from Tashkent, brings the Cossack up the Murghab to within 140 miles of Herat. As Quetta is 145 miles from Candahar, Russia, as soon as she has organized her annexation, will be able to occupy Herat from her new Merv base before you can even occupy Candahar. This is a very serious matter, even if we exclude the incorporation of Khiva, now at length consummated, and the enclosure of the Ersari Turcomans, between Merv and Bokhara, thus giving the annexation of a "few mud huts" the true proportions of the annexation of a province as large as France, with 100,000 splendid horsemen within a few days' march of Herat. These considerations have evidently produced a very powerful effect on Her Majesty's Government; they displayed their anxiety clearly enough the other night. But how do they propose to meet the situation? They have annexed Quetta. Quetta was practically annexed beforehand, so that this is no new measure. They have established a protectorate over Beloochistan; but we have practically exercised a protectorate for two or three years, so that this also is nothing as a set-off against the Russian advance. The only other measure I could catch, and I hardly think you will consider it meets the situation—the only other measure was, that Government would lay papers before the House as soon as possible.

Now, to my view, we must do something more than this, and that something is, that we should get back to Candahar as soon as possible. Go back we must some day, and it would be only right that a Government that blundered so terribly in giving up that city should itself acknowledge and repair its error. The Government, let me say in its defence, trusted too much to the advice of the Duke of Argyll, who is now, thank heavens, out of the Cabinet, and who has become utterly discredited by the progress of events in Central Asia. You have heard what I have told you to-night of the growth of Russia's power in the Caspian; let me quote what the Duke of Argyll said on January 10th, 1881, when the country was agitated about the retention of Candahar: "We are told by the late Government that the danger they wished to guard against was the danger of a new military basis to be formed by Russia on the Caspian. I hold that to be one of the wildest dreams ever entertained." Well, in three short years the Russians have established that new military basis the Earl of Beaconsfield wished to guard against, and the "wildest dream" has become a practical reality.

Another point politicians of the Argyll and Northbrook school were continually parading was, that the Russians were only annexing deserts in Central Asia. But a desert, or rather steppe-land, for many of these so-called deserts are prairies half the year round—a desert, I say, is not always a valueless possession. Let me give you an instance, without reminding you what you already know, that in annexing the desert inhabitants of Merv, the

Russians have annexed the finest breed of horses in the world. The instance I will give you is this:—A short distance inland of Michaelovsk, on the Caspian, in the midst of one of these barren Russian deserts, a Russian exploring party two years ago came upon a hill sodden with petroleum and ozokerit, computed to be worth thirty-five millions sterling. While I was at Baku I met a Russian official who had recently returned from this locality. He told me that it furnished sufficient oil-fuel for all the locomotives on the Transcaspian railway, and that consignments were being exported to Khiva. This locality was only one of a series that was being discovered; yet it contained sufficient deposits to furnish annually 250,000,000 gallons of crude petroleum, or enough to light every lamp, grease every machine, and drive every locomotive in the whole Russian Empire. Yet you are requested by professional purveyors of humbug—Russian as well as English—to believe that Russia is only annexing dry sand and scorpions in Central Asia.

Bearing, then, these things in mind, you have got to take measures, not only against the present position of Russia in Central Asia, but against her prospective position. Five years ago Herat was quite safe from sudden seizure; even Merv was practically secure. Before this year has run its course you will have Russians posted not only at Merv, but closer to Herat than your Quetta garrison is to Candahar. In face of this great revolution, can any one seriously pretend that Russia cannot occupy Herat whenever she likes, in defiance of all our threats? Do you know that the presence of only 7,000 Russian troops in the Transcaspian region is more significant than 70,000? And why? Let me answer in the words of a Russian general, with whom I discussed the matter during one of the balls at the Tsar's coronation. "We have now," said he, "such a good road to the heart of Afghanistan, and our communications with the Caspian base, and from the Caspian base to Askabad, are so perfect, and admit of such a ready movement of troops, that we only need a handful of men to garrison the Turcoman region. It is cheaper to maintain 70,000 men in the Tiflis district than at Geok Tepé and Askabad, and we can throw them from the one point to the other at a moment's notice."

Such was his opinion, expressed perfectly good-humouredly, and without any desire to give offence. Let me, as a final word, clench it with a very serious fact. You know that Russia invaded Turkey from Kishineff in 1877 with a force that ultimately grew to half a million men. Now, from Kishineff to Constantinople the troops of the Shipka column had to march 750 miles, and of the Sophia column 970 miles. Russia, as I have told you, could assemble on the Caspian a similar army with greater ease than she could at Kishineff. Treating Kizil Arvat as a Kishineff, the distance thence to Herat is only 523 miles, as compared with the 750 and the 970 traversed by the Russian troops in 1877. But, perhaps you object to Kizil Arvat being treated as a Kishineff. Then start from the Caspian, from the decks of the steamers at Port Michaelovsk. The distance even then is only 667 miles as compared with the 1,000 miles many Russians trudged on foot before they got to Constantinople. And, mark this difference. Russia, in invading Turkey, had Austria to threaten her flank. There would be no such enemy in the Caspian. Russia, further, had to cross the Danube—one of the largest rivers in Europe—in face of the Turks; she had to encounter large armies at Plevna, and traverse the almost impregnable Balkan range, meeting on the other side armies again before she got to Constantinople. In the case of Herat, nothing of the kind exists. There is not a single river of any magnitude the whole distance from the Caspian to Herat. There is no mountain range whatever—only a few hills that the fattest alderman could toddle up without difficulty. And, instead of great armies, the Russians would meet no enemy, but sweep along in their course 50,000 Turcoman cavalry to assist them in their undertaking. Finally, the Russians, instead of having to commence operations from Kishineff, 800 or 900 miles from the objective point, would be already posted at Merv, within 240 miles of it; at Sarakhs, within $202\frac{1}{2}$ miles; and at Penjdeh, within 140 miles of the Key of India. Such being the case, I hold you have entered upon the most critical period of the Centra. Asian Question; and unless you insist upon a firm, clear, decisive, patriotic policy on the part of the Government, you will have a repetition of the Egyptian muddle, with this difference, that your opponents will not be the sheep-like fellaheen, but men who will take advantage of every blunder—and your statesmen, at the best, are sure to blunder a good deal—to seek to accomplish their schemes of aggrandisement in Europe by upsetting your power in India.

THE RUSSIAN ANNEXATION OF MERV.*

BY CHARLES MARVIN.

TAKING advantage of a moment when England's hands are full with complications in Egypt, South Africa,

* This was penned for the debate following upon the annexation of Merv, and circulated in a pamphlet form. Respecting it a London correspondent wrote to the *Newcastle Daily Chronicle*, February 28, 1884 :—" I have read your admirable review of Mr. Marvin's pamphlet on Merv, and it has occurred to me that the circumstances under which it was produced and the influence it exercised on the debate may interest your readers. Mr. Marvin had contemplated issuing a pamphlet this week, as announced in the *Athenæum*, and was taken by surprise on Thursday morning to find the debate fixed for the next day, and not later on, as generally anticipated. At eleven o'clock nothing was ready but the MS., but Messrs. Allen placed the whole of their resources at his disposal, and, thanks to the rapid photo-engraving process and the never-ceasing energy of all concerned, 25 advance copies of the pamphlet, with the three maps and the frontispiece of Merv, were completed by seven o'clock at night, and within an hour were circulating in the London press and in the House of Commons. In connection with the wholesale distribution of copies in the House the next day a difficulty now presented itself. The whole edition could not be finished in sufficient time to ensure its delivery by post by the time the House assembled. This obstacle Mr. Marvin overcame by making an arrangement with one of the lobby messengers, who agreed to distribute them by hand. By one o'clock the next day the messenger already had the batch, and soon after the House assembled half the persons in the lobby might have been seen with the orange pamphlet in their hands. As the House filled, a demand arose for copies on the part of minor members who had not received them, and to meet this, Mr. Marvin, who was in the lobby, despatched a special messenger for a hundred more. In this manner, when the debate actually did come off, nearly everybody used it as a handbook, and there can be hardly a doubt that it exercised a very important effect upon the speeches ; observable in the unanimity with which the members of both Parties insisted on the necessity of trusting Russia no more, and the imperative need of a firm attitude and decisive measures on the part of the Government. During the debate, Mr. Marvin sat under the gallery watching the effect of his pamphlet."

Madagascar and Tonquin, Russia has suddenly annexed the oasis of Merv. That a *coup* of this description had been long meditated was well known to experts, but the general public reposed implicit confidence in the pacific and anti-aggressive manifesto ushering in the Tsar's reign, and believed Alexander III. had chosen a different policy from that of his father. Even experts were sufficiently impressed by the Imperial assurances to doubt whether Russia would openly seize the long-coveted oasis. Rumour favoured the belief that the annexation would be masked by coercing Merv into accepting the suzerainty of the Khan of Khiva. But these expectations have not been realised. At a moment when the Merv Tekkés were quieter than they had been for ages, and when Russia at least had no cause for complaint against them, the people have been compelled to accept her direct rule, and His Imperial Majesty has proved himself as little to be trusted in his Central Asian policy as his aggressive and unreliable father. Merv has been won, but Alexander III. has lost what he can never regain— the confidence of the English people.

That a formal protest will be entered against this fresh and unwarrantable advance towards India is too much to expect from a Ministry which has involved England in humiliation in every land, and a Parliament too infatuated with extreme views of Party allegiance to demand a bolder and more patriotic attitude on the part of its leaders. But the annexation of Merv is something more than an act merely calling for condemnation. Herat, the Key of India, is placed in peril. The Cossack is brought into actual contact with the Afghan, and England is compelled to decide, and to decide at once, whether the future frontier separating the two empires in Asia shall be left to the exclusive selection of Russia, or whether she shall take instant measures to render the annexation of Merv the final step in the Russian advance in the direction of India. The public have to face this fact, and it is a fact which no amount of web-spinning can deprive of its significance, that if we do not immediately take in hand the safe-guarding of Herat, that key of our Indian Empire will be annexed in a few years' time as surely as Russia has now incorporated Merv.

Yes, the conquest of Merv is something more than the annexation of a mid-desert oasis. It means the complete junction of the military forces of the Caucasus (nearly 150,000 men in time of peace) and Turkestan (27,000), itself a political fact of great magnitude. It means, with the annexation of Akhal, the absorption of 100,000 of the best irregular cavalry in the world, at a week's march from the city of Herat. It means the meeting, for the first time, of the Cossack and the Afghan. It means the complete enclosure of Khiva within the Russian Empire, and the reduction of Bokhara from the independent position of a border State to the dependence of an incorporated province. It means the acquisition of more than 200,000 square miles of territory, and the addition to the Russian Empire of a region as large as France. It means the completion of the conquest of the Central Asian deserts, and the commencement of the annexation of the great fertile mountain region of Persia and Afghanistan. It means the deliberate occupation of a strategical point, fraught with political entanglements of such a widespread nature, that, whether Russia desire it or not, she will inevitably be led, unless forestalled or checked by England, to Meshed, to Herat, to Balkh, and Cabul. And she will not remain there. She will continue her swift advance until she triumphantly lays down her Cossack border alongside the Sepoy line of India.

What question can be more appropriate than that which Alayar Khan, one of the Perso-Turcoman border chiefs put to General Valentine Baker in 1873: "How do you expect to prevent Russia from taking Herat when once she is at Merv? The Murghab river runs from Afghanistan to Merv. You know well that, in this country, where there is water, troops can move. The banks of the Murghab are fertile. How near to Herat along this river do you intend to let Russia advance and settle?"*

From Merv to Herat, *viâ* this Murghab road, is 240 miles.

From Quetta, our present outpost, to Herat is 514 miles.

The Russians, then, being nearer Herat by 274 miles than the English, can the latter let themselves be deceived by political web-spinners and excusers of the evacuation of Candahar into the belief that the Key of India is safe from a Russian *coup de main?*

* "Clouds in the East." London, 1875

On this point the opinion of General Valentine Baker is worth a whole session of Parliamentary discussion: "Merv, with its water communication nearly complete, lies only 240 miles from Herat, to which place it is the key. There can be no doubt that Merv is the natural outwork of Herat, with the advantage of a water-supply all the way between the two cities. Strategically, the Russian occupation of Merv would be, so to say, the formation of a lodgment on the glacis of Herat. It would place Herat completely at her mercy."

Undeterred by the splendid success achieved by the Russian army, in face of fearful difficulties, in crossing the Balkans in the winter of 1878, compared with which crossing the Paropamisus ridge, separating Merv from Herat, would be child's play, politicians exist who consider this ridge a sufficient barrier between the two strategical points. Let us humour such men, and treat the direct road along the Murghab and over the Paropamisus as non-existent. What then? There is another, altogether practicable, only twelve miles longer.

Of this General Sir Charles Macgregor, the Quartermaster-General of India, wrote in 1875: "A Russian authority M. Tchichacheff, declares that Herat would be in no danger, even if the Russians were in possession of Merv, because the road between these places lies over an impracticable range of mountains. I must, however, take leave to deny this statement in the most decided manner. I have been to the Herat valley, and have followed a considerable part of one of the roads to Merv, and I have made the most careful inquiries from people on the spot who were in the constant habit of riding over the rest of the distance. Yet there is so little impression of difficulty in my mind that I would undertake to drive a mail coach from Merv to Herat by this road."

This opinion of a general, who may well be described as the Skobeleff of India, was pooh-poohed at the time by Radical politicians, and has since been totally ignored by Radical Cabinet Ministers; but the opinion was a true one, and has been altogether confirmed by the Russian engineer explorer, Lessar, after a personal examination of the road in question. He says: "The entire length is 252 miles. It entirely avoids the Paropamisus range, the pass across which has caused the road from Merv to Herat to be regarded as unfit for wheeled traffic, and traverses the Barkhut hills at Chesmeh-sebz by a pass similar to that of Khombôu, 900 feet above the level of the surrounding country, which is quite fit, even in its present condition, for wagon traffic. The section of 100 miles, including the passage of the Barkhut hills, is exactly of the same character as the country through which our Russian railways usually run—flat in some places, slightly undulating in others. The hill crossings for a railway would be of the easiest description. There would be engineering works, of course, but of rapid construction. Where essential, sharp inclines could be made that would not delay the rest of the line to Herat."

"Herat," therefore, to quote Macgregor's words, "is easily accessible from Merv, for guns, cavalry, and infantry. How soon 5,000 men could be transferred from one place to the other I leave my readers to work out for themselves. All I contend is, that to do so, would be a perfectly feasible, nay, an easy military operation."

There is, thus, no physical difficulty to prevent Russia occupying Herat from Merv at any moment. We could not possibly prevent her. Let us see what kind of base Merv offers for such an operation.

According to the latest Russian surveys of Alikhanoff, Lessar, and others, the oasis possesses an area of 1,600 square miles under cultivation. The soil is famous throughout Central Asia for its fertility, and yields wheat 20-fold, sorgo 200-300-fold, countless melons—the staple food of the hardy Tekkés, and a large article of diet of the South Russians themselves — and sufficient cotton to be able to export 54,000 lbs. annually. The population consists of 48,000 *kibitkas* or tents, or 240,000 souls; and its wealth comprises 160,000 sheep, 7,800 camels, 12,000 horses, 24,000 donkeys, and 48,000 head of cattle. The fortress of Merv has a circumference of five miles, and a height of eighty feet. It contains thirty cannon taken from the Persians. By developing the irrigation system the oasis could be largely extended, as the country for hundreds of miles round consists of the same soil as the oasis itself, lacking simply a broader diffusion of water to give it life.

Merv is thus well adapted as a place of arms. But the annexation of Merv does not mean simply the annexation of the oasis itself—1,600 square miles—nor yet the tens of thousands of square miles of steppe land and desert stretching away from Merv to Khiva and Bokhara. Russia, in incorporating Merv, takes with it the country of the Sarik Turcomans, lying along the Murghab river in the direction of Herat. The Sarik Turcomans number 13,000 tents, or 65,000 souls, gathered at Youletan and Penjdeh; the former thirty-five miles from Merv, the latter sixty-five from Youletan. After the fall of Geok Tepé in 1881, they sent a deputation offering to submit to Russia, and since then they have manifested the friendliest feelings towards them. Having no rulers, and no notion of nationality, it is a most improbable circumstance that Russia will encourage them to remain independent after occupying Merv, and thus we have to face this fact:—

THAT THE ANNEXATION OF MERV, BEING INEVITABLY ATTENDED WITH THE INCORPORATION OF THE SARIK TURCOMANS, WILL EXTEND RUSSIAN RULE 100 MILES UP THE MURGHAB TO PENJDEH, AT THE FOOT OF THE PAROPAMISUS, OR TO WITHIN 140 MILES OF HERAT.

England at the same time being still posted at Quetta, 514 miles from Herat.

This is a fact which no amount of Russian diplomatic perfumery will keep from stinking in the nostrils of England. The *coup de main* that has captured Merv has, in reality, virtually hooked Herat.

Posted at Penjdeh, 140 miles from Herat, what will intervene between the Russians and that city? The two tribes, the Djemshidis and the Hazaras, unwillingly acknowledging the Ameer's rule, and having no tribal or national feeling to prevent them falling under Russia's influence. Besides, the Russians will be alongside them, while their suzerain will be twenty days' distance from their tents. If the Ameer can hardly maintain his rule at Herat, what must be the character of his sway over the wild tribes outside it? The Djemshidis number, according to Grodekoff, who was the last European among them, 5,000 families; the Hazaras, 4,000. Collectively they can put in the field 2,000 badly-armed horsemen. What barrier is that to a Russian force crossing the Paropamisus to enter Herat? Yet it is the only living obstacle lying between the Russians at Merv and the "Key of India."

But suppose they fall in with the Duke of Argyll and

the Northbrook school, and treat the trivial barrier of the Paropamisus ridge, with its 2,000 horsemen, as impracticable; they have then, as I have pointed out, the Barkhut road, surveyed by Lessar, which is only twelve miles longer. By using this they could penetrate to Kusan without meeting a soul, and in traversing the fruitful Hari Rud valley to Herat, a matter of two marches, the Russian troops would encounter only a few well-disposed villagers.

"Herat," wrote General Grodekoff in 1879, after surveying the place, "Herat contains nothing that would call to mind the fortifications of a European city. It is not in a condition to defend itself against a European army, since at a mile to the north it is commanded by heights from which it could be bombarded by artillery."

In a word, there is nothing to prevent a small raiding party of Russians from taking Herat whenever they choose. The sudden seizure of Merv is a proof that the present Emperor and his Ministers are not to be trusted not to do it, whenever they care to exercise their own sweet will upon this undefended side of Afghanistan.

But the incorporation of Merv is accompanied by a declaration which ushers in danger in another quarter. The *Journal de St. Pétersbourg*, the organ of the Russian Foreign Office, declares the Atak to be Turcoman and not Persian territory, despite a title as clear as Russia's own title to the possession of Moscow. This Atak is a natural extension of the Akhal oasis annexed by Skobeleff in 1881. It is a long narrow oasis stretching along the foot of the Khorassan highlands, commencing near the Russian outposts beyond Askabad and terminating at Sarakhs. This Sarakhs is another outpost of Herat, 202½ miles from it. It is garrisoned by a Persian force. Russia magnanimously assures England that she is not going to take Sarakhs, "to which English strategists attach so much importance," and therefore England may profoundly bow and express her thanks. Russia is not going to take Sarakhs, no, she is only going to occupy all the country (Turcoman steppe-land and the Atak oasis) up to its walls, so as to be able to turn the corner there, and advance along the Hari Rud whenever she likes! The Merv Tekkés recently established settlements close to Sarakhs, on the east side of the river. These will become Russian property by the submission of "all the Merv

Tekkés," and Russia will acquire a lodgment 202½ miles from Herat at this point, as well as at Merv and Penj-deh. This is the real significance of the annexation of the Atak. Once it is realized, the assurances about Sarakhs disappear into the depths of bunkum.*

Russia cannot maintain good communications with Merv without annexing the Atak. The surveys of Alikhanoff and Lessar have shown that the direct road to Merv from Gyaoors, avoiding the Atak (210 miles), is impracticable. It is necessary to proceed fifty-seven miles beyond Gyaoors to the Atak settlement of Kahka, and then strike off across the steppe to Merv by way of the Tejend oasis. From Kahka to Merv is 143 miles. The Tejend oasis, which is touched at the fiftieth mile from Kahka, is "almost larger than that of Merv," to use Alikhanoff's words. It contains 25,000 people, and their number is daily increasing by arrivals from Merv.

This Tejend is the same river that washes Herat, called by the Afghans the Hari Rud. From the Tejend oasis, itself a base that can be made as good as that of Merv, troops can march all the way alongside water to Herat itself. The Russians accepted the submission of the Tejend Tekkés in 1881, and have treated the oasis as Russian territory since, repeatedly sending reconnoitring parties thither to assist the people in extending the irrigation canals, and, while surveying the country as far as Merv, establishing firm relations with the people. The final settled point of the Tejend oasis is distant only thirty miles from Sarakhs, or 232½ from Herat. Lessar computes the entire distance as consisting of eight marches. The Tejend oasis is distant ninety-five miles from Merv; Sarakhs seventy. Caravans are constantly crossing the intervening expanse.

Connecting as Merv does Bokhara, Khiva, Afghanistan, and Turkestan, it must become a great commercial centre. General Abbott designates it "the granary" of the country stretching up to Herat; Colonel Burnaby a "magnificent *étape*"; Captain Terentieff "a splendid base of operations against India." In his minute on Candahar in 1880, Lord Napier of Magdala said: "If the Russians are about to occupy Merv, of which they

---

* My anticipation that Russia would annex Old Sarakhs was justified by events. The English Government have thus no excuse that they were not forewarned.

make no secret; if they have an easy road to Herat, which is a fact well known, and a fortress there before them, in a fertile country, held by a people without unity and without leaders, who that regards the course of Russian progress can doubt that, if we are timid, apathetic, or consenting, a few years will see them in possession of a fortress which, in their hands, will be rendered impregnable, and will command the road to India with a facility for aggression which may be measured by Ayoob Khan's rapid march to Candahar?"

And now, respecting the roads to Merv. There are three: from opposite the mouth of the Volga to Khiva, and thence to Merv; from Krasnovodsk, *viâ* Askabad and the Tejend; and from Samarcand through Bokhara and Tchardjui. The last lies too far away from European communications to excite much attention, and, my space being limited, I will concentrate what I have to say upon the two Transcaspian routes. The first, from the Mertvi Kultuk bay, opposite the mouth of the Volga to Khiva, is the new route to Turkestan opened up by General Tchernayeff last year. It is fit for wheeled traffic all the way, and the Khan of Khiva has bound himself to provide transport animals to keep it up. This year the recruits for the Turkestan army are to be sent by this route instead of *viâ* Orenburg. The entire distance from the Caspian to Merv by it is a little over 600 miles. Kouropatkin's successful march with the Turkestan column from Khiva to Geok Tepé in 1880 proves that forces can be thrown into Merv from this direction.

The second is from Krasnovodsk, opposite Baku, where a vast industrial centre is rising, owing to the development of the Apsheron petroleum deposits, the richest in the world. The army of the Caucasus on a peace footing consists of nearly 150,000 men, mostly gathered near Tiflis. From Tiflis to Baku the railway train can take troops, at the slowest pace, in twenty-two hours. At Baku there are twenty-five piers for shipping oil, &c., all accommodating several vessels apiece. On the Caspian are fifty steamers; twenty new ones are being added every year. There is thus transport for the largest army without touching the 700 steamers of the Volga. From Baku to Krasnovodsk is sixteen hours' run. Thence to Michaelovsk, the railway starting-point across the bay, is a few hours' journey in smaller steamers, From Michaelovsk to Kizil Arvat is 144 miles' railway journey, which can be performed in six or seven hours. At this point the soldier leaves steam behind him, and he has the following distances to do on foot:—

			Miles.
Kizil Arvat to Askabad	...	...	135
,,	,, Sarakhs	...	320½
,,	,, Merv	...	368
,,	,, Herat	...	523

The country as far as every one of these places is flat; the only elevation to cross is the Barkhut Hills, 900 feet high, in penetrating Herat. Arriving in three days from his Caucasus base, the Russian soldier can rapidly move from Kizil Arvat over the fertile oasis-plains of Akhal, Atak, and Tejend, to his destination.

But what about Tommy Atkins, who is to confront them at Herat? England's steam communication terminates at Sibi, at the entrance of the Bolan pass, *more than three weeks' instead of three days' distance from her shores.* He has then before him the difficult Bolan pass, and a whole series of heavy hilly roads to Herat, taking him twice as long to do the 600 miles of marching as the Russian soldier.

		Miles.
Kizil Arvat to Herat	...	523
Sibi to Herat	...	599

Thanks to the evacuation of Candahar, we stand in this position: that though we may protest, we cannot enforce compliance with our wishes. Had we retained Candahar we could have held over Russia's head the threat of occupying Herat, as a retort to the occupation of Merv. That power is gone from us for ever. The Gladstone Government flung it heedlessly away, together with all other fruits of the £18,000,000 sterling invested in the Afghan War. The threat to occupy Herat is a weapon which is now in Russia's hands. Before a single sepoy could arrive before Herat to defend it, Russia even now, before she has posted a garrison at Merv, could thanks to the Transcaspian Railway and the annexation of Askabad, be mistress of the Key of India an entire fortnight, any fraction of which period would be sufficient to put the fortress in a condition to resist an English siege; while, at the same time, Russia could pour reinforcements into Herat from the Caucasus a clear month of English succour arriving on the scene from this country. In this manner, Herat is already more within the control of Russia than within the control of England; and her occupation of Merv will render the control complete.

The Russians posted at Merv, 240 miles from Herat, the Russians posted at the Sarik Turcoman stronghold of Penjdeh, 140 miles from Herat, the Russians posted within sight of Sarakhs, 202½ miles from Herat—what power on earth can prevent those Russians from meddling with the Key of India? It is a question I have been asking for years; it is a question I am sick of asking. Not without reason did a great Continental writer point out to me in 1880, after a brief stay in London, the inutility of writing political works: "I am amazed at your political leaders," he said; "they all of them possess most positive opinions about Central Asia; but they really know nothing about it. Every one has his views about Merv; but when I question them they have no idea of what Merv is like, where it is actually situated, and what relations the people have with Afghanistan. I have not met any statesman yet with a grasp of the Central Asian Question based upon clear and accurate information. It is no use advising; your statesmen will not listen. It is no use writing books; your statesmen will not read them. The future of your Empire appears lost in the conflict of party—public opinion is of no avail. English statesmen never read, but always pass opinions; the public always read, but possess no opinions to pass."

"The Central Asian Question is all humbug." These historical words of Skobeleff to the writer are acquiring a fresh significance. The Central Asian Question is all humbug to England. But I cannot decide in my mind whether England is more humbugged by her own statesmen or by those of Russia.

No; it will not do to persist in attempting to build up, in a mud-pie fashion, a solid independent state in Afghanistan. Russia will never allow it; and Russia's power of disintegration in Central Asia is infinitely stronger than our power of creation. Posted as we are, by the will of God and the folly of Gladstone, so far from Herat, what can we do to check the intrigue and the unscrupulosity of Russian generals?

It is only a few months ago that the writer touched at Kertch, on his way to visit the Caspian region. While waiting for the steamer to proceed, he went ashore, and, accidently entering a jeweller's shop, came across a man who had acted as interpreter to a recent secret Russian mission to Cabul. Early in 1882, he and two other persons—Captain Venkhovsky, of the Engineers, and Prince Khilkoff, head of the Transcaspian Railway—left Askabad in disguise, and successively visited Merv, Bokhara, Herat, and Cabul. The Ameer, to whom we are giving £10,000 a month, received the Russians well; and not only entertained them, and carried on negotiations with them, but offered his assistance in surveying the road to Candahar! And what was worse, this mission went to Herat and Cabul, and stayed at both places, and England never heard of it. There were rumours, indeed, that certain secret Russian agents had been to Cabul; but if a series of chance coincidences had not brought the writer in contact with Samuel Gourovitch at Kertch (of all places in Russia) we should have never been able perhaps to have defined one of them at least with precision, until Roberts went a second time to Cabul, and discovered there another "Secret Cabul Correspondence" between the Ameer and Russian Generals.

The discovery of this mission proved that the Russia of the present Emperor is not to be trusted in not tampering with Afghanistan; the sudden annexation of Merv demonstrates that no stronghold in Central Asia is safe from a *coup de main.* "Russian assurances to respect the integrity of Afghanistan!" Only Englishmen who consider the honour of England unsullied after Majuba Hill and Sinkat can put up with any more kid-gloved mendacities like these.

"If the Central Asian Question does not enable us in a comparatively short time to take seriously in hand the Eastern Question itself, why, the Asiatic fleece is not worth the tanning."

"The Eastern Question will be partly solved behind the walls of Akhal Tekké. It is a great link in our chain."

"It is my conviction that if England and Russia should have to knock against each other, the nearer the better."

Such convictions of Skobeleff, expressed at different times, ought to sink deep into the heart of every Englishman. What they really meant he exposed in his plan of invasion of India, published a few weeks ago.

"We have to consider, in the event of our enterprise wholly succeeding, that we could destroy the British Empire in India, which for England would involve incalculable consequences. But, even in the event of our enterprise not wholly succeeding—that is to say, if India herself does not rise, and we do not manage to get into the country—we shall, nevertheless, tie the whole Indian army to Hindostan, and prevent the English from transporting part of the army to Europe—nay, we should even compel England to send some portion of her European troops to India. Without going into details, the campaign, in my opinion, ought to fall into two periods—first, that of swift action and diplomatic negotiations with Afghanistan, the latter to be supported by pushing forward our active corps towards Cabul. The second period after the occupation of Cabul would be one of waiting, when we should have to enter into relations with all the disaffected elements of India, and convert them to our interests. The main cause of the failure of the rebellion of 1857 was the fact that the insurgents were not properly organized and led. And, finally, it would be our chief duty to organize masses of Asiatic cavalry, and, hurling them on India, as our van-guard, under the banner of 'Blood and Rapine,' thus bring back the times of Tamerlane. The Hindoo Koosh once crossed, I believe the conviction would be kindled in the breast of each combatant that he had come to Afghanistan to conquer or to die. This the Emperor demands of him, and there would be no reproaches made if our banners remained in the hands of the foe beyond the Hindoo Koosh after every Russian soldier has fallen."

To sum up: the annexation of all the Merv Tekkés and the Sarik Turcoman tribe gives Russia three points whence she can fall on Herat at any moment, the nearest being within 140 miles of the Key of India; it gives her the control over a sufficient native cavalry force, aided by a few guns, to carry the place by a *coup de main*; and, finally, the means of insidiously decomposing the influence of the Ameer and of England throughout the whole of the contiguous part of Afghanistan. If we take no measures to counteract this advance, we shall enter upon the next Eastern conflict fettered hand and foot in India, and unable to stretch forth a hand to protect our interests in Europe.

The time has arrived to leave off discussing the Central Asian Question, and to apply ourselves to decisive action. We must complete our railway to Quetta at once. We must exact from the Ameer, as a return for the £10,000 a month we are giving him, the permission to extend the railway to Candahar. We must abrogate the foolish Government regulation forbidding English officers entering Afghanistan. We cannot keep the Russians out on the Herat side, and the simplest way to nullify their influence is to let English officers go wandering about on the Cabul side; we shall at least get to hear, then, of the movements of Russian secret agents. Ignoring Cabul for the moment, we must insist upon England being represented by a political resident at Herat; employing a trustworthy Indian prince, if an English officer be too obnoxious to start with. At Saraks, either the Foreign Office must place a consul or the India Office an agent, to watch the Russian operations at Merv, Penjdeh, and the Atak; and Colonel Stewart must be kept stationed at Khaf, to watch them at Herat. Finally, a diplomatic note must be presented to Russia, informing her that what England has hitherto regarded as the true boundary of Afghanistan on the Turcoman and Persian side must be scrupulously respected, and that any attempt to occupy the country beyond it, or to enter Herat, will be treated as a *casus belli*.

WHAT THE ANNEXATION OF MERV MEANS.

Russia has annexed Merv.

But Merv is merely a "mud fortress," says the Duke of Argyll; "why, therefore, be 'mervous' about it?"

To annex Merv, however, the surrounding region must be annexed also.

In reality, therefore, Russia in annexing Merv has made a whole series of annexations:—

Enumeration and Area.

1. The Merv Oasis.
2. The Tejend Oasis (as large as Merv).

3. The Atak Oasis, as far as Sarakhs.
4. The Sarik settlements, to within 140 miles of Herat.
5. All the steppe and desert lying between Merv and Persia.
6. All the steppe and desert lying between Merv and Khiva.
7. All the steppe and desert lying between Merv and Bokhara.

Total area annexed; more than 200,000 square miles, or a province as large as France.

POPULATION.

	People.
1. Merv Oasis	240,000
2. Tejend Oasis	25,000
3. Atak Oasis	20,000
4. Sarik settlements	65,000
5. Ersari Turcoman settlements between Merv and Bokhara, &c.	250,000
	600,000

This population is not scattered over the desert, but is massed in oases within striking distance of Herat. Collectively it can place over 100,000 horsemen in the field.

Between the new Russian frontier and Herat, the only impediment to the attack of these 100,000 horsemen upon the Key of India is the 2,000 horsemen of the Djemshidi and Hazara tribes subject to the Ameer.

DISTANCES TO BE REMEMBERED.

	Miles.
Russian post at Penjdeh to Herat	140
Quetta to Candahar	145
Quetta to Herat	514

The country between Penjdeh and Herat, *viâ* the Barkhut Hills, being easier than the country between Quetta and Candahar, Russia will be able to occupy Herat before we can even occupy Candahar.

THE CAUCASUS VIEW OF THE INVASION OF INDIA.

Considerable attention was excited in May this year by the appearance of the following article in the semi-official Tiflis newspaper *Kavkaz* (April $\frac{14}{26}$, 1884), which may be said to have represented very frankly the views on the subject of Prince Dondukoff-Korsakoff, the Governor-General of the Caucasus. It should be noted that it was published after the announcement in the same paper of the annexation of Sarakhs, and when that advance was therefore known to the official writer of the article.

"Our readers cannot have failed to observe the happy coincidence that at the very moment when England, in her endeavours to get hold of the Suez Canal, has entangled herself in difficulties in Egypt and the Soudan, so as to be almost compelled to abandon General Gordon at Khartoum, a victim to the exasperated natives, our Prince Governor has started for Merv with the absolutely pacific object of organizing the civil administration of that territory, the population of which has hitherto supported itself only by marauding expeditions against the surrounding countries.

"It is impossible not to applaud such a wise direction of our policy in the distant depths of Southern Turkestan. It is quite enough for us that we take our stand upon a line of frontier, for the inviolability of which the neighbouring State can answer to the same degree that we in future answer for the peaceable conduct of our new subjects the Mervis and Tekkés. Even this simple task presents not a few difficulties. Opposite Merv, on the upper reaches of the Murghab, and more particularly of the Hari-rud (Tejend), on the borders of Afghanistan, dwell the Mongol tribes, the Hazaras and Djimshidis, which were not only able to defend themselves against the attacks of the Mervis, but not unfrequently made raids upon the latter in turn. It is obvious that in future the Afghans must divide with us the responsibility for the good conduct of the Hazaras and Djimshidis.

"As to India, it is our decided opinion that its possession is in no way necessary for the development of our national prosperity. India is rich in wheat, cotton, tea, dyes, and spices. But with the present extension of the productive area of the Kirghiz Steppes (where the black earth zone, just as in Little Russia, attains a depth of three-and-a-half feet, and extends from the Rivers Ural and Tobol almost to the Aral Sea), we shall not know what to do with our own wheat; and as to cotton, the utmost demand can be met with ease by developing irrigation in the Caucasus and in Turkestan.

"Then comes tea. But what hinders us even now obtaining it from India, where it is prepared by machinery, and not, as in China, by an objectionable use of the feet, as observed by Dr. Pyasetsky, whose testimony will doubtless be confirmed by the Potanin Expedition, now on its way thither? Even if we were to conquer India nobody would give us tea for nothing, and our countrymen would have to pay all the same for this national beverage. Besides, the question of tea-planting in the Caucasus must now be considered settled in the affirmative as far as theory goes, and it wants only enterprise on the part of our capitalists to put it into practice.

"Then we come to dyes, of which indigo is the most important; but in all probability aniline dyes, obtained from petroleum refuse, will destroy the indigo trade as they have already destroyed with us that of madder. It follows therefore that India will retain but one unquestioned product—spices. But is it worth while for that alone to think seriously of undertaking the conquest of this country, with its 230,000,000 inhabitants? Without a doubt we could take India, but what would be the effect on our Budget; and what difficulties should we not have to overcome to maintain the country in subjection? We have only to remember its open coasts and the want on our side of a fleet comparable with that of England.

"Besides we must do justice to the English. India

at the present moment has reached a very considerable degree of civilization. The English have covered it with a wide network of railways (20,000 versts—*i.e.*, as much as we have in Russia), irrigation canals of enormous length, and telegraphs. They support three Universities, &c.

"In our opinion, therefore, our approach to India is important only in the sense that we have at last achieved a position that will enable us at any time, in case of absolute necessity, to strike a blow at England, which has hitherto been so far as we were concerned simply invulnerable. It is evident that by far the most advantageous policy for us to pursue in regard to India is not that of conquest, but of freeing the Hindoos from the British yoke. Such a policy, too, is morally a much higher one than that of mere conquest, which could only be justified by the irresistible force of circumstances.

"Taking our stand at Merv, on the borders of Afghanistan, we are near enough to India for our purpose—that is: to strike a blow at England if necessary. Afghanistan, which separates us, may be compared in position to Roumania, which in like manner separated us before the last war from Turkey.

"The one did not prevent our movement on the Danube, nor will the other stop our march to the Indus.

"Thus the conquest of Afghanistan is also quite unnecessary—the more so, since in regard to our position at Merv and on the Oxus that country is more defenceless than on the side of British India. The population is about equal to that of Roumania—some five million souls all told.

"The whole of the available strength of this population can be concentrated against India, but not against us. There are two roads leading from Turkestan into Afghanistan—the one from Bokhara through Afghan Turkestan straight to Cabul; the other from Merv to Herat and Cabul. The first is available only in summer, since in winter, owing to the deep snows in the lofty Hindoo-Koosh, all communication between Mazar-i-Sherif or Balkh and Cabul is interrupted, and Afghan Turkestan in consequence isolated. On the other hand, its connection with Cabul by the side road through Maimene and Herat we can always cut without much trouble. Besides, owing to local physical conditions, it is much easier for us to invade Afghanistan by way of Herat than for the English to do so by way of Quetta; they would have to scale mountains, we merely to work along the sides over the spurs of them. It seems to us, therefore, that the subsidies paid by the English to the Afghans are merely so much money thrown away. Owing to its natural position Afghanistan must inevitably take sides with a powerful army, which, advancing upon India, should reach Herat from the North-West."

THE END.

POPULAR EDITION.

The Region of the Eternal Fire;

TRAVELS IN RUSSIA, THE BLACK SEA, CAUCASUS, AND THE CASPIAN.

BY CHARLES MARVIN.

With 16 Maps, Plans, and Illustrations, Crown 8vo, 406 pp., price 7s. 6d.

Opinion of the Right Honourable the Earl of Ravensworth, President of the Institution of Naval Architects.

"It is with great pleasure that I am able to announce that we have present to-day the distinguished traveller and writer, Mr. Charles Marvin, the author of that most interesting book—more fascinating than any novel I know of—'The Region of the Eternal Fire.'"—*Conference of Naval Architects, Liverpool, July 27th, 1886.*

Opinion of The Right Hon. Sir Lyon Playfair, K.C.B., M.P.

"The accounts given of Baku, by Mr. Charles Marvin, have made the district familiar to us. A formidable competition to American oil is arising in Russia."—*Good Words, February, 1884.*

Opinion of Arminius Vambery.

"The leading authority of the English Press on the Central Asian Question is Charles Marvin, a man of iron industry, who has wielded his comprehensive knowledge of the region in such a manner as to render eminent service to his country."

Opinion of Professor A. H. Keane, Vice-President of the Anthrpooloogical Society.

"Charles Marvin is unquestionably the leading authority of the day in all matters appertaining to the operations of Russia in Central Asia. He has no equal, and can hardly be said to have any rival."

Opinion of Colonel Malleson.

"Charles Marvin's services in respect of the Russo-Afghan Question have been invaluable. He has heard with his own ears the opinions expressed on the subject by Russian generals and diplomatists, and, for the love of England, has spent his own money to warn England's people."—*The Russo-Afghan Question, p. 55.*

Opinion of Alderman A. B. Forwood, M.P. (First Secretary to the Admiralty).

"His writings and his works are so well known, that I have only to mention the name of Charles Marvin, the Russian traveller, and writer on this great question, to ensure him a warm welcome to Liverpool."—*Speech, May 4, 1885.*

Opinion of Commander Verney Lovett Cameron, C.B.

"Charles Marvin stands out prominently to-day as the representative of non-party public feeling in England on the Russo-Indian Question."

Opinion of the Chief Surveyor, Lloyd's.

"Almost every day I am having applications addressed to me, with regard to Petroleum steamers, from English shipbuilders, and I find that the inspiration is invariably due to Mr. Marvin's 'Region of the Eternal Fire.'"—Mr. MARTELL (*Meeting of the Lewisham and Blackheath Scientific Association, May 3, 1886.*)

Opinion of the Imperial Russian Technical Society.

"Charles Marvin has been elected Corresponding Member of the Imperial Russian Technical Society, in recognition of his writings on Petroleum."—*Academy, August 6, 1887.*

The Gold Medal of the Balloon Society.

"At a meeting of the council of the Balloon Society held yesterday, it was resolved to present the gold medal of the society to Charles Marvin, in recognition of his valuable writings on petroleum, and his unwearied efforts to establish the industry in Burma and other parts of the Empire."—*Daily Chronicle, Jan. 5, 1888.*

Opinion at the Society of Arts.

"I need not tell the members of this Society of the inexhaustible stores of oil at Baku, as this information has already been given in a masterly manner by Charles Marvin, whose patriotic labours merit national recognition."—*Lecture by J. B. Hannay, Nov. 30, 1887.*

Opinion of Sir Henry Tyler, M.P.

"No one is more entitled to speak on matters connected with Central Asia and Afghanistan than Charles Marvin, who has made a special study of those points which have a particular interest at the present moment."—*Speech, March 6, 1885.*

Opinion of the Special Correspondent of the "Illustrated London News."

Mr. William Simpson (attached to Sir Peter Lumsden's Mission) specially recommends "The Region of the Eternal Fire," in his articles on the Baku oil region, in the *Illustrated London News*, June, 1886.

Opinion of English Working Men.

"At a meeting of the Portsmouth Working Men's Club, Feb. 29, 1884, a resolution was passed expressing hearty sympathy with Charles Marvin in his works and lectures on Central Asia, and trusting that he would be supported by working men throughout England."—*Portsmouth Times, March 12, 1884.*

Charles Marvin and his Policy.

"Charles Marvin's political mission has been summed up by himself in one word—'To *Imperialise* the working man.' He says: 'The working man has the largest vote, and the welfare of the Empire is largely in his keeping.' His object in life is to create a consciousness of Empire in his mind—when this is done, the masses will insist on a strong foreign policy, and the federation of the Colonies with the Mother Country will follow as a matter of course. He does not write for any *Party*, but for the whole people, and he always strives to keep himself in harmony with the national sentiment."—*Newcastle Examiner.*

www.ingramcontent.com/pod-product-compliance
Lightning Source LLC
Chambersburg PA
CBHW032006300426
44117CB00008B/925